ENVIRONMENTAL EDUCATION

ENVIRONMENTAL EDUCATION

Principles, Concepts and Management

K.K. Shrivastava

KANISHKA PUBLISHERS, DISTRIBUTORS
NEW DELHI-110 002

KANISHKA PUBLISHERS, DISTRIBUTORS
4697/5-21A, Ansari Road, Daryaganj
New Delhi -110 002
Phones : 2327 0497, 2328 8285
Fax : 011-2328 8285
E-mail : kanishka_publishing@yahoo.co.in

Enviornmental Education:
Principles, Concepts and Management
First Published- 2004

Edition- 2020

ISBN: 978-81-7391-702-7

PRINTED IN INDIA

Published by Madan Sachdeva for Kanishka Publishers, Distributors, 4697/5-21A, Ansari Road, Daryaganj, New Delhi-110 002, Typeset by Sunshine Graphics, Delhi, and Printed at Rajdhani Printers, Delhi.

Preface

The concept of environmental awareness and study of environment as an academic discipline in a new phenomenon, which has its roots in the developed western world, though in India the concept of environmental preservation is as old as Rigveda. Yet at present we are faced with grave environmental problems because most of our people are illiterate, hence, they are not aware of the adverse effect of human activities on ecology, ecosystem and the entire environment. In this situation environmental education is of vital concern for us, therefore, we are evolving an educational system having due emphasise on environmental understanding, environmental awareness, environmental planning and management. Some aspects of environmental education are also included in non-formal education to create environmental awareness in large masses through distance education.

The concept of environmental education is very wide and interdisciplinary in nature, which includes geosciences, physical and biological sciences—such as Bio-chemistry, Environmental Botany, Environmental Geography, Ecology, Population Biology or Human Ecology, Psychology, Statistics, Forestry, Eco-development and problems related with socio-economic and socio-political aspects of human life.

In view of the interdisciplinary nature, as discussed above of the environmental education, it is a difficult task to prepare a book to be used by each discipline as mentioned above because each discipline has its own point of view for the study of problems concerning man and environment.

However, with the help of the basic concepts of each of the above subjects concerning environment, I have tried to make this book useful for the majority of the readers in various Indian Universities because it has not been designed to suit any particular university.

The work at hand on 'Environmental Education' among several books written on the subject claims to be most comprehensive. In this book the description and analysis of the subject is in the Indian context and it covers basic concepts of the syllabi of almost all the Indian Universities on the subject in simple and lucid language drawing examples from Indian environmental and educational system.

This includes chapters:

1. Approaches to the study of man-environment relationship;
2. Man's interaction with nature through ages,
3. Current nature of man-environment relationship;
4. Ecosystem and education;
5. Exclusive chapters on Air, Water, Soil, Noise and Radio-active pollutions;
6. Environmental Management—A social concern;
7. Global Perspective on Environmental Management; and
8. Status of Environmental Education in India.

Thus this book contains 30 chapters, while most of the other books do not have more than 20 chapters. It is because I have tried to make it useful for the students of all Indian Universities.

Planned as a text book for the students and reference book for the specialists, scholars and teachers of the subject. This book is a critical constructure of the subject.

While I have tried my best to make this book the best for the intellectuals, the readers are the best judge of its merits, therefore, suggestions for improvement are cordially invited.

K.K. Shrivastava

Contents

Preface v

1. INTRODUCTION 1
   - Basic Ingredients of Environment and Its Pollution
   - Meaning of Environment
   - Basic Components of Environment
   - Cycles of Carbon, Nitrogen, Oxygen and Hydrogen in Ecosystem
   - The Food Chain
   - The Soil
   - The Acid Rain
   - Pollution
   - Losing Forest
   - New Species
   - Wildlife under Threat

2. APPROACHES TO THE STUDY OF MAN-ENVIRONMENT RELATIONSHIP 17
   - Deterministic Approach
   - Teleological Approach
   - Possibilistic Approach
   - Economic Deterministic Approach
   - Ecological Approach

3. MAN'S INTERACTION WITH ENVIRONMENT THROUGH AGES 23
   - Hunting and Food Gathering Period
   - Period of Domestication of Animals and Pastoralism
   - Period of Plant Domestication and Agriculture
   - Period of Industrialization—Science and Technology

4. CURRENT NATURE OF MAN-ENVIRONMENT RELATIONSHIP 35

5. BASIC ASPECTS OF ENVIRONMENT 39
- Introduction
- Meaning of Environment
- Definition of Environment
- Basic Characteristics of Environment
- Classification of Environment
- Components of Environment
- Biological and Physical Component of Environment
- Environment Related Subjects
- Determinants of Personality
- Socio-Cultural Conditions
- Environment—The Social Aspect
- Environment—The Political Aspect
- Environment—The Geographical Aspect
- Environment—The Aspect of Natural Resources
- Environment—The Educational Aspect

6. BASIC CONCEPTS OF EDUCATION 61
- Introduction
- Meaning of Education
- Data of Education
- Nature of Modern Education
- Parts of Education
- Aims of Education
- Some Conclusive Aims of Education
- Importance of Synthesizing the Aims into an Inclusive Aim
- Inter-Disciplinary Approach of Education
- Growth and Development
- Meaning and Definition of Growth
- Development
- Maturation
- The Task of Education

7. BASIC CONCEPTS OF ENVIRONMENT EDUCATION 91
- Introduction
- Definition of Environmental Education

- Environmental Awareness—Development and Contents
- How do Environmental Education and Environmental Awareness Differ
- Education Develops Environmental Awareness
- Characteristics of Environmental Education
- Utility and Need of Environmental Education
- Aims And Objectives of Environmental Education
- Teacher's Role in Environmental Education

8. ENVIRONMENTAL EDUCATION AS AN ACADEMIC DISCIPLINE 106
- Meaning of Discipline
- Characteristics of a Discipline
- Environmental Education Qualify to be an Academic Discipline
- Objectives of Study
- Components of Study
- Stagewise Course Contents
- Newman's Four-Fold Environmental Education Programme
- Non-Formal Agencies/Programmes and Environmental education
- Environmental Education for Teacher Education
- Methods and Techniques of Teaching Environmental Education
- Educational Excursion or Field Trips
- Co-curricular Activities
- Present Status of Environmental Education

9. ECOLOGY AND EDUCATION 125
- Definition of Ecology
- Basic Characteristics
- Is it Science or Art
- Basic Fundamental Principles
- Aims and Objectives of Study
- Branches and Areas of Study
- Area or Field of Study
- Tools and Techniques of Study
- Ecology and Education

10. ECOSYSTEM AND EDUCATION 136
- Meaning and Definition
- Fundamental Characteristics
- Classification of Ecosystem
- Ecosystem—The Functioning Process
- The Components
- Kinds of Aquatic Ecosystem
- Difference between Ecology and Ecosystem
- Ecosystem and Education

11. CONCEPTS OF ENVIRONMENTAL POLLUTION, DEGRADATION, HAZARDS AND DISASTER 146
- Introduction
- Definitions of Pollution
- Pollutants
- Sources of Pollution
- Classification/Types of Pollution
- Environmental Degradation
- Classification/Types of Degradation
- Causes of Environmental Degradation
- Hazards and Disasters
- Pollution—Role of Education

12. AIR POLLUTION 166
- Meaning and Definition of Air Pollution
- Nature of Air Pollution
- Sources of Air Pollution
- Air Pollutants
- Detection and Measurement of Air Pollution
- Adverse Effects of Air Pollution
- Control and Prevention of Air Pollution
- Health Effects of Exposure to Air Pollutants
- Education for Control and Prevention of Air Pollution

13. WATER POLLUTION 177
- Introduction
- Meaning and Definition
- Sources of Water Pollutants
- Classification of Water Pollutants

- Nature of Water Pollution
- Sources of Water Pollution
- Ecological Effects of Water Pollution
- Assessment of Water Quality
- Pollution Prevention Measures
- Laws for Water Quality Management

14. SOIL OR LAND POLLUTION 189
- Introduction
- Definition of Soil Pollution
- Sources of Soil Pollution
- Effects of Soil Pollution
- Control of Soil Pollution
- Solid Waste Pollution
- Sources of Solid Waste
- Types of Solid Waste Substances
- Management of Solid Waste

15. NOISE AND RADIOACTIVE POLLUTION 200
- Introduction
- Sound and Noise
- Definition of Noise Pollution
- Sources of Noise Pollution
- Types of Noise Pollution
- Measurement of Noise Level
- Noise Pollution Level in India
- Effects of Noise Pollution
- Control of Noise Pollution
- Radioactive Pollution
- Sources of Pollution
- Prevention and Control of Pollution

16. HUMAN ECOLOGY AND ENVIRONMENTALISM 211
- Man and Environment and Human Activities
- Social and Cultural Determinism
- Humanistic Philosophy of Environment
- Human Activities
- Impact of Man on Environment—An Assessment

17. ENVIRONMENT: THE INTERDEPENDENCY—THE FOOD CHAIN, FOOD WEB AND REMEDIES 221

- Environment—The Functional Aspect
- Ecological Production And Productivity
- The Food Chains And Food Webs
- Factors Affecting Food Chains and Food Webs
- Education—The Best Remedy

18. EXPLOSION OF HUMAN POPULATION: THE ECOLOGICAL ASPECTS 235

- Ecology Through Ages in Population Growth
- Ecology of Human Needs and Problems
- Problems of Population Explosion
- Population Explosion in India
- Features of Indian Population
- Impact of Population Growth in Environment
- How to Control Population Growth
- India—The Population Policy
- Population Education—The Only Way
- Need of Population Education
- Objectives of Population Education
- The Course Contents
- Importance of Population Education
- How to Make Population Education Effective

19. EDUCATIONAL ENVIRONMENT: THE SCHOOL 255

- Introduction
- Areas of Educational Environment
- Social Ecology and Organizational Climate
- Definition of Organizational Climate
- Main Characteristics of Organizational Climate
- Determinants or Dimensions of Educational Climate
- Organizational Health
- Dimensions of Development of Organizational Climate
- Factors Influencing Organizational Climate
- Evaluation or Assessment of Organizational Climate

20. EDUCATIONAL ENVIRONMENT: THE TEACHER AND CLASSROOM 268

- Teacher
- Teacher—The Classroom Leader
- Class Structure—The Teacher's Place
- Teacher's Role in the Classroom
- Classroom Climate
- Definition of Class
- Characteristics of Classroom
- Problem of Identification and Interaction in the Classroom Climate
- Classroom Climate

21. ENVIRONMENTAL ASPECT OF HUMAN GROWTH AND DEVELOPMENT 279

- Introduction
- Nature of Development
- Dimensions of Development
- Physical and Motor Development
- Emotional Development
- Affection—Two Way Process
- Humour and Laughter
- Social Development
- Motor Skills and Social Development
- Educational Implications
- Mental Development
- Development of Moral Concepts
- Educational Implications of Mental Development

22. PSYCHOLOGICAL AND ECOLOGICAL ENVIRONMENT FOR MENTAL HEALTH 296

- Introduction
- Human Ecology
- Definition of Mental Health
- Mental Health and Education
- Mental Ailments
- Attributes of Mental Health
- Attributes of Superior Mental Health
- Theory of Mental Health
- Education and Mental Health

- Factors Influencing Mental Health of Child
- Problems of Adjustment—The Cause of Mental Ailment
- Mental Health and School
- Teacher's Mental Health
- How to Ensure Teacher's Mental Health

23. ENVIRONMENTAL EDUCATION IN TEACHER EDUCATION PROGRAMME 319
- Need of Environmental Education in Teacher Education
- NCERT's Emphasis on Environmental Education
- Environmental Education—The Modular Programme and Identification of Environmental Needs of Training
- Identification of Training Needs
- Objectives of Environmental Education and B.Ed., M.Ed Courses
- Environmental Education—Course Contents
- Environmental Education—Teaching Strategies
- Group Discussion
- Project Work
- Classification of Project
- Teacher Education Institutions
- Co-curricular Activities
- Environmental Education for Distance Teachers
- Need for Training
- Nature of Training
- The UGC and the National Council of Teacher Education (NCTE)
- Government's Approach
- Concerns of UGC and NCTE

24. MASS MEDIA: THE INSTRUMENT OF ENVIRONMENTAL EDUCATION 339
- Instructional Media
- Approaches of Instruction and Use
- Educational Radio
- Educational Radio—The Characteristics
- Educational Television (As Non-print Instructional Media)

25. CHILD AND HIS ENVIRONMENT 364
- Impact of Environment in Child Development
- Social Development
- What Makes Family, School, Community and Social Environment Effective for Child's Development

26. ADULT EDUCATION FOR ENVIRONMENTAL AWARENESS AND SOCIAL FORESTRY 375
- Introduction
- Environmental Awareness and Adult Education
- Environmental Awareness and Non-formal Education
- Afforestation and Social Forestry
- Social Forestry
- New Strategy Needed
- An Estimate for Proper Consideration

27. ENVIRONMENTAL MANAGEMENT: A SOCIAL CONCERN 391

28. GLOBAL PERSPECTIVES ON ENVIRONMENTAL MANAGEMENT 397
- Global Issues and Concerns
- Tools of Environmental Management

29. ENVIRONMENTAL MANAGEMENT: MEANING AND DEFINITION 403
- Aspects and Approaches to Environmental Management
- Components
- Approaches to Environmental Management
- Ecological Basis of Environmental Management
- Approaches to Resource Management
- Environmental Management Functions and Characteristics
- International Agencies and Programmes of Environmental Management
- India's Environmental Policies
- Environmental Management in India
- Working Structure of the Ministry of Environment and Forests

- Assessment of Environmental Impact
- Control of Environmental Pollution and Degradation
- Environmental Education and Training
- Environmental Management—Vital Priority Areas
- The Role of the Judiciary
- Citizens' Protests

30. STATUS OF ENVIRONMENTAL EDUCATION IN INDIA **436**

- Introduction
- Heritage and Tradition
- Environmental Studies: ideal and the Real
- Imperatives
- Model Curriculum of Masters Degree in Environment and Ecology
- Conclusions

BIBLIOGRAPHY **447**

INDEX **452**

1

Introduction

BASIC INGREDIENTS OF ENVIRONMENT AND ITS POLLUTION

Environmental education is a new concept but its basic nature is as old as human civilisation since early days. Before we discuss the nature and concept and all other aspects of environmental education, we must have the basic ingredients of natural environment and its pollutants which should be included in the study of environmental education at various levels of our education system. Hereunder, we will discuss these basic ingredients of environment and its pollution, very briefly.

MEANING OF ENVIRONMENT

Environment is taken to mean all those which are physical, chemical, organic and non-organic components of the atmosphere, lithosphere and oceans. Environment is the aggregate of external conditions that influence the life of an individual or the population, specifically the life of man; environment ultimately determines the quality of survival of life. The importance of management of such a vital, natural phenomena needs little elaboration. However, with threat to the environment being realised by the people across international community, the growing consciousness among them is justified. With this, the concern for Environmental management is catching up fast the imagination of even the last man in the society thereby reducing the threat to the environment. Having concern for the environment, its preservation is every individual's responsibility. It is the responsibility of every one of us to care our environment if we aspire for sustainable development.

BASIC COMPONENTS OF ENVIRONMENT

The meaning of the environment as given above clearly states of some components, therefore, hereunder we will discuss the basic components, the natural nature of environment, which consists of the following concepts:

Ecology

Human civilisation has developed very slowly. In the ancient times man was totally dependent on nature for his needs but as he learnt about agriculture he started interfering with the laws of nature. He shaved off the forests for agriculture and tamed many wild animals for his food and clothing. He left the caves and started living in houses. With the development in man's lifestyle several civilisations of Sumaria, Egypt and Indus Valley spread over the vast areas of the world. It is a general belief that man has conquered the nature but still he cannot control natural disasters.

All the living beings on the earth utilise solar energy and get essential elements from atmosphere, lithosphere and hydrosphere. Animals and plants either depend on plants or on other animals for their food. A balance exists between living and non-living things in the nature. Whenever any element of nature increases or decreases in large proportions, ecological balance gets disturbed. The study which deals with the relationships of life forms with each other and with their surroundings is called ecology. A group of animals living in a particular physical environment is called *ecosystem.*

Causes of Imbalance

Today rapid industrialisation and ever increasing human requirements have disturbed these natural elements and created an ecological imbalance. Increasing population, emission of carbon-dioxide and other toxic gases by factories and vehicles, occurrence of acid rain, nuclear tests and poisonous chemicals have posed a serious threat to the ecological balance. The entire earth and its inhabitants are affected by pollution. Life an earth is endangered. Now, the man has realised the need of ecological conservation and sefety of environment. Public awareness is being created for the protection of life on the earth. Many programmes for a better environment and conservation of nature resources are being carried out all over the world. The scientific conservation programmes are mainly based on the principles of ecology. We can get a better environment only when every body, specially the children, becomes aware about it.

Earth—The Living Planet

Among the nine planets of the solar system, earth is the only one where life exists. Plants and animals exists on earth because it has all the favourable conditions required for survival of life.

Even on earth life is not found every where because survival requires a particular type of environment. That part of the earth where plants and animals exist is called biosphere. Biosphere is further divided into three parts: Lithosphere, Hydrosphere and Atmosphere. Lithosphere is that part of earth where rocks, sand, soil, plants, animals, etc., are found. That part of the earth where water is present is called *Hydrosphere.* All the animals and plants need water to live. The blanket of air which surrounds the earth up to a height of about 100 km is called *atmosphere.* Atmosphere is a balanced mixture of several gases like nitrogen, oxygen and carbon dioxide. The major atmosphere extends upto 320 km above lithosphere and hydrosphere. About 10 km below and 10 km above the surface of the earth is biosphere. In reality 90 per cent living beings live in the area between 1 km below and 1 km above the earth's surface.

Biosphere or ecological framework always remains in a dynamic equilibrium. In this many biological and physical elements are present in a balanced state. Air, water, soil, animals, plants and bacteria are all linked to each other or to their surroundings by some means or the other. This system is called *Environment*. Environment includes all those conditions which affect our life. Plants, animals, water, air, land are important parts of our environment because living being cannot survive without them. Our houses, villages, towns etc., all are included in the environment. Man has created an imbalance in the environment by its haphazard exploitation to fulfil his needs. The trees are being cut mercilessly, water and air are becoming highly polluted. If environmental pollution keeps on increasing with the present rate, the very existence of the life on earth is endangered.

CYCLES OF CARBON, NITROGEN, OXYGEN AND HYDROGEN IN ECOSYSTEM

Innumerable kinds of plants and animals are found on earth which are different from each other in shape, size and structure. All these are basically made up of carbon, nitrogen, oxygen and hydrogen. Animals get these elements from nature only. The processes like formation and decay, growth and decomposition normally occur in nature. Various cycles are going on in the nature as a result of these processes. Due to these cycles—plants, animals and their environment are linked to each other and a balance is established between them.

Carbon Cycle

Carbon is an essential element found in all living beings. Plants and animals get this element from carbon dioxide present in the atmosphere. Plants take carbon dioxide from air and in the presence of water and sunlight they make their food by the process of photosynthesis. Plants are consumed by other animals as food. In this way they get compounds of carbon. Energy is produced by digestion of these carbon compounds. Carnivores get carbon from flesh of herbivores. Omnivores like man get carbon from both plants and animals. Carbon cycle shows that all the animals absorb carbon dioxide directly from atmosphere or from the plants. Animals convert carbon into carbon dioxide during respiration or oxidation and again this carbon dioxide is released into the air. Carbon dioxide is also liberated during decay of plants and animals and burning of fuels which enters into the atmosphere and completes carbon cycle.

Nitrogen Cycle

In nitrogen cycle, nitrogen circulates continuously through soil, water, air and living beings. All living beings need nitrogen. It is found in proteins and nucleic acid. Though 80 per cent of air is nitrogen, yet most of the plants and animals cannot use it in gaseous state. It is utilised by plants or animals in the form of several compounds like ammonia or amino acids. Many bacteria of soil like Azotobacter and Clostridium convert the atmosphere nitrogen into nitrogenous compounds which can be absorbed by the plants. Many small nodules are present in the roots of leguminous plants which contain bacteria named Rhizobium leguminosarum. These bacteria convert atmospheric nitrogen into nitrates. Plants absorb nitrate salts through their roots and synthesize proteins in their cells. Nitrogen enters into the body of the animals when they eat these plants. Bacteria and fungi decompose the dead bodies on earth. Nitrosomonas bacteria convert ammonia into nitrites and nitrobacter bacteria convert nitrites into nitrates. In this way plants absorb nitrates again. Some other bacteria like Thiobacillus denitrificans and Micrococcus denitrificans convert nitrates and ammonia of soil into nitrogen gas. Apart from this, a fraction of nitrogen in atmosphere changes into nitric acid during lightning which forms nitrates with rain water in soil that is absorbed by the plants. In this way atmospheric nitrogen moves through many food chains and again comes into the air through a cycle. Though this process takes billions of years but each atom of nitrogen comes back into the air.

Oxygen Cycle

Life is not possible without oxygen. About 20 per cent of air is oxygen. All the living beings on earth need oxygen for respiration. Oxygen is essential for burning. You will think that the constant use of oxygen from the atmosphere will bring its end some day. But in nature the oxygen cycle is constantly going on and no disturbance has occurred to the balance of this gas. This cycle like nitrogen-cycle is a continuous one. Green plants absorb carbon dioxide gas from the atmosphere and convert it into oxygen by the process of photosynthesis.

Hydrogen Cycle

Water is very important for all plants and animals. The hydrosphere gets its most abundant element, the hydrogen, from water only. Water is formed by the combination of oxygen and hydrogen. During photosynthesis hydrogen is produced by the dissociation of water which forms glucose after combining with carbon dioxide. Plants provide food for herbivores and these animals get glucose and proteins from plants only. Hydrogen forms carbohydrates which is an important source of energy for living beings.

THE FOOD CHAIN

All the animals, directly or indirectly, depend on plants for their food. Horbivores get their food directly from plants. Carnivores eat small and weaker herbivores. The inter-relationship between plants and animals is very interesting and is an important subject in ecological studies. This inter-relationship is called *food chain.* Food chains can be observed in places like grazing lands, deciduous forests, rivers, seas, deserts etc. which are inhabited by plants and animals.

Insects eat plants, and insects are themselves eaten by shrew and shrew is eaten up by the owl. In this way a food chain (Plant-Insect-Shrew-Owl) is formed. Zebra eats grass in African Savana and lions consume zebra (Grass-Zebra-Lion food chain). Similar food chains exist in sea also. For example, small fish eats algae and it is eaten by bigger fish, bigger fish is eaten by gull and gull is further consumed by seal. This cycle does not end here. When many food chains combine then a food web is formed. Most of the food chains start from plants.

Food chains are very delicate and they can be broken easily. If one relationship in the food chain is broken it becomes dangerous for the whole chain. If the farmer uses pesticides to kill the pests then shrews will also die of starvation because pests are food. Owls, which eat shrews will also die in want of their food. At the Peru coast, extensive hunting of anchobi fish led to a decrease in the number of carmorent birds which ate anchobi fishes only. Vanishing carmorent birds caused lack of their faces which were consumed by plankton. And decreasing planktons caused food deficiency for anchobi fishes which led to the reduction of anchobi fishes.

Man is also an important member of several food chains because he eats plants (vegetables) as well as meat, fishes, eggs etc. For the animal conservation we should have the knowledge about food habits and food webs of the animals.

THE SOIL

The uppermost layer of the earth is called soil. It is made up of rocks, organic substances, minerals, water and air. Soil is essential for life on earth. Plants grow in soil which are eaten by other animals. Various insects, worms and other organisms breathe in the air present inside the soil.

About 300 million tiny creatures live in every one hectare of soil. Rodents, insects, millipedes, mites, sea bugs, snakes, spiders, earthworms and other types of worms, reptiles and protozoa are commonly found in soil. They grow due to base exchange capacity of soil in the presence of potassium and phosphorus. These creatures produce organic substances for soil by decay of their dead bodies and waste products.

When man learnt about importance of soil for the production of food, he shaved off jungles, built dams for water and worked against laws of nature. In this way, he progressed a lot but forgot that excessive crop cultivation, cutting of forests and overgrazing will cause soil erosion, and consequently turn fertile land into deserts. The area where ancient civilisations of Nile Valley, Mesopotamia, Sindhu Valley and Vi-ho Valley of China were flourished, have been converted into barren lands today. Only 20 per cent area of the old Iraq civilization is under cultivation now. Today, even after knowing the importance of the soil, we are destroying more than 3,000 tons of soil every second. For good growth of crops we have to conserve the soil and this can be done by controlling erosion. Soil erosion is caused by wind and water. Erosion is also caused by overgrazing, forest fires and growing same crops repeatedly. Erosion makes the soil waterless and causes the death of wild animals. It increases the possibility of floods. Erosion can be controlled by planting trees, bushes and grass. It can also be stopped by controlling soil flow with the help of dams and retaining walls. Contour ploughing, deep ploughing, step farming and mixing of organic matter in the soil is also helpful in controlling soil erosion. The repeated use of chemical fertilizers also reduces the fertility of the soil. It can be controlled to some extent by the use of compost and home made manures.

THE ACID RAIN

The term acid rain refers to the fall of acids mixed with rain and snow. The main cause of acid rain are the gases emitted by the factories and motor vehicles which pollute the atmosphere. Mainly sulphur dioxide is responsible for acid rain which is produced in the burning of fossil fuels. This gas is also produced by natural phenomena like volcanic eruptions, forest fires etc. Sulphur dioxide reacts with water vapour and forms sulphuric acid in the presence of sunlight. This acid gets mixed with rain water or snow flakes and falls on to the earth. Similarly, motor vehicles burn petrol and diesel and produce oxides of nitrogen. These oxides produce nitric acid with rain water.

The acid rain may occur thousands kilometres away from the source of gas emission. During the Gulf war many oilfields caught fire and the smoke produced was so much that it reached even up to the Kashmir Valley and turned the snow into black. Acid rain badly affects the marine life. The reproduction capability of fish gets reduced. Trees defoliate before time and the crops having edible roots get destroyed. The Taj Mahal at Agra and New York's 'Statue of Liberty' have lost their lustre due to acid rain.

POLLUTION

The term pollution refers to the contamination of the environment—air, water and land—with harmful wastes resulted from human activities. Environmental pollution has become a major world wide problem. It has badly affected the whole biosphere.

Pollution has been caused by man. Man has been polluting the air with smoke and poisonous gases; rivers, lakes and oceans with sewage and harmful chemicals. During loading and unloading of crude petroleum in huge tankers millions of tons of oil spills in the oceans adversely effecting the aquatic life. You can observe the dead bodies of birds and fishes near sea shores or floating on the water.

Increasing human population of the world and industrialisation are the major causes of environment pollution. The jungles have been shaved off to accommodate the increasing population. This has considerably reduced the vegetation and forest cover over land. During the last 50 years industries have multiplied manifold. The harmful chemical discharge of factories are polluting the rivers and oceans. The smoke produced by automobiles is increasing the air pollution and the noise produced by the engines of motor vehicles is aggravating the noise pollution. Modern means of agriculture have increased the use of pesticides which have also added to land and water pollution.

The marine life in the big lakes like Ari has vanished due to pollution. The sewage water, industrial wastes and the water from agricultural farms containing extensive amount of fertilizers had filled this lake with too much of phosphates and nitrates. These chemicals have permanently distorted the biological balance of the lake. All the fishes of the lake have died. The water of Ganga and Yamuna rivers is also becoming bodily polluted. Pollution has affected mankind adversely. For the improvement of degradation of biosphere only man is responsible.

Air Pollution

Air not only supports the human life but is also essential for the survival of plants and other animals. Polluted air can cause many diseases such as cancer and lung malfunctioning. The main pollutants of air are the smoke, dust, ash, pollen grains, poisonous gases and tiny particles of materials. The air pollution is mainly caused by burning fossil fuels like coal, petrol, natural gas etc. Industrial plants, electric plants and automobile engines also add to air pollution. They produce oxides of nitrogen, sulphur dioxide, carbon monoxide particulate matter etc. and pollute the air. The smoke emitted by factories, automobiles, trains, ships etc. also release poisonous particles in the air. The smoke of jet planes pollute the upper atmosphere. Air pollution causes many diseases like allergy, cough, cold, heart troubles and many types of cancers. Green leaves turn yellow due to air pollution. The growth of the plants is slowed down. The paint of the buildings gets faded and the colours of various materials and clothes get bleached due to air pollution.

The increasing quantity of carbon dioxide has posed a serious threat to the environment. Prior to industrial revolution the amount of carbon dioxide was 275 to 285 parts per million in the atmosphere. By 1980s this increased to 338 parts per million. The neat energy radiated from the earth is in the form of long waves. About 90 per cent of this heat is absorbed by the atmosphere. Atmosphere heats up mainly due to this terrestrial radiation. The complete absorption of solar radiation by the atmosphere is called *Green House Effect*. The Green House Effect was explained for the first time by the Swedish chemist Arthenius in 1986. In a green house, the glass walls and roof allow the sunlight to reach the earth but they do not allow the terrestrial radiation to go out. This causes the temperature to rise.

On the global scale, carbon dioxide in the atmosphere acts as a green house. The carbon dioxide is largely transparent to incoming light energy but outgoing infrared radiation from the earth is absorbed by carbon dioxide leading to a warming of atmosphere. If the amount of carbon dioxide continues to increase in the atmosphere then the atmospheric temperature will become so high that ice of polar regions will melt and water level in oceans will rise, leading to flooding of coastal areas. The air pollution also affects direction of wind, temperature, climate and weather.

Ozone Deplition

According to meteorological researches the atmosphere is divided into five thermal zones—the troposphere—10 km above the sea level; stratosphere 10 to 40 km; mesosphere 40 to 70 km; ionosphere 70 to 400 km; and exosphere above 400 km.

Stratosphere contains negligible amount of water vapour and dust. Strong jet streams blow in this layer which affect the weather of the earth. For convenience this layer may be divided into two parts called stratospheric layer and ozonosphere. Stratosphere layer exists only up to 25 km height and its temperature remains almost constant. Ozonosphere contains ozone and it exists between 25 km to 40 km. Ozone is essential to life on earth because it acts as a safety shield for the earth. Ozone forms a hot layer by absorbing about 99 percent of short ultraviolet rays of sun which are harmful for the life on earth.

In nature ozone is formed from oxygen by ultraviolet radiations of the sun. These two gases remain in equilibrium or balanced condition. But recently oxygen-ozone balance has been upset by the excessive presence of chemical pollutants in the atmosphere. Scientists believe that ozone layer is becoming thin over Antarctica.

Man-made chemicals specially chlorofluorocarbons adversely affect the ozonosphere. Freon gas is also a chlorofluorocarbon which is used in refrigerators. These chemicals are also used in airconditioners, aerosol spray and plastic foams. Free chlorine atoms of these compounds have disturbed the ozone equilibrium. Ozone depletion will cause dreadful diseases like skin cancer and skin allergies. It may also have hazardous effect on plants and other animals. To save our earth we have to discover substitutes for chlorofluorocarbons which do not cause ozone depletion in atmosphere.

Water Pollution

The earth, from a spacecraft, looks blue, because its two-third part is covered with water. This part is called hydrosphere (hydro means water and sphere means region). Water is elixir of life. Neither plants nor animals can survive without it.

These days rapidly increasing population and industrial units have been polluting the water. The water coming from the factories and homes contains liquid and solid wastes. This is called sewage. The river sources and sea coasts all are polluted by sewage. This polluted water contains organic compounds of mercury and lead which enter into the body of aquatic animals. Eating such fishes is harmful for the eyes and brain of the man. In Minamata Bay of Japan, mercury was deposited in the body of the sea animals through industrial wastes. These animals were eaten by local people. It is horrifying to know that 10 thousand people were poisoned by mercury, and 100 people died the cause of their poisoning could be known. In muddy polluted water sun rays cannot penetrate and light does not reach the aquatic plants. This halts the process of photo synthesis and plants die. Consequently the fishes which are dependent on such plants also die.

Oil pollution is very harmful for the ecological balance of the oceans. The spilled oil spreads widely on the water surface and badly affects the aquatic life. About 30,000 aquatic birds can die due to the oil spill from a big tanker. Fishes do not get sufficient oxygen due to oil pollution and they start dying in large numbers. The oil spill during the Gulf war has been the worst in the history of mankind.

Agricultural fertilizers and insecticides are also adding to water pollution. Heat of nuclear power plants too poses a danger to aquatic life. The river water in large quantity is used to control the nuclear reactions in nuclear power plants. The river water gets heated to very high temperature and is again fed into the river after use. This waste water increases the temperature of river water at the point where it goes into the river. The hot water kills many aquatic plants and animals.

Every nation is striving to provide clear drinking water to its citizens. This can only be done by controlling water pollution.

Noise Pollution

Today, noise pollution has become a serious health hazard in the big cities. Automobiles, trucks, motors, factory machines and even the means of entertainment produce loud, irritating sounds. Man feels disturbed by such sounds. The harmful effects of intense sounds are referred to as noise pollution.

The intensity of sound is measured in decibels. It is based on a logarithmic scale which means that ten decibel is ten times more powerful than one decibel and 20 decibels are 100 times more powerful, and so on. Man's ears can tolerate the sound of upto 80 decibels. The sounds of higher intensity than this are harmful for ears. Normal human voice is of about 60 decibels. People living in noisy places become accustomed to high intensity sounds but their ears lose the sensitivity and capacity to send sound waves to the brain. This leads to deafness.

Studies reveal that in India ten per cent people living in cities and seven per cent in the villages are suffering from auditory defects. Abnormally high noise disturbs the sleep and increases heart beat. Noise pollution causes gastric problems, dilation of pupil of eyes, ulcers in stomach, weakening of teeth and defects in kidney. It is also harmful for the nerves of the womb and adversely affects the embryo of a pregnant woman. Noise pollution can only be checked by the people who are aware of its ill-effects.

LOSING FOREST

Forests are the homes for various plants and animals. There was a time when about 40 per cent of land was covered with forests. Today only one-third part of land has forests. Twenty-two per cent of the world forests are present in the republics which formerly comprised the Soviet Union, 22 per cent in South America, 20 per cent in North America, 17 per cent in Africa, 15 per cent in Asia and the Pacific area and 4 per cent in Europe.

Man has been destroying the forests to meet his needs. According to some surveys about 40 hectares of forests are shaved off per minute. Temperate forests have suffered immense destruction. About 42 per cent of tropical rain forests have been destroyed by man. Such forests are mainly destroyed in Africa where they have reduced to half. In South America 37 per cent and in Asia about 41 per cent of forests had been cut down.

Destruction of forests will not only result in vanishing of greenery on earth, but the whole ecological balance will be disturbed.

Forests provide us with wood, raw materials and protect our environment against pollution. Forty-one per cent land of Soviet Union, 32 per cent of America, 50 per cent of Brazil, and 69 per cent land of Japan is covered with forests. These forests are mainly used for furniture wood, pulp and fuel. Forests are useful in many other ways also. They prevent floods by controlling the flow of rain water. This increases underground water and soil erosion is reduced. Forests prevent fast evaporation of water from land and increase the humidity of air by transpiration. The destruction of forests by man, if not stopped, will one day lead to a catastrophe.

NEW SPECIES

The beauty of earth lies in plants and greenery. Grasslands, fragrant pine forests, evergreen forests and shady deciduous trees contribute to this beauty. Various kinds of animals are also found with plants. The natural groups of plants and animals found in big areas are known as biomes. Biomes are found at those places where environment is favourable for vegetation. The natural vegetation areas and the biomes found in them are interdependent on each other.

The vegetation of any place depends on the climate of that place. The animals found in any area adjust with the climate and vegetation of that place. Today bison grass is not found in Great Plain of North America so the antelope, the animal dependent on this grass, had also become extinct. Hilly goats and sheeps are also lost from conifer biomes. White pine and red wood of California have become extinct in the same way. The unnatural environmental changes brought about by man's lifestyle are responsible for this destruction. Environmental activities all over the world are campaigning to stop all such human activities which are dangerous for biomes.

Rain Forests

Scientists are now concerned about rain forests are found in Amazon basin of South America and coastal regions of Brazil, coastal parts and western islands of central America, Congo basin in Africa, Gini coast and eastern Madagascar, New Guinea island of Asia, Sri Lanka, India's Western coast and north eastern states, countries of South East Asia and southern China.

Rain forests are dense and high. Epiphytes like ferns, archids, algae, lichen etc. are commonly found among them. These plants remain attached to the stems, leaves and branches of trees. A unique feature of rain forests is that different varieties of trees in large numbers grow at one place. Surprisingly more than 1,200 kinds of trees can be found in just one square kilometre area of a rain forest. We do not know exactly how many species of plants and animals exist on the earth. Scientists know about 1,150 million species and they are working to discover more. About many species of plants and insects we are still ignorant. Rain forests are main source of new species. If these forests are destroyed then probably all these species may be lost forever.

The number of mammals is very small in rain forests because mammals cannot easily roam in dense forests. Monkeys, bear, jaguars are commonly found in these forests. The number of crocodiles, gharial and hippocerous in rivers is also very small. Mainly reptiles, insects and birds are found here in large numbers. Besides animals, in these are hidden treasures of useful produce forests would be a great source of useful not yet touched by man.

Today about 40 per cent medicines are obtained from plants. A new fascinating plant Rosy Periwinkle has been discovered from Amazon rain forests which can cure a kind of cancer. Still there are many undiscovered plants in these forests which can be of great help to medical science.

Another plant known as petrol plant is also discovered from Amazon rain forest. The juice of this plant can be used in place of petrol in car engines. Jojoba plant is a similar type of plant recently discovered which can yield good quality oil. Its oil can be used in place of whale oil in many industries. It is expected that in future many more useful products can be obtained from these forests.

WILDLIFE UNDER THREAT

The destruction of forests, pollution, climatic changes and extensive hunting have resulted in the extinction of some species of plants and animals, and many more are approaching towards extinction. Man has realised today that destruction of wild life means end to his own survival.

The Aak bird of northern polar region which was commonly seen some 100 years ago has been so extensively hunted for meat and feathers that its whole genus has vanished. Some 300 years ago the Moa bird of New Zealand became extinct. Dodo was a bird found on Mauritious island which became extinct about 300 years ago as a result of merciless hunting. Thylacine, an animal with pouch which was also known as Wolf of Tasmania, is reported to have become extinct some 300 to 400 years ago. Indian tiger, Indian rhino, pink headed duck are the animals which have become extinct in our country during the present century. The number of rare and endangered animals has been increasing with time.

The destruction rate witnessed during the last few years was never seen before. In a period of 400 years from 1,550 to 1,950, on an average one species of animals have become extinct every year due to ignorance of man. By 1,985 this rate increased to one species per day. If such trends continue, then by the end of present century 50,000 species will become extinct. Studies show that during 1980 to 2,000 about 5,00,000 species of plants and animals will face extinction, *i.e.* 10 per cent of total plants and animals will become extinct.

Wildlife has been under threat of extinction all over the world. Nothing but man's modern lifestyle is responsible for this situation. Today about 1,000 types of animals and 20,000 types of plant species are endangered. Some rare vertebrates like Gila Trout, Houston Toad, Gharial, Californian Condor, Javan Rhinoceros, Lion, Puma, Polar Bear, Antelope, humpback Whale and Panda have reached the stage of extinction.

Among the plants species, Monkey Orchid, Alpine Catchfly and Snakes Head Fritillary are under threat of extinction. The species of following Vertebrates are also facing the danger of extinction:

Fishes	190
Amphibians	40
Reptiles	150
Birds	430
Mammals	320

To control pollution, the effort is on all over the world to bring new areas under forest cover. Cutting of forests is banned to prevent further destruction of forests. The wild animals are saved by keeping them in natural environment. In this direction Yellow Stone National Park was set up in 1872 in USA, which was the first Conservation Area of the world. Canada's Wood Buffalo National Park, Alberta is the world's biggest conservation park, with an area of 45,480 square km. It was established in 1922. Today, there are 1,200 such national parks and animal reserves in the world. India has 59 national parks. Now, zoological parks are also used as conservation areas. About 500 zoos all over the world have saved many animal breeds from extinction.

International Union for the Conservation of Nature and Natural Resources (IUCN) has done pioneering work for the cause of healthy environment and World Wildlife Fund (WWF). This society has helped to lot to save wildlife.

QUESTIONS FOR ANSWER

1. *Give in brief an account of various ingredients of environment and its pollution.*
2. *Write a note on Air and Water Pollution.*
3. *"Losing forest are cause of extinction of wildlife." Justify.*
4. *Write short notes on:*
   (*a*) *Environment and new species.*
   (*b*) *Ozone Depletion.*
   (*c*) *Acid Rain.*
   (*d*) *The Food Chain.*
   (*e*) *Ecology.*

2

Approaches to the Study of Man-Environment Relationship

Environment education consists of many aspects, therefore, study of basic ingredients of environment and its pollutants as discussed in chapter one of this book is the basis of all the aspects we will go through in this book but before we attempt to do so let us understand the following three concepts:

1. Approaches to the study of Man-Environment Relationships.
2. Man's Interactions with the Environment through Ages.
3. Nature of Man-Environment Relationship.

We will discuss these aspects in chapters 2, 3 and 4 respectively. This chapter deals with approaches to the study in a brief manner as follows.

The study of relationships between man and environment has always been, a focal theme of geography as environmental science and facets of man-environment relationship changed through time with the development of human society and the dimension of environment. In the beginning of the process of evolution of man and his society physical elements of the planet earth *e.g.* terrain, soil, water, climate, flora and fauna formed man's environment and man was basically a 'physical man' because of his limited wants, requirements and total dependence on nature.

As the man become social, economic and technological man, he broadened his environment by creating his own environment through his design and skill to have provision for better food, shelter, access and comfort. The man environment relationships, thus, can be perceived and evaluated in a variety of ways and approaches, as discussed hereunder, in brief.

1. DETERMINISTIC APPROACH

This approach is based on the basic tenet of 'earth made man' and pays more attention on the complete control of physical environment on man and his activities. In fact, according to deterministic perspectives of man-environment relationships, man in subordinate to natural environment as all aspects of human life *viz.* physical (health and comfort), social, economic, political, ethical and aesthetic etc. not only depend but are dominantly controlled by physical environment.

Though this deterministic or environmentalistic approach blossomed in the writings of E.C. Semple (1910) in the second decade of the present century but its seeds were already sown in the second half of the nineteenth century. In fact, the publication of 'The Origin of Species' of Charles Drawin in 1859 laid the foundation stone of the concept of environmental influences on man and other organisms.

Fredrich Leplay demonstrated the effects of physical environment on society through his dictom, PLACE (environment)—WORK-FOLK, which shows that environment (PLACE) conditions the type of work, and work shapes, atleast in part. The concept was further elaborated with the tone of firm determinism by Demolins (1901 and 1903). He postulated that 'society is fashioned by environment'.

He attempted to analyse social structure in terms of 'geographical environment'. Three American geographers *e.g.* W.M. Davis, E.C. Semple and E. Huntington strengthened the concept of environmentalism. W.M. Davis, though more known as a geomorphologist, attempted to link nature with man. He classified human elements in terms of physical elements and pleaded for the control of physical elements over human elements.

The concept of environmentalism culminated in 1910 when American geographer E.C. Semple published her book 'Influences of Geographic Environment' wherein she opined that 'man is the product of the earth's surface. This means not merely that he is a child of the earth, dust of her dust, but the earth has mothered him, fed him, set him tasks, directed his thoughts, confronted him with difficulties that have strengthened his body and sharpened his wits, gives him his problems of irrigation and navigation and the same time whispered hints for their solutions.

Deterministic/environmentalistic approach was fully organised on scientific plane by E. Huntington. His 'Civilisation and Climate' (1915), 'The Human and Habitat' (1927), 'Season of Birth' (1938) etc., clearly demonstrate the influences of physical environment on man. His postulation that 'climate not only influences human life but also his birth' proves that he was a strong advocate of environmentalism.

According to Grossman (1977) the first two decades of the twentieth century was influenced by three aspects of contemporary scientific thoughts. (*i*) Darwinian concepts of natural selection, adaptation and survival of the fittest. Darwin's argument that 'gradual modification and diversification of organisms stems from a process of natural selection and adaptation to environmental factor both being slow but on going over long period of time'.

2. TELEOLOGICAL APPROACH

Teleological approach is based on religious faith of man being superior to nature and all other creatures. This school emanated from the teachings of Judeo-Christian religious tradition which preached that 'man is superior to all creatures and every thing is created for his use and enjoyment'. This ideology of man-environment/nature relationship fostered the man to exploit natural resources and to subdue nature without considering the after effects of reckless and uncontrolled plundering of natural resources.

This approach of man-environment relationship led to excessive and rapid rate of exploitation of natural resources in North America and Western Europe as well as in other parts of the world which were their colonies. A host of scientists and environmentalists have held this religious tradition responsible for present-day ecological crises.

3. POSSIBILISTIC APPROACH

Possibilistic approach to the study of man-environment relationships emerged through the criticism of environment determinism and overtone of teleological approach. Right from the very inception of the school of environmental determinism there was dissenting voice raised by those who believed that 'no doubt physical environment influences man and his activities but there is ample scope for man to change the environment so much so that it becomes suitable for man and his society'.

The German philosopher Hegal, fed up with physical determinism remarked, 'Don't talk to me about environmental determinism. Where the Greeks once lived, the Turks live now, that settles the matter'. White reviewing man-environment relationships, Kirchoff concluded that 'man is not an automation without a will of his own. The suggestions thrown out by the nature of his birth place some times find him a docile, some times a different people'.

They believed in the capacity of man to modify and mould the nature in their own ways. This concept of possibilism was founded by Febvre who has remarked, "man is a geographic agent and not the least. He everywhere contributes his share towards investing the physiognomy of the earth with those 'changing expressions' which are the special charge of geography to study".

Two French geographers, Vidal de la Blache and Jeans Bruhnes and American geographers Isiah Bowman and Carl Sauer founded the school of possibilism which is based on the philosophy of possibilism in nature at every stage in a given space and time as remarked by Febvre. 'There are no necessities, but everywhere possibilities and man as a master of these possibilities is the judge of their use'.

Possibilists were quite aware that man cannot fully tame the nature and is not always victorious. Febvre, a staunch believer and advocate of possibilism has accepted that 'Man can never entirely rid themselves, whatever they do, of the hold their environment has on them. Taking this into consideration they utilize their geographical circumstances more or less according to what they are and take advantage of their geographical possibilities. But here as elsewhere there is no question of necessity'.

Possibilists replaced more determinaistic terms 'Control' by 'Influence' and 'Influence' by more moderate terms 'Response' or 'Adjustment'. G. Tantham while bridging the gap between environmental determinism and possibilism maintained that 'the maxim should not be conquest of not submission to, but cooperation with nature'. Harlan Barrows (1923) presented an alternative approach and defined geography as 'human ecology' wherein he pleaded for the study of mutual interaction between man and environment, the study of human societies in relation to their environment and environmental adaptation in place of environmental control.

4. ECONOMIC DETERMINISTIC APPROACH

This approach is based on the basic ideology of Man's mastery over environment and continued economic and industrial expansion through the application of modern technologies. The basic thesis of the growth (affluence) school is that because economic growth is required for political, social and economic stability, the 'quality of environment' normally assumes lower priority in formulating planning proposals and in long-term planning because the deterioration of the environment is generally protracted and socially less oblique than a deterioration in the economy'.

In fact, 'economic determinism' based on two fallacious assumptions of (*i*) positive correlation between the population of a given region and the level of economic development and activity in that region, and (*ii*) the interactions of people, resources and society being governed by universal economic principles as observed by W. Zelinsky, believes in man's ability to solve environmental problems arising out of continued economic growth and industrial expansion.

It may be pointed out that this extreme concept of economic determinism led to rapacious exploitation of natural resources in the western developed countries and thus created most of the environmental and ecological problems of global dimension.

5. ECOLOGICAL APPROACH

Ecological approach to the study of man-environment relationships is based on the basic principle of ecology which is the study of mutual interactions between organisms and physical environment on the one hand and interactions among the organisms on the other hand in a given ecosystem. Thus, man is considered as an integral part of nature/environment.

The relationship of man 'with the natural environment should be symbiotic and not exploitative nor suppressive'. This school recognises man, being most skilled and intelligent, as the leader of all biota and steward of the earth. This approach further lays emphasis on wise and restrained use of natural resources, application of appropriate environmental management programmes, policies and strategies keeping in view the ecological principles so that already depleted natural resources are replenished (wherever possible), degraded environment is set right and ecological balance is maintained.

It may be pointed out that man-environment relationships should be viewed taking into account the multi-dimensional aspects of environmental problems which are the result of complex series of several factors *viz.* physical, economic, social, political ethical etc. but any positive approach adopted for the study of man-environment relationships must take into account the fact that there should be harmony and not hostility between man and environment.

It is obvious that the relationship between man and environment is two-directional as the environment affects and influences man and in turn man also influences and modifies the environment. This type of mutual interactions and relationship between man and environment is symbiotic in character.

QUESTIONS FOR ANSWER

1. *Give a brief account of various approaches of the study of man-environment relationship.*
2. *Discuss in detail the possibilistic approach to the study of man-environmental relationship.*
3. *Write short notes on following approaches of the study of man-environmental relationship:*
   (*a*) *Ecological Approach.*
   (*b*) *Economic Deterministic Approach.*
   (*c*) *Deterministic Approach.*

3

Man's Interaction with Environment Through Ages

The fundamental aim and objective of education is to make man a real man in all aspects—social, political, economic and cultural etc. The basis of the development and growth of these aspects is the process of human interactions with environment, therefore, as a part of environmental education we must understand this process. Hereunder, we will discuss this concept very briefly.

Man is an important part of the biotic component of the environment and simultaneously he is also an important factor of the environment. Thus man plays important roles in the natural environmental system in different capacities such as 'biological or physical man', 'social man', 'economic man' and 'technological man'. All the natural functions of human beings such as birth, growth, health and deaths are affected and determined by the natural environment in the same manner as the cases of other organisms but man being most developed and advanced animal, both physically and mentally and hence technologically, is capable of making substantial changes in natural environment so as to make it suitable for his own living.

The role of most primitive biological or 'physical man' in the functions of natural environmental system was fundamentally that of user of environmental resources and thus he played the role of a factor of the environment but as the skill and technology of man developed with cultural development has roles towards natural environment also changed progressively such as from user through modifier and changer to destroyer of the environment.

So, it is the technology of man which has drastically changed the man-environment relationship from prehistoric period to the present most advanced industrial period. In fact, 'the industrial and scientific revolutions' have led to rapid changes in our environment, but all technology, from the most primitive to the most advanced, causes some changes in the environment.

It may also be stressed that religious ideas and materialistic outlook of man have also played significant roles in changing man-environment relationships on a large-scale. Modern technological man, intoxicated by highly advanced technology and materialistic viewpoints, has changed and is changing the environment for his vested interests to such an extent that even the very existence of human beings is threatened.

Thus if we look at historical progression of man-environment relationships it becomes clear that purely natural relationship between 'physical primitive man' and natural environment during prehistoric period has changed to hostile relationship between 'technological man' and the environment at present. This substantial change and shift in the nature and magnitude of man's interactions with the natural environment has given birth to numerous environmental problems of serious consequences because the changes effected by man in the environment have become unadjustable by the in-built self regulatory mechanism of the natural environmental system/ecosystem.

The study of changing relationships between man and environment in historical prespective may help in demonstrating the increasing adverse impacts of human activities on the environment. The changing relationships of man with the natural environment from prehistoric to modern periods may be divided into four stages as given below.

HUNTING AND FOOD GATHERING PERIOD

This period is related to most primitive man when he was basically a part of natural environment and his function was like other animals. Thus the primitive man was functionally a 'biological man' or 'physical man' because his basic requirements were limited to food only which he could collect from his surroundings. Thus the primitive man used to satisfy his hunger by fruits which were easily obtained from plants and trees and he spent his nights in the caves or on the trees.

The relationship between man and the environment was very

friendly, cordial and sweet. The natural environment provided all requirements of early man (food and shelter) and thus man was totally dependent on his environment. Though even early man used to derive resources from the nature (only food) but this did not make any change in the natural environment because only fruits were used.

With the march of time man learned to hunt animals for his food. This led to first attempted intentional step of man in the exploitation of natural resources. Even the hunting of animals (significant component of biotic components of natural environment) by early man did not make any change in the natural environmental system because of his limited requirement and very low population and unorganised society.

The discovery of fire made a significant change in the attitude of man because now he learned to cook animal flesh before eating. This practice required wood which he used to derive easily from the forest. The demand of wood for burning purposes to roast animals make another significant starting point in the technology as the man had to invent some divice to cut and chop trees and their branches to get firewood.

He also invented some tools to kill animals. Thus the discovery of fire and invention of tools and weapons made the man capable of exploiting natural resources from the forest through fruit gathering and animal hunting.

The first destruction of environment started with inadvertent burning of forests due to carelessness of man while cooking and roasting the animals with fire. This led to a chain of effects by man on his environment. He might have seen the destruction and clearing of dense forests and running of animals away due to inadvertent man-induced fire. He, thus, might have intentionally used fire to drive away dangerous animals from his surroundings.

At a much latter date he also might have used fire to clear the forest for different purposes. Since the early man depended exclusively on fruit gathering and animal hurting to satisfy his hunger, he was very much mobile because he had always to move in search of food. This mobile tendency of early man was also responsible for least interference with the environment interms of its destruction.

It may be concluded that "fire was one of the first major ecological tools used by human beings to change the environment for their own benefit. Indeed, fire has been used around the world by early peoples to clear the land for improved travel and hunting or for farming."

PERIOD OF DOMESTICATION OF ANIMALS AND PASTORALISM

With the march of time early man learned to domesticate animals for his own benefits. He might have domesticated some milch cattle and some animals for meat in the beginning. Slowly and slowly his herd of domesticated animals might have substantially increased. This trend might have necessitated to create habitats though for temporary stay for the domesticated animals.

Thus early man used to burn forest to create temporary home for the domesticated animals, to exploit forest resources to gather fodder for his animals and food for himself. Domestication of animals might have also given birth to group or community life among the early peoples inorder to protect their animals and themselves from wild animals.

With the march of time the early peoples might have gathered larger herds of domesticated animals. They still stuck to nomadic way of life as they had to move from one place to another place in search of water and fodder for their animals and food for themselves.

Thus increase in the population of domesticated animals also led to increase in the population of early peoples which ultimately led to meaningful exploitation of environmental resources but this could not change the natural state of the environment because the population of early peoples and their domesticated animals was still under mangeable size and the changes brought in by human activities in the environment were well within the limit of self-regulatory mechanism of the natural environmental system/ ecosystem.

D.B. Botkin and E.A. Keller have maintained that prehistoric people changed the environment (*i*) by the hunting (of animals for his food); (*ii*) by decreasing the abundance of some animals through hunting; (*iii*) by increasing the abundance of others when they altered the habitats and made them more favourable to those species; (*iv*) by burning (of the forests for making his and his domesticated animal's movement easy, for creating homes for his animals etc.); (*v*) by domesticating plants and animals; (*vi*) by changing erosion rates by agricultural and other land clearing practices and thus altering soils as well as vegetation; and (*vii*) by transporting organisms into new areas from which they had been isolated by geographical boundaries.

PERIOD OF PLANT DOMESTICATION AND AGRICULTURE

Domestication of plants for food was a hallmark in the development of human skill of taming and controlling the biotic component of the natural environmental system or ecosystem. Domestication of plants initiated primitive type of agriculture and sedentary settled life of people who previously were nomads and wanderers.

But still many of the people used to live nomadic life. It may be pointed out that initiation of cultivation of mainly food crops resulted into the formation of social groups and organizations which gave birth to early human civilization known as 'river valley civilization' because most of people settled in the river valleys due to availability of water and fertile land for cultivation.

Thus the emergence of socially organized human communities, human civilization and farming practices changed the existing almost friendly and cordial relationships between man and his natural environment. Gradual but continuous improvement in farming practices resulted into gradual increase in human population and in the number of domesticated animals and thus more and more virgin forest lands were cleared through felling of trees with the help of more advanced tools and weapons and through burning of forest in order to increase the agricultural land so that increasing number of human beings could get food.

People also move from the area of greater concentration (of people) to other areas in search of new fertile land. This led to spread of human population and thus destruction of natural ecosystem. Shifting or Jhuming cultivation, which was most prevalent form of primitive cultivation, was responsible for more destruction of natural forest. Such farming practice is still in operation in many of the hilly regions of south and south-east Asia. North-eastern hill states of India are still characterized by Jhuming cultivation.

With the march of time man developed his own environment known as, 'the cultural environment' by building houses and thus creating villages and towns and cities, by developing social institutions like schools and colleges by building places of worships like temples, churches, mosques etc., by constructing roads, railroads, bridges, canals etc. It may be pointed out that all these and many more elements of 'cultural environment' were evolved through various stages of agricultural development upto 1860 or say before industrial revolution.

All these could be possible because of development in technologies which changed the physical and social man into 'economic man' but no serious damage was done to the natural environment though significant changes, no doubt, were brought in the environment. Though man became successful in transforming the natural environmental resources in his way but the nature was still supreme and master and man continued to be guided by physical environment.

PERIOD OF INDUSTRIALIZATION—SCIENCE AND TECHNOLOGY

The dawn of industrial revolution in late nineteenth century (say precisely since 1860 A.D.) with the emergence of science and development of more efficient and sophisticated technology initiated the hostile relationship between man and his natural environment. Extreme concept of the western world, advanced technologies and scientific techniques of the modern 'technological man' led to reckless and indiscriminate rapacious exploitation of natural resources for industrial expansion and urban growth which have altogether created most of the present day environmental and ecological problems of global dimension.

The impacts of modern technological man on natural environment are varied and highly complex as the transformation or modification of one natural condition and process leads to a series of changes in the biotic and abiotic components of biospheric ecosystems.

The man's impacts on environment fall into two broad categories *viz.* (*i*) Direct or Intentional Impacts, and (*ii*) Indirect or Unintentional Impacts. Direct or intentional impacts are preplanned and premediated because man is aware of the consequences, both positive and negative of any programme which is launched to change or modify the natural environment for economic development of the region concerned. Such changes include land use changes (clearing of forests and burning of grass lands for crop cultivation; felling of trees for commercial purposes; changes in cropping patterns in relations to new farming techniques, new high yielding seeds, irrigational facilities etc.) constructions and excavations, agricultural practices (mechanisation of agriculture, use of chemical fertilisers, pesticides and insectisides), weather modification programmes (cloud seeding to induce precipitation, dispersal and clearing of clouds and fogs, checking of hailstroms etc.), nuclear programmes etc.

It is significant to point out that the effects of such anthropogenic changes in the natural environment are noticeable within short period and may continue to affect the environment for long time but these effects are reversible because both before and after studies (which are possible) may enable the man to set the adverse effects right to certain extent if so intended by making suitable changes in the initial programmes.

For example, deforestation (either for cropland or for commercial purposes) leads to accelerated rate of soil erosion resulting into gully erosion and loss of soil fertility on the one hand and enormous increase in sediment load in the river which causes severe floods on the other hand. These chain effects can be effectively stopped by reforestation of the deforested areas. Similarly, changes in farm practices, which introduce adverse changes in the environment, may be rechanged to suit the environment and ecological situations.

As regards weather modification and transformation of climate at local and regional levels through purposive human action, the after effects are seldom pre-mediated. It is important to note that it is not possible to master meteorological processes because 'there is no permanent channels of control in the atmosphere as in machines and living organism' but man can control or divert undesirable natural atmospheric processes and disturbances as cyclones, hailstorms, precipitation, clouds etc.

One of the intentional or purposive actions of man to modify meterological phenomena is 'cloud seeding' to stimulate clouds and precipitation through crystallisation of supercooled drops through the application of solid carbon dioxide and certain compounds of iodine.

'A few hundred grams of solid carbon-dioxide or a few grams of an iodine compound are enough to crystalise a cubic kilometre of a super-cooled cloud of water drops'. The second area of weather modification is prevention of hailstorms. Such practices are being carried in Soviet Union, Bulgaria, Hungary, Yogoslavia, Switzerland etc.

The third area is of dispersal of low, supercooled clouds and fogs to clear airports in winter for smooth landing and take off of aircrafts. In all the cases enormous heat energy employed to induce precipitation, to prevent hails and to disperse and clear clouds and fogs is released and it causes additional heating of the lower layer of the atmosphere and thus changes the natural meteorological processes.

Withdrawal of groundwater for drinking water and irrigational purposes is a general practice in almost all the countries but some times the impact is so enormous that it becomes disastrous and pounds back on man and society.

This resulted into the formation of big cavity beneath the city, consequently saline sea water leaked into the cavity and the wells became contaminated due to salty water which forced the city authorities to close down these contaminated wells.

Excessive withdrawal of groundwater also results in land subsidence. A land subsidence of 1 metre to 3 metres has been reported in a few localities of San Joanquin valley in California because of drop in water table from 30 m to 150 m due to pumping of groundwater from the basins filled with alluvial sediments (A.N. Strahler and A.H. Strahler, 1976, p. 127).

The cases of land subsidence due to withdrawal of groundwater have occurred in several localities and cities all over the world *e.g.* Houston City (Texas, U.S.A., 0.3 to 1.0 m), Mexico city (ground subsidence from 4 m to 7 m between 1891 and 1959), Venice (Italy) etc. Ground subsidence also occurs due to mining activities.

Constructional activities, like construction of dams and reservoirs, upset the equilibrium of the rocks below and thus is triggered off seismic events because the load of water of lakes and reservoirs constructed behind the dams on majro rivers increases hydrostatic pressure which causes disturbances in the underlying rocks. The earthquakes of Denver since 1962 (Denver, Colorado, U.S.A., due to pumping of fluids under pressure into disposal well upto the depth of 3,600 m and associated release of strains within the already disturbed rocks), Los Angeles earthquake of 1963 (California, U.S.A. caused due to raising of the hydrostatic pressure through pumping of fluids into the oil field so that the production of mineral oil could be increased.

This resulted into the movement of pre-existing faults and triggered off tremors which fractured the wall of the Baldwin Hills Reservoir), Lake Mead earthquake (Hoover Dam in Arizona and Nevada, U.S.A., due to weight of accumulated water in the Mead Lake Reservoir), earthquakes occurring around Lake Kariba (on Zambezi river in Zambia), Koyana earthquake of 11 December 1967 (Satara, Maharashtra, India, due to weight of water in the Koyana Reservoir) etc.

Man changes the river regime and ecology through flood control measures, reservoirs, construction of dykes and flood walls to restrict the water into river valleys, flood diversion systems and stream channelization (strenghthening, shortening, widening, deepening of river channels to prevent seasonal overbank flooding).

The indirect impacts of man on the environment are not premediated and planned and these arise from those human activities which are directed to accelerate the pace of economic growth, especially industrial development. Though such economic activities may be economically important but the after-effects are certainly socially undesirable.

The indirect impacts of human economic activities on the environment are not immediately noticeable because of time-lag because the effects of economic activities bring in slow rate of changes of moderate nature in a few components of the ecosystems and these changes take long time to cross the sensitivity of the system.

Moreover, the indirect impacts are experienced after long time when they become cumulative. Sometimes, such effects are not reversible and therefore it becomes very difficult to identify and evaluate them. These effects may change the overall natural system and the chain effects some times become suicidal for human being. Majority of the indirect impacts of human activities on the environment are related to pollution and environment degradation.

The release of toxic elements into the ecosystem through their uses as insecticides, fertilizers etc., changes the food chains and food webs (*e.g.* introduction of D.D.T.). Similarly, the release of industrial wastes into stagnant water, rivers and seas contaminates water and causes several diseases and deaths of organisms and thus disturbs ecological balance (*e.g.* washing and dumping of tailings or waste sludges from factories, release and concentration of specks of asbestos, release of mercury in its toxic methyl form, leakage of crude oil from oil tankers, release of lead, mixing of different quantities of dissolved inorganic matter etc.).

M.C. Saxena (1989) has cautioned the people against the environmental pollution caused due to indiscriminate and excessive use of pesticides, fertilizers and a number of other chemicals (about 2,000 chemicals are released to the environment each year). According to him these toxicants are transported across the placenta and reach the developing foetus of woman and cause abortions and premature labour.

Increasing urbanisation and industrial expansion are responsible for the release of enormous quantities of pollutants (ions of chlorine, sulphate, bicarbonate, nitrate, sodium, magnesium, phosphate etc.) through sewage effulent into the river and lakes and thus contaminating the water. 'The basins of rivers flowing through thickly populated and industrially developed regions (and there are almost all the rivers of the U.S.A., Japan and European countries, including two-thirds of the rivers in the European part of the U.S.S.R.) have long lost their natural state and been converted into transport, power and water—main systems of sorts and at the same-time into sewers'.

The Yamuna river at Delhi has, in fact become a sewage as 323 million gallons of sewage enter the Yamuna per day through 17 open drains, while the capacity of all treatment plants of the Municipal Corporation of Delhi (MCD) is only 184 MGO (million gallons per day). 'Before the Yamuna enters the capital, 100 millilitres of its water contain more than 7,500 disease causing bacteria but after receiving Delhi's share of sewage carries 24 million bacteria according to pollution control experts'. The tanneries (151) of Kanpur city are heavily polluting the Ganga by discharging 5.8 MLD (million litres per day) of untreated effluents. The pollution of the Gomti river at Lucknow has resulted into the death of all useful organisms.

Urbanisation, industrial expansion and land use changes very often change weather and climate though in long-term perspective. Economic activities of man are capable of affecting the heat balance of the earth and its atmosphere which in turn transforms weather and climate at regional and global scales. Infact man changes the atmospheric conditions through (*i*) changes in the natural geseous composition of the atmosphere mainly in the lower part, (*ii*) changes in the water vapour content of the troposphere and the stratosphere through direct (cloud seeding) and indirect means (deforestation), (*iii*) changes and alteration of land surfaces (deforestation, mining, urbanisation etc.), (*iv*) introduction of aerosol in the lower atmosphere, and (*v*) release of additional heat in the atmosphere (from urban and industrial sources) etc.

The burning of hydrocarbon fuels has increased the concentration of CO_2 in the atmosphere. The natural content of CO_2 in the atmosphere was fixed at 0.029 per cent or 290 ppm (part per million) before industrial revolution (before 1860) but at present the atmospheric level of concentration of CO_2 is estimated to be 0.0319 per cent (319 ppm, an increase of 10 %) and it is expected that by the turn of the present century it would increase to 0.0370 per cent (370 ppm, an increase of 25 per cent over the pre-industrial level).

The increase in CO_2 content of the atmosphere may change heat balance by increasing the level of sensible heat in the atmosphere because CO_2 allows more absorption of incoming short wave solar radiation and out going long wave terrestrial radiation. Release of chlorofluorocarbon in the atmosphere through the propellants used in spray can dispensers and fluids used in refrigerators and air conditioners and of nitrogen oxides emitted from the engines of supersonic jets (flying at the height of about 60,000 feet with a speed of more than twice the speed of sound) is capable of depletion of ozone.

It may be pointed out that ozone gas in the atmosphere (ozone layer is concentrated mostly at the height of 15 km–36/55 km) absorbs ultraviolet rays of the sun and thus protects the earth from becoming too hot. Depletion in ozone layer means less absorption of ultraviolet rays and thus increase in the temperature at the earth's surface.

Thus increase in air temperature through increased solar ultra-violet radiation due to decrease in the concentration of O_3 (ozone) would cause skin cancer, immuno-suppression in human body, decrease photosynthesis, water use efficiency and crop yield. The marine environment would also suffer drastic damages as the productivity of phytoplankton would be reduced due to decrease in photosynthesis and therefore zooplankton feeding on phytoplankton would starve.

This will also affect the mortality of larvae of zoophankton. The species composition of marine ecosystem may change as certain species are more vulnerable to ultraviolet radiation. Ultraviolet radiation also accelerates the photochemical processes that create urban smogs.

QUESTIONS FOR ANSWER

1. *"Man plays important role in the natural environmental system in different capacities such as 'biological or physical man', 'social man', 'economic man and 'technological man'." Justify this statement in brief.*
2. *"During the period of hunting and food gathering relationship between man and environment was very friendly, cordial and sweet." Justify this statement.*
3. *"During the period of plant domestication and agriculture the emergence of socially organised human communities and human civilisation changed the almost friendly and cordial relationships between man and his natural environment". Justify this statement.*
4. *"Extreme advanced technologies and scientific techniques of modern 'technological man' led to reckless and indiscriminate rapacious exploitation of natural resources for industrial expansion and urban growth which have altogether created most of the present day environmental and ecological problems of global dimensions" Justify this statement to highlight the need of environmental education.*

4

Current Nature of Man-Environment Relationship

Current nature of man-environment relationship is the subject matter of environmental education, therefore, hereunder we will discuss this concept very briefly because in the last chapter under sub-heading—Period of Industrialization—Science and Technology, we have already discussed basic nature of current human interaction with environment.

The environment affects man through (*i*) biophysical limitations, (*ii*) behavioural controls, and (*iii*) resource availability. Weather and climate affect human well-being and health. The study of reactions of human body to changes in the atmospheric environment is known as 'human biometeorology' which lays emphasis on to 'establish how much of the overall biological variability is the result of changes in weather, climate and season.

According to M. Bates (1966) three levels of climatic environment affect human behaviour *viz.* (*i*) 'microclimate' (which represents weather conditions surrounding an individual organism), (*ii*) 'ecological climate' or 'ecolimate' (represents weather elements of the habitat of the organisms, in the case of man the habitat may be his house and working places like factory, office, mine, agricultural farms, pasture or forest), and (*iii*) 'geographical climate' or 'geoclimate' (weather conditions of larger areal unit and longer span).

Biologically, human body can function properly only in certain suites of environmental conditions in terms of oxygen, heat, light, humidity and precipitation, wind, lightning, fog, clouds, atmospheric electricity and space. Even the survival of human body depends on the above factors. Lack of required amount of oxygen at higher attitudes makes human survival impossible. Excessive heat and humidity retard body and mental growth whereas very high or very low temperature on the one hand adversely affects human body and on the other hand makes food a scarce commodity to support human life.

Micro-climate affects leisure, recreation, comfort etc. Certain non-infectious diseases and medical disorders have been correlated with environmental factors such as geochemistry of rocks, soils and water. Concentration of a few traceminerals in the racks, soils and water in the U.P. Himalaya causes stomach disorders through diarhoea, dysentry etc.

M. Cole has shown correlation between certain forms of cancer and cardio-vascular troubles and geochemical properties of soils and water whereas B.E. Davies and R.J.F.H. Pincent's study of 'minerals and morbidity' has revealed relationships between stomach cancer and hardening of tissues and arteries of human body (sclerosis) and certain trace minerals in the soils and water.

Certain diseases and illnesses have been related to atmospheric conditions. E.H. Derrick has related seasonal, annual and short-term variations in asthma in Brisbane (Australia) to variations in weather conditions. He has related weeks with high incidence of asthma with decrease in mean and minimum temperature, due point, relative humidity and rainfall but increase in sunshine hours whereas low incidence of asthma has been found in those weeks which are characterised by higher due points and relative humidity, more rainy days, low temperature ranges and fewer hours of sunshine.

Many more investigators have established evidences to demonstrate close association between asthma and cold *e.g.* L. Greenburg, F. Field, J.I. Reed and C.L. Erchardt relationship between asthma and temperature change in New York), S.W. Tromp and J. Bouma (1965, increase in asthma among 16 years old children during periods of cooling in the eastern Netherlands), M.J. Spodnik, concluded that airflow resistance of 100 students of Baltimore, U.S.A., increased with decrease in temperature, etc.

J.B. Hansen and S.A. Pedersen's (1972) study of relation between barometric pressure and certain ailments has demonstrated that there is positive correlation between rapid changes in the atmospheric pressure and the incidence of perforated duodenal ulcers and peripheral arterial embolism. F.K.

Davis has found close relationship between temperature changes and frequency of haemorrhaging from duodenal ulcers.

A few researches have revealed seasonal occurrences of many diseases and ailments *e.g.* scarlet fever, diptheria, and jaundice are more prevalent during winter whereas measles, influenza and chicken pox are most common in spring in Switzerland (J.E. Hobbs, 1980).

Various combinations of environmental factors have not only affected but conditioned racial characteristics in different parts of the earth's surface. Environment also influences and conditions thoughts, ideologies and culture of human being. Even the social, economic and political behaviour is influenced to certain extent by man's perception of environmental factor and his responses to these factors.

Frequency and magnitude of extreme natural events and environmental factors like vulcanicity, earthquakes, floods, droughts, landslides, atmospheric storms etc. influence man's perception of natural environment and decide his reactions and responses to these events.

For example, the inhabitants of riparian tracts of major alluvial rivers of the Ganga plain of North India are largely adversely affected by recurrent floods and riparian decay and thus they conceive that rivers are sources of perpetual disasters but the inhabitants of equatorial rain forest living in the riverine tracts are seldom aware of floods and disastrous role of rivers.

The ravinous tracts of the Chambal valley (India) have not only moulded the social behaviour of the local people but also of the people of the adjoining areas as the circuitous network of ravines provides ideal hideouts and the people after committing crimes easily escape to these ravines which extend standing invitation to criminals by providing safe shelter though with least comfort. Many more examples may be cited to demonstrate the impact of environment on human behaviour, his perception and responses to environmental factors.

The most significant aspect of the environment in influencing human activity is the availability of resources. The richness or poorness, quality and quantity and above all the availability of renewable and non-renewable resources decide the type of human activities, economic viability, social organisations, political stability, international relations etc.

Very rich reserve of mineral oil in the Middle East is the main reason for political instability in the Gulf Countries. The inter-state disputes sharing river waters are because of location of rivers in more than one country. In fact, the level of economic development largely depends on natural resources.

QUESTIONS FOR ANSWER

1. *Write a note on environmental affects on man.*
2. *"Various combinations of environmental factors have not only affected but conditional racial characteristics in different parts of earth is surface." Justify this statement.*
3. *Write a note on the relationship between environment and human health.*

5

Basic Aspects of Environment

The study of environmental education as a discipline—the object of this book, requires fundamental knowledge of man-environment relationship as discussed in chapters 1, 2, 3 and 4 of this book as well as a clear understanding of the basic aspects of environment, which we will discuss in brief hereunder.

INTRODUCTION

Environment is a broad concept encompassing the whole range of diverse surroundings in which we perceive, experience and react to events and changes. It includes the land, water, vegetation, air and the whole gamut of the social order. It also includes the physical and ecological environment. It concerns man's ability to adapt both physically and mentally to the continuing change in environment.

Environment is not static. It is dynamic and changes occur event if there in no human interference. In its natural uninterfered conditions, the environment of any region is in state of dynamic equilibrium. This is what is called the balance of nature. It is when human's in their greed or say ego to conquer nature for higher and still higher standard of life for the ever increasing population try to over exploit and interfere with nature that this equilibrium is disturbed and in most class to the detriment of all forms of life.

Ultimately it is the condition of our land and water resources and the quality of the air which we breathe that determine the wealth of nation.

Generally speaking the environment is equated with nature wherein physical components of the planet earth, *viz.* land, air, water etc., support and affect life in the biosphere. A. Goudie (1984) in his book *'The Nature of the Environment'* has, in fact, taken environment as the representative of physical components of the earth wherein man is an important factor affecting the environment.

Environment is defined more comprehensively by others as holistic view of the world as it functions at any point of time, with a multitude of spatial element and socio-economic 'systems distinguished by quality and attributes of space and mode of behaviour of physical and biological forms.

Our immediate concern is the quality of space we live in, the air we breathe, the food we eat, the water we drink and the resources we draw from the environment to support our economy'. He has also pleaded for the inclusion of only 'air-land-water-plant' in the concept of environment, thus excluding man and human society from the ambit of environment.

There has been a constant debate on heredity and environment as regards their influence, in the development of personality of an individual. Behaviourists are of this view that environment is all in all in the development of personality and heredity is nothing to do in it. Others say that heredity has an important role in the personality development.

The main focus of educational process is to develop the child personality, therefore main job of education is to create conducive environment for the child in educational institutions. The development of any type—physical, social, economic, cultural, etc., require an appropriate or desirable environment.

MEANING OF ENVIRONMENT

The dictionary meaning of the word 'environment is a surrounding; external conditions influencing development or growth of people, animals or plants; living or working conditions etc. This involves three questions what is surrounded? by what surrounded? and where surrounded?

Decidedly the answer to the first question is living object in general and man in particular. If man is taken to be surrounded, physical attributes become the answer to the second question which become environment and where surrounded is the space or habitat. Primarily, the concern of all educationists is with the environment of man. But man cannot exist or be understood in isolation from the other forms of life and from plant life' and so environment of all biological population should be the concern of teachers. 'Environment refers to the sum total of conditions which surround man at a given point in space and time'.

In the beginning the environment of early man consisted of only physical aspects of the planet earth (land, air and water) and biological communities but with the march of time and advancement of society man extended his environment through his social, economic and political functions.

Thus we see that there are several difficult ways in which the world environment is used, most people are aware that there is a need for all of us to care of the environment, if we wish not to threaten the ability of the earth to support future generations. This can only be done by imparting instructions concerning environmental education.

DEFINITION OF ENVIRONMENT

Environment covers all those circumstances which assert their influence on the individual since conception to death. Whatever found around the individual, may be covered by the term environment. It has been defined by various psychologists as follows:

> 'A person's environment consists of the sum total of the stimulation which he receives from his conception until his death'.
> —*Boring*

> 'The environment is everything that affects the individual except his genes'.
> —*Anastasi*

> 'The term environment is used to describe, in the aggregate, all the external forces, influences and conditions, which affect, the life, nature, behaviour and the growth, development and maturity of living organisms.'
> —*Douglass and Holland*

Environment consists of various types of forces like, physical, intellectual, social, moral, economic, political, cultural and emotional forces. 'Environment is the aggregate of all the external forces, influences and conditions, which affect the life, nature, behaviour and the growth, development and maturation of living organisms.

The term mental environment means the atmosphere necessary

for the mental development of person. All the things helpful in the mental development of a child constitute his mental environment. Thus, for a child in school, the mental development consists of the libraries, laboratories, recreational, co-curricular as well as curricular activities. If these are properly organised, the child would achieve the desired intellectual development. Therefore, teachers should try their best to provide the best mental environment in the schools.

The term 'Environment' refers the surroundings of an organism which includes both living and non-living components. The word meaning of environment is to surround and to develop. The words 'surround' and 'develop' raise two basic questions:

- What is surrounded and developed? The answer is that man and other organism.
- Man and other living organism are surrounded by what? The simple answer is that all non-living components—Land, water, air, atmospheric pressure, etc, and living components—plants, social, cultural and economic surroundings.

Thus environment consists of natural as well as socio-cultural environment. Man has to improve the quality of his environment, because there is environmental pollution or crisis. It is due to over consumption of natural resources, over population, urbanization, industrialization and unscientific attitude of human beings.

Natural resources have been utilised to meet the demand of better living to such an extent that has caused serious ecological and environmental imbalances. Man's participation is the only way to improve environment protection. The best insurance for the environment is a commitment to prevent the deterioration of land, water and air and hence introduction of environmental education at various levels of our educational system.

Environment is viewed in different ways with different angles by different groups of people but it may be safely argued that 'environment is an inseparable whole and is constituted by the interacting systems of physical, biological and cultural elements which are inter-related individually as well as collectively in myrid ways.

Physical elements (space, landforms, water bodies, climate soils, rocks and minerals) determine the variable character of the human habitat, its opportunities as well as limitations. Biological element (plants, animals, micro-organisms and man) constitute the biosphere. Cultural elements (economic, social and political) are essentially man-made features which go into the making of cultural milieu'.

BASIC CHARACTERISTICS OF ENVIRONMENT

Above definition underline basic characteristics of environment, which may be listed as follows:

1. The sum total of the stimulation from his birth until his death.
2. It is the every thing which affects the individual excluding genes.
3. All the external forces which affect the growth, development of living organism.
4. It consists of physical, intellectual, social, moral, cultural, emotional, economic and political forces which affect the life and nature of behaviour.
5. It refers to sum total of conditions which surround man at given point in space and time.
6. It includes physical (land, air and water) and biological (plants, animals including man and his several functions, organizations and institutions) components.
7. It involves, physical, chemical, biological, social, economic, political and cultural processes.

CLASSIFICATION OF ENVIRONMENT

Kurt Lewin has enumerated three types of environment which influence the personality of an individual—

1. Physical Environment,
2. Social and Cultural Environment, and
3. Psychological Environment.

Kurt Lewin includes biological components in physical environment.

1. Physical Environment

It refers to geographical climate and weather or physical conditions in which an individual lives. The human races are greatly influenced by the climate. The white, black and yellow races are due to climatic conditions. In the cold countries, the people are of white colour and in hot countries people are of black colour.

The human working efficiency depends on the climatic conditions. The physique of an individual depends on climatic conditions. The individual tries to adjust in his physical environment. Even heredity is also influenced by the physical environment.

2. Social and Cultural Environment

It refers to the social, economic and political conditions of an individual in which he lives. The moral, cultural and emotional forces affect the life and nature of individual behaviour. It may be of two types—closed and open society. The open society is very conducive for the individual development, whereas closed society is not very conducive for the development. Even the classroom climate should be more open which contribute for the development of individual potentialities. Every individual tries to adjust in his social environment.

3. Psychological Environment

Kurt Lewin has given main emphasis to the psychological environment of individual. The physical and social environment are common to the individual in a specific situation while every individual has own environment, in which he lives. He has used 'life space', topology for explaining psychological environment. It refers to the definition of personality. The man within man is the personality.

Psychological environment is very important to understand the personality of an individual. The person and his goal form the psychological environment. If a person can not achieve his goal, unable to overcome the barriers it may account to frustration or he has to change his goal for a new psychological environment. This mechanism will help the individual for the adjustment.

COMPONENTS OF ENVIRONMENT

Since this aspect has been discussed in chapter one of this book, therefore, hereunder only a brief account is given.

Land

Land is one of the most important components of our environment as the soil is vital for life. An inch of soil takes anything from 500 to 1,000 years to build whereas it may take only one rainy season to erode. The soil erosion is a natural process, but in its undisturbed condition the existing plant cover of grasses, shrubs and trees not only check soil but also replenish soil.

As human activity disturbs this balance of soil and vegetation, soil erosion is accelerated, Pollution starts its existence, in India nearly 175 million hectares or about 50 per cent of our land area; suffers from one type of degradation or the other and comes under the definition of waste land, which means the productivity from this area is much less than what it should be.

Another about 27 millions hectares are degraded by floods, salinity and alkalinity. It is estimated that our national soil loss is about 6,000 million tons annually, and with this soil we loss about 6 million tons of nutrients. This is more than the quantity of fertilisers applied to our soil every year. If we do not take adequate the timely care of our oil resources the time is not far when there will be famine and hunger stalking us.

The application of inorganic fertilizers to our crop-lands and using highly toxic insecticides and pesticides to control crop diseases, has the harmful effects of indiscriminate use of the toxic chemicals in agriculture over a long period is contaminating food and feed. It is absolutely essentially to be cautious with the modern technology in agriculture if we want to sustain to our crop production at a reasonable high level to feed the rising population.

Another problem is incorrect land use and this is mainly responsible for land degradation. Good agriculture land and forest are being destroyed for faulty irrigation practices or are being used for brick manufacture or for urban development scheme. What is required is scientific land use planning policy for the country.

Water

Water is vital for all forms of life on this earth. In our country, the main source of water is in the form of precipitation, which is roughly of the order of 400 million hectare metre per year. Nearly 50 per cent of it percolates into the soil. About 30 per cent of it runs as surface run off and another 20 per cent evaporates into the atmosphere.

Pure and clean water is necessary for healthy environment. We cannot afford to waste our valuable water and resources through faulty land and water management practices. But whatever water bodies we have in India about 70 per cent of them are polluted.

Pollution of water may be by different sources. Soil erosion in the catchment of the rivers, streams and ponds leads to excessive sediments load thus polluting the water system. Streams and other water systems are also polluted by municipal waste and industrial effluent, particularly.

The responsibility for maintaining civil amenities like water supply, drainage, slum clearance, open spaces and streets in the cities rests with our municipal bodies. Unfortunately there has been a dismal failure on the part of our municipal bodies to keep the cities and nearby streams clean. Similarly industries have taken up anticipation measures only haltingly causing severe pollution to our water bodies.

Forests

Forests influences local and regional climates besides their productive uses *viz.* supply of energy in the form of wood and timber for construction purposes. They make the climate milder, help to ensure a continuous flow of clean water, reduce soil erosion, and reduces chances of floods and droughts. We all know these: but in spite of this, forests are being divested in the name of development.

The satellite imagery has indicated that the total extent of forest cover in 1986 was only 46 million hectare which is hardly about 14 per cent of the total land area as against the recorded area of about 23 per cent. We are losing about 1.5 million hectares of forest cover every year. At this rate India will have no real forest cover left in another 40-50 years. This is a very alarming picture.

Mining

Extraction of minerals for industrial development and better living standard is inevitable. Mining, however, has a serious disturbing effect on the ecology and environment leading to pollution. Generation of various pollutants, directly and indirectly are in built features of mining activity. Mining ruins the land, water, forests and air.

The pollution of natural resources degrades the quality of human life in these areas. Air pollution in mining areas causes respiratory diseases and eye ailments. A study has indicated that chronic exposure to sulphur dioxide and nitrous oxide has an effect on mortality rate of cancer.

Hence, like the developed countries like U.S.A., U.K. etc. there should be low requiring that reclamation of the mine area has, to be undertaken by the mining company and the land must be stored in original condition after mining within a specified period of time.

Air

Air is life itself but pollutants are being added into the atmosphere. An Expert committee of the W.H.O. warns: "Earth's atmosphere is finite, and its capacity to cleanse itself seems to be limited." Industries like Oil Refineries, Fertilisers, Paper and Cement etc. produce hydrogen sulphate, oxides of sulphur, organic vapour and dust. Steel plants emit metal fumes, fluorides, oxides of sulphur and particulates. All these are health hazards. The Central Board for Pollution Control and scientist like Prof. Trivedi and his associates from our state in collaboration with State Board of Pollution conducted a study and have found that the consumption of motor spirit containing LEAD has increased by almost twice the anticipated rate after 1983 in surrounding air at street crossing in Patna. According to Central Board it is 8 to 10 times than those in Delhi and Calcutta, because of the Oil Refineries in the East and North East which produces motor spirit with TEL (Tetra ethyl lead).

So unless we stop using the atmosphere as dustbin for our toxic industrial and vehicular emissions the atmosphere will lose its life sustaining property. It is also high time that the industries should reorientate their attitudes and consider pollution control as a part of their corporate and social responsibility. They must learn to concentrate on 3Ps namely Production, Profit, and Pollution, Control instead of 2 Ps *i.e.* Production and Profit only.

It is necessary that every development programme/project

should have in built provision for environmental protection (Pollution control) and should take into consideration the consequences of the project/programme on the Environment (Pollution load). In case of an adverse consequences, appropriate remedial measures have to be provided in the project itself. Environmental Education based on scientific studies and social system approach will generate awareness in the common masses as well as to government for better developmental planning.

So, if we have to maintain the ecological balance and sustainable development for the posterity, an integration of environmental conservation and development is important. Unless we protect and conserve our natural resources of land, water, vegetation, and air, it will be impossible to meet the rising demands of the present day population without fore-closing the achievements of tomorrow.

BIOLOGICAL AND PHYSICAL COMPONENT OF ENVIRONMENT

Experts devoted to the study of environment are of the opinion that the environment is both physical and biological concept, it includes both living and non-living components. Thus, on the basis of basic structure the environment may be divided into two basic types. (1) Physical or abiotic environment, and (2) Biological or biotic environment. On the basis of physical characteristics and state, the physical environment is subdivided into three broad categories *viz.*, (*i*) solid, (*ii*) liquid, and (*iii*) gas which represent the lithosphere (solid earth), the hydrosphere (water component) and the atmosphere respectively.

Thus the three basic divisions of physical environment may be termed as (*i*) lithospheric environment, (*ii*) atmospheric environmental, and (*iii*) hydrospheric environment. These may be further broken into smaller units based on different spatial scales, *e.g.*, mountain environment, plateau environment, plain environment, lake environment, river environment, maritime environment, glacier environment, desert environment, coastal environment, etc.

Biological Component

The biological component of the environment consists of plants (flora) and animals (fauna) including man as an important factor. Thus the biotic environment may be divided into floral environment and faunal environment. All the organisms work to form their social groups and organisation at several levels and thus is formed social environment wherein the organisms work to derive matter from the physical environment for their sustenance and development. This process generates economic environment. It may be pointed out that of all the organisms man is the most skilled and civilized and hence his social organisation is most systematic.

It is significant to note that three aspects of man, *e.g.*, physical, social and economic, have different characteristics and functions in the biotic environment as 'physical man' is one of the organismic populations or biological community and thus requires basic elements of the physical environment, *viz.*, habitat (space), air, water and food like other biological, populations and releases wastes into the ecosystem; 'social man' establishes social institutions, forms social organisations, formulates 'laws, principles and policies to safeguard his existence, interest and social welfare and 'economic man' derives and utilises resources from the physical and biotic environments with his skills and technologies. These may be termed as physical, social and economic functions of man.

It is the third function (economic) which makes the man an environmental/geomorphic process as well because he transports matter and energy from one component of the ecosystem to the other. This aspect/function does not necessarily involve change in the working of the ecosystem so long as the exploitative functions are an harmony with the natural environment but when these exceed the critical limit, the equilibrium of the environment/ecosystem is disturbed and several environmental and ecological problems crop up which become detrimental not only to man himself but to whole population (of spacies) in a given ecosystem.

Physical Component

The physical environment may also be viewed in terms of climatic conditions providing certain suites of habitat for the biological communities, *viz.*, tropical environment, temperate environment, polar environment, etc., which may be further sub-divided into smaller but specific divisions. Physical/abiotic and biotic environments fused together form 'biome environment' like tundra biome, temperate biome and tropical biome which are further sub-divided into second and third order biomes.

In environmental geography the physical environment is the most outstanding feature and thus should be given more significance than the social or cultural environment. The economic function of man becomes more significant than his other functions as it is more concerned with the functioning of ecosystem. Thus, the interaction of man through his economic function and hence as an environmental process, with natural environment and resultant human response to the environment is the fundamental concern of environmental education.

In addition to the above following components are considered as vital too by some scholars of environmental studies:

1. *Social components* are population, social system, social changes and social relations, urbanization, etc.
2. *Cultural components* are political, economic, moral and values of life religion, industries, etc.
3. *Psychological components* are facts, self concepts, level of aspiration, life space, topology, goals of life.
4. *Energy components* are includes solar energy and geothermal energy.

Social components are very important to determine the role of educational institutions. Environment and society are closely related and they are interdependent. Different social groups and social structures like industrial, agricultural, political, cultural, religious, aesthetic, etc., have evolved and developed during various stages of development of human civilization and there social structure represents man's accumulated cultural experiences and resources primarily based on natural environment. The educational process helps in the development of different structures of society, on one hand, the quality of environment on the other hand.

'Education is the creature and creator of society.' The structure of the society is evolved by the process of education. The educational process utilizes the natural environment and its resources. Different social structures depend on the natural resources and environment. Education is the powerful instrument for social

change and social control. The social changes are essential to utilize the natural resources of the environment.

ENVIRONMENT RELATED SUBJECTS

The components of the environment are broadly classified into two major categories—

1. Physical components or aboitic components, and
2. Biological components or boitic components.

The environment is composed of biotic (biological) and aboitic (physical) components. This can be shown with the help of chart.

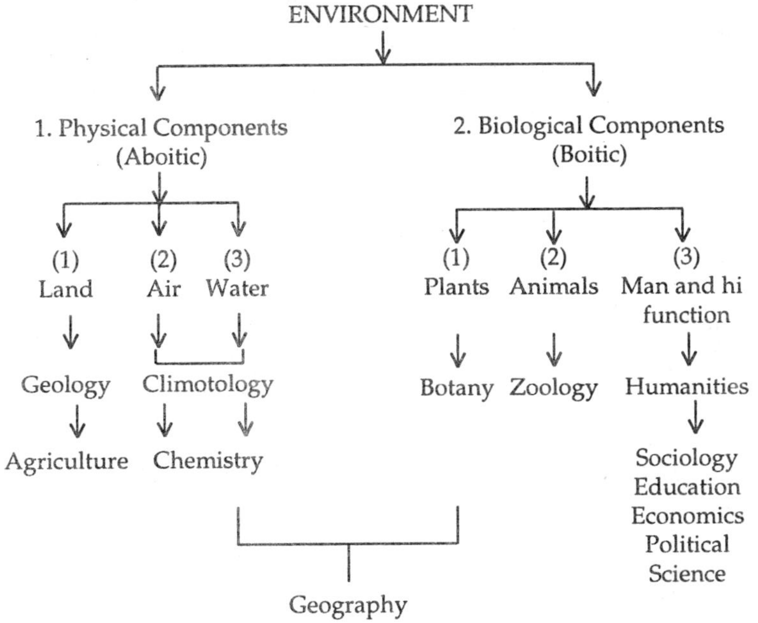

Every independent field of study or discipline has its own area of study.

DETERMINANTS OF PERSONALITY

Heredity and Environment

Heredity is defined as the totality of biologically transmitted factors that influence the structure of the body and environment is the totality of conditions that serve to stimulate behaviour or act to bring about modification of behaviour. Both the heredity and environment are important in the life of individual, both are the determinants of development. According to Ruch "The action of these factors in determining the level of an individual's biological, psychological, and social development".

Heredity works only in some sort of environment. Without environment it is useless and the environment without heredity means nothing. It means both are very important in the development of an individual. Heredity gives us the body structure, complexion or features, etc., and the environment provides the opportunities to develop them. Macver and Page state, 'Every phenomena of life is the product of both'.

There are individual differences in attitude, aptitude, interest, personality, values and behaviour. Different reasons have been assigned by different psychologists and biologists. One group of psychologists is of the view that heredity is everything in determining the personality of an individual, and the environment can not make the child bright if he is dull while the other group believes that environment is retractable.

An individual gets something from the heredity which is fostered by the specific environment and which results in the specific individual. Heredity sets the limits, environment tries to fulfil these limits through education.

In school we can provide right type of environment which may be favourable to the growth of the 'child because maximum growth of personality demands ideal environment. The powers of mind remain idle in absence of education and of an environment, bearing the stamp of intellectual, moral, religious and aesthetic accomplishments.

Heredity and environment both are important factors in the education of the children. He may develop his all the native abilities to his best in favourable environment. T.P. Nunn concludes beautifully, 'The human organism, body and mind, is a centre of creative energy that uses endowments and environment as its working material, so that the elements, it receives from nature and nurture, do not make it what it becomes.' Murphy has rightly pointed out, 'Heredity is known only by the liberation of the heredity potentials through specific environmental forces, and what is liberated is as much as function of the environing pressures as it is the latent or potential disposition'.

SOCIO-CULTURAL CONDITIONS

Several studies have been conducted in psychology and education on social and cultural factors as the determinants of personality development. Under these studies the following aspects have been taken into consideration:

1. Role of home and family,
2. Role of school,
3. Role of parents,
4. Role of teachers, and
5. Role of peers.

All men are born alike with respect to their biological needs and physical environment. The differences are due to social and cultural environment, in which the needs are fulfilled. Social and cultural environment of family contributes significantly in the development of personality. The child comes in the close contact with his parents and other members of the family. The mother of a child is considered the first teacher to shape his behaviour. The family morale influences the moral of a child.

An economic factor influences the personality development. The family poverty affects adversely in the development of personality.

A significant part of child's life is spent in school and college. The educative process play an important role in developing the personality of children. Education is considered as a process of all round development physical, social, emotional and intellectual. A conducive environment is generated for the development of children by the teachers and principals.

Ryan has enumerated the following roles of a teacher:

1. He should employ democratic method of teaching specially question-answer method should be prepared.
2. He should encourage and praise students behaviour.
3. He should be open-minded and create open climate in the classroom and in school.

4. He should have full awareness about the objectives and behavioural changes among students.
5. Teaching should be an interactive process.

The main objective of education is to develop cognitive, affective and psychomotor aspects of children. It emphasized on cognitive development. The cultural aspect is related to affective aspect. The child's early experiences of his family help in their cultural development. The cultural aspects include values, feelings, attitudes, beliefs and customs.

On the basis of above discussion of determinants of personality, the following dimensions or factors have been identified by psychologists:

1. *Intellectual dimension* includes intelligence, aptitude, creativity, achievement.
2. *Social dimension* includes values, attitude, beliefs, feelings and interest moral.
3. *Emotional dimension* includes needs, motives, aspirations, instincts, temperament.
4. *Physical dimension* includes height, colour, complexion and physique.

Several empirical studies have been conducted by measuring the personality factors. In the second part of the chapter assessment of personality has been discussed in detail.

ENVIRONMENT—THE SOCIAL ASPECT

The society is now awakened towards environment problems and the public concern about the quality of environment has reached the emotional peak but can this tempo be sustained for long time? Can this be translated into practice? The environmental improvement measures being costly and long-term investment of time, money and resources may eclipse the tempo, jeopardise the public interest in the implementation of environmental improvement programmes. According to Downs public interest in environment changes through time and the whole sequence of changes is completed in five stages termed as 'Issue Attention Cycle'.

(*i*) *First Stage* or *Pre-problem Stage:* is characterised by no public attention towards environmental problems except a few experts and interest groups who are seized with such problems.

(*ii*) *Second Stage*: Stage of alamed discovery and euphoric enthusiasm—when the issue of environmental problems catches the public attention and the public are so alarmed and become so enthusiastic that they readily respond to solve the problems without having any care for the cost of investment.

(*iii*) *Third Stage*: is marked by realisation of the cost of significant progress. That is to say that the public become aware of the cost of investment. It is also realised that the technological development may not always be the best solution to the environmental problems.

(*iv*) *Stage Four*: is characterised by gradual decline in public interest towards environmental improvement programmes due to realisation of higher cost of solution of environmental problems and difficulty in implementing the environmental improvement programmes.

(*v*) *Post Problem State*: is marked by lessening of public interest in the issues of environmental concerns but the public interest occasionally surges and again keeps a low ebb thus the public interests in environmental problems occur in spasmodic manner.

ENVIRONMENT—THE POLITICAL ASPECT

The interaction between environment and society depends largely on the social and political systems within which arise the environmental and ecological problems. The capitalistic and socialistic systems perception and reactions to the environment are quite different. Even the ecological situation varies from one country to the other and one region to the other because of uneven distribution of natural resources, uneven economic and social development, dissimilarity of demographic factors, varying view, points of the government and individuals towards environment, etc.

The capitalistic system of government of the west is full of contradictions regarding the exploitation of natural resources, rate of development, use of modern technologies and conservation of environmental resources and maintenance of ecological balance. Continuous but exceedingly increasing rate of rapacious exploitation of natural resources and uncontrolled development by the developed western world, monopolistic groups and selfish international companies, are responsible for alarming situation of grave environmental crises and ecological imbalance not confined to the limits of their own countries and regions but to the whole globe. The inherent ideology of capitalism is to increase production with minimum production cost but for maximum profit leading to accumulation and hoarding on the one hand and to shift the responsibility of environmental crises to developing and under-developed countries on the other hand. In fact, the pessimistic ideology of the western world about environmental degradation is painting a gloomy picture of ecological problems before the developing and under-developed world, so much so to discourage the use of modern technology and launching of developmental programmes so that they may remain perennial markets where the factory produce from western world may continue to be dumped.

It may be pointed out that intensive researches in the field of non-polluting and ecologically safe technologies are being conducted and policies of conservation of nature are being pursued through appropriate legislations even in the western world but these are blocked by vested interest of monopolistic groups.

The socialistic system of government mainly of the Communist Block lays more emphasis on the social importance of natural resources and environmental and ecological problems and on the urgent need to tackle these problems. 'Fundamental tradition of investigating ecological problems have matured in Marxism, which disclosed the dialectic of interaction of society and nature in demonstrating the sources of the unity and opposition of man and his habitat.

ENVIRONMENT—THE GEOGRAPHICAL ASPECT

The field and study of geography is Earth and Man. Earth includes physical, biological, social, cultural and economic components of the environment with reference to man. Thus, geography is the only discipline that can pursue the study of environment and organisms as whole because:

1. It studies the spatial attributes of all the phenomena including man in a given space and highlights complex man-environment relationships at different stages and phases in a time-

space continuum while other sciences study individual phenomenon and do not bother for spatial organisation.

2. Being an integrating science geography synthesises all the elements and components of planet earth into one body and links the social sciences with the natural sciences.

3. It lays stress on 'synthesis of all near surface spheres into one interacting system' (Annuchin, 1974). That is to say geography studies the biosphere (the interface of air, land and water) in totality (all components of biosphere-abiotic and biotic, their characteristics and interrelationships).

4. As regards the physical system it is geography that excels other sciences because geographers have the knowledge of structure, geomorphic processes, climate, vegetation and soils while other scientists specialise in only of those aspects.

5. The geographers besides identifying complex relationships between man and physical environment have the capability of locating the distribution of such relationships in space, mapping them and exploring the causes of variations in distribution.

6. The 'geographers recognise that the quality of life layer varies from place to place in terms of richness or poverty of life forms capable of being supported' (A.N. Strahler and A.H. Strahler, 1976). Geographers are the only scientists who can recognise and identify the environmental regions, locate them in space and present them on maps.

The themes of geography irrespective of the dichotomy of 'earth made man' *versus* 'man made the earth', right from the beginning 'man and the land', man and the nature, man's relationships to his earthly environment; etc., have been recurring. Thus, geography discipline directly and widely concern with environment.

ENVIRONMENT—THE ASPECT OF NATURAL RESOURCES

Though natural resources are vital part of study, but because resources have significant role in environment, therefore, a brief account of this aspect is hereunder.

The environment and resources are of most concern to the present society and also for future generations. The present society has to educate the future generation in the light of resources of the country which are to be utilized adequately.

The resources are fundamental base for the economic growth and development of human society but their withdrawal from the nature, mode of their uses by human being and their disposal have enormous adverse effect on the environment. It is, thus, imperative to study the linkages between resource use and the environment so that proper management of resources, both effective resources and resources out of place (waste material after use) and remedial measures of environmental pollution and degradation arising out of resources use and disposal of waste materials may be made possible.

The term resource is very wide in the present context. There are various type of resources—social resources, physical resources, natural resources, human resources, etc. It is the responsibility of education to prepare personnel in various fields to utilize these resources of a country.

The natural resources in the form of matter and energy are of vital significance for the successful survival of all types of life on the planet earth in general and for human being in particular. In fact, all aspects of human society (social, cultural, political and economic) depend on resources.

Therefore, the meaning, classification, assessment and evaluation, uses and abuses, conservation and management of all sorts of resources either natural or cultural, renewable or non-renewable, are very significant aspects of environmental geography. The very fundamental principle of resources is that resources, even renewable, are finite. For example, air and water are in abundance and are very much renewable but when they are polluted and degraded, they become unusable and non-renewable because it becomes very difficult to restore the original quality of air and water if they have been degraded beyond a certain critical limit.

A student of geography studies the earth and man as whose while other scientists have limited field of study. A geographer can explore the areas of new resources or natural resources but he can utilize the resources properly. He provides the awareness about these new resources of his country, it requires an interdisciplinary approach for the use of new resources. Mishandling of resources and negligence of the upkeep of the resources also affect the environment adversely.

ENVIRONMENT—THE EDUCATIONAL ASPECT

Environment is a holistic view of the world as it functions at any point of time, with a multitude of spatial elemental and socio-economic systems distinguished by quality and attributes of space and mode of behaviour of physical and biological forms.

The physical and biological components of the environment contribute and influence for social and economic development. Sometime, it has the adverse effect on social and economic growth and development.

Education is an independent field of study or discipline which is concerned with process of development, *i.e.*, teaching-learning, training and instruction. It has the focus on physical, social, mental and emotional development of a child, *i.e.*, all round development. The job of a teacher is to create conductive environment in the school and in the class room to have the desirable change in the behaviour of child.

A child gains experience from the school environment (physical and social) and from the classroom climate (social and emotional). Gates has defined, 'learning is the modification of behaviour through experience and activities.' Experience means learning or modification of behaviour. The experience can only be provided through environment. In the classroom a teacher, performs some activities or teaching to generate social and emotional climate with the help of some content for providing new experiences to his students. The educational institutions are located out-side the locality to have good physical and biological environment for the students.

The heredity and environment are the two major factors in the development of personality of an individual, but behaviourists are of the view that environment is all in all in the development of personality and heredity is nothing to do in it. It is the environment which helps in developing heredity traits of the personality.

The environment can not induce the traits and abilities which are inborn of an individual. Environment can develop inborn abilities and traits. The physiologists and anthropologists explain the nature of physical development of an individual. Thus, the new area of study has evolved under the discipline of education which is termed as 'Environmental Education'.

The area of environmental education includes both formal and non-formal education. In the formal education four different but inter-related components are recognised:

1. Awareness of environment,
2. Environment and real life situation,
3. Conservation of resources, and
4. Sustainable development of an individual.

These components are related to the four levels of education—

1. Primary education—awareness.
2. Secondary education—real life situation.
3. Higher Secondary education—conservation.
4. Higher education—sustainable development.

QUESTIONS FOR ANSWER

1. *Describe the structure and components of the environment. Compare the role of heredity and environment in the development.*
2. *Explain the following terms and concepts:*
   (*a*) *Environment and Society.*
   (*b*) *Environment and Politics.*
   (*c*) *Environment and Resources.*
   (*d*) *Environment and Geography.*
   (*e*) *Environment and Education.*
3. *Describe the role of Environment in human, social, physical, emotional and mental development.*
4. *Define 'Environment' and write a note on its basic characteristics.*
5. *Write brief notes on the following:*
   (*a*) *Classification of Environment.*
   (*b*) *Land and Water as Components of Environment.*
   (*c*) *Biological Components of Environment.*
   (*d*) *Heredity and Environment.*

6

Basic Concepts of Education

INTRODUCTION

Education aims at the physical, social, emotional and intellectual development of the child in which environment too has a significant role. Biological process of environment is an important aspect in the process of educational development. The environmental process has both positive and negative ingredients but educational process has only the positive ingredient in the growth and development of the child therefore, it is through education only that the impact of the process of environment may be formed to be only positive, hence, we must have a system of education to be apt for the purpose. Hereunder we will discuss basic aspects of education, which we should mould aptly for environmental education.

MEANING OF EDUCATION

Etymological Meaning of Education

The Latin word 'Educatum' means to train. 'E' means from inside and 'Duco' means to draw out, to lead out or to bring up. By combining the two education comes to mean to draw from within. Education is a process which draws from within. Each child is born with some innate tendencies, capacities and inherent powers.

Education draws these powers out and develop them to the full. Latin words 'Educare' and 'Educere' mean to bring up, to lead out and to develop etc. In this way the word education means to develop the inborn qualities of a child to the full.

Narrower Meaning of Education

In its narrow sense, school instruction is called *education*. In this process, the elders of society strive to attain pre-determined aims during a specified time by providing pre-structured titbits of knowledge to children through set methods of teaching.

The purpose is to achieve mental development of children entering school. In the process, the teacher is the most important factor and the child is assigned a subsidiary role. The teacher is expected to instill readymade dozes of knowledge in the child's mind.

Following opinions of some educationists represent the narrow meaning of education:

1. "In narrow sense, education may be taken to mean any consciously directed effort to develop and cultivate our powers." —*S.S. Mackenzi*
2. "Education is a process in which and by which knowledge, character and behaviour of the young are shaped and moulded." —*Prof. Drever*
3. "The influence of the environment on the individual with a view to producing a permanent change in his habits of behaviour of thought and attitude." —*G.H. Thompson*

Wider Meaning of Education

In its wider sense, education, is not the communication of information by the teacher or the acquisition of knowledge by the child but the total development of child's personality. Education consists of all those experiences in the process by which an individual freely develops his self according to his nature in a free and uncontrolled environment. It is a life long process of growth and development. It is not confined to the limits of time, place and individual.

Any person who gives the child a new experience is a teacher and any place where this giving and receiving takes place may be termed as a school. Thus, education is essentially a process of growth and development which goes on throughout the whole life. Rousseau developed his philosophy of naturalism keeping this wider concept of education in his mind. Following eminent scholars interpret education in the wider context.

1. "In the wider sense, it is a process that goes on throughout life, and is promoted by almost every experience in life."
—*S.S. Mackenzi*
2. "By education, I mean the alround drawing out of the best in child and man—body, mind and soul". —*M.K. Gandhi*

Analytical Meaning of Education

1. *Not Limited to Knowledge Imparted in Schools:* Education cannot be confined to the processes of giving knowledge to children in schools. Its programme goes on from birth till death. Everyone learns something or the other throughout life by various experiences and activities. All this is education.

2. *Education as the Development of Child's Innate Power:* Education is developing the native endowments of a child rather than something forced into the mind from outside. Addison, has rightly remarked, "Education, when it works upon noble mind, draws out to view every latent virtue and perfection which without such help are never able to make their appearance."

3. *Education as a Dynamic Process:* Education is not a static but a dynamic process which develops the child according to changing situation and times. It is a purposive activity always pursuing some aim of life to which an individual devotes himself fully.

4. *Education as a Bipolar Process:* In his book *Evolution of Educational Theory* Adams has interpreted education as a bipolar process. He analysed education as under—

(*i*) "It (Education) is a bipolar process in which one personality acts upon another in order to modify the development of the other.

(*ii*) "The process is not only a conscious one but a deliberate one. The educator has the clearly realized intention of modifying the development of the educand."

(*iii*) "The means by which the development of the educand is to be modified are two folds:

(*a*) The direct application of the educator's personality to the personality of the educand, and

(*b*) The use of knowledge in its various forms."

According to Adams, the bipolar education has two poles. At one end is the teacher and at the other is the child. Both are equally important in education. If the teacher instruct, the child follows.

If the teacher gives, the child receives. Thus, in the process of education there is interaction between the teacher and the child.

The teacher tries to mould and modify the behaviour of the child so that the latter develops his personality to the full. With the active cooperation of the teacher and the child, the process of education goes on smoothly and efficiently.

5. *Education as a Tripolar Process:* Like Adams, John Dewey also regards education as a process of development. But while accepting the psychological view, Adams emphasizes the importance of teacher and the child, John Dewey emphasizes the sociological view point.

Hence, according to John Dewey, education has two aspects—(1) Psycological, and (2) Sociological. He accepts the contention that education of the child should be according to his native endowment.

He further asserts that the development of a child does not take place in a vacuum. It takes place in and through the society in which the teacher and the child both live. It is the society, which will determine the aims, contents and methods of teaching. In this way, the process of education contains three poles, namely—(1) the teacher, (2) the child, (3) the society. These three factors actively co-operate in the efficient and successful working of the educational process.

Broader and True Meaning of Education

In its true meaning, there is dynamic coordination between narrow and wider meaning of education. It is because the education in narrow meaning is limited to its conservative nature. This meaning considers education as keeping the pupil in controlled environment and forcibly imposed education to lead a particular life style. This suppresses his interest, attitude, capacities, abilities and needs.

In broader meaning, education is liberal. According to this broader meaning, natural development of the pupil is emphasized by keeping him in uncontrolled environment. If the broader meaning of education is accepted, the social and spiritual development of the pupil is necessarily difficult, if not impossible.

In such condition, both narrow and broader meanings of education are not correct. Both need co-ordination. After co-ordination in both the meanings, education is presented as that dynamic process which brings the changes in the behaviour of the pupil and develops him intellectually, socially, culturally and spiritually in such a way by allowing reasonable independence and keeping in view, consciously or unconsciously the personal interests, attitudes, capabilities, abilities, social ideals and needs of the pupil so that both the individual and the society may touch the peaks of the progress.

T. Raymont, a well known educationist, has similar idea that, "Education is the process of development which consists the passage of human being from infancy to maturity, the process whereby he adapts himself gradually in various ways to his physical, social and spiritual environment."

Thus, education is a process of development. To understand its nature and rate of progress, one must know the data of education.

DATA OF EDUCATION

The data of education consists of the following four factors:

1. *The Child*: The foremost data of education is the child. Each child has certain innate powers. His natural development is possible only according to these native endowments. As such, the child's nature should be known to those who provide education for his development.

2. *Heredity*: Hereditarians believes that education of a child is predetermined by heredity. According to them, hereditary impressions influence a child from his infancy before any formal education begins. As the impressions are often indelible, therefore education has to follow the lines laid down by these impressions generated and formed by parents and other related elders of society.

These innate tendencies and qualities are the firm foundations for his education. These also delimit and define the highest achievements to be achieved by him. Without hereditary traits and impressions of a musician, a child can never be developed into a noted musician of repute by education or any other process. Thus, to be hereditarians, education is development according to lines pre-determined and prelaid by the heredity of a child.

3. *Environment*: Another factor of education is environment.

Every child is born in a family at a particular place and time. His upbringing also takes place in a specific environment. This environment is either controlled or uncontrolled. Both types of environments exert their influence upon the growing child in different ways. Controlled environment leads to controlled growth and uncontrolled environment promotes uncontrolled growth.

According to environmentalists, heredity factor is only a myth. They assert that if the environment is not desirable, no amount of heredity will be able to develop the child according to desirable lines and standards of growth. According to them, environment is a powerful factor which influences the development of child consciously or both. One cannot escape its influence at any cost.

Thus, according to environmentalists, education is a process based on and conditioned by the environment in which the child is brought up.

4. *Time*: During the process of development, specific activities are indulged by the child at specific times. To understand this process of development, one must have a clear understanding of the various stages of development. As different and specific tendencies sprout out of these various stages, education must correspond its plans and programmes to these budding capacities. Then only, the development of the child will be normal and natural. Hence, education should correspond and suit the mental level of the child, otherwise it will create complexes and mar the development.

Both the hereditarians and the environmentalists assert one side of the truth. The two factors are not contradictory. They are mutually complementary and supplementary. Both work together to develop the child smoothly and in a balanced way. Both are essential for the proper development of child.

The above discussion brings out the following points:

1. Education is a life-long process.
2. Education is unfolding process of knowledge.
3. Education is based on child's psychology.
4. Education is individual as well as social.
5. Education is a process of total development.
6. Education is an instrument of social change and social control.

7. Education is for future or futurology.
8. Education is an art as well as science.
9. Education is the positive science.

NATURE OF MODERN EDUCATION

To understand the modern concept of education, one has to make a comparative study of the old and modern concepts. Following are the differences between the old and the new concepts.

1. *Meaning of Education*: Education is derived from the Latin word 'Educatum' which, means to draw out, to foster growth and to develop. Hence, the modern concept of education seeks to develop the inherent capacities of a child in the social environment. In the old concept, education was taken to mean as a process to thrust ready made titbits of knowledge into the mind of a child as if it was an empty vessel. The old concept has exploded under the weight of psychological researches and democratic values. The mind is a dynamic self-adjusting and self-learning force needing proper guidance for wholesome growth and development. Modern education seeks to develop the mind according to its own inherent capacities in a social environment.

2. *Aims of Education*: Ancient education emphasized scholarship and mental development. It kept an indifferent attitude towards other aspects of personality. Acquiring more and more knowledge was regarded as the prime aim. On the contrary, modern educationists lay equal stress upon other aspects of development *viz.* physical, mental, emotional and social. Thus, the aim of modern education is to develop individuality to the full and attain social efficiency and dynamism.

3. *Curriculum*: In the old curriculum, only subjects promoting mental development were included and emphasized. Thus, old curriculum got rigid and stratified. It was confined mostly to classroom activities and experiences. Modern curriculum is flexible, varied and progressive in the sense that it tries to meet the needs of the developing child as well as the demands of ever-changing modern society.

4. *Methods of Teaching*: As the methods emphasized cramming and stimulated rote memorization education was a lifeless, dull and drab process. Modern methods condemn rote memorization

and promote the adoption of lively and effective methods life Play way, Learning by doing, Learning by experience etc. These methods stimulate motivation, interest and attention.

5. *Discipline*: Old concept of discipline emphasized the use of rode and punishment to enforce obedience and discipline in children. This concept of enforced discipline through repression has now been given up. The modern concept is self discipline leading to natural obedience.

6. *Examination*: The old method of essay type examination encouraged cramming and rote memorization. Modern techniques evaluate as well as examine. These include objective tests, progress reports, cumulative records, interviews and practical performances.

7. *Agencies of Education*: According to old beliefs, school was the only agency for the education of children. According to modem views, all formal and informal agencies are harnessed to the task of education.

8. *Teacher*: Old education put the teacher at the top of the educational process. In modern times, a teacher is considered as a friend, philosopher and guide.

9. *Child*: According to old concept, the child was a mere passive recipient of whatever the teacher instructed. Modern education is child-centred. The entire educational process is to cater to his needs and develop him according to his nature. He is to interact actively with the teacher and his class-mates to achieve effective learning promoting his own development and the development of the society of which he is an integral part.

10. *School*: According to old concept, school served as a shop for selling knowledge. Everything was pre-planned in advance. Teachers were concerned with the input and bothered little about output. Modern concept of education regards school as miniature of society laying emphasis more on output in comparison with input.

11. *Educrtion as a Discipline*: In ancient times, education meant only training of something for some aim. Modern education is a separate discipline of deep study, investigation and research. It is a very important process of human development in all fields of human activities. It has its own distinct special feature and factors to promote it as a vital formative process.

PARTS OF EDUCATION

According to John Dewey, education is a tripolar process. It has following three important ingredients:

1. *The Teacher*: In ancient times, the teacher had the main role to play while the learner's role was subsidiary. In modern time, the role has been reversed. Though the place of teacher has now become secondary, yet his responsibility has increased because a teacher is not only an important factor in the educational environment of the learner, he is also a builder of the whole educational environment which is very comprehensive and all inclusive.

In the process of education, a teacher's role is of two fold. First, being the important factor of the educational environment, he influences the personality of the learner through his own magnetic personality. Second, as a builder of the educational environment, he provides suitable experiences to the learner to develop and use fully his skills and capacities to achieve the good of his ownself and the welfare of his society, of which he is integral part. Besides, by his own attitudes and behaviour, the teacher builds the character of learners and infuses in them respect for moral and spiritual values.

This is only possible when the teacher is himself a man of strong moral character. He must be well aware of the modern strategies, tactics and techniques of teaching. He should be capable of using them to the best of his knowledge to make teaching-learning most effective. Thus, to develop the learner as well as the society, a teacher is a very important factor in the educational process of today.

2. *The Learner*: According to psychological findings and democratic feelings, education starts from the child. Thus, education has become child-centred today. Adams was the first educationist to point out this truth by his remark, "The teacher teaches Latin to John". John is more important than Latin.

Modern educationists are unanimous about the importance of child in the educational process. Education should develop the personality of the learner according to his interests, inclinations, abilities and capacities. Everything concerning education is now child-centered. Aims, curriculum and methods keep the child at the centre of their formulation and planning of educational programmes.

No teacher can be successful in his activities if he fails to understand the learner with which he is to deal. To make teaching-learning normal, natural and effective, the teacher should not only be the master of content but also know fully well the stages of child development and their characteristics.

3. *Curriculum*: The essential link between the teacher and the child is the curriculum. It serves as a vehicle for the realization of educational aims. The teacher uses the items of curriculum according to modern methods of teaching to educate children to realize the predetermined aims of education. In the wider sense, curriculum means all the experiences and activities from which a child learns something or the other.

The teacher and the child both co-operate in building and formulating experiences conducive to learning. Curriculum is structured according to the ever-growing needs of children and changing demands of dynamic society.

This is the difference between the curriculum of despotic as well as democratic countries. In the former type, all activities are rigid, predetermined and fully controlled by the state, while in the latter pattern, there is flexibility, freedom and adjustment.

AIMS OF EDUCATION

Since educational aims are not directly related to environmental education, therefore, hereunder some points are given to provide basic knowledge to the readers.

Meaning of Aim

An aim is a predetermined goal which inspires an individual to do certain activities to achieve it. *Importance of Aim*—For success in life. *Need of Aim*—An aim inspires the individual with courage and confidence. It also helps in the construction of curriculum and selection or teaching techniques. *Classification of Aims—Four Categories*—(1) Particular, (2) Universal, (3) Individual, and (4) Social. *Bases of Formulation of Educational Aims*—(1) Idealistic, and (2) Realistic. *Relation of Educational Aims to the Life of Individual*—It is in ten forms—(1) Nature or human spirit, (2) Achievement of the values of life, (3) Achievement of perfection, (4) Mental and spiritual growth, (5) Development of conduct and moral character, (6) Development of balanced personality,

(7) Attainment of right judgement, (8) Preparation of self-preservation, (9) Building of social organization, and (10) Promotion of social feeling. *Relation of Educational Aims to Ideals of Society*—There is a close relation of educational aims to ideals of all societies' namely idealistic society, materialistic society, pragmatic society, communistic society and democratic society.

Points concerning individual and social aims of education are as follows:

Meaning of Individual Aim

Development of individual interests, inclinations, aptitudes and capacities.

Narrow Meaning—In its narrow meaning it is known as self-expression, alround development of the child and natural development. In this sense it is based on the philosophy of naturalism. Thus education should develop the child according" to his basic instincts. *Wider Meaning*—It signifies self-realization. Hence education should make the child a superior human being. *Meaning of Social Aim*—Development of social values in the child. *Narrow Meaning*—Equates state socialism and advocates absolute control over individual by the state. *Wider Meaning*—Believes in democratic socialism—welfare of all. *Synthesis Between the Individual and Social Aims*—Both are unacceptable in their narrow meanings. But in their wider meaning both agree on one aim that self-realization means the development of the individual as well as the society to which he belongs. It involves the development of both simultaneously.

SOME CONCLUSIVE AIMS OF EDUCATION

There are twelve conclusive aims of education, a brief account of each one is as follows:

1. Knowledge Aim

Meaning of Aim: In its narrow sense knowledge aim means "knowledge for the sake of knowledge." Even common people have received their education inspired by this aim. As such, it is the duty of teachers to impart knowledge to children as much as possible. According to its protagonists, education is that knowledge which only the scholars know. Experiences gained in day-to-day activities of life is not taken as knowledge. A majority of patents and teachers think that knowledge is received through the cult and exercise of the mind. Hence bookish knowledge is eagerly sought for and given a high rating in society.

In its wider sense, knowledge aim means 'mental development'. In this sense, it is not only the craming of various subjects or a body of information but it means to develop all the mental powers, namely thinking, reasoning, discrimination, judgement and memory under a discipline. Such knowledge gives insight to judge between proper and improper and also increases the capacity to do more and more work. In reality true knowledge co-operates actively in making the life of an individual quite happy and successful. But this kind of knowledge may be gained by the child when he learns through his own initiative, efforts and research. This will endow him with full confidence and insight to face the future problems of life boldly and solve them by his own experience gained by earlier efforts. It is why some educationists emphasize knowledge for 'mental development' instead of only 'knowledge for the sake of knowledge.'

2. Cultural Development Aim

Meaning of Aim: Some scholars, hold that the aim of education should be cultural development. This aim means to culturize an individual. It may be noted that the word culture has been interpreted variously in various countries at various times. In some countries, it signifies only a high degree of efficiency in some particular languages. Some times it is interpreted in terms of ways of living, varieties of entertainment, general behaviour and standard of fine arts in society. There are some countries where culture is made synonymous with love of music, dancing, literature and refined social behaviour. Some regard smoking, drinking, gambling and free mixing with sex as items of culture. Thus cultural development aim of education includes the inculcation of noble ideas, attitudes and patterns of behaviour.

3. Character Development Aim

Meaning of Aim: A number of noted educationists have emphasized character development as an aim of education. Among these educationists, the German educationist Herbart tops the list. According to him, character means the inner stability and strength. A man of character always acts according to his ideals and principles. These principles may be moral or immoral.

Herbart speaks of character as a character based on moral ideals and values. The development of the individual as well as of the society depends upon this moral character. Thus Herbart says—"The one and the whole work of education may be summed up in the concept of morality."

According to Herbart, the conduct of an individual often creates disorder in society because it is guided by his inherent tendencies and basic instincts. Hence education should sublimate and purify these basic instincts into moral qualities of thinking, feeling and action so that his conduct becomes morally desirable.

At the time of birth a child does not possess a sound moral character. To achieve this aim his innate tendencies have to be purified and moulded into desirable channels of moral conduct and healthy attitudes. Education is the only potent means to inculcate in children all the moral qualities namely love, sympathy, co-operation, sacrifice and social service in such a way that he easily learns what is bad, evil and unfair and gradually forms a good moral character.

4. Vocational Aim

Meaning of Aim: Some educationists are of opinion that only knowledge and culture aims of education are not sufficient to provide for all the needs of the individual and that of the society. They emphasize that the aim of education should be vocational. According to them, livelihood is a very important problem before every individual today. Such education is useless if it makes the individual a parasite on others even for the fulfilment of his basic needs of life.

Hence in modern times, the chief aim of education should be to provide vocational education to each child so that he is able to solve his economic problems without any difficulty. Parents also send their children to schools so that; after receiving education, they become capable to earn their livelihood, maintain themselves and their families. The government have also made suitable provisions for the vocational guidance for children in all the developed and developing countries of the world.

Full use of these services should be made and the teachers should guide children into right channels. Since vocational aim of education emphasizes upon the problem of livelihood ensuring the fulfilment of the economic needs of the individual, this aim is often called as Bread and Butter Aim, Blue Jacket Aim and White Collar Aim also.

5. Harmonious Development Aim

Meaning of Aim: By harmonious development aim of education, we mean that all aspects of child's personality namely physical, mental, emotional, spiritual, moral and aesthetic should be developed equally. It may be noted that this aim is based on the psychological foundations which assert that each child is born with some innate tendencies, aptitudes and capacities. To develop his individuality in a harmonious way, it is greatly essential to develop his native endowments in a balanced way. If his native potentialities are not developed harmoniously, it will effect adversely upon his balanced development.

To develop his individuality in a balanced and effective way, harmonious development of all aspects of his personality is a must. It is with such a harmonious development of his inherent powers that he will be able to play his part well in life and achieve success in all fields. Eminent educationalists Rousseau and Pestalozzi are the chief supporters of this aim. Thus Rousseau speaks out—*"The spontaneous development of our organs and faculties constitutes the education of nature."* Pestalozzi says—*"Education is the natural, harmonious and progressive development of man's innate power."*

6. Citizenship Aim

Meaning of Aim: Socialists hold that in a democratic country, creation of true, honest and dynamic citizens is most essential. Hence they have laid great emphasis upon citizenship as an aim of education. But for good and dynamic citizenship many qualities namely, mental, moral and social are necessary. Thus education should be organized in such a way that these qualities develop in each child to fullest according to his interests, inclinations, aptitudes and capacities. Then only, the individual will be able to understand fully well the problems of society with a clear understanding of his rights and duties. Not only this, he will also be able to confront the problems with courage and determination and ultimately solve them to his own welfare and good of the society.

In short, according to this aim, a fully developed individual will be a really dynamic, resourceful, enterprizing and responsible citizen. Hence all democratic countries of the modern age emphasize citizenship as an aim of education. Throwing light on the meaning and importance of this aim H.H. Horne speaks out—*"citizenship is man's place in the state. As the state one of the permanent institutions of society and as man must ever live in organized relations with his fellows citizenship can not be omitted from the constituency of the educational ideal."*

7. The Complete Living Aim

Herbert Spencer, an eminent educationist of the nineteenth century emphasized that the aim of education is to provide completeness to life. Spencer advocated full development of individuality in all spheres rather than only one dimension. He was of view that education should bring about the wholesome development which enable an individual to face all problems of life in all spheres and solve them with great courage and insight.

At one place Spencer says—*"Education must tell us, in what way to treat the body, in what way to manage our affairs, in what way to behave as a citizen, in what way to utilize those sources of happiness which nature supplies. How to use all faculties to the greatest advantage of ourselves and others."*

Discussing this topic he further adds that—*"To prepare us for complete living is the function which education has discharged and the only rational mode of judging any educational course is to judge in what degree it discharges such function."*

Herbert Spencer, criticising vehemently the academic education of his times in his article 'What knowledge is of most worth' lays down very clearly that scientific subjects should be given prime importance in the curriculum of education. Not only this, he has divided human activities into five categories according to their value and importance.

8. Physical Development Aim

Meaning of Aim: Some educationists have laid stress upon the development of the body of an individual. They insist that physical development should be the aim of education. According to this aim, education should be organized in such a way that it develops a sound and handsome physique of all children. In ancient times and also in the middle age physical development aim of education was accepted in many countries. The state of Sparta in ancient Greece kept this aim in the forefront of its educational system. One still reads with taste the stories of physical powers and daredevil deeds of the Spartan's heroes.

The famous educationist Plato also kept this aim in his scheme of education. Not only this, the great naturalist philosopher Rousseau also prescribed a scheme according to natural surroundings which make the body and its organs healthy, robust and efficient. He insisted on free physical drills, sports and out door activities as much as possible. Emphasizing this aim Rabelais emphatically speaks—"*Without health life is not life, it is only a state of languor and suffering, an Image of death.*"

9. Leisure Utilization Aim

Meaning of Aim: Leisure time means that time when one is not engaged in any activity concerning livelihood. According to Ranganathan—"*Leisure is that time that is unoccupied with work forced by physical, economic, hygenic and spiritual necessities.*" In modern times, science has invented such techniques of production, brought out so efficient invention and varieties of time saving gadgets that an individual finishes his daily routine work in a very short period of time.

Hence a new problem has emerged as to how to spend this extra time at the disposal of an individual. Keeping this problem in view, some educationists have advocated leisure utilization as an aim of education so that individuals are educated to spend their spare or leisure time usefully.

10. Adjustment Aim

Meaning of Aim: Some educationists emphasize that education should inculcate the capacity to adjust one self to the ever changing environment. They hold that individual is always engaged in a struggle with his environmental conditions or surrounding situations of nature and society. Those, who are unable to adjust decay and disappear. Only those who adjust well survive and develop.

11. Self-Expression as Aim

Meaning of Aim: Individualists have advocated the aim of education as self-expression. This aim signifies free and natural development according to one's interests, inherent tendencies and capacities. To achieve this aim society should provide the necessary freedom, customs and situations so that the child is able to develop his innate capacities to the full extent after fulfilling his diverse needs of sex, curiosity and self-glorification in proper and effective ways.

12. Self-Realization as Aim

Meaning of Aim: Self-realization means to understand Nature, Human Being, God and their inter-relationship. Hence some educationists advocate that the aim of education is to develop the spirit in child so that he is able to inculcate high moral qualities and achieve spiritual ideas. In this sense self-realization is quite different from self-expression. In self-expression, the spirit means only the animal instincts but according to J.S. Ross— *"The self-realization is not the present unsatisfactory or indisciplined self, but the potential, fully developed self that is to be."*

IMPORTANCE OF SYNTHESIZING THE AIMS INTO AN INCLUSIVE AIM

An intelligent perusal of the above detailed discussion clearly shows that education should develop all the aspects of individuality, namely—physical, mental, moral, emotional, social and spiritual. None should be neglected. With such a wholesome development, the individual will be able to use to the full all the natural means to fulfil all the basic needs and necessities of life. He will not like to be a parasite on others and will do maximum good to self and to others with a spirit of selfless devotion and sincerity. Modern education should elevate us from all narrow considerations, namely—feeling of caste, creed, colour, provincialism, linguistic jingoism, religious fanaticism and nationalistic chauvinism. An individual should learn to respect his own culture and national heritage and also bestow the same feelings of respect to other cultures, ways of thinking and acting. He should try to imbibe the spirit of world citizenship so that he is able to achieve the good of his own country as well as the welfare of other countries also. He should firmly believe and act according to the spirit of international brotherhood.

INTER-DISCIPLINARY APPROACH OF EDUCATION

Education is a full-fledged academic discipline and has opted for inter-disciplinary approach to solve various human problems by giving help to and by taking help from other disciplines for that purpose. Education, through this approach has developed into an important discipline in humanities. Its relationship and interaction with psychology and political science are well established.

An example which illustrates the interaction of three disciplines in the area of behavioural sciences. The education is for both boys and girls and they would like to serve in any department. Thus, husband and wife both are in job who will look after their children during office time. This problem has been identified by an expert of sociology and refers to an educationist to provide the solution. He has proposed a new ladder to the system of education. There should be pre-primary education, it is meant for 2 to 6 years children.

A child psychologist can suggest the method, content and technique to deal with 2 to 6 years children. Thus, the experts of three disciplines: Education, sociology and psychology are interacting on this problem. The solution of the problem will be the new knowledge of these disciplines. It will be termed 'social psychology of education'.

The financial aspects of these problems can be suggested by the expert of Economics. The Nursery and KG schools have been started. These are self-supporting institutions. The parents can afford to pay fees. This knowledge is termed as economics of education.

The education has its foundation on other disciplines. The aims of education are given by philosophy and methods of teaching and techniques are devised by psychology.

GROWTH AND DEVELOPMENT

In effective educative process, teacher must know his student and the environment. A teacher has to teach with children of different age groups, socio-economic and cultural background. They have wide variety of difference with regard to social, emotional, intellectual and physical aspects among themselves. It is very challenging for teacher to bring desirable changes in their behaviour so that they may contribute in national and social development.

Individual differences among students play an important role in teaching-learning situation. Not only the difference but a teacher has to keep in view the potentialities and capacities of the students at different age levels. This concept is dealt under the heading of 'Growth and Development'. A teacher must know the basic principles of growth and development and the characteristics which develop at different age levels.

The most potent fact in education is that of growth and development. "An understanding of the nature and principles of human growth and development is very essential for the realization of the aims and objectives of education." The teacher has to stimulate and direct physical, social, emotional and intellectual growth and development of the students. He may be able to do it only when he has thorough knowledge and understanding of growth and development at various stages of human life.

MEANING AND DEFINITION OF GROWTH

Growth means increase in size, height and weight of child. It implies growth of heart, brain, muscles and body in general. It can be easily observed and measured. It is generally confined to quantitative changes.

According to Arnold Gessell:

> "Growth is a function of the organism rather than of the achievement as such. The environment furnishes the foil and the milieu for the manifestations of development, but these manifestations come from inner compulsion and are primarily organized by inherent mechanics and by a intrinsic physiology development. Growth involves limiting and regulatory mechanisms. Growth is a process so intricate and so sensitive that there must be powerful stabilizing factors, intrinsic rather than extrinsic, which preserve the balance of the total pattern and direction of the growth trend. Maturation is, in a sense, a name for this regulatory mechanism."

Arnold Gessell has enumerated the following features of growth in his definition:

1. It is a function of the organism,
2. The environment helps in its manifestation,
3. It is intrinsic physiological development,
4. It has limited and regulatory mechanism,
5. It is an intricate and sensitive process,
6. It maintains the balance of the total pattern and direction, and
7. The regulatory mechanism is known as maturations.

DEVELOPMENT

Development refers to change in structure form or shape and improvement in functioning, *e.g.* hands only grow large but they also develop, because they also improve in their functions.

Thus development can be defined as "a progressive series of changes in an orderly coherent pattern. The term progressive signifies that the changes are directional leading forward rather than backward. These changes include change in size, proportions, disappearance of old features and acquisition of new features at physical, social, emotional and intellectual and of daily living."

Development can be defined as "the emerging and expanding of capacities of the individual to provide greater facilities in functioning such as development of motor ability from uncertain step to proficiency in games. Development as a matter of fact is achieved through growth."

"By the term development, we mean the changes in the shape of the parts of the body and the integration of the various parts into the functional units as growth goes on." —*Boring*

Development refers to interaction of person and his environmental surroundings whose after-products alter existing response tendencies in such a way as to increase:

1. Their strength,
2. The degree of differentiation, and
3. The organization of personality.

Development is confined to qualitative changes in the organism, and has the following main characteristics:

1. It is an interaction between person and his environment.
2. It is confined to qualitative changes in form and functions of the organism.
3. It involves a progressive series of changes leading forward not backward.
4. It refers to acquisitions of new features at physical, social, emotional and intellectual and daily living.
5. It is the emerging and expensing capacity of the individual.

According to *Arnold Gessell*, the role of physical change is important in development. He used the word maturation to describe growth processes that are governed by automatic, genetically determined signals. He believed that major changes in the organism are based on maturation. The cognitive growth in each year is characterized by certain behaviour changes rather than biological. Thus development contributes in maturation.

Development and Learning

Development is the result of maturation and experience. The maturation concerns with growth, while experience concerns with learning.

Baev has defined development as,

> "Behaviour change which requires programming and programming requires time or duration but not enough of it to call it age."

Programming refers here to sequences of learning may be arranged in the life of an individual. Development is a collection of learning experiences.

Principles

There are some psychologists who emphasize the environmental influences in the growth and development of a child, and there is another group of psychologists who claim the superiority of heredity over environment in the development of children. There is no definite line of demarcation which can be drawn between the contribution of heredity and environment in the development of a child.

The development of an individual is the by-product of constant interaction of heredity factors are more important for growth whereas environmental factors are essential for development processes. Genetic factors are basic that determine the development of an individual. There are three basic principles of the development:

1. Principle of Maturation,
2. Principle of Instinct Approach, and
3. Principle of Reflex Approach.

1. *Principle of Maturation*

Maturation and learning are the two main aspects of development; they are very close to each other. The maturation is highly influenced by the heredity and learning is the result of environment but depends on the individual potentialities. Any specific task is performed by the individual with his abilities and maturation. Maturation is usually stable. Learning is also influenced by maturation level of an individual.

2. *Principle of Instinct Approach*

Mc Dugall has analysed the instinctive behaviour with reference to the development of an individual. He believes that there are some basic instincts which influence the development of a person. The learning does not occur in the absence of the basic instincts. The social behaviour are also governed by the harmones of male and female. Thus development of an individual is caused by the development of basic instinct.

3. *Principle of Reflex Approach*

Watson believes that all the children are equal at the time of birth. They have definite structure of their bodies. They have three emotions love, fear and anger and have manipulative tendencies. The child uses them according to his environment. These functions and activities help in his development and also indicate the direction of his developmental process. Thus, environment contributes significantly in the development of a child.

Characteristics

The variation or individual difference is universal in nature and is known as the principle of variability of inheritance. There are two principles, one is of resemblance and another is of variability. The development process is governed by both the principles. It has the following main characteristics:

1. It is a product of the interaction between person and the environment,
2. It is a continuous and life-long process,
3. It is individual process but takes place in a group,
4. Different aspects of development are inter-related,
5. It proceeds from general to the specific,
6. It is cumulative and positive process,
7. It is bilateral to unilateral trend,
8. It follows an orderly sequence,
9. It has a uniform pattern,
10. It is an intergraded process, and
11. It has the variation of differentiation.

Stages

There is great dispute among psychologists and scientists regarding the stages of human life. The age group is for class organization in schools, but it is system of solving problems of different age group subjects. A person tries to solve his problems by inventing ways and means. Development is process which has various stages.

According to Saily

1. Infancy—(1 to 5) years—Pre-primary education
2. Childhood—(5 to 12) years—Primary and secondary
3. Adolescence—(12 to 18) years—Higher secondary education.

According to Ross

1. Infancy—(1 to 3) years;
2. Pre-childhood—(3 to 6) year—Pre-primary education
3. Post-childhood (6 to 12) years—Primary and secondary
4. Adolescence (12 to 18) years—Higher secondary education.

According to Kalsnik

1. Pre-natal period

2. Neo-natal 3 or 4 weeks before birth
3. Early infancy (1 to 15) months
4. Post infancy (15 to 30) months
5. Early childhood (3 to 5) years—Pre-primary education
6. Middle childhood (6 to 12) years—Primary and secondary
7. Adolescence (12 to 18) years—Higher secondary.

Thus, there are various stages of development, but from educational point of view four stages are taken into consideration.

1. Pre-natal period upto birth.
2. Infancy stage from birth to 5 years—Pre-primary education
3. Childhood stage 6 to 12 years—Primary and secondary
4. Adolescence stage 13 to 19 years.
   Also known as 'Teen Age'—Higher secondary education.

The last two stages are most important for a teacher to understand the nature of development with regard to physical, social, emotional and, mental development. The first two stages are most significant for parents specially for mother to understand the nature of development of pre-natal period and infancy stage of the children.

Forms

Development is a process and it has some specific characteristics. The characteristics of development help or guide us to understand nature of development of a child. The following changes are observed during the process of development:

1. *Structural Change*: Growth concerns with the changes in height, weight, form of the body. It can be observed and measured.

2. *Changes in Proportion*: The child is the miniature of the adult. There is proportionate changes or growth in structure of an adult. The proposition is also noted in mental, social and emotional development.

3. *Changes in Old Features*: Some changes are observed in old features of an individual. These changes are caused by thynus and pinial glands.

4. *Acquisition of New Features*: The old features gradually vanish and new features are acquired. There is change in teeth and growth

in sexual organs. Maturation is the stage that an individual is ready to function.

5. *Predictability of Development*: The rate and speed of development provide the basis for the prediction of development.

6. *Definite Pattern of Development*: Whatsoever the form of development but it has definite pattern. It is the law of nature.

7. *Development has Specific Characteristics*: Each stage of development has some traits or specific characteristics. The most effective traits of each stage emerge in process of development. Every individual has to go through these stages. The behaviour which appears unique behaviour during the process of development, are normal.

Factors Influencing Development

Growth is natural and automatic process but development is planned and deliberate efforts to bring desirable changes among children. Development process depends on heredity and environmental factors. Thus, it is influenced by these factors:

1. *Heredity factors* are intelligence, sex, race, secretion of glands, height, weight, structural features.

2. *Environmental factors* are nutrition, fresh air and light, open environment, family status, culture, diseases and injuries.

(*a*) *Intelligence*: The most important aspect of development refers to mental development. It depends on the intelligence of child. All other types of development are also influenced by the intelligence. All intelligent child acquires new behaviours quickly and early maturation. The body moments and behaviours of a child reflect his level of intelligence.

(*b*) *Sex*: There is difference between boys and girls with regard to their growth and development. The body constitution and structural growth of girls are different from boys. The functions of boys and girls are also of different nature.

(*c*) *Secretion of Glands*: The para-thyride glands make the body more sensitive and more emotional. The thymus glands influence the mental and chest development. It brings an early maturity among children.

(*d*) *Races*: The racial factor has great influence on height, weight, colour feature and body constitution. A child of white race will be white, tall and smart. Even hairs and eyes colour are governed by the concerning race.

(*e*) *Nutrition*: Growth and development of a child mainly depends on his food nutrition. The malnutrition has adverse effect on their structural and functional development. The balance diet is very essential for the proper development of a child.

(*f*) *Family Status*: Nutrition and family status have similar influence. The poor family can not provide balance diet to their children. It will effect adversely.

(*g*) *Social and Cultural Factors*: The behaviour and functional aspect is greatly influenced by social and cultural environment in which a child lives. They acquire values, feelings and attitudes.

(*h*) *Disease and Injuries*: The mental injuries and other type of long disease have adverse effect on the development of children.

MATURATION

Growth process is described with the help of maturation. It is governed by automatic, genetically determined signals. The major changes in structure and functions of an individual are based on maturation. The term maturation has been defined by several psychologists and child psychologists.

> "Maturation is the process by which underlying potential capacity of the organism reach at the stage of functional readiness. This process involves both type of changes—structure and function. The structural changes are with growth and progressive exercise by structures that provide ground work for later performances or functions."
>
> —*T. Jersild and others*

> "Maturation is an autonomous process of somatic physiological and mental differentiation and integration spread over developmental stages and phases which are correlated to one another in a course of time, as the result of this process the individual's growth is completed and consolidated emotionally, mentally and spiritually as well as socially and he can thus adapt life." —*H.S. Eysenck*

"Maturation means the growth and development that is necessary either before any unlearned behaviour can occur or before learning of any particular can take place."

—*Boring and others*

In the above definitions of maturation, the following characteristics have been emphasized:

(*a*) Maturation is the process for describing underlying potential capacity of an individual.
(*b*) Maturation means the growth and development.
(*c*) Maturation is an automatic process of somatic, physiological and mental differentiation and integration.
(*d*) Maturation involves both type of changes—structural and function or performance.
(*e*) Maturation helps an individual with structural change to reach at the stage of functional readiness.
(*f*) Maturation is stage of completion of growth and consolidating of emotional, mental and social development.

Characteristics

Some of the characteristics of maturation have been listed above and some other characteristics are described in the following paras:

1. *Maturation is the Basis of Learning*: It is an essential condition for learning process.

"If we analyse learning process carefully without regard to its different forms, we shall discover first of all that it is a continuous process of modification of behaviour involving changes and development in the mental and behavioural patterns of an individual." —*S. Alexander*

2. *Factors of Maturation influencing Learning*: The basis of learning is process of maturation which involves several factors but its following factors influence learning:

(*a*) Acquisition capacity of the learner.
(*b*) The retention power of the individual.
(*c*) The potential of recall of the learner.
(*d*) The necessary skills of learning.

3. *Maturation is the Complete Behaviour of an Individual*: It is the stage of completion of growth and consolidating the social, emotional, and mental development.

4. Maturation is the complete change in an individual which assist him to reach at the stage of functional readiness.

Growth and development are both the aspects of maturation and they help in learning.

THE TASK OF EDUCATION

The task, therefore, is to start building upon edifice of knowledge pertaining to education taken in its comprehensive meaning an edifice of thought and practice which will be grounded in our national aspirations and which can totalize and rejuvenate our thinking in all fields of educational efforts.

An appropriate set-up which would be actively engaged in producing men and material for the whole educational machine (and not just teacher) has also been lacking. The group or body of workers would create and dispense knowledge at the highest level and would be in a position to infuse vitality and realism into our education.

The widening of scope is essential if we are to come out of the narrow groove into which we have fallen. The liberalizing influence of other fields and discipline should be permitted freely to enrich our understanding of education in all its implications.

A student of philosophy may become interested in education and its why and where for; a sociologist can perhaps better contribute to our understanding of how social forces affect education and are in turn affected by it, an expert in public health can study problems of school health, etc. There are some other area in which workers from other fields or disciplines can cooperate and contribute materially to overall task of building-up the edifice of education.

The present training colleges are fully occupied with training teachers and the duties which envelop the staff in their day-to-day work as a teacher rather than education. The curriculum of these colleges is professional and persons involved are naturally more concerned with problems of a practical character, but for the edifice of education the growth of different thinking and reflecting their educational thought is necessary.

The task of a teacher is to satisfy the society but it is next to impossible task. Because training colleges concentrate their efforts on evolving and perfecting a system of training into effective school practice. Therefore, training college goals should be reciprocated so that teacher would be able to satisfy the society and able to do expeditiously, economically and with efficiency.

The task broadly conceived is the extension of educational thinking and the creation thereby of a body of knowledge which may serve as a source and fountain head of inspiration for all spheres of education, including the training of teachers. Thus, it is submitted, is a primary national need. Speaking again in broad terms, the study of education as a field of intellectual effort, in our circumstances to-day may have the following broad objectives:

1. The study and pursuit of cognate disciplines and field of study with a view to bringing out their full implications for education in the Indian context.
2. The study of specialized fields of work already chalked out by workers in other countries with a view to understanding their technique and methodology and developing out own material where needed.
3. The creation of new knowledge and literature relevant ourselves and our needs.
4. Encouraging and involving workers and scholars in other disciplines to contribute to education.

In slightly less general terms, the area of work may be suggested as comprising:

(*a*) Sociology and its bearing on education.
(*b*) Philosophy and education.
(*c*) Planning of finance.
(*d*) Political ideology and education.
(*e*) Psychology and its various applications to education.
(*f*) History of education.
(*g*) School health.
(*h*) Public administration in relation to school.
(*i*) Education to teachers.
(*j*) Study of education at all levels, professional as well as liberal, in other countries of the world.

QUESTIONS FOR ANSWER

1. *Discuss various meanings of education and write a note on 'Data of Education'.*
2. *Write a note on the concept of nature of modern education.*
3. *Write short notes on the following:*
   (*a*) *Parts of Education.*
   (*b*) *Task of Education.*
   (*c*) *Inclusive Aim of Education.*
4. *Write a note on conclusive aims of education.*
5. *Define the concept of 'Growth and Development' and its significance in education.*
6. *Write short notes on the following:*
   (*a*) *Principles of Development.*
   (*b*) *Characteristics of Maturation.*
   (*c*) *Factors Affecting Development.*

7

Basic Concepts of Environment Education

INTRODUCTION

Environmental Education is the new area of study of the discipline of education. With recent developments and advances, 'environmental education' is virtually a new source of concern for educators, teachers and students.' The area of 'environmental education' has been discussed thoroughly at several national and international seminars, workshops and conferences. Most of the people have recognized the urgent need of environmental education. Therefore, an attempt has been made in this chapter to explain the concept of 'environmental education'.

The meaning of the terms 'Environment' and 'education' have been provided in the earlier chapters. It is evident from the discussion that the process of 'development' is common in both the concepts. Education is defined as the process of development, and environment is the aggregate of all the external conditions and influences affecting the life and development of man and other living organism. Man's environment consists of natural as well as socio cultural environment. Education can change and improve the quality, of man's environment for desirable modification of his behaviour.

Education deals with the various problems and principles which govern the relationships between students and their environment which is created by school and teacher formally and informally. Similarly ecology is a new science which deals with the various principles which govern the relationship between o ganisms and their environment. Thus education may be termed as 'Human Ecology' which deals the relationship of man and material in context of growth and development.

DEFINITION OF ENVIRONMENTAL EDUCATION

The term 'Environmental Education' has been discussed in various national and international seminars who tried to define it. Some of the definitions have been provided here to understand the concept.

> "Environmental education is the process of recognizing values and clarify concepts in order to develop skills and attitude necessary to understand and appreciate the interrelatedness among man, his culture and his bio-physical surroundings. It also entails practice in decision-making and self formulation of a code of behaviour about problems and issues concerning environmental quality."
>
> —*UNESCO* (*1970*) *Working Committee*

> "Environmental education is a way of implementing the goals of environmental protection. It is not a separate branch of science or field of study. It should be carried out according to the principles of the life-long integral education."
>
> —*UNESCO* (*1976*) *Seminar at Jammi*

> "Environmental edcation appears to be a process that equips human beings with awareness, knowledge, skills, attitudes and commitment to improve environment."
>
> —*Mishra* (*1993*)

> "Environmental education involves a comprehensive, life-long education, one responsive to changes in a rapidly changing world. It prepares the individual and communities for life, through an understanding of the major problems of the interaction of the biological, physical, social, economic and cultural aspects of the individual and communities. It provides skills and attitudes needed to play a productive role in improving life and values: In order to enable people to enjoy good health and high quality of life."

Environmental education is a process of providing learning experiences to obtain knowledge, understanding, skills and awareness with desirable attitudinal changes about man's relationship with his natural and man-made surroundings which includes the relation of population, pollution, resource allocation, transportation technology and urban and rural planning to the total human environment. Environmental education must utilize diverse learning environments and a broad array of educational approaches to teaching learning about and from the environment with due stress on practical activities and first hand experience.

> "Environmental education is problem-centred, inter-disciplinary, value-oriented, community-oriented, and concerns with man's survival as species, based on student-initiated activities and involvements present and future oriented". —*Cook and Hearn (1971)*

> "Environmental activities will lead to the study of natural and physical sciences, social sciences. Construction and creative skills will provide the basis for the practice of healthy living will serve as the basis for the practice of healthy living and will serve as the basis for environmental education."

The study of natural and physical sciences, social sciences and geography provides the awareness of the environment. Similarly the study of psychology provides the awareness about learning but educational psychology provides the awareness about learning as well as practice the methods and techniques for improving learning. The environmental awareness is limited to the understanding aspect while environmental education has the productive role in improving life and values.

ENVIRONMENTAL AWARENESS— DEVELOPMENT AND CONTENTS

The terms environmental education and environmental awareness are used interchangeably for the same meaning but there is significant difference in these two terms. The study of physical and biosciences, geography, agriculture provides the environmental awareness. But the awareness does not help in developing skills and attitudes for improving environment.

Therefore it is essential to understand the concept of environmental awareness and differentiate it with educational environment. Environmental awareness may be defined as to help the social groups and individuals to gain a variety of experiences in and acquire a basic understanding of environment and its associated problems.

At the Belgrade International Workshop (1975) working documents were provided by the trend papers that described the state of the art of Environmental Education in all parts of the world and provisions to extend and explore the Environmental Awareness. It also states—Environmental Awareness may provide power and understanding:

- To recognise the interdependence among materials into physical environment, plants and animal life for survival, growth and development.
- To take decisions individually and collectively and initiate actions for social, cultural and economic survival, growth and development and for conservation of nature and natural resources.
- To identify human, material, space and time resources in the environment.
- To recognise ways of making effective use of environmental resources for social economic and cultural survival, growth and development.
- To take decisions for the effective use of resources, to recognise the special significance of conservation of natural resources and initiate or support community efforts for the purpose.

Development

The United Nation Conference of Human Environment (Stockholm, June, 1971) was a major event for those concerned with the quality of the world's environment. One of the recommendations of the Conference resulted in the creation of United Nations Environmental Programme (UNEP) while other recommendations specially constituted the foundation of framework for co-operative effort in International, which states that Environmental Awareness may be developed by:

- Indentifying; analysing and understanding the needs and problems of personal life including health, vocation, etc.

- Social li:e at different levels *viz.* family, caste, community, religion, town or village life, state and country.
- National life including civic, economic, etc.

Environmental awareness may also be developed when we:

- Appreciate, promote and use the environment to improve health, vacation and social and national life.
- Interact with government and social agencies and utilise the development facilities provides by these agencies in his/her individual capacity and also for organizing certain community activities.
- Develop the aesthetic sense to appreciate beauty and adopt it in personal and social life.

Environmental awareness provide the understanding and competence to recognize environmental resources and interdependence between physical and biological components of the environment for the growth and development. The areas and content of environmental awareness have been enumerated in the following para.

Contents

Awareness to environment is a horizon-sweeping word and presents the totality of social, biological and psychochemical factors individually or collectively that comprise the natural and man-made surroundings. Environment can be classified into basic components:

(*i*) *Physical Components*: Water, air, land, light, temperature, humidity etc.

(*ii*) *Biological Components*: Aquatic and terrestrial flora (plants) and fauna (animals).

(*iii*) *Human Uses*: Agricultural, Industrial, Residential, Forestry, Transportation, Water supply, Navigation, Hydropower and Recreation.

(*iv*) *Human Values*: Traditional life style, Religious status, Arachaeological and economic base, Community structure. Hence the term 'Environment' therefore can cover the whole spectrum of science and humanities.

HOW DO ENVIRONMENTAL EDUCATION AND ENVIRONMENTAL AWARENESS DIFFER

Environmental education (EE) is an effective process to develop the understanding of environmental awareness. Environment awareness (EA) is the most important aspect of environmental education but not the whole. These may be differentiated in the following ways:

1. The cultural and psychological environments are crucial in EE because organization, climate and health of an institution is governed by the psychological principles and social and emotional climate of classroom teaching is generated by the psychology of the subject teacher, while EA provides the knowledge and understanding of interdependence of physical and biological components and the ecology of the organism.
2. The EA provides the understanding of natural, physical and biological environment of an organism and to identify human, material, space and time resources in the environment, while EE includes the awareness of physical, biological, cultural and psychological environment of man. It investigates the methods and techniques for modifying and improving quality of man and community as whole.
3. The EE has the main task of having the productive function in order to improve the quality of life and values, whereas EA has the main task of providing the understanding of physical and biological components of the environment and their interdependence.
4. EE plans and generates the conducive environment for desirable changes in man. It manipulates the environment whereas EA involves the knowledge of both natural and manipulated environment, but it confines itself only upto the theoretical aspect.
5. Environmental education is an effective process for developing environmental awareness through classroom interaction between teacher and taught and through the following activities:

- Provide sanitary facilities in school.
- Keeping school, home and surroundings clean.
- Making provisions for deposition of waste.
- Controlling the pollution of air and water.

- Keeping the body healthy and clean with games and sports facilities in schools.

6. The EE provides the opportunities and situations for performing certain tasks and activities at all levels for solving environmental problems, while EA is limited to the problems and their solutions but does not involve task and activity.

EDUCATION DEVELOPS ENVIRONMENTAL AWARENESS

Several seminars and conferences have been organized at national and international level on "environment". Most of the experts and scientists of different disciplines have realized the importance of 'environmental awareness'. They also recognize the urgent need for an introduction of 'environmental education'. Under the environmental education theoretical and practical aspects are emphasized. The awareness confines to cognitive level whereas educational environment includes cognitive, psychomotor and affective levels. The involvement and indentification with a field study based on affective development *i.e.* feelings, attitudes and values.

In order to help children grow in knowledge, skills and values, attitudes and awareness relevant to environments teacher is expected to be dispenser of information and knowledge, through teaching learning situations. For the purpose of profitably utilizing the time and taking care of the interests of children, teacher should resort to group activities and bear with a certain amount of active involvement and talking in classroom. Therefore the concept of discipline in the classroom has also to be changed. They should look for the positive development in the children rather than the acquisition of bookish information.

The environment and the experiences of the children outside the school, vary from place to place, consequently the activities provided them in the school by teachers would also vary so that knowledge, attitudes, skills and commitment can be built on the solid foundation of experiences the child draws from the environment.

The teacher can enjoy greater autonomy in organising such experiences by providing them chances to explore their activities in regard with environment through plantation, through forest conservation, etc. Teacher should show them documentary films in the school time by time and organise an excursion programme to watch and observe the nature and natural resources—how badly they are crushed and acted upon by their own race monsterly?

Teacher should also suggest the students to see T.V. programmes, to read newspapers and to hear the radio news as regard with environment. He should show environmental teaching aids such as charts, models of environment in which it is bitterly going to be polluted and damaged.

CHARACTERISTICS OF ENVIRONMENTAL EDUCATION

Following are the main characteristics of environmental education:

1. It refers to the knowledge and understanding of physical, biological, cultural and psychological environment and to perceive its relevance for real life situation.
2. It identifies the imbalances of environment and tries to improve it in view of sustainable development.
3. It entails practice in decision-making and self formulations of a code of behaviour about problems and issues concerning environmental quality.
4. It involves child's investigation and systematic exploration of his own natural and social environment and prepares himself to solve problems for improving his life.
5. It develops skills, attitudes, feeling and values needed to play productive role in improving life and values.
6. It provides the basis for construction and creative skills for the practice of healthy living and improvement.
7. It is problem-centred, interdisciplinary, value and community oriented and concerns with man's survival and development. It concerns with the present and the future.
8. It utilizes educational approaches, methods and techniques of teaching to identify the real causes of environmental problems and practice problem solving skills in formal and non-formal situations.
9. It is a process of recognizing the interrelatedness among man, his cultural and biological surroundings.

10. It involves both theoretical and practical aspect of environment to improve the imbalances and prevent the deterioration or pollutions.

11. It appears to be a process that equips human beings with awareness, skills, attitude, values and commitments to improve environment.

UTILITY AND NEED OF ENVIRONMENTAL EDUCATION

Rigveda is the oldest of all four Vedas. It has been stated in the Rigveda, "The dust (*Dhula*) of mother earth and light of father sky should remain be associated with full brightness for our welfare". According to Rigveda, there are three kinds of god—the celestial, the aerial and terestrial *i.e.* land, air and water. *Brihaspati* is most important, means awareness of these mandals. The whole *Brahmanda* was full of peace and happiness because life and environment were so closely related that it was difficult to think man and organism as something separate from nature or environment.

In present situation man and environment are considered interrelated and there is interdependence in them. The nature or environment becomes a source of sorrow and in happiness, because the dust of earth, light and air of sky have the adverse effect on human beings. Therefore, there is need of introduction of 'environmental education'.

The country has accepted the need for environmental education, with the recommendations of the Tiwari Committee (1980). Many people recognize an urgent need for environmental education', Besides introducing the subject of 'Environmental science' at all levels of education, we must give much emphasis on the new approaches and programmes of environmental education, thus the idea is to bring environmental concerns in all subjects.

Most people recognise the urgent need for environmental education, but only some have clear ideas about what needs to be done, and very few have either the actual experience or the knowledge about the courses that need to be taught. The chief objective of environmental education is that individual and social groups should acquire awareness and knowledge, develop attitudes, skills and abilities and participate in solving real-life environmental problems.

The lay public in rural, tribal, slum and urban areas, women and students and teachers in schools, colleges and universities as well as planners and decisions and policy makers, programme implementators and workers need to be educated about the environment.

The area of 'environment education' is very wide as compared with the environmental science. It can be illustrated with the help of the following statements:

"If you want to grow a crop, you have to plan for a year." It is the job of agriculture scientists.

"If you want to grow a plant, you have to plan for ten years." It is the task of plant scientists.

"If you want to grow or educate a man, you have to plan for one hundred years." It is the responsibility of an educationist.

The agriculture and plant scientists are also educated and trained for their area of study. In fact education is considered as the highest order investment which becomes an asset in time to come.

The need of environmental education (EE) has been thoroughly discussed at several national and international seminars, workshops, conferences. After the deliberations at Fourex in 1971 and at Stockholm in 1972, an International Workshop was held on Environmental Education.

"The Belgrade Charter at Belgrade (Yugoslavia) in 1975 organised by UNESCO and later an Inter Governmental Conference on EE (UNESCO, UNEP) at Tbilisi, USSR in 1977. Belgrade workshop formulated the guiding principles to achieve the objectives of Stockholm Conference, whereas Tbilisi Conference followed closely the foot steps of Belgrade Workshop.

In a national seminar, organised by the Indian Environmental Society in collaboration with the International Programme on Environmental Management at the Indian National Science Academy, New Delhi in 1979, emphasis was given to incorporate Gandhian thought and values as a part of environmental education. A number of recommendations were made in the seminar.

In the First International Conference on Environmental Education held at New Delhi, in 1987, the late Mrs. Indira Gandhi observed that EE is to help arouse social consciousness and make community aware of the fact that the good of the individual and that of community are both harmed by ecological disruptions. In 1985, there was the Second International Conference on EE at New Delhi. Several important points could emerge from the deliberations of the international, regional, national and even local conferences on EE.

AIMS AND OBJECTIVES OF ENVIRONMENTAL EDUCATION

There are several governmental and non-governmental organizations to educate people and to create awareness of environment. A department of environment has been set-up in (1982) for this purpose. There is a Centre for Environmental Education (CEE) at Ahamedabad. There are more than two hundred private organizations working for environmental education.

The environmental education aims at developing in the child an awareness and understanding of the physical and social environment in its totality. Fortunately 'environmental education' has been introduced in the curriculum from an early stage in our country. Kothari Commission (1966) recommends:

"Environmental activities will lead to study of natural sciences, physical sciences, geography, history and civics; construction and creative skills will provide the basis for the practice of healthy living will serve as the foundation for environmental education."

A number of objectives of environmental education have been formulated for both formal and non-formal education at all levels at the International Conference of UNESCO (1977) held at Tbilisi. These are as follows:

1. To develop an awareness of environment and sensitivity (feeling and attitude) to the total environment and its allied problems.
2. To help in acquiring knowledge and variety of experience of the environment and associated problems.
3. To develop a basic understanding of structure, processes and problems of environment; interdependence of environmental components.

4. To help in acquiring skills for identifying and solving environment problems.
5. To develop attitudes, a set of values and feelings of concern for the environment and encouragement or motivation for active participation in protection and improvement of environment.
6. To provide an opportunity for an active participation or practice at all levels in working for the solution of environmental problems.
7. To develop an ability for evaluating environmental components and educational programmes in terms of ecological, economic, social, cultural aesthetic and educational factors.

The above objectives are related to all levels and both formal and non-formal system of education. In the formal system of education four different but interrelated components have been recognized which are noted below.

Objectives	*Level*
1. Awareness of environment	• Primary education (knowledge)
2. Relevance for real-life situation of environment (understanding)	• Secondary education
3. Conservation of natural resources of environment (skills)	• Higher Secondary Education
4. Sustainable development by solving problems of environment (Attitude and Evaluation)	• College and University Education.

Environmental Education Aims

1. To consider the environment in its totality (natural, artificial, technological, social, economic, political, moral, cultural, historical, aesthetic).

2. To consider a continuous life process (from pre-school to all higher levels—formal as well as non-formal).

3. To be interdisciplinary in approach in EE.

4. To emphasise active participation in prevention and solution to environmental problems.

5. To examine major environmental issues and problems from local, national, regional, and international point of view.

6. To focus on current, potential environmental situations.

7. To consider environmental aspects in plans for growth and development.

8. To emphasize the complexity of environmental problems and need to develop critical thinking and problem-solving skills.

9. To promote the value and necessity of local, national, and international co-operation in the prevention and solution of environmental problems.

10. To utilise diverse learning about environment and different approaches to teaching and learning about environment.

11. To help learners to discover the symptoms and the real causes of environmental problems.

12. To relate environmental sensitivity, knowledge, problem-solving and values clarification at every grade level.

13. To enable learners to have a role in planning their learning experiences and provide an opportunity for making decisions and accepting their consequences.

14. To develop the abilities of doing and understanding growth, structure approaches and programmes of environmental education.

These objectives and assumptions are the guiding principles for developing content course of environmental education.

TEACHER'S ROLE IN ENVIRONMENTAL EDUCATION

Environmental education consists of curricular courses that is formal one and co-curricular activities that is non-formal one. So far as the first part is concerned our whole syllabi is full of topics relating to environment. There is no need to increase the already overburdened school children by introducing additional course. An integrated, inter-disciplinary and holistic perspective is to be adopted. Environmental bias must permeate into all facets of human life and, therefore, environmental concern should be taught in all subject areas.

But so far as the second part is concerned a teacher has to perform a lot of work. Hence co-curricular activities must be linked with formal teaching relating to real life situations. In order to cope with this a teacher should play the following roles:

1. While teaching his own subject matter he would correlate the topics of environmental issues.

2. He can help individuals in awareness of and sensitivity to the total environment and its allied problems.

3. A teacher may create an awareness regarding renewable and non-renewable resources of environment.

4. He can help his pupils to acquire basic understanding of the total environment, its associated problems and humanity's critically responsible presence and role in it.

5. A teacher can use play way techniques to make them understand the significance of food chains and food web on ecological balance.

6. A teacher can help his students to acquire social values, strong feelings of concern for the environment and the motivation for actively participation in its protection and improvement.

7. A teacher should conduct activities like drama on environmental conservation.

8. A teacher should help individuals to acquire the skills for solving environmental problems.

9. He may organize field trips to zoos, national parks, polluted cities, polluted rivers, birds sanctuary etc.

10. A teacher should help his pupils to evaluate environmental measures and education programmes in terms of ecological, social and aesthetic factors.

11. He should organized seminars, workshops on environmental issues like soil erosion or population explosion etc.

12. He may help students to develop a sense of responsibility and urgency regarding environmental problems to ensure appropriate action to solve these problems.

13. He should arrange lectures on topics of environmental concerns.

14. He should always teach the interdependence of living things as the relationship between the needs of society and the interaction with environment.

15. A teacher should discuss environmental issues along with simple teaching activities through which pupils understand the significance of environmental resources.

16. He should motivate and train to acquire and spread knowledge and skills that will help society solve interrelated environmental problems and prevent their occurrence.

QUESTIONS FOR ANSWER

1. *Define 'Environmental Education' and write a note on its main characteristics.*
2. *What do you mean by 'Environmental Awareness'? Discuss the role of education in the development of environmental awareness.*
3. *Write shot notes on the following:*
   (*a*) *Difference between environmental education and environmental awareness.*
   (*b*) *Need of environmental education.*
   (*c*) *Objectives of environmental education.*
4. *Write note on teacher's role in providing environmental education.*

8

Environmental Education as an Academic Discipline

Environmental education is a new field of study under the discipline of education which is concerned with the advancements and development in each area. The problems are interdisciplinary in nature which can be resolved by employing interdisciplinary approaches. Environmental education field is also inter-disciplinary in nature. Therefore, the concept of discipline, rationale for environmental education, its content and area of research have been discussed in this chapter.

MEANING OF DISCIPLINE

A discipline in the generally accepted sense of the word means a field of study which has a well defined content and a technique of its own together with a unique system of values. Most of the subjects taught in universities and colleges are 'discipline' in this sense. These have been traditionally accepted by the academic world.

When new directions of thought emerge from man's struggle and efforts with life and environment through his creative mental efforts and acquire in time a degree of stability in a new discipline, but during the course of its development it involves its own distinct characteristics and acquires status in the intellectual world.

There may be a social and professional activity which on account of its importance becomes an area of application for several disciplines, and this common area in course of time may come to be recognised as an independent field of study or an academic discipline.

The important thing to realize is that the necessary conditions for the growth of discipline are:

(*a*) Freedom to develop: New ideas,
New synthesis, and
New horizons.

(*b*) Increasing opportunities to experiment with them. When a number of discipline converge into an important field of social activity, this activity gives a new meaning a two-way-flow of ideas and resulting in the enrichment of both. It is an inter-disciplinary approach in different disciplines.

CHARACTERISTICS OF A DISCIPLINE

Every discipline has some specific features and has the following characteristics:

1. *Own Content*: Every discipline has its own specific content or subject-matter or course of study at a different level of teaching.

2. Every discipline has its own method of study. For example, physics and chemistry content matter is studied through laboratory or experiment method. History requires another method such as library method.

3. It is related to some professional and social activity. For example—Agriculture is related to 'farming'; psychology deals with the 'behaviour'; chemistry is related to 'matter'.

4. Every discipline has its methods of research. The science subjects usually employ the experimental method whereas social science subjects use survey method.

5. Each discipline has its own field of research. For example—researches of botany are concern with plants and zoology with animals or species.

6. The scholar of each discipline has unique idea, conduct, horizon of thinking and have impact of the discipline on his way of life style.

7. The content of each discipline is being advanced by conducting researches in the discipline.

8. The content of every discipline is transmitted by organizing separate departments in the colleges and universities.

9. The content of each discipline is preserved in the libraries separately.

ENVIRONMENTAL EDUCATION QUALIFY TO BE AN ACADEMIC DISCIPLINE

Academically, 'Environmental Education' is unquestionably related to and can be assigned a place under, the comprehensive discipline of Education. It seems to be an independent entity as it has wide relevance for the recent problems.

So it makes sense as a special educational discipline. It is considered a power instrument for improving the quality of the environment

> "Environmental education is a powerful instrument to maintain ecological balance that equips human beings with awareness, knowledge, skills, attitudes and commitment to improve the quality of environment"

An academic discipline is an area of academic interest and one that poses sufficient problems to stimulate research, and one that leads to the publication of journals in the subject area.

Environmental Education has its own independent content like other disciplines. The following structure of the discipline of 'Environmental Education' would qualify it for independent status as a discipline:

Concept of Environmental Education

1. Concept of Environment and its Components.
2. Concept of Education.
3. Meaning of Environmental Education and relationship with other subjects.
4. Environmental Education as a Discipline.

Concept of Ecology and Environmental Pollution

5. Concept of Ecology and Ecosystem.
6. Quality of Environment—Pollution and Degradation.
7. Environmental Pollution—Air, water, land and noise.
8. Human Ecology and Environmentalism.
9. Interdependency in Environment—Food chains and food web flow of energy and biochemical cycles.

Concept of Educational and Psychological Environment

10. Concept of Educational Environment.
11. Growth and Development.

12. Psychological Environment and Mental Health.
13. Population Explosion and Environment.

Concept of Environmental Management

14. Meaning of Environmental Management.
15. Teacher Education and Environmental Education.
16. Role of Media in Environmental Education.
17. Social Forestry and Environmental Education.
18. Problems and Remedies of Environmental Education.
19. Evaluation of Environmental Education.

The core content of Environmental Education is highly interdisciplinary in nature but the difference lies in the level of objectives. The purpose of other subject is to provide the awareness of environment and environmental studies, but environmental education has to develop cognitive, affective and psychomotor abilities and efficiencies.

OBJECTIVES OF STUDY

The following objectives were formulated in the international conferences of Environmental Education:

1. To develop an awareness of environment and sensitivity to the environment and its problems.
2. To help in acquiring knowledge and various type of experiences of the environmental problems.
3. To develop the basic understanding of structure, processes, problems and interdependence of environmental components.
4. To help in acquiring skills for identifying and solving environmental problems.
5. To develop attitudes, a set of values and feelings of concern for the environment and to encourage for active participation.
6. To develop ability for evaluating environmental components and educational programmes in terms of ecological, economic, social, cultural, aesthetic and educational factors.

The above contents of 'Environmental Education' is directly; and indirectly related to 'Environment'. It concerns with physical, social, biological, psychological and educational environment as whole. The core is the understanding of ecology and ecosystem and interdependency of biotic and abiotic factors. Various factors have to be studied which are polluting the environment.

The content of 'Environmental Education' is interdisciplinary in nature. Therefore, various methods of teaching and research are used. The experimental and non-experimental methods are used, even philosophical and historical methods are employed. Some legal laws are formulated to protect the quality of the environment.

The research areas of Environmental Education are also interdisciplinary. There are two types of environmental problems—natural and man-made. For natural problems (disasters and hazards), we can forecaste and develop effective media of communication preventive and relief measures can be made effective and prompt.

Human activities have created several types of environmental problems which are very harmful at present and also in future. The programmes and projects are to be evaluated in terms of their adverse effect on man. Thus, the problems are related to 'environmental management and evaluation'.

(*a*) *Human Activities*: Agriculture, industries, urbanization transportation, forestry, power plants, navigation and recreation, etc.

(*b*) *Human Values*: Traditional and modern life style, religious; status, economic status, public health, education, population, character and tourism.

Environmental Education as a leading subject from primary to university level. Some universities are organizing courses, seminars and conferences on environmental education, but the content relates to all levels of education. The inter-related components are to be taught for different levels.

Thus, the curriculum for environmental education is to be developed in the graded forms from the primary to the university level, so as to realize the objectives of environmental education.

Areas of Research

The university education has recognized three major components: teaching, research and extension work. At postgraduate level four major study areas are identified:

(*a*) *Environmental Engineering*: It includes civil engineering, planning, human settlement, industrial design, urban ecosystem studies.

(*b*) *Environmental Health*: It concerns with public health and hygiene, sanitary, chemical engineering, occupational health, institutional health, nutrition, etc.

(*c*) *Conservation and Management*: It includes land use, agriculture, energy flow, waste management, wildlife management, national parts, water management, non-polluting renewal energy development.

(*d*) *Social Ecology*: It includes human sociology, human ecology, population explosion, urbanization, social planning, cost-benefit, community organization and services guidance and counselling and environmental ethics.

Environmental education involves both theoretical and practical aspect of environment to improve the quality, imbalance and prevent the deterioration. It utilizes educational approaches, methods and technique of teaching, learning, and instruction, to identify the real causes of environmental problems and practices problem solving skills in formal and informal situations.

COMPONENTS OF STUDY

The content of environmental education has four, integrading and interrelated components—(1) Awareness, (2) Real-life situations, (3) Conservation, and (4) Sustainable development. The brief description of these components has been given in the following paragraphs.

1. *Awareness*: That include making the individual conscious about physical, biological, social and cultural aspects of environment. The environment is linked with the life support system which in itself has six components: air, land, water, flora, fauna and sunlight. These components have dynamic relationship. Man is most important organism and has great responsibility.

2. *Real-life situations*, that link environment to life, these conditions are location-specific, thus problems and priorities of each area are different.

3. *Conservation*, means utilization of natural resources not only by the present generation but also by the future generations. It does not include the process of exploitation.

4. *Sustainable Development*: It aims at utilization of resources for development. Therefore resources should be used in a wise manner. All resources are finite and there is also a limit to the growth of living system. Thus, the efforts are to be made to utilize the resources wisely and intelligently.

STAGEWISE COURSE CONTENTS

1. *Primary Education Stage*: Here the emphasis should be mostly (75%) on building up awareness, followed by real-life situations (20%) and conservation (5%). Thus attempt should be to only sensitise the child about environment. The content to be used are surroundings from home to school to outdoor situations. Teaching strategy includes audio-visual and field visits.

2. *Lower Secondary Education Stage*: From the lower secondary stage onwards, the quantum of awareness must decrease and there should be increased knowledge of real-life. situations, conservation and sustainable development. At lower secondary level, objective must be real life experience, awareness and problem identification. The contents to be used are those used at Primary School level supplemented with general science. Teaching, practicals and field visits are to be done.

3. *Higher Secondary Education Stage*: Here the emphasis must be on conservation, assimilation of knowledge, problem identification and action skills. The content used may be science-based and action oriented work. There should be proper teaching, practicals and field work.

4. *College Education Stage*: At this level, the picture would be almost reverse of the primary level, as maximum emphasis would be here on knowledge regarding sustainable development based on experience with, conservation followed, in a descending order, by conservation, real-life' situations and awareness. The content must be college/university based on Science and Technology. Teaching, practicals and action-oriented field work is to be done.

In the school education NCERT has been playing vital role in designing, syllabi, text books, help books, guide books, charts, kits, teaching materials and aids both for students and teachers.

5. *University Education Stage*: Environmental education at this level is being looked after by the University Grants Commission. There is a high powered Committee to suggest areas of EE at post-

graduate level. There are about 10 universities teaching courses in environmental areas.

Besides these, there are also research institutes and professional institutions as Indian Institute of Technology, Engineering Colleges, Schools of Planning and Architecture, which offer courses in environmental engineering. The University education has three major components: teaching, research and extension. At post-graduate level, four major areas are recognised:

(*a*) *Environmental Engineering*: It includes the subjects like architecture, civil engineering, town and country planning, including human settlement, slum improvement, landscape architecture, industrial design, regional science and urban ecosystem studies.

(*b*) *Conservation and Management*: It includes fields like land use, forestry, agriculture, energy, waste management, wildlife management, national parks, biosphere reserves, biological diversity, water management, mining management, non-polluting renewable energy development etc.

(*c*) *Environmental Health*: This deals with public health and hygiene, sanitary and chemical engineering, occupational health, toxicology, nutrition and drug use etc.

(*d*) *Social Ecology*: It includes subjects like human ecology, sociology, social planning, cost-benefit, community organisation and services, psychology and counselling, environmental ethics and related areas of humanities.

There are some institutes, centres assisted by the Department of Environment, which provide formal education/training in environmental areas. For instance, Centre for Environment Education (CEE), Ahmedabad; Indian Institute of Forest Management, Bhopal and Indira Gandhi National Forest Academy, Dehradun.

The main objectives of EE in our country are as follows:

1. To improve the quality of environment.
2. To create an atmosphere in the school and classroom so that students can participate in problem-solving and decision-making plans and procedures.
3. To develop an awareness among students on environmental problems and conservation.
4. To develop the capabilities to evaluate the effectiveness and workability of developmental programmes.

NEWMAN'S FOUR-FOLD ENVIRONMENTAL EDUCATION PROGRAMME

Newman (1981) proposed a four-fold classification of Environmental Education (EE) programmes based on different disciplines:

1. *Environmental Studies*: This is, concerned with the environmental disturbance and minimisation of their impacts through changes in the society (Social Sciences).
2. *Environmental Science*: It deals with the study of the procession water, air, soil and organisms which lead to pollution or environmental damage and to know a scientific clean, safe and healthy for human and the natural ecosystem (Physical and Natural Sciences).
3. *Environmental Engineering*: This is the study of the technical processes which are used to minimise the pollution and the assessment of impact of these on environment (Engineering Sciences).
4. *Teacher Education Programmes*: It develops the awareness, skills, attitudes and values about the environment or surroundings, plan and practice some activities to solve the problems, to improve the quality of environment. The area of teacher-education is different from social science because they are limited to awareness only.

NON-FORMAL AGENCIES/PROGRAMMES AND ENVIRONMENTAL EDUCATION

Governmental Organisations have to Play a Significant Role

In the directory of the Department of Environment, there are nearly two hundred private organisations of which 150 work in the area of environmental education and awareness. Moreover, children are to be told the real meaning of wildlife. Most children think only tiger, lion or elephant as wildlife. They are to be educated for plants, smaller animals, microbes etc. *i.e.* holistic approach to wildlife.

The environment education is designed both formally and non-formally. The formal environmental education has been discussed and an outline has been given in the above paragraphs. The EE is the lifelong process for the welfare of mankind and the development of the society. Therefore, it is designed for any age group, participating in social, economic, cultural development of the community. They form groups or clubs and arrange exhibitions, public lectures, meetings, environmental campaigns. The following constitute main content of this education:

1. *Adult Education*: Adult may influence other members for better ways of life. In local language, information packs, posters, slides, audio, audio-visuals etc. may be generated.

2. *Rural Youth and Non-student Youth*: They may organise into groups. The programmes of education can be taken up by involving their community leaders, women and youth. They are an important content of our forest wealth, for tribals and forest dwellers.

3. *Children Activities*: This can be ensured through essay competitions of different age groups. Department of Environment with the help of United School Organisation of India organised such activities. On the spot painting, modelling and poster design contents are conducted for children by the National Museum of Natural History (NMNH). Short-term courses are also given by NMNH in EE every year.

4. *Eco-development Camps*: They help in sound rural development involving youth. A set of guidelines has been prepared by (1984) Department of Environment. The main objectives are to create awareness in student and non-student youth about basic ecological principles; to identify root cause of ecological/environmental problems; and to develop a spirit of national integration and emotional integration.

5. *Non-governmental Organisations (NGOs)*: There are over 200 NGOs, of which most are involved in EE and awareness, others in nature conservation, pollution control, afforestation and social forestry, floristic and faunal studies, rural development, wildlife conservation and waste utilisation and eco-development.

6. *Public Representatives*: India has Environmental Forums for M.Ps and M.L.As to discuss environmental problems facing the country. They may build up sound public opinion and stimulate public interest.

7. *Training Senior Executives Administrators*: Regular courses should be arranged for various institutes imparting such training. These are general environmental management, industry-specific environmental management etc. It should be included in M.B.A. courses.

8. *Foundation Courses*: The courses for the probationers selected for the I.A.S., I.F.S., I.P.S., and cadets and three wings of Armed Forces need to be supplemented with foundation courses on environment relevant to their area of work.

9. *Research and Development Programmes*: Such programmes are supported by Department of Environment in Man and Biosphere and basic and applied environmental problems.

10. *Centres of Excellence*: Department of Environment has established two Centres of Excellence in the country. They generate knowledge and methodology and training in areas of Tropical Ecology (Bangalore) and Environmental Education (Ahmedabad).

11. *Development of Trained Manpower*: There must be training programmes for the trainers, professionals, technical personnel, and legal experts.

12. *Development of Educational Material and Teaching-aids*: Audio, audio-visual materials, materials for media (TV, radio, films newspapers etc), mobile exhibitions etc. must be designed by competent manpower. One such centre is Centre for Environment Education, Ahmedabad.

13. *World Environment Day*: All Governments in the States, Union Territories, academic institutions, universities, colleges, schools and voluntary organisations organise suitable activities on this day (June 5). Department of Environment support this financially.

14. *National Environment Awareness Campaign (NEAC)/National Environment Month (NEM)*: Commencing from 1986, Department of Environment conducts NEAC and NEM; from November 19th to December 18th every year is observed as NEM. Each year there is a major environmental theme.

ENVIRONMENTAL EDUCATION FOR TEACHER EDUCATION

The universities and educational institutions have designed the course content of Environmental Education for B.Ed. and M.Ed. levels. The review of the courses indicates that main emphasis has been given on physical and biological components of the environment. The problems, inter-relationship and interdepen-dence of these components have been emphasized, but the main focus of education is to develop the integrated personality of a child. It involves physical, social, emotional and mental development of the child which requires conducive social, cultural and psychological environment alongwith physical and biololgical environment. A comprehensive course of EE for teacher education is as follows:

1. *Historical Development of E.E.*: Ancient viewpoint and recent concept of EE.

2. *Concept of Environment*: Meaning, structure and processes. Types of environment and components.

3. *Concept of Education:* Meaning, objectives, content and status, interdisciplinary approach to education.

4. *Concept of Environmental Education*: Relationship between Environment and education; meaning and definition, characteristics, objectives, content, method and techniques, productive function of EE.

5. *Concepts related to EE.*: Ecology, Ecosystem, Autocology, Bioms and Pollution, Environmental Degradation.

6. *Physical Environment and Education*: Meaning components: Air, water, sound/noise pollutions. Meaning structure, components, factors affecting environmental, industry, urbanization, traffic etc and role of Education and interdependency of various factors of the environment.

7. *Social and Cultural Environment and Education*: Meaning and structure. Population, colonization, urbanization due to social changes and mobility. Development of media, factors influencing the environment and role of teacher and school, mental health and community health.

8. *Psychological Environment and Education*: Meaning structure, components-feelings, interests, attitudes values and level of aspirations. Factors affectings the psychological environment-family, social system, organization climate of school and classroom social and emotional climate.

9. *Agencies of Environmental Protection and Information*: Steps take. The governmental organizations, private organizations, legal steps, role of educational institutions.

10. *Environmental Planning and Management*: Need, meaning, organizations, components and role of Education and Evaluation System of programme.

METHODS AND TECHNIQUES OF TEACHING ENVIRONMENTAL EDUCATION

The content of EE is largely interdisciplinary in nature as discussed in the earlier paragraphs and presented an outline briefly. It is both 'art (doing) and science (understanding), organized from primary to university level. The objectives of EE are not confined upto knowledge and understanding (awareness) but include skills, attitudes and values. The problem solving and development of quality of man and environment are the major functions of E.E. Thus strategies of teaching and learning have wide coverage, based on content, its components, levels of education and the objectives of EE.

The major objectives of EE are awareness, attitude and action. It covers cognitive psychomotor and affective domains of teaching learning objectives. Therefore a student should be allowed and asked to observe simple phenomena of earth and the sky. He acquires awareness about the living and non-living components and develops awareness about one's well being in the context of social and natural environment.

He begins to form positive feelings and attitudes of environmental protection. He may utilize this awareness, skills attitudes in his actions as personal habits. Personal habits can contribute in improving the quality of the environment. The teacher should also translate the awareness in his actions which will be the model for the students.

Thus, the doing part is much more important for the teacher. The role of teacher is very significant in realizing the above objectives of EE. A number of projects can be assigned to students in school situations for making herbarium, plantation in school campus. It is the teacher who can sensitize his students for improving the quality of environment.

The objectives of EE can be realized through formal and non-formal system of education. In view of above objectives and levels of education, educational excursions or field trips are very effective methods.

EDUCATIONAL EXCURSION OR FIELD TRIPS

Ryan developed 'Educational Excursion Method' of teaching which is commonly used in geography, botany, zoology, study of nature and history teaching. There are certain topics in Environmental Education which can be taught effectively by this method.

Rouseau has emphasized the need and importance of this method. "Natural observation is the best method of teaching as compared with classroom teaching learning and studying books." This method provides the real awareness by local observation, regional and natural observation, geographical conditions observation, observing historical places, and remains, industrial area, natural vegetation which are the major components of the environment related school subjects.

The following are the theoretical basis of this method:

1. It is based on psychological principles, the awareness of environment is provided through the perception of the students.
2. It involves the observations, imagination and ability of discovering the cause-effect relationship among the environmental components.
3. It provides the real experiences about the environmental education to the learners.
4. It develops the feeling of cooperation and group work/ team work as social principles.
5. The observation tourist place develops the feeling of appreciation.

The following are the main objectives of this method.

1. To provide the awareness about their environment.
2. To develop the tendency of excursion and its utility for the understanding.
3. To develop and enrich the ability of observation, imagination and discovering.
4. To develop the ability for interpreting his own experiences and observations.
5. To develop the ability of appreciation of natural beauty and tourist places.
6. To develop the ability of cooperation and group-work.

The following steps are essential in organizing educational excursion.

1. The specific objectives are to be formulated.
2. The ways and means are to be identified to that objectives may be realized.
3. *A schedule*—date, time, number of students, duration and financial aspect should be finalized.
4. The visiting organizations are to be contacted for the arrangement.
5. The means of transportation are to be organized and time schedule is to be finalized.
6. A guide sheet is prepared and supplied to students.
7. The students are instructed to prepare a report about their observations and visiting different places.

The success of excursion depends on the selection of places and points of observation by the students. The important aspects of observations should be—plants and other vegetation and farming, land scape or soil, animals, industries, panchayat activities, social poverty, water resources, electricity supply; voluntary organizations, adult education and non-formal education programmes. Every student should prepare a report about his observations. The excursion should be followed by group discussion to highlight the environmental components and sources of pollution.

The following are the main advantages of the method.

1. Teaching can be made effective and interesting by real experiences.
2. It develops the ability of appreciation of natural environment.
3. It helps in developing the ability of observations and imagination.
4. The objectives of teaching can be realized by this method.
5. It develops the feelings of co-operation and group work or team work.

CO-CURRICULAR ACTIVITIES

The strategies of teaching of EE can be used for providing awareness, developing skills and attitudes for the environmental consciousness but action and participation is equally important in the area of environmental education. The co-curricular activities of education are the most appropriate means for providing opportunities for the action.

The teacher is the principal means for implementing the programmes and realizing the objectives of environmental education and organization of co-curricular activities in the school and out-side the school because a student has complete trust and faith in his teacher. Most of the teachers are still held in esteem by their students and the community.

Hence a teacher should possess the abilities of organizing effectively curricular and the cocurricular activities. In this context there are two main educational programmes recommended by the Education Commission *i.e.,* National Social Scheme (NSS) and Socially Useful Productive Work (SUPW). The co-curricular activities are organized through these programmes.

- To clean the environment through NSS camps.

- To grow plants and develop garden for protection.
- To clean the public places, parks, etc.
- To construct the roads and dig pits for the waste in the village by organizing NSS camps and also scout camps.
- To develop the sense of sanitation among the people by organizing cultural programmes.
- To develop the consciousness about population education by organizing camps of population education or family planning.
- To encourage the students for preparing charts related to the environmental pollution and its protection.
- To motivate the students for using stories and essays on the environmental education.

PRESENT STATUS OF ENVIRONMENTAL EDUCATION

The review committee (1977) on Curriculum of Environmental Education has stressed the need for more environment based education. The committee has recommended that physical and bio-sciences, life sciences curriculum should be made environment oriented with emphasis on problems related to environment. B.Ed and M.Ed courses of universities have special emphasis on environmental education. Brief account of the progress of EE is as follows.

A centre of environmental education has been set up at Ahmedabad. The educational teaching material and teaching aids are developed at this centre. Audio-visual materials for media mobile exhibitions are organized by the experts. The regular courses are organised for various institutions imparting training to senior executives and administrators. The foundation courses are developed for I.A.S., I.P.S., I.F.S. and I.E.S. candidates to their area of work.

Department of Education has established two Centres of Excellance in the country. They generate knowledge and methodology of training in the areas of Tropical Ecology, Banglore and Environmental Education at Ahmedabad: The education department has prepared guidelines to help in sound rural development youth. The main purpose is to identify root cause of ecological problems as related, to human activities and solve the local environmental problems.

Environmental Information System was set-up in (1982) under the Department of Education plan programme. There are ten such centres on diverse areas of environment, established in specialized institutions in the country.

There are more than two hundred non-governmental organizations which are engaged in environmental education awareness and training youths on different areas—pollution control, rural development, wildlife conservation, afforestation, floristic and faunal studies, waste utilization and eco-development.

To highlight the present status of environmental education in India following two tables are enlisted for the benefit of the students who may desire to go for higher studies in environmental science or Environmental Education.

Table 8.1: Representative List of Institutions Dealing with Higher Education in Ecology and Environment

Central Universities	**Deemed Universities**
Aligarh Muslim	Avinashalingam Institute
Banares Hindu	Ghandhigram Rural Institute
Hyderabad	Gurukul Kangri
Jawahar Lal Nehru	Indian School of Mines
North Eastern Hill	School of Planning & Architecture
Pondicherry	Sri Satyasai Institute of Higher Learning
	Thapar Institute of Engineering & Technology
State Universities	
Andhra	**Specialist Universities**
A.P. Singh	Anna
Baroda	Birsa Agricultural
Berhampur	G.B. Pant Agricultural
Bharathiar	Jawahar Lal Nehru Technological
Calcutta	Punjab Agricultural
Cochin	Tamil Nadu Agricultural
Guwhati	Y.S. Parmar Agricultural
Jadavpur	
Jiwaji	**Autonomous National Institutions**
Kuvemp	Indian Institute of Forest Management
Madurai Kamaraj	Indian Institute of Science
Manonman Sundaranar	Indian Institutes of Technology
Marathwada	Forest Research Institute of India
Mysore	Wildlife Institute of India
Poona	
Rajasthan	
Roorkee	
Shivaji	
Sukhadia	
Venkateswara	

* Ecology is taught as a full or part paper in the departments of Botany and Zoology in all Universities. Environmental Biology is offered as an elective in some Universities; Natural Resources are covered in geography curricula. Colleges are excluded because the scenario is same as in the Universities and they are so innumerable.

Table 8.2: Representative List of Indian Universities/Institutions offering Educational Programmes in Environmental/Ecological Sciences and Allied Subjects at Postgraduate Level

University/Institution	*Subject*	*University/Institution*	*Subject*	*University/Institution*	*Subject*
Ahmedabad (Gujarat)	Environ. Sci.	Coimbatore (T.N. Agri.)	Environ. Sci.	Panjim (Goa)	Marine Science
Aligarh	Wildlife Biol.	Coimbatore (Bharathiar)	Environ. Sci.	Patiala (Thapar Inst. Tech.)	Env. Eng.
Aurangabad (Marathawada)	Environ. Sci.	Dehradun (Wildlife Inst. India)	Wild life	Patiala (Punjabi)	Env. Tech.
Bangalore	Environ. Biol. Marine Biol	Delhi	Envinron. Biol.	Pondicherry	Ecology
Bangalore (Ind. Inst. Sci.)	Ecol. Sci.	Delhi (Ind. Inst. Eco. & Env.)	Eco. & Env.	Poona	Environ. Sci. Climatology
Behrampur	Marine Science	Delhi (Ind. Inst.Tech.)	Env. Sci. Eng.	Raipur (Ravisankar)	Water Res. Dev.
Bhopal (Barkatullah)	Limnology	Delhi (Jawaharlal Nehru)	Environ. Sci.	Rajkot (Saurashtra)	Wildlife Biol
Bhopal (Id. Inst Forest Manag.)	Forest Management	Dharwar (Karnataka)	Marine Biol	Rewa (A.P. Singh)	Environ. Sci.
Bhubaneswar (Utkal)	Marine Sci Marine Zoology	Guwahati	Environ. Sci.	Roorke	Env. Eng.
Bilaspur (Guru Ghasidas)	Forestry, Wildlife & Ecodevelopment	Gwalior (Jiwaji)	Environ. Sci.	Sambalpur	Environ. Sci
Bombay (Bombay Natural History Society)	Wildlife Biol Field Botany, Mammalogy & Ornithology	Jadavpur	Environ. Sci.	Shimla (Himachal Pradesh)	
Bombay (Ind. Inst. Tech).	Envi. Sci. Eng	Kalyani		Solan (Horticulture & Forestry)	
Calcutta	Environ. Sci. Biol.	Kolhapur (Shivaji)	Environ. Sci. Environ. Man.	Srinagar (Garhwal)	
Chitrakoot	Environ. Sci	Madras	Env. Toxicoi Environ. Sci. & Management Ocean Life Sci Environ. Sci.	Thiruchirapalli (Bharathidasan)	Environ. Sci. Wildlife
Cochin	Environ. Sci.	Madurai	Environment, Natural Resources	Tirupati (Sri Venkateswara)	Environ. Chem Environ. Eng.
Pantnagar GB Pant)	Marine Biol Environ. Biol			Trivandrum (Kerala)	Aquatic Biol
				Waltair (Andhra)	Marine Science

Most of the above offer doctrol programmes. Some offer M. Phill also. A few offer only M. Phill/Ph.D. courses.

QUESTIONS FOR ANSWER

1. *What makes 'Environmental Education an academic discipline? Explair ?*
2. *Write a note on the objectives and contents of environmental education.*
3. *Describe the non-formal environmental education for children as well as rural and urban youth.*
4. *Write a note on the course contents of environmental education for teacher education programmes in Indian Universities.*
5. *Write short notes on the following:*
   (*a*) *Characteristics of a discipline.*
   (*b*) *Components of environmental education.*
   (*c*) *Stagewise course contents of environmental education.*
   (*d*) *Educational excursions or field trips.*
   (*e*) *Present status of environmental education in India.*

9

Ecology and Education

Environmental study is interdisciplinary in nature and interacts with all physical bio and behavioural sciences. Each discipline and field of study has its own words and terms to communicate the concepts involved in it. There are several words and terms used in environmental studies. The two terms 'Ecology' and 'Ecosystem' are most important and basic for understanding the environment. Some times these terms are used interchangeably, but they have different meanings. Hereunder, we will discuss various concepts and aspects concerning 'Ecology' and 'Ecosystem'.

DEFINITION OF ECOLOGY

Ecology, in a very simple term, is a science that studies the interdependent, mutually reactive and interconnected relationships between the organisms and their physical environment on the one hand and among the organisms on the other hand. Though the term 'oecology' was first coined and used by the German biologist, Ernst Haeckel in 1869, a few conceptual terms were already proposed to reveal relationships between organisms and their environment. For example, French zoologist, Isadore Geoffroy St. Hilaire used the term 'Ethology' for the study of the relations of the organisms within the family and society in the aggregate and in the community.

British naturalist St. George Jackson Mivart proposed the term 'Hexicology' for the study of the relations which exist between the organisms and their environment as regards the nature of the locality they frequent, the temperatures and the amounts of light which suit them, and their relations to other organisms as enemies, rivals, or accidental and involuntary benefactors'.

It may be pointed out that Darwin's concepts of the 'evolution of species' through natural selection involving interactions between biological species and habitat was the key stone of the formulation of various terms and concepts of inter-relationships between organisms and their physical-environment in one way or the other.

Thus, Ernst Haeckel coined the term 'oecology' or 'oekology' (derived from two Greek words, 'Oikos' meaning house or dwelling as habitat and 'Logos' meaning the study of) to understand the relationships between organism and their environment.

Ecology was considered by American ecologist Frederick Clements (1916) as 'the science of community' while Charles Elton defined ecology as 'a scientific natural history'. Thus the science of ecology was endowed with two overlapping areas of study *e.g.* (*i*) the study of organisms in relation to their environment, and (*ii*) the evolutionary history of the organisms.

British ecologist Macfadyen (1957) emphasised to discover the principles which govern the relationships between plants or animals and their environment while K. Friederichs (1958) defined ecology as 'the science of living beings as members of the whole of nature' but he ignored the effects of the organisms on environment and those of the environment on the organisms.

F. Fraser Darling (1963) broadened the field of ecology by defining the subject as 'the science of organisms in relation to their total environment, and the inter-relationships of organisms inter-specifically and between themselves'.

This definition of ecology led to the development of two approaches to the study of ecology and its divisions into two branches *viz.* (*i*) 'autecology' wherein ecological relations of individual species in a given ecosystem are studied, and (*ii*) 'synecology' which is the study of plant communities in relation to their habitats of a given ecosystem.

More recently, the concept of ecology has been extended to the corresponding range of phenomena, research and problems. In that connection 'ecology' has been quite logically extended as well to the field of the interaction of society and its physical environment' (Y.P. Trusov, 1983).

E.P. Odum (1963, 1964, 1969, 1971) pleaded for remodelling the conventional definition of ecology (the science of inter-relationships between organisms and environment) on the ground that biotic and abiotic components of nature are not only interrelated in reciprocal manner but these two components also function in an orderly manner as a definite system. So, Odum presented a new definition of ecology as 'the study of the structure and function of ecosystems' or the 'study of structure and function of nature'.

The scope of ecology and its aims have expanded enormously with development of ecological concepts and thoughts consequent upon growing interests in man-environment relationships due to increasing pressure on natural/ecological resources to sustain and enhance economic development in view of ever-increasing human population.

The above discussion makes it clear that "ecology is the study of structure and functions of nature". Hereunder, some other important definitions are given:

C.J. Krebs (1985) defined ecology in simple and in comprehensive way as "Ecology is the scientific study of the interactions between organisms and nature that determine the range/distribution and abundance of organisms."

Macfadyen (1957) defined ecology as, "a science which concerns itself with the inter-relationships of living organisms, plants, animals and their environment".

G.L. Clarke (1954) defines ecology as "the study of inter-relations of plants and animals with their environment which includes the influences of other plants and animals as well as those of the physical features."

L.R. Taylor (1967) have defined ecology as "the study of the way in which individual organisms, populations of some species and communities respond to those changes."

Alles *et al.* (1949) considered ecology as, "the science of inter-relation between living organisms and their environment, including both the physical and biological environments and emphasizing inter-species as well as intra-species relations."

The modern ecologists have given somewhat more comprehensive and broader definitions of ecology as follows:

Southwide (1976) defined ecology as, "the scientific study of the relationship of living organisms with each other and with their environments." He further explained his definition of ecology by stating that, "it is the science of biological interactions among individuals, populations and communities, and it is also the science of ecosystems—the inter-relations of biotic communities with their non-living environments."

Pinalea (1973) deemed ecology as, "the study of relations between organisms and the totality of the biological and physical factors affecting them or influenced by them."

BASIC CHARACTERISTICS

Basic characteristics are as follows:

1. It is the scientific study for analysing the relations between organisms and environment.
2. It is the study of inter-relationships and interdependence between organisms and environment.
3. It includes the structure and function together for full understanding of this vast nature.
4. It is also a philosophy in which the world of life is interpreted in terms of natural processes.
5. It is the scientific approach for controlling and regulating the welfare of living organisms.
6. It is the science of all the relations of all organisms to all their environment.
7. It is the study of organisms in relation to their environment.
8. It is the science of ecosystems. The ecosystem is an important ecological unit.
9. It is the science of inter-relation between organisms and their environments and also emphasises inter-organisms as well as intra-organisms (within) relations.

IS IT SCIENCE OR ART

The above definitions and characterirstics of ecology indicate that it is science as well as art. The science includes observations and experiences which leads for understanding. The art is more concerned with doing things.

The awareness and informations collected through observation and experiences which provides the understanding of various principles and theories that govern the function of nature (the science of ecology) are then applied for the welfare of mankind that is the art of ecology. Advancement in art depends on science, as more we learn and understand. Indeed science and art go side by side and are studied best together. The ecology is both science as well as art.

Education discipline is also both science as well as art. With reference to the conceptual meaning of ecology, the education may be termed as human ecology or child ecology. Education is interaction between child and his environment (physical, social, cultural and psychological environment). The science of ecology concerns with all phases of development and helps in the process of development of its art, as conservation of nature and natural resources, solution of pollution problems. It is a basic division of biology and is an integral part of any and all the taxonomic divisions.

BASIC FUNDAMENTAL PRINCIPLES

There are basic fundamental principles which govern the various aspects of organisms and components of environment. The following are the fundamental principles of ecology:

1. All living organisms and physical environment are mutually reactive. The organisms interact among themselves and affect each other and physical environment.
2. Environmental principles of holistic nature of natural environment which largely affect the biological communities in a biospheric ecosystem.
3. Sustained life on earth is a characteristic of ecosystem, not of individual organisms or population.
4. The physical and biological processes follow the principle of uniformitarianism which states the same physical and biological processes, as the environment is influenced by human activity.
5. Natural hazards affect adversely the biological communities in general and in particular. When biological processes are associated with physical events, yet severe hazards are created.
6. Ecosystem is a fundamental unit of ecological study because it comprises both biotic and abiotic components.
7. The ecosystem productivity depends on two factors:

(*a*) The availability of the amount of solar radiation to the primary producers.
(*b*) The efficiency of plants to convert solar energy into chemical energy.

8. Ecosystem functions through the input of energy mainly solar radiation which is trapped by green plants and is used to prepare food through the process photosynthesis. The solar radiation is the main driving force of the ecosystem. In any system of constant mass, energy is neither created nor destroyed but it can be transformed from one type to another type.
9. Man being an active agent of environmental change, modifies the ecosystem through the exploitation of natural resources.
10. Ecosystem instability results when an ecosystem becomes unable to adjust with environmental changes.

AIMS AND OBJECTIVES OF STUDY

Ecology is an independent field of study as it has a body of knowledge not similarly organised in any other science subject. Ecology has a special set of methods, techniques and procedure. Theme of ecology has its own. The following are the main objectives of ecological studies:

1. To study the relationships between living organism and environment.
2. To provide the true understanding of the structure and functions of the vast nature.
3. To analyse the interdependence between organisms and environmental components.
4. To interpret the world life in terms of natural processes.
5. To evolve scientific approaches for controlling and regulating the welfare of living organisms.
6. To explore the evolutionary development of the inter-relations between living organism and environment.
7. To evolve mathematical models to relate interaction of environmental components and predict their effects by employing system analysis approach.
8. To provide the comprehensive awareness of all the relations between all the living organisms and their all environments.

9. To study the conservation and management of natural resources and environmental pollution. It is the main focus of applied ecology.
10. To observe the biological productivity of physical environment or nature and how the products may best serve the mankind or improve the quality of man. It is the main aim of ecosystem ecology.

The objectives are related to different areas of ecology and the other disciplines—population ecology, geography, physiology, evolutionary, ethology, ecosystem, system analysis and applied ecology. There is not one ecology but several ecology to understand the relationships.

BRANCHES AND AREAS OF STUDY

The scope of ecology is very vast, therefore, various kinds of ecology. Early scientists have classified into two major kinds: (*i*) animal ecology, and (*ii*) plant ecology. When equal emphasis is given to animals and plants, it is termed bioecology.

Further ecology is broadly divided into (*i*) Autecology, and (*ii*) Synecology.

(*i*) Autecology deals with the relationship, of one species of organism. An autecologist studies the life history, population, dynamics, behaviour, home range of single species *e.g.* bull frog of India.

(*ii*) Synecology deals with the ecological studies of communities or entire ecosystem. A synecologist study deserts, caves or tropical forests. He describes the overall energy and materials flow through the system.

There are the following specialized branches of ecology:

	Branch of Ecology		*Area of Study*
1.	Habitat Ecology	:	The study of different-habitats on earth and their effects on the organisms.
2.	Geographic Ecology	:	The study of geographical distribution of plants and animals.
3.	Ethology	:	The interpretation of animal behaviour under natural surroundings.
4.	Human Ecology	:	The study of man and man's relation to the environment and man's effects on biosphere and implication for man.

(*Contd.*)

	Branch of Ecology		Area of Study
5.	Community Ecology	:	The study of the local distribution of animals in various habitats.
6.	Population Ecology	:	The study of growth, structure and regulation of population of organisms.
7.	Applied Ecology	:	The study of the human needs and the applications of ecological concepts *e.g.* agriculture, forestry, land use etc.
8.	Production Ecology	:	It deals the production of different ecosystems like fresh water, crops sea water etc.
9.	Sociology	:	The study of ecology and ethology of mankind.
10.	Radiation Ecology	:	The study of effects of radiation on environment and organisms.
11.	System Ecology	:	It deals the analysis and understanding of the structure and function of ecosystem. It employs mathematical models.

AREA OR FIELD OF STUDY

The field of study of ecology is very vast. It not only confine to biological sciences from where it has evolved but it has reached the social sciences and, also upto behavioural sciences of edifice of knowledge. Ecology has been viewed as 'a state of the mind' on the basis of its holistic nature, as a unifying social movement. It accelerates the rate of economic development to meet out the demands of ever-increasing human population at global and regional levels.

Ecology is the science that requires minimum time and labour for its introduction to a layman. Present day problems varied nature in human life are directly and indirectly very much related to the field of ecology, and their solution needs an ecological knowledge. The ecology has been contributing these days very much to socio-economic, industrial, technological, political and other policies and plans of the worlds.

Ecology indeed plays an important role in human welfare. The field of study of modern ecology is concerned with the fundamental interdependences between organisms and their environment.

Ecology is an interdisciplinary discipline and it includes not only the life sciences but also chemistry, physics, geography, geology, meterology, mathematics, statistic, sociology, climatolgy, anthropology, hydrology etc. An ecologist has to collect the data for interpreting the behavoiur of an organism in given environment which are obtained from many sources: morphology, geology, taxonomy, genetics, physiology, soil science, climatology, physics and chemistry.

Many practical applications of this area are found in agriculture, horticulture, forestry, limnology, fishery, biology survey, oceanography, public health, mental health and hygiene. Ecology helps in discovering new sources of food, source of energy (solar energy) and new method of pest control such as biological control which causes no environmental pollution.

TOOLS AND TECHNIQUES OF STUDY

Ecology is an interdisciplinary approach for studying environment. It is considered both art and science. It concerns both the aspects doing and understanding. An ecologist has to work with living systems and various environmental components. In ecology, various types of tools and techniques are used. It employs both longitudinal as well as cross-sectional approaches. It involves scientific and non-scientific methods, tools and techniques. An ecologist has to begin with observations of living organisms and environmental components. The observation tool and correlation techniques are commonly used by ecologists.

Following qualitative and quantitative methods and tools are employed in ecology:

Qualitative Method	*Quantitative Method*
(*a*) Observation	(*a*) Observation
(*b*) Historical	(*b*) Experimental
(*c*) Longitudinal	(*c*) Cross-sectional
(*d*) Descriptive	(*d*) Project method
(*e*) Sampling technique	(*e*) Sampling technique

Statistical Techniques: In physical sciences mathematics is used to analyse and interpret the observations and the data. In biosciences, biostatistics is employed to analyse and interpret the observations. Biostatistics may be defined as the applications of statistical technique to the solution of biological problems. It is also termed as biometry. The various biological observations are randomly taken and these are normally distributed, therefore, inferential statistics can be easily applied for the formulations and generalizations.

The biological variable, are of two kinds—continuous variables and discrete variables. Thus, elementary statistics, parametrics and non-parametric statistical tests and techniques are used.

ECOLOGY AND EDUCATION

The concept of 'ecology' has been widely used in physical and biosciences but it has very broad areas of its application in social sciences as well as behavioural sciences. It is considered both art and science. Education is the process of development or all round development. Behaviour psychologists have claimed that environment is all in all in the development of a child and heredity has nothing to do in the process of development. Behaviourists have given much more importance to environment. This school of psychology is also termed as Environmental psychology.

Educational processes create environments for the students to gain experiences which result in learning. Both types of environment, natural and the man-designed, are essential in education. Thus education is the study of interaction between child and his environment.

The ecology includes the structure and function together for with understanding of the environment. Similarly education also designed the structure for the functions of students which helps in their development. Education is a scientific approach for controlling and regulating the behaviours for the desirable change among the students.

The teaching is an art and learning is the science. The teaching is the doing or action part whereas learning is the understanding aspect in the educational process. Ecology has also both doing and understanding aspects.

Education is also philosophy which helps in formulating aims and objectives for the human welfare whereas ecology interpret world of life in terms of natural processes.

Education includes several systems. A school is a unit of the system which has its own organizational climate which is same as ecosystem of ecology. Every institution has its own input and output or productivity, it functions like ecosystem. Education and ecology have their broad areas of doing and understanding.

QUESTIONS FOR ANSWER

1. *Define 'Ecology and justify that it is science as well as art.*
2. *Enumerate fundamental characteristics and basic aims and objectives of ecology.*
3. *Write a note on the principles and branches of study of ecology.*
4. *Write short notes on the following:*
   (*a*) *Area or Field of study of ecology.*
   (*b*) *Tools and techniques of ecological study.*
   (*c*) *Ecology and education.*

10

Ecosystem and Education

Ecosystem is a fundamental ecological unit because it is a particular category of physical systems consisting of organisms and organic components in a relatively stable equilibrium. Sometimes ecology and ecosystem are used interchangeably, but in real sense they differ with each, though they are complimentary to each other. Hereunder, we will discuss various aspects concerning ecosystem including how it differs from ecology.

MEANING AND DEFINITION

Any unit that includes all the organisms in a given area, interact with physical environment so that flow of energy leads clearly defined trophic structure, biotic diversity and material cycle within the system is known as an ecological system or ecosystem.

The recent development in economical studies has been to undertake besides structure, the similarities and differences in food and energy relationships among living components of ecosystem that is generally referred to as the bioenergetic approach in modern ecology. Modern ecology is broadly defined as the study of ecosystems.

Human ecology or applied ecology is the use of ecological concepts to describe human activities and determination of ways in which people can best obtain their needs from ecosystems. Ecosystems which are substantially altered by human activities are called managed whereas those free from such disturbances are referred to as natural.

According to Tansley the ecosystem is comprised of two major parts:

(*i*) The first part is biome which includes the whole complex of plants and animals of particular spatial unit.

(*ii*) The second part is habitat which involves the physical environment of the particular spatial unit.

All parts of an ecosystem—organic and inorganic, biome and habitat may be regarded as interacting factors which, in a mature ecosystem, are in approximate equilibrium, it is through their interactions that the whole system is maintained.

> "The ecosystem as functioning, interacting system composed of one or more living organisms and their effective environment, both physical and biological".
>
> —*A.G. Tansely & F.R. Fosberg* (1963)

An ecosystem may be defined as fundamental functional unit occupying spatial dimension of 'earth space ship' characterised by total assemblage of biotic community and abiotic components and their mutual interactions within a given time unit.

The ecosystems are units of organisms connected to one another and to their environment. The ecosystem is the sum total of all natural organisms and substances within an area, and it can be viewed as basic example of an open system in physical geography.

> "The term ecosystem applies to, 'any system composed of physical, chemical and biological processes within a space-time unit of any magnitude." —*R.L. Linderman* (1942)

> "The total assemblag of components interacting with a group of organisms is known as ecological system or more simply an ecosystem."—*A.N. Strahler & A.N. Strahler* (1976)

Living organism can use energy in several forms, but all forms can be grouped into categories—radiant and fixed.

(*i*) Radiant energy is in the form of electromagnetic waves such as light.

(*ii*) Fixed energy is chemical energy in various organic substances which can be broken down to release energy.

FUNDAMENTAL CHARACTERISTICS

We may enlist the characteristics as follows:

1. Any system composed of physical, chemical and biological processes with in a space-time unit of any magnitude.

2. The ecosystem is a unit of organisms connected to one another and to their environment within given space and time unit.
3. It is composed of three basic components—biotic (biome), abiotic (habitat) and energy components.
4. Ecosystem of any given space-time-unit represents the sum of all living organisms and physical environment.
5. It occupies certain well defined area on the earth-space, and time unit.
6. There are complex sets of interactions between biotic and abiotic components including energy component on the one hand, and among the organism, on the other hand.
7. It is an open system which is characterised by continuous input and output of matter and energy.
8. It is powered by energy of various sorts but the solar energy is the most significant (radiation) and tends to be relatively stable equilibrium. It has the natural resources system.
9. Ecosystem has its own productivity which is the process of building organic matter based on the availability and amount of energy passing through ecosystem. The productivity refers to the rate of growth of organic matter in a space unit per time unit.
10. It is well organized and structured system. The study of ecosystem development is helpful in the environmental planning from ecological point of view.

CLASSIFICATION OF ECOSYSTEM

There are different types of ecosystem of nature. These may be classified broadly into three categories:

1. *Natural Ecosystems* operate by themselves under natural conditions without any major interference by man and based upon the particular kind of habitat, these are further divided into two sub-categories.

(*a*) *Terrestrial Ecosystem* as forest, grassland, desert etc.
(*b*) *Aquatic System*

  (*i*) Fresh water-running, spring, waterfalls, rivers and standing as lake, pond, pools, ditch.

(*ii*) Marine or ocean water such deep bodies as sea, ocean, estuary etc.

2. *Artificial Ecosystem* (*man-engineered*): These ecosystems are managed by man where, by addition of energy and planed manipulations, natural balance is disturbed regularly *e.g.* croplands, wheat, maze, rice field etc. Man tries to control biotic components and physio-chemical environment which are common as artificial ecosystem.

3. The space-ecosystem is the recent development which comes under artificial ecosystem.

Ecosystems has also been classified on the following bases:

(*i*) Habitats,
(*ii*) Ecolines,
(*iii*) Spatial scales,
(*iv*) Uses,
(*v*) Source and level of energy,
(*vi*) Stages of ecosystem development, and
(*vii*) Stability and instability.

The physical conditions determine the nature and characteristics of biotic communities and therefore, there are spatial variations in the biotic communities. The biological or social features of human beings and their language pronunciation are determined by physical conditions. The low land, desert mountain are the types of ecosystem.

There are two broad categories on the basis of uses of ecosystem: (*i*) cultivation, and (*ii*) non-cultivation or natural ecosystems. The cultivated ecosystem is concerned with the various types of crops production.

The ecosystem has been classified into four categories on the basic source of energy: (*i*) Natural solar-powered ecosystems, (*ii*) Natural subsidized solar-powered ecosystem, (*iii*) Man-subsidized solar-powered ecosystem (human tastes and activities) mechanised farming ecosystems, man increases the productivity through the use of chemical fertilizers, irrigational water, and (*iv*) Fuel-powered ecosystems the industrial areas where fuel energy fully replaces solar energy. An ecosystem is dynamic equilibrium state is that which represents balance between the input and output of energy.

ECOSYSTEM—THE FUNCTIONING PROCESS

Functioning of an ecosystem basically depends on the pattern of energy flow, because all aspects of living components of an ecosystem depends on energy flow. The following are the main functions of ecosystem:

(*i*) Transformation of solar energy into food energy,
(*ii*) The circulation of elements through energy flow,
(*iii*) The conversion of elements into inorganic forms, and
(*iv*) The growth and development of plants.

The first-law of thermodynamics states that any system of constant mass, energy is neither created nor destroyed but it can be transformed from one type to another type *e.g.* electrical energy can be converted into chemical energy. In terms of ecosystem energy inflow or energy input into the system will be balanced by energy outflow from the system.

The second law of thermodynamics states that when work is done, energy is dissipated and the work is done when one form of energy is transformed into another form. In this context the lost energy is not again available to the ecosystem.

1. *Transformation of Solar Energy into Food Energy*: There are two types of energy as mentioned earlier, the solar radiation is major source of energy in the ecosystem.

The solar radiation is the basic input of energy entering the ecosystem. The radiant solar energy is received by the green plants. Most of the received solar energy is converted into heat energy and is lost from the ecosystem to the atmosphere, through plant communities. Only a small proportion of radiant solar energy is used by plants to make food through the process of photosynthesis. Thus green plants transform a part of solar energy into food energy or chemical energy which is used by the green plants to develop their issues and thus is stored in the primary producers at the bottom of trophic levels.

The chemical energy stored at trophic level one becomes—the source of energy to the herbivorous animals at trophic level two of the food chain. Some portion of energy is lost from trophic level one through respiration and some portion is transferred to plant eating animals (herbivores) at trophic level two.

2. *The Circulation of Elements through Energy Flow*: The energy flow is the main driving force of nutrient circulation in the various biotic components of the ecosystem.

The materials that make up the biosphere are distributed and re-distributed by means of an infinite series of cyclic pathways motored by the continuous input of energy.

3. *The Conversion of Elements into Inorganic Flow*: The organic elements of plants and animals are released in a variety of ways *i.e.* (*i*) decomposition of leaf falls from the plants, dead plants and animals by decomposers and their conversion into soluble inorganic form, (*ii*) burning of vegetation by lighting, accidental forest fire or deliberate action of man.

The portions of organic matter on burning are released to the atmosphere and these again fall down, under the impact of precipitation, on the ground and become soluble in organic form of element to join soil storage, while some portions in the form of ashes are decomposed by bacterial activity and join soil storage. (*iii*) The waste materials released by animals are decomposed by bacteria and their way in soluble inorganic form to soil storage.

4. *The Growth and Development of Plants*: The biogeochemical cycles include the uptake of nutrients of inorganic elements by the plants through their roots in solution form from the soil where these inorganic elements derived from sedimentary phase, are stored.

The decomposition of leaves, plants and animals and their conversion into soluble inorganic form are stored into soil which helps in the growth and development of plants. The decompositions are converted into such elements which are easily used in development of plant tissues and plant growth by bio-chemical processes, mainly photosynthesis.

5. *Ecosystem Productivity*: The productivity of ecosystem refers to the rate of growth of energy or organic matter per unit time by autotrophs at trophic level one through the process of phototsynthesis with the help of solar energy. The production of organic matter of energy by autotrophs is known as primary production and the green plants involved in the production activity are called as primary producers. The ecosystem

productivity depends on two factors *e.g.* (*i*) the availability of the amount of solar radiation to the primary producers at trophic level one, and (*ii*) the efficiency of the plants to convert solar energy into chemical energy which is used by green plants to build up their tissues.

6. *Stability of Ecosystem*: There are two models of the nature of ecosystem stability or equilibrium: (*i*) equilibrium model, and (*ii*) non-equilibrium model.

The equilibrium model states that an ecosystem always tends towards stability. Whenever the community of an ecosystem is disturbed due to external environmental change, it quickly returns to original state whereas the non-equilibrium model states that ecosystem stability is rarely attained because disturbances caused by frequent external environmental change do not allow to develop ordered state of species assemblages in an ecosystem.

The stability of ecosystems refers to balance between production and consumption of each element in the ecosystem. In other words, ecosystem stability means balance between input and output of energy and normal functioning of different biogeochemical cycles and stable conditions of concentration of all elements.

There is self-regulating mechanism within the system, and the system returns to stability. This mechanism increases more protection available to the organisms against external environmental changes. It so happens when the changes are continuous and enormous and these changes are beyond the capacity of ecosystem *e.g.* deforestation and subsequent grazing. Man causes instability in the ecosystem.

THE COMPONENTS

There are three major components of ecosystems:

(*i*) *Energy Components*—Radiant and fixed energy.
(*ii*) *Physical Components*—Land water and air and sunlight.
(*iii*) *Biological Components*—Plants and animals including human beings.

The physical component comprises—land, soil, water, air and sunlight. Some organic substances are carbohydrates, protein, fat and liquid substances. These have been summarized in Table 10.1.

Table 10.1

	Types		*Components and Substances*
1.	Abiotic (Physical)	:	Land, soil, water, air and sunlight.
2	Biotic (Biological)	:	Plants and animals—Carbohydrates, protein, fat and liquid substances
3.	Biogenic (Biotic)	:	Carbon, nitrogen, hydrogen, calcium and potassium.
4.	Energy	:	Radiant (Solar energy, and fixed energy).

The producer of green plants, act as intermediaries between biotic and abiotic kingdom and the consumers are men and animals, they obtain their food.

KINDS OF AQUATIC ECOSYSTEM

The water is a most important and essential abiotic factor of all kinds of ecosystems and it also forms the habitat for an enormous variety of organisms. The water forms the biggest ecosystem, the aquatic ecosystem of the biosphere. These can be broadly classified into four sub-divisions of aquatic ecosystems.

1. *Aquatic Ecosystems*: Fresh water ecosystem-pressure, density buoyancy physio-chemical nature of fresh water—lakes and ponds.
2. *Aquatic Source Ecosystems*: Estuaries and marine ecosystem *i.e.* ocean or sea region biotic communities of coral reef.
3. *Terrestrial Ecosystems*: Physio-chemical nature of terrestrial and their comparisons with aquatic ecosystems—biome, forest, tundra, alpine and grassland.
4. *Biogeography*: Distribution pattern of biota major plants of the world, chief vegetation, regional geography.

DIFFERENCE BETWEEN ECOLOGY AND ECOSYSTEM

The basic differences are as follows:

	Ecology		*Ecosystem*
1.	It is a science of environment.	1.	It deals with a system of a environment.
2.	It is the study of population and communities as whole.	2.	It is the study of an organism with reference to specific time and space unit.
3.	It has two components— organism and environment.	3.	It has three components—organism, environment and energy.
4.	It includes structure and functions of environment.	4.	It concerns with a functional unit with in a given time unit.
5.	It is composed of biotic and abiotic components.	5.	A system is composed of physical, chemical and biological process (material and energy) with in a space time unit.
6.	It is the science of ecosystems.	6.	It is an important ecological unit.
7.	The analysis of relationship between organisms and environment is done in ecology.	7.	It attempts to analyse the relationship and interdependence of any system within space and time unit.
8.	The ecology is science and art. It is also considerial philosophy 'world of life'.	8.	Ecosystem is purely science which helps in controlling and regulating the system.
9.	It is a science of all relations of all organisms to all their environment.	9.	It is applied science of an organism to his environment within space time unit.
10.	Ecology concerns with welfare of organism and mankind but not energy.	10.	It is open system of input and output of matter and energy.
11.	It is the study of changes and development of vast nature.	11.	It has its own productivity, *i.e.*, role of growth of organic matter in space-time per unit.
12.	It usually refers to organism and environment.	12.	It generally refers to an organism its environment and energy.

ECOSYSTEM AND EDUCATION

The ecosystem is used mostly in ecology. The ecosystem is the study of any unit of ecology within given space and time unit. It is a functional aspect of ecology which includes interacting system composed of living organisms and their effects on one another. Ecology is defined as the study of ecosystems. Ecosystem includes biotic, abiotic and energy components and has its own productivity.

The ecology and ecosystem are the new areas of study which are broadly concerned with interaction and interdependence of organisms and environment. The theme and concepts which have been interepreted according to their own but theme and concepts are applicable also to interpret educational concepts. Education is also an applied aspect of ecosystem.

Recently in the discipline of education, new concepts of organizational climate and organizational health of educational institutions have evolved. A school is the functional unit of education process which has its own input as the man power of teachers and output in terms of students, results and performances in co-curricular activities.

The organizational climate of school or college includes physical, social and cultural environment which is mainly created by the psychology of the head of institution. The teachers and head of institution are the energy or power components. If head of institution is changed the whole organizational climate is changed.

Similarly in the classroom, the teacher generates social and emotional climate by performing certain activities in which students gain new experiences which result in desirable behavioural changes. The school has its own ecosystem which is governed by the principal and classroom unit has its own ecosystem which is regulated by the teacher.

The term 'feedback' has been widely used in teaching and instruction. It is a device for providing energy in the instruction and teaching system for realizing the objectives of education.

QUESTIONS FOR ANSWER

1. *Define and illustrate the term 'Ecosystem'. Enumerate the characteristics of ecosystem.*
2. *Enumerate the types of 'Ecosystem' and indicate the bases of classification of ecosystem. Mention the components of ecosystem and their types.*
3. *Describe the functions and diversity of ecosystem.*
4. *Differentiate between 'Ecology' and 'Ecosystem'. Indicate the similarity between them.*
5. *Write a note on characteristics of ecosystem.*
6. *Ecosystem and education are co-related for better human life. Justify.*

11

Concepts of Environmental Pollution, Degradation, Hazards and Disaster

Ecological imbalance caused by man or nature according to the quality and quanity of imbalance may be termed as pollution, degradation, hazard or disaster. Hereunder we will discuss these aspects in brief.

INTRODUCTION

Unlimited exploitation of nature by man disturbed the ecological balance between living and non-living components of the biosphere. The adverse conditions created by man himself threatened the survival not only of man himself but also other living organisms. Due to progress industries, technology, chemicals, atomic energy, there are a number of industrial effluents and emissions of poisonous gases in the atmosphere and also added solid waste which has lowered the quality of environment.

Environmental *pollution* and degradation are used interchangeably by most of the people because both are concerned with the lowering of the 'quality of environment'. There are two aspects (*i*) lowering the quality of environment, and (*ii*) deterioration of the quality of environment. The deterioration of environmental quality referes the magnitude or intensity of the area covered.

Environmental *pollution* means lowering of the quality of environment at local level caused by human activities for exploitation of resources.

Environmental *degradation* means deteriorating the

environmental quality at global, regional and local levels by both natural processes and human activities.

The *pollution* is a necessary evil of all development. Due to lack of development of a culture of pollution control, there has resulted a heavy backlog of gaseous, liquid and solid pollution in our country. Thus pollution control in our country is a recent environmental concern. There is race in developed countries to exploit every bit of natural resources to convert them into goods for their use and confort and to export them to other needy countries. The industrialised countries dump lot of materials in their environment which becomes polluted. The environmental pollution has lowered its quality.

However, it may be restated that environmental pollution means lowering of environmental quality at local scale caused exclusively by human activities whereas environmental degradation means lowering of environmental quality at local, regional and global levels by both natural processes and human activities. Both, environmental degradation and pollution, are considered in terms of man. Since the realization of environmental pollution has now become of global concern and there is growing awareness about pollution as *'VICIOUS CIRCLE'* situation, a comprehensive study of pollution involving definitions and perception of pollution, types of pollution, sources of pollution, causes and processes of pollution, environmental and ecological effects of pollution, monitoring of pollution and pollution abatement programmes is not only desirable for environmental geographers and environmental scientists but is also necessary so that future strategies for resource utilization and comprehensive environmental management programmes may be formulated and implemented.

Since pollution is viewed from different angles as an environmental problem by the geographers in general and environmental geographers in particular and natural scientists; as a social problem by the sociologists; as an economic problem by the economists; as an ecological problem by the ecologists etc. and thus it may be defined in a number of ways. It is commonly agreed that pollution is, without doubt, the outcome of urban-industrial technological revolution and rapacious and speedy exploitation of natural resources, increased rate of exchange of matter and energy and ever increasing industrial wastes, urban effluents and consumer goods.

DEFINITIONS OF POLLUTION

Hereunder we enlist few definitions of pollution.

1. According to the report of the Restoring the Quality of Our Environment, President's Science Advisory Committee, Washington, USA, pollution may be defined as "unfavourable alteration of our surroundings wholly or largely as a by-product of man's actions through direct or indirect effects of changes in energy patterns, radiation levels, chemical and physical constitution and the abundance of organisms".

2. According to D.M. Dixon (1972) pollution includes "all those activities conscious or unconscious of human beings and their domestic cattle and the result thereof, which detract in any way....in the long-term or short-term, from enjoyment of his environment and his ability to derive full benefit therefrom".

3. Pollution is viewed as "the release of substances and energy as waste products of human activities which result in changes, usually harmful, within the natural environment".

—Natural Environmental Research Council (NERC), 1976.

4. "Residuals, or wastes, are generated in all stages of production and consumption of goods or services. Residuals become pollutants or an environmental problem of some kind and in some degree when they have harmful effects in the atmosphere, the oceans or the terrestrial environment. Harmful effects are effects that are harmful to man, or to animals, plants or inanimate objects or conditions that are important to man. Their importance to man may be biological, economic, religious, moral, aesthetic or intellectual".

—Massachusetts Institute of Technology (MIT), 1970.

5. Pollution is defined as "the presence at large of substances, or energy patterns which have been involuntarily produced, have outlived their purpose, have escaped by accident, or have unforseen effects, in quantities which harm his (man's) health or do offend him".

—Lord Kenett

6. R.F. Dasmann (1975) had defined pollution as "the accumulation of substances, or forms of energy, in the environment

in the quantities, or at rates of flow, which exceed the capacity of ecosystems to either neutralize or desperse them to harmless levels. Pollutants are not necessarily harmful in themselves".

It is apparent from the above definitions of pollution that there are three criteria, as mentioned by N. Lee and C. Wood (1972) for defining pollution *viz.* (*i*) the waste materials resulting from human activities and disposal of wastes, (*ii*) damages caused by disposed wastes whether directly or indirectly, and (*iii*) the circumstances where the effect of damage is met by third parties.

On the basis of above definitions we may define pollution as follows:

Pollution is an undesirable change in the physical, chemical and biological characteristics of air, water and soil that may harmfully affect the life or create a potential health hazard of any living organism. Pollution is thus direct or indirect change in any component of the biosphere that is harmful to living organisms and man, affecting adversely the industrial progress, cultural and natural resources or general environment.

POLLUTANTS

Any substitute which causes lowering the quality of environment or pollution in called pollutants.

> "Every human society, be it rural, urban, industrial and most technologically advanced society dispose of certain kinds of by products and waste products which are injected into the biosphere in great quantities and they affect the normal functioning of ecosystems and have an adverse effect on plants, animals and man are called *pollutants*"—*Smith* (1977).

A pollutant is defined as any form of energy or matter that causes degradation and pollution in the existing natural balance of ecosystems. On the basis of source of genesis pollutants are divided into two main types *e.g.* (*i*) *NATURAL POLLUTANTS* and (*ii*) *MAN-MADE POLLUTANTS*. 'Natural pollutants are manageable because of the laws of cybernetics or homeostatic mechanism. But unfortunately man is not making any permanent arrangement for pollutants made by himself'. Pollutants are further divided on the basis of VISIBILITY in two types *viz.* (*i*) *VISIBLE POLLUTANTS* and (*ii*) *INVISIBLE POLLUTANTS*. Visible pollutants include smoke, gases, dusts coming out of 'human volcanoes' (chimneys), waste water or sewage water coming out from factories and urban areas, heaps of garbages, animal and human wastes etc. whereas invisible pollutants include several types of bacteria, toxic chemicals mixed with water and soils etc.

Pollutants may be classified on the basis of their nature and state such as (*i*) SOLID PARTICULATE POLLUTANTS *e.g.* aerosols, industrial wastes such as lead, mercury, tailings, asbestos etc. (*ii*) GASEOUS POLLUTANTS *e.g.* chlorofluorocarbon gases, carbon dioxide, sulphur dioxide, nitrogen oxide etc. and (*iii*) LIQUID POLLUTANTS *e.g.* leaked oil slicks in sea water, dissolved solids, ammonia, urea, nitrate, chloride, fluoride, carbonates, insecticides and pesticides—all in dissolved form, oil and grease etc.

Pollutants are also divided into (*i*) *PHYSICAL POLLUTANTS*, (*ii*) *CULTURAL POLLUTANTS*, and (*iii*) *BIOLOGICAL POLLUTANTS*. Physical pollutants include all natural as well as man-made pollutants in gaseous, solid and liquid state as referred to above. Cultural pollutants include over-population or say explosive population, poverty, crime, richness, cultural backwardness etc. whereas biological pollutants include entrophication, locust swarms etc.

Pollutants may also be divided on the basis of areas polluted by specific pollutant and ground of pollutants such as (*i*) *AIR POLLUTANTS e.g.* sulphur oxide, nitrogen oxide, carbon dioxide, carbon monoxide, hydrocarbon, ammonia, lead, aldehydes, asbestos, aerosols etc.; (*ii*) *WATER POLLUTANTS e.g.* dissolved and suspended solids, chlorine ion, sodium ion, calcium and bicarbonate ions, sulfate ion, nitrate ion, potassium ion, magnesium ion, insecticide and pesticide residues, toxic metals such as lead, mercury an cadmium, radioactive wastes etc., and (*ii*) *LAND POLLUTANTS e.g.* human and animal wastes/excreta, garbages, pesticides, insecticides and chemical fertilizers, machines and tools, radioactive substances etc.

The Massachusetts Institute of Technology (MIT, 1970) has identified more than a million kinds of products produced by man which are both waste and useful products that eventually turn to be wastes after their uses. MIT has also specified a series of key pollutants which create critical environmental problem. They may be listed as follows:

1. Carbon dioxide.
2. Particulate matter.

3. Sulphure dioxide.
4. Oxides of nitrogen.
5. Toxic heavy metals (lead, mercury, arsenic, cadmium, nickel, manganese, copper, zinc).
6. Oil.
7. Chlorinated hydrocarbons (especially DDT and Polychlorinated biphenys-PCB).
8. Other hydrocarbons.
9. Radionuclides.
10. Heat.
11. Nutrients.
12. Domestic sewage and other oxygen-demanding wastes.
13. Infectious agents.
14. Plant nutrients.
15. Organic chemicals which are highly toxic at very low concentrations (such as insecticides, pesticides, detergents, and petrochemicals).
16. Minerals and chemicals (including chemical residues, salts, acids, silts and sludges).
17. Sediments from land erosion.
18. Radioactive substances.
19. Heat from power and industrial plants.

Thus *pollutant* may be defined as 'any solid liquid or gaseous substance present in such a concentration that may have adverse harmful effects or may be injurious to the environment. Pollutants are the residues of things we makes use or throw away. The rivers are polluted by wastes from factories, air by gases, thermal power plants etc. In fact, in countries where there have been the greatest technological and industrial advances, the worst pollution occurs.

Environmental Pollutants

On the basis of above discussion main environmental pollutants, which pollute our air, water and land, are as follows:

1. Deposited mater—dust, smoke, tar, grit, etc.
2. Gases—nitrogen, carbon monoxide, sulphur, oxides.
3. Solid waste.
4. Radioactive waste.

5. Noise.
6. Complex organic substances—ether, acetic acid benzene, etc.
7. Metals.
8. Fluorides.
9. Photo chemical oxidants.
10. Agrochemical—fungicides and fertilizers.

SOURCES OF POLLUTION

The pollutants, as described earlier, are produced by both natural and anthropogenic processes and therefore the sources of pollution on this basis are divided in two categories *viz.* (*i*) *NATURAL SOURCE* of pollution and (*ii*) *ANTHROPOGENIC SOURCE* of pollution. Natural source of pollution includes pollutants such as volcanic ashes and dusts from volcanic eruptions (volcanic dust layers in the atmosphere reduce air temperature); undesirable substances brought to the surface because of fracture and faults caused by seismic events; flood water in low lying areas causes diseases etc. Anthropogenic source of pollution is varied and is the main culprit of environmental pollution because the nature takes care of natural pollutants because of in-built mechanism of absorbing any change brought in the nature by natural processes.

Anthropogenic sources of pollution include (*i*) industrial source, (*ii*) urban source, (*iii*) agricultural source, (*iv*) population source etc. Most of the pollutants come from industrial and urban sectors. The industrial source contributes a host of pollutants such as gaseous pollutants (nitrogen oxides, sulphur dioxide, carbon monoxides, hydrocarbon as methane and numerous toxic gases), solid pollutants, dissolved and suspended solids, waste water having numerous chemical ingredients, heat etc. Urban sources of pollution contribute sewage water, solid waste, gaseous exhausts, liquid effluents, pollutants coming out of chimneys of factories located within the urban centres etc.

Agricultural source of pollution includes the pollutants related to chemical fertilizers, pesticides and insecticides. Human population is the most important source of pollution because all forms of anthropogenic pollution are the creation of human activities. On an average the increase in the population of a nation has been positively correlated with pollution. The ever increasing population in the developing countries is posing as much the problem of pollution as in the developed countries through industrial growth and urban expansion. Poverty and underdevelopment are yet other sources of pollution.

CLASSIFICATION/TYPES OF POLLUTION

The classification of environment pollution is a difficult task because the pollutants and the media through which the pollutants are transported and diffused (such as air, water and land) are all interconnected and inter-related and thus all types of pollution, identified so far, are arbitrary in character. In spite of the drawback of arbitrariness in the typology of pollutions they are classified in a number of ways on various grounds as elaborated below:

1. On the Basis of Nature of Pollution

Pollution is divided into two categories *viz.* (*i*) *PHYSICAL POLLUTION*, and (*ii*) *SOCIAL POLUTION*. Physical pollution means lowering of the quality of physical components of the environment such as land, air and water. Thus physical pollution is further divided into (*a*) land pollution, (*b*) water pollution, and (*c*) air pollution. Social pollution means degradation of human communities due to a variety of factors and through a number of processes. Social pollution is further divided into (*a*) economic pollution based on economic poverty and underdevelopment, (*b*) religious pollution (communal riots and violence), (*c*) political pollution (wars), (*d*) ethnic pollution (ethnic riots such as in Sind, Pakistan, northern peninsula of Srilanka, Punjab and Kashmir in India etc.), (*e*) social pollution (several types of crimes such as robbery, rape, dacoity, murders etc.)

2. On the Basis of Medium of Pollution

Pollution is divided on the basis of media through which pollutants are transported and diffused into three categories *e.g.* (*i*) land pollution, (*ii*) water pollution, and (*iii*) air pollution.

3. On the Basis of Area and Source of Pollution

Pollution is divided on the basis of area affected by pollution and sources of major pollutants into (*i*) urban pollution, (*ii*) rural pollution, (*iii*) industrial pollution, and (*iv*) agricultural pollution.

4. On the Basis of Location of Pollution

Pollution is divided into two major types on the basis of locational aspect *e.g.* (*i*) *POINT POLLUTION*, and (*ii*) *NON-POINT POLLUTION*. Point pollution is always visible and hence can be easily identified. Discharge of effluent from a drain or pipe into a river channel is termed *POINT SOURCE POLLUTION* or simply a point pollution. Infact, point pollution means coming out of pollutants from a specific location such as outfall of sewer drains in a river or a creek, outfall of drains of industrial waste water, chimneys of factories etc. whereas nonpoint pollution means pollution of the area from unspecified location. Nonpoint pollution includes washing of fertilizers and pesticides from agricultural land into streams. Thus nonpoint pollution is seldom visible. For example, chemical fertilizers and pesticides and insecticides used in the agricultural fields are washed out during rains and thus are brought to the streams.

Nonpoint pollution mostly occurs from agricultural practices. The chemicals used in the form of plant nutrients as fertilizers and in the form of pesticides and insecticides in the agricultural farms are brought to the tanks and ponds, lakes and streams in dissolved and solid forms. The main medium or agent of nonpoint pollution is surface runoff resulting from atmospheric rainfall. The rainwater transports pollutants in two directions *viz.* (*i*) lateral movement of pollutants through surface runoff, and (*ii*) downward movement of pollutants through infiltrating and percolating water.

Thus nonpoint pollution involves both surface water and groundwater. Infact, nonpoint pollution is a slow poisoning of our physical environment mainly surface and subsurface waters and soils. The polluted water in turn adversely affects biological communities in general and human community in particular and soil pollution results in phenomenal decrease in fertility and productivity which causes drastic reduction in agricultural production and hence consequent substantial shortage of food supply may cause economic pollution through poverty, starvation and deaths.

Besides chemicals, eroded sediments and silts brought down by the surface runoff from the land to lakes, reservoirs and rivers are also significant pollutants and causes nonpoint pollution of lakes and rivers through increased proportion suspended solids, and sediment loads in the water and consequent sedimentation and siltation of lakes, reservoirs and river beds.

The rainwater after having numerous chemicals in dissolved forms (rainwater receives several chemicals from the agricultural farms which are treated with chemical fertilizers and pesticides and insecticides) infiltrates downward and hence these chemicals are also moved downward to pollute groundwater.

Nonpoint pollution is further divided into two types viz. (*i*) *RURAL NONPOINT POLLUTION*, and (*ii*) *URBAN NONPOINT POLLUTION*.

(i) *Rural Nonpoint Pollution*

The major source of nonpoint pollution in rural areas is agricultural activity. Since rural nonpoint pollution is basically related to agricultural activities, it is also called as *AGRICULTURAL POLLUTION*. Nature and amount of chemical fertilizers, pesticides and insecticides applied to the farms, types of soils, amount and intensity of annual rainfall, other climatic conditions, methods of ploughing and farm management techniques, nature and slope of ground surface, nature of crop etc. are the factors which determine the nature and magnitude of non-point pollution in rural areas.

(ii) Urban Nonpoint Pollution

Though the sources of urban nonpoint pollution are varied and uncertain yet these are divided into 3 categories *viz.* (*a*) pollutants coming from residential areas, the amount of which depends on the density of houses, (*b*) pollutants coming from small-scale industries, and (*c*) pollutants coming from large-scale industries.

ENVIRONMENTAL DEGRADATION

Environmental degradation means overall lowering of environmental qualities because of adverse changes brought in by human activities in the basic structure of the components of the environment to such an extent that these adverse changes affect adversely all biological communities in general and human society.

Environmental *pollution* and environmental *degradation* terms are used interchangeably but these are different concepts. Pollution is the cause for the degradation of air environment. The *degradation* of environment is caused by pollution and *hazards/disasters*. The *hazards* or *disasters* are sudden by natural processes or by human activities which require the immediate relief.

Environmental pollution is taking place due slow and gradual human activities, *e.g.*, increase of human population, establishing factories and industries, development of transportation facilities, etc. The pollution degrades the *quality of the environment* which can be protected by proper environmental management and assessment.

Environmental degradation leaves direct impact on the ecology and thus is caused ecological imbalance because of marked reduction in the ecosystem and ecological diversity. The ecological imbalance is the sign of environmental degradation. It can be easily observable in living organisms.

Causes of Environmental Degradation

The following are the basic causes for the environmental degradation:

1. The development of modern technologies.
2. The increase in the human population.
3. There is pressure on natural resources.
4. The high rate of exploitation of natural resources.
5. Growing industries and factories.
6. Increasing settlement of urbanization.
7. The development of economic functions of man.

All these causes are to be modified of the components of the environment to such an extent that the adverse effects on the environment are reduced to minimum by *'Homeostatic Mechanism'*. The physical and biological processes of the natural environmental system are self regulatory to compensate the negative feedback.

If the physical and biological processes can not compensate and regulate the adverse effects on living organisms and man, it refers to *'Environmental Degradation'*. It can not be set right by the self regulatory mechanism or homeostatic mechanism of the environment.

The *environmental degradation* is a wider concept than environmental pollution. It includes both natural processes and human activities while pollution is limited to lowering the quality of environment by human activities only.

CLASSIFICATION/TYPES OF DEGRADATION

Environment is wider and comprehensive term which refers to lowering and deterioration of environmental quality which is caused by natural processes and human activities from local level, regional and global level.

The natural processes bring immediate adverse changes in the environment or damage and loss to the quality of environment and living organisms and man are called *Hazards* or *Events.*

Environmental degradation is divided into two categories on the basis of factors responsible for the lowering of environmental quality.

1. Environmental pollution, and
2. Hazards and Events.

1. Types of environmental pollution have been enumerated in above paragraphs under the heading of *types of Pollution.*

2. Extreme Hazards and Events—This category may be divided into two sub-categories on the basis of causative factors.

(*i*) Natural Hazards and (*ii*) Man-induced Hazards.

(*i*) *Natural Hazards*

These are caused by natural factors which are further divided into 3 sub-categories.

(a) *Terrestrial Hazards:* These occur on the earth's land surface, *e.g.*, earth quakes, volcanic eruption, etc.
(b) *Atmospheric Hazards:* These are caused by atmospheric processes, *e.g.*, tropical cyclones, typhoons, forest-fires, hurricanes.
(c) *Cumulative Atmospheric Hazards:* These are caused by certain atmospheric imbalance, floods and drought.

(*ii*) *Man-induced Hazards*

These are caused by sudden effects of human activities.

(*a*) *Physical man-induced Hazards*: forest fire by man and large scale land slides.

(*b*) *Chemical and Nuclear Hazards: e.g.*, nuclear explosion, gases from chemical factories (Bhopal gas, hazards, fire in gas cylinders or godown, etc.).

(*c*) *Biological Hazards:* e.g., Explosion of human population, hunting of wildlife by man, increase in toxic elements.

The above factors, processes and mechanisms which disturb the stability of ecosystem and balance of ecology of the environment are called processes of environmental degradation. There inbuilt self regulatory mechanison is called Homestatic Mechanismn.

CAUSES OF ENVIRONMENTAL DEGRADATION

Environmental and ecological changes are the result of developmental processes of the 'economic and technological man'. With the socio-economic, scientific and technological development has emerged the serious problems of environmental degradation or several types of environmental pollution. Some significant causes are as the following:

1. *Religious,* Economic and philosophical factors.
2. *Deforestation:* Conversion of forest land into agricultural land and pastures.
3. *Agricultural Development:* High concentration chemicals and fertilizers pollute the soils or degrade the soils.
4. *Population Growth:* Ever increasing human population places greater demands on the finite resources of earth.
5. *Industrial Development.*
6. *Urbanisation:* The formation and growth of big slum areas, air pollution, smoke, dust.
7. *Modern Productive Technology:* Construction of huge dams, and reservoirs upset the equilibrium of rocks.

The interaction between the environment and society depends largely on the social and political systems within which arise the environmental and ecological problems. The capitalistic and socialistic systems perception and reactions to the environment are quite different. Socialistic system lays main emphasis on the social importance of natural resources and environmental problems. The capitalistic system has selfish international motive, regarding the exploitation of natural resources.

The *Environmental Management Plan* (EMP) includes the following aspects to maintain the *quality of environment.*

1. Safeguard and to prevent the adverse environmental impacts.
2. Contingency plans for dealing with accidents, or disaster.
3. Plans for rehabilitation of project ousters.
4. Monitoring and feedback mechanisms on implementation of necessary safeguards.

HAZARDS AND DISASTERS

Environmental hazards may be stated as those extreme events caused by natural process or man's activities which exceed the tolerable magnitude within or beyond certain time limits, make adjustment difficult, result in losses of property and lives.

The terms environmental *hazards*, environmental *stresses* and environmental *disaster* are used for extreme events which are caused by natural process or human activities.

The environmental *hazards* are the abnormal processes which cause environmental disasters or the results of environmental hazards or extreme events. The intensity of environmental *disasters* are assessed in terms of damages done to the human society. The environmental quality is lowered and deteriorated by these extreme *events* which are termed hazards and *disasters.*

The environmental or ecological balance is disturbed, the resultant state of the highly disturbed natural environment is called '*Environmental Stress*'. The natural sudden physical processes and events become hazards and disasters when humans live near a danger.

Type of Environmental Hazards and Disaster

The extreme events are divided into two categories on the basis of causative factors—

1. Natural hazards and disasters, and
2. Man-induced hazards and disasters.

Natural Hazards and Disasters

Natural hazards and disasters involve rare high-intensity processes and extreme events caused by terrestrial or endogenous hazards and atmospheric or exogenous hazards. Thus natural hazards and disasters are of two types.

(*a*) *Terrestrial* or endogenous hazards and disasters.
(*b*) *Atmospheric* or exogenous hazards and disaster.

(*a*) *Terrestrial or Endogenous Hazards and Disasters*—These normally include those extreme events which are caused by endogenetic forces evolving from within the earth. The causative factors of such extreme events and hazards are hidden deep within earth which are not observable, only their effects are observed and experienced. These can be classified into three categories—

(*i*) Volcanic Eruptions,
(*ii*) Earthquakes, and
(*iii*) Land slides.

These extreme events are caused by endogenetic thermal conditions of the interior of the earth. It is the result of disequalibrium in any part of the earth crust. In India earthquakes are along the Himalayas and foothill zones and Bihar. The three types of hazards and events are inter-related to each other. The land slides are in hilly regions due to earthquakes.

These hazards and disaster have resulted in great damages to human constructions—buildings, roads, rails, factories, dams, heavy loss to human property. On the other hand there is great disaster for human lives and other organisms. The *quality of environment* is deteriorated and great damage to human structures, towns and cities, dams and human settlement as a whole.

These extreme events can not be prevented or checked because these are beyond human control and management. The *prediction* of these hazards can be possible by the continuous efforts of scientists.

(*b*) *Atmospheric or Exogenetic Hazards:* These are normally related to weather and climatic extreme conditions. These natural hazards are caused by atmospheric processes or forces which generate from within the atmospheric so these are known as *'exogenetic natural hazards'*. The causative factors are not observable but are recorded by meterorologists to forecast about the weather conditions. These are classified into two categories.

(*i*) *Abnormal or Infrequent Events:* (1) Cyclones (2) Lightening, (3) Hailstorms, and (4) Fires.
(*ii*) *Cumulative Atmospheric Hazards and Disaster:* (1) Floods, (2) Droughts, (3) Cold wave, and (4) Heat waves.

(*i*) *The Tropical Cyclones,* our country is an example of abnormal exogenetic hazards. It comes from over the Bay of Bengal, become hazardous to the east coastal lands of India which effects West Bengal, Orissa, Andhra Pradesh and Tamil Nadu states of our country. The November, 1977 cyclonic storm struck Andhra Coast when the biggest surge of 6 metres height was recorded and moved with a speed of 175 kilometres per hour.

It damaged human lives and other organisms and made the coastal land barren and wasteland by the deposition of salt on the soils by the storm. The strongest cyclone hit the Andhra Coast on May, 1990. It was 25 times stronger than the cyclone of November 1977. The destructions by the tropical cyclones include loss of human lives, other organisms and human constructions, agricultural crops, vegetation, wildlife and power supply and communication system and so on.

(*ii*) *The floods and droughts* are cumulative atmospheric hazards. The floods means comming out of huge volumes of water from the river banks and spread over the extensive land area for several days in continuation. This may be caused by natural factors, *i.e.,* heavy rain and by man-induced dams and reservoir. These floods damage the human lives and property also the natural environments. The large scale deforestation is the most important factor which causes the river floods in upper catchment area of rivers.

The cumulative atmospheric hazards are of two types as discussed in the above paragraphs on the basis of causative factors (*i*) *Natural processes and forces,* and (*ii*) *Man-induced.* The Environmental Management Plan (EMP) may include two types of safeguards.

The scientists can *predict in advance* about natural atmospheric hazards, the safety measures can be used for these hazards and contingency plans can be made effective for dealing with the hazards. Some atmospheric hazards are caused by human activities such as dams, reservoirs and deforestation. The human activities should be evaluated in terms of *impact assessment.*

The alternative plans and projects may be introduced to avoid these atmospheric hazards. The monitoring and feedback mechanism on the implementation are necessary measures for the safeguards.

Extra Planetary Hazards. Earth scientists are of the opinion that several cases of collision between the earth and other plants—asteroid meteorite and comet have taken place in the past history. The *disaster* caused by the collision between earth and other extra planetary bodies of space are called *'extra planetary hazards'*.

The astrologists can *predict* about the occurrence of collisions, but nothing can be done to prevent from these hazards which may cause the damage to human lives and environment as a whole at global level.

Man-Induced Hazards

The environmental *degradation* is also induced by human activities which cause irreparable loss to human community. The man-induced environmental hazards and disasters are caused through a variety of human activities both deliberate and spontaneous character. These can be classified into *three* categories—.

1. *Physical hazards* such as earthquakes, landslides and soil erosion.
2. *Chemical hazards* such as toxic chemicals, poisonous gases nuclear explosion, tankers leakage into the ocean, leakage of gases and crude oil.
3. *Social hazards* such as population explosions and downfall in moral and religious values. The use of chemical and organismic weapons during wars. The construction of multi-storied buildings.

Man is the product of his social as well as his physical environment, and it is in times of disaster that these strong bonds with his origins manifest themselves and take precedence over his ordinary behaviour.

Social response to natural and man-induced disasters is increasing in positive direction and immediate relief measures are provided from within the country and from outside the country. Several nations and voluntary social organizations involve themselves immediately in extending relief measures, helping and serving the victim of disasters is terms of food, clothes, medicines, volunteers, doctors, nurses and engineers. There are some anti-social elements as well who resort to looting and robberies, etc. even developing countries. It is the impact of education and social values.

Environmental degradation and pollution are directly related to increase in human population during present century. At the beginning of 20th century, the world population was about 1.50 billion and by the end of the century it will be about 6 billion, *i.e.*, four times. It has caused the pressure on agriculture for more food, deforestation, industries and further development. It has degraded the quality of environment and created environmental problems.

Man should give up the idea of exploitation of nature and have a check on human population by introducing family planning programmes and moral check.

POLLUTION—ROLE OF EDUCATION

The environmental hazards and disasters are generally in terms of lives and property. There are a few benefits as well from the natural hazards, *e.g.*, floods renew the soils fertility, landslides sometimes result in the formation of lakes, volcanic eruptions enrich the soils, sometimes earthquakes cause ground water, barriers so that ground water may be localized.

The reduction of natural hazards and disasters and relief measures are taken up by *environmental management* for immediate relief, prediction and adjustment of these natural hazards. Education plays an important role in the programme of management for the reduction of hazards and disaster.

The *education* must be broad based and it should reach everyone including the scientists, the engineers, administrators, policy and decision makers as well as general public through popular and common media such as newspaper, radio, television and documentary films. It is the responsibility of the government to reduce and manage for these events. The teachers and scientists must educate the decision makers through the following steps:

1. To provide information about the occurrence of these extreme events and disasters through the *various media* well in advance. Every one should be mentally prepared and can plan for the protection. The communications are of crucial importance in the assessment and reduction of disasters.
2. To provide and arouse *awareness* about the hazards and disasters among general public and train the

administrators and policy makers to handle the situation created by a disaster by providing detailed maps of the problem area.

3. To explain the techniques and measures of *immediate relief* for the reduction of disasters. The attitudes and perceptions are to be changed about the natural hazards.
4. To persuade the people to improve the *standard* of *construction* so as to the escape the disaster by providing history of past experiences of the disasters.
5. To assess the *impact of plans,* projects, dams, reservoirs, factories, deforestation in view of their adverse impact on human life.
6. To educate the people for *moral and religious values* and discourage for economic values to maintain the quality of environment.

The *environmental education* concept has its roots in academic and intellectual pursuit from our vedic period. It is difficult to think of man as something separate from physical environment because life and environment are interdependent. It was the firm belief that to harm nature or environment is to harm oneself. *According to Vedas* a relationship between man and nature is of mutual respect and kindness.

Several animals have been considered as vehicles of God or Goddess. Preservation of animals and plants are clearly mentioned and some of the plants are worshipped by Hindus. Ecology was sacred science for them. The people of that period protected the environment from *pollution* and *degradation* by all means. Not only they protected the external environment but also the conducive environment is generated by *habbans* and *yagyas.*

At the same time they protected their psychological and cultural environment (*internal environment*) from pollution by obeying the moral and religious norms and maintained high values of life and quality of the environment as well. Environment is the part and parcel of human life because the quality of the environment has the direct impact on the quality of man.

Hence, systematic, *environmental education* is essential for maintaining harmony between man and his environment—*'Environmental education'* is a way of thinking, doing and feeling pertaining to natural as well as social sciences and behavioural science.

It suggests a way out to integrate moral values and cultural education to environmental education. It is the need of the day that educationists must have full understanding of physical, biological, social, cultural and psychological environment—its components and their operations. In other words the ecological studies are of great importance in our education.

Note: Please a separate chapter on environment education in India.

QUESTIONS FOR ANSWER

1. *Define the term* 'pollution.' *Enumerate the type of pollution and their bases of classification.*
2. *Explain the term-*pollutants *and* pollution. *Describe environmental pollution and their kinds.*
3. *Explain the term* 'environmental degradation' *and differentiate it with* 'environmental pollution'.
4. *Enumerate the types of* 'environmental degradations'.
5. *Define and explain the term* 'environmental hazards and disasters. *Indicate the types of environmental hazards and disaster.*
6. *Explain* 'Man-induced Haszards'. *Enumerates the causes of Environmental degradation which are lowering the quality of the environment.*
7. *Describe the role of Education in (a) Environmental pollution, (b) Environmental hazards and disaster, and (c) Quality of the environment.*
8. *Write the causes of environmental degradation.*
9. *Write a note on the classification of environmental degradation.*
10. *Write short notes on the following:*
    (*a*) *Man-made pollutants.*
    (*b*) *Environmental pollutants.*
    (*c*) *Environmental disaster.*

12

Air Pollution

The pollution is a necessary evil of all development because in a mad race to exploit every bit of natural resource to convert them into goods for their comfort and to export them to needy developing people, the nature balance of environment get disturbed. There are many types of environmental pollutions as discussed in chapter one of this book, very briefly, but the most devastating of them is air pollution because one can go without food for a day or so and without water for a few hours if food and water of desired quality is not available when needed but one can not stop breathing even for ten minutes. Therefore, it is rightly said that the quality of air determines the quality of man, hence, hereunder we will discuss various aspects of air pollution to enable the readers to protect their health.

MEANING AND DEFINITION OF AIR POLLUTION

The atmosphere is a gaseous envelope which surrounds the earth from all sides and the air is a mechanical mixture of several gases, mainly nitrogen (78.09%), oxygen (20.95%), argan (0.93%) and carbon dioxide (0.03%). Besides, other trace gases like neon, krypton, helium, hydrogen, xenon and ozone are also present. Air is very important for all types of life in the biosphere. Human life is not possible without air because man can live for a few days without water or for a few weeks without food but cannot survive even for a few minutes without air. It constitutes about 80 per cent of the total intake of all things by a person every day as a person breathes 22,000 times a day inhaling 35 gallons or 16 kilogrames of air which he obtains from the oxygen-rich atmosphere surrounding the earth.

It may be pointed out that air is never pure because some gases such as sulphur dioxide, hydrogen sulphide, carbon monoxide; emissions from volcanoes and swamps, windblown dusts, salt spray, pollens from plants etc. are continuously added to the air by the natural process. Thus the air becomes polluted when its natural composition is disturbed either by natural or man-made sources or by both.

H. Perkins (1974) has defined air pollution as "the presence in the outdoor atmosphere of one or more contaminants such as dust, fumes, gas, mist, odour, smoke or vapour in quantities of characteristics and of duration such as to be injurious to human, plant or animal life and to property or which unreasonably interferes with the comfortable enjoyment of life and property."

According to World Health Organisation (WHO) air pollution is defined as limited to situation in which the outdoor ambient atmosphere contains materials in concentration, which are harmful to man and his surrounding environment.

In a general sense air pollution may be defined as the disequilibrium condition of the air caused due to introduction of foreign elements from natural as well as anthropogenic sources to the air so that the air becomes injurious to biological communities in general and human community in particular.

On the basis of above discussion we may define air pollution as follows:

The *air pollution* is generally accomplished through the pollutants of gases and solid and liquid particles of both organic and inorganic chemical. It is true that air is never pure because some gases such as sulphur dioxide, carbon monoxide, hydrogen sulphide emissions from volcanoes, swamps, dusts, salt spray, pollens from plants, etc., are continuously added to the air by these natural processes. Thus the air becomes polluted when its natural composition is disturbed either by natural or man-made sources or activities or by both.

NATURE OF AIR POLLUTION

Man-made pollutants are injected and concentrated in certain localities of their sources mainly in highly industrialized and urbanized pockets of the world. In other words, the pollutants coming out of natural sources are generally absorbed by the natural environment and no pollutional problem arises but man-made pollutants being concentrated in certain parts of the atmosphere pollute the air.

The nature, dimension and magnitude of air pollution depend on a variety of factors such as residence time of pollutants in the atmosphere (duration of stay of pollutants in the atmosphere), sources of pollutants, nature of pollutants, amount of pollutants etc. "The residence time of pollutants in the atmosphere (also) vary considerably, depending upon the nature of the pollutant itself, upon the way emission has taken place, on meterological factors, and on sink mechanism (absorption of pollutants such as nature of vegetation, water bodies etc.)" (H.E. Hobbs, 1980).

SOURCES OF AIR POLLUTION

Many sources of air pollution are *NATURAL SORUCES* (volcanic eruption, deflation of sands and dusts, firest or wild fires of natural vegetation etc.) and *MAN-MADE SOURCES* (industries, urban centres, automobiles, aircrafts, agriculture, power plants etc.). A brief summary of the pollutants of natural and anthropogenic sources (man-made sources) is given below:

1. Pollutants from Natural Sources

(*a*) from volcanoes: dust, ashes, smoke, carbon dioxide and other gases;
(*b*) from extra-terrestrial bodies: cosmic dusts, dusts produced due to collision of asteroids, meteors, comets etc. with the earth;
(*c*) from green plants: vapour through evapotranspiration, pollen of plant flowers, carbon dioxide from bacteria;
(*d*) from fungi: fungal spores, viruses,
(*e*) from land surface: salt spray from seas and oceans, dusts and soil particles from ground surface.

2. Pollutants from Man-made Sources

(*a*) gases from kitchen and domestic heating, industries, incineration of municipal and domestic garbages, automobiles, railways mostly from coal and diesel engines, aircrafts etc;

(b) solid or particulate matter from industries, mines and urban centres;
(c) radioactive substances from nuclear plants, nuclear fuel releases, nuclear explosions;
(d) heat from industries and domestic kitchen etc.

AIR POLLUTANTS

From the different sources of air pollution, a variety of pollutants are released into atmosphere. The principal air pollutants emitted from these different sources are as follows:

1. *Carbon compounds:* These are mainly carbon dioxide and carbon monoxide, the former released by complete combustion of fossil fuels and the latter by automobile exhaust.

2. *Sulphur compounds:* These include SO_2 H_2S and sulphuric acid, mostly released by fossil fuel (coal, etc.) based power generating plants (thermal plants) and industrial units as refineries.

3. *Nitrogen oxides:* These include chiefly nitrogen monoxide, nitrogen oxide, nitric acid mostly released by automobiles, power plants and industries.

4. *Ozone* (O_3): Its level may rise in atmosphere due to human activities.

5. *Fluorocarbons:* These come from industries, insecticides spray, etc.

6. *Hydrocarbons:* These are chiefly benzene, benzpyrene, etc. which are mostly discharged by automobiles and industries.

7. *Metals:* These include chiefly lead, nickel, arsenic, beryllium, tin, vanadium, titanium, cadmium, etc., present in air as solid particles or liquid droplets or gases. They are produced mostly by metallurgical processes, automobiles, seaspray, etc.

Classification of Air Pollution

Air pollution is classified on two bases as follows:

1. On the basis of types of *pollutants,* and
2. On the basis of types of *sources of pollutants.*

1. On the basis of types of pollutants pollution is divided into two categories:

(*a*) *Gaseous* pollution, and (*b*) *Particulate* air pollution.

2. On the basis of sources of air pollution is sub-divided into six categories:

(*a*) *Automobiles* Pollution,
(*b*) *Industrial* Pollution,
(*c*) *Thermal* Pollution,
(*d*) *Urban* Pollution,
(*e*) *Rural* Pollution, and
(*f*) *Nuclear* Pollution.

Generally these approaches are used to describe the air pollution. There is overlapping among the various ways used for this purpose.

Automobiles Air Pollution

There is very rapid increase of cars, trucks, buses and two wheelers. It has raised the traffic density in our towns and cities. The vehicles create tones of gaseous pollutants into the air daily. The brief idea of gaseous pollutants has been given in the following paragraphs.

The toxic vehicular exhausts are a source of considerable air pollution, next only to thermal power plants. The ever increasing vehicular traffic density posed continued threat to the ambient air quality. There are over 500 million cars, trucks and buses the world over and their number is increasing rapidly. India is likely to have over 4.8 million vehicles by 2005 of which more than 65 per cent will be two-wheelers operating on petrol. In all the major cities of the country about 1600 to 2,000 tonnes of pollutants are being emitted into the air daily, of which 50 per cent come from automobile exhausts. In the major metropolitan cities, vehicular exhaust accounts for 70 per cent of all CO, 50 per cent of all hydrocarbons, 30-40 per cent of all oxides and 30 per cent of all SPM. During peak traffic hours automobiles of all classes emit as much as 1,700 kg of CO, 1250 kg of hydrocarbons and 120 kg of nitrogen oxides. The two-wheelers and three-wheelers contribute 60 per cent of the total CO and 83 per cent of total hydrocarbons, whereas heavy traffic vehicles 55 to 80 per cent of the oxides of nitrogen.

Industrial Air Pollution

India is the agricultural country but there is rapid development in the agricultural technology and engineering. The economic development is based on both agricultural and industrial development of nation. There is also rapid industrial development in our country.

There are a number of industries which are source of air pollution. Petroleum refineries are the major source of gaseous pollutants. The chief gases are SO_2 and NO_2. *Mathura based petroleum refinery is posing threat to Taj Mahal in Agra and other monuments at Fatehpur Sikri complex.* Cement factories emit plenty of dust, which is potential health hazard. Stone crushers and hot mix plants also create a menace.

The SPM levels in such areas of stone crushing are more than five times the industrial safety limits. There are many food and fertilisers industries which emit gaseous pollutants.

There are also chemical manufacturing industries which emit acid vapours in air. During last 10 years the number of industrial units in Delhi; increased from about 50,000 to 85,000. Nearly 60,000 of these are located in predominantly residential areas.

Kanpur city of Uttar Pradesh is the biggest industrial city of the state which has the heaviest air pollution due to dust and smoke of the factories.

Thermal Air Pollution

There are a number of thermal power stations and super thermal power stations in the country. The *National Thermal Power Corporation* (NTPC) is setting up four mammoth coal powered power stations to augment the energy generation. These are at Singrauli in U.P., Korba in M.P., Ramagundam in Andhra Pradesh and Farakka in West Bengal. The coal consumption of thermal plants is several million tonnes. The main pollutants are fly ash, sulphur oxide and other gases and hydrocarbons.

The three thermal power stations at the Indraprasthra Estate, Rajghat and Badarpur in Delhi are the main source of air pollution. The Indraprastha plant consumes about four thousand tonnes of coal in the fire units. Badarpur, the largest consumes daily about 10 thousand tonnes of coal. The gaseous pollutants from these thermal power plants are aldehydes, carbon monoxide, hydrocarbons, oxides of sulphur, particulate matter and ash.

The different sources of air pollution release a variety of pollutants into the atmosphere.

(1) Carbon compounds, (2) Sulphur oxides and compounds, (3) Nitrogen oxides, (4) Ozone gas, (5) Fluorocarbons, (6) Hydrocarbons, (7) Metals, (8) Phetochemical products, (9) Particulate matter, and (10) Toxicants other than heavy metals.

DETECTION AND MEASUREMENT OF AIR POLLUTION

Air pollution is usually measured by sampling of air by thermal and by electrostatic, Sonkin impactor and electrostatic and dust collectors. The particulate pollution is examined by the instrument which is called *deposit gauge* or by *Owen's dust counter.* The thickness of the smoke measured by *Liegean sphers* and by Ringelmann chart. The rough estimate of sulphur dioxide in air by laboratory chemical analysis of the dust collected in a deposit gauge or by bubbler method. Fluorides are estimated by colour reaction.

There is separate department at *Bhava Atomic Energy Centre at Bombay* which is known as *'Air Monitoring Department'* to measure and estimate about atomic experiments conducted by any country of the world. The dust collected in a deposit gauge on *International Aeroplanes* which travel over the world. The dust is analysed for several purposes as to how far the atomic particle are harmful for man and what will be the remedy for the adverse effect on man.

ADVERSE EFFECTS OF AIR POLLUTION

The effects of air pollution on the environment (both components-abiotic and biotic) may be grouped in three broad categories *viz.* (1) Effects on Weather and Climate., (2) Effects on Human Health, and (3) Effects on Biotic Community.

Effects on Weather and Climate

Different types of air pollution caused by gaseous and particulate pollutants modify weather and climate at local, regional and global levels. A few of the climatological effects of air pollution are given below:

Depletion of ozone caused by chlorofluorocarbons (CFCs) emitted from airconditioners, refrigerators, foam plastic, hair driers, spray can dispensers, fire extinguishers and many cosmetic goods and nitrogen oxides released by large fleets of supersonic zets travelling at more than double the speed of sound and at a height more than 15,000 m may change the tradition balance at global level. The overall effect of ozone pollution (depletion is also a form of pollution) would be increased in the ultra-violet solar radiation reaching the earth's surface and therefore rise in air temperature. Substantial increase in the surface temperature of the earth would cause global warming of the environment which would cause climatic changes at regional and global levels. Increased temperature would cause melting of continental glaciers and ice caps such as those of Antartica and Greenland. This would in turn cause rise in sea level and consequent submergence of coastal lands of lowlying countries.

Briefly we may enlist the adverse effects of air pollution as follows:

Air pollution causes several kinds of damages to man, animals, plants and also on weather, climate and atmospheric processes. Some significant effects have been enumerated here in the following paragraphs.

1. Air pollution has very serious types of pathological effect on man. It causes several types of diseases to man.
2. It causes obstruction to vision of pilots and have caused air craft accidents.
3. Air pollution has damaged both agricultural crops and natural plants and vegetation.
4. There has been injury to agricultural livestocks; particularly from air borne fluoride and arsenic pollution.
5. Air pollution also takes its role of buildings and other man-made objects such as famous buildings, monuments and art treasures.
6. Air pollution also effects weather and climate on regional, continental or global basis.
7. The increased amount of carbon dioxide in atmosphere causes to increase the temperature of earth. It is known by the phrase *'Green house effect'*. It has tends to prevent the long wave radiation from earth. Thus it has atmospheric effect. The intensity of *radiation* will cause skin cancer.
8. The jet engines of supersonic aircraft flying at high atitude release nitrogen oxide which destroy ozone molecules. It has also atmospheric adverse effects.

CONTROL AND PREVENTION OF AIR POLLUTION

The several types of air pollutions can be controlled by employing modern technology and scientific researches, but the costs to be borne by the public in the form of higher prices for manufactured goods, higher taxes, reduction of profit margins in industry and more restriction on human activities. It involves the benefits to improve the quality of the environment and human health, agriculture, vegetations. It will also improve the ecological balance and stability of ecosystem.

The main *sources* of air pollutions are: (1) Automobiles, (2) Industrial development, (3) Power plants—coal based and thermal power plants. Thus steps are to be taken to control air pollution at source and after the release of pollutants.

1. *Automobiles Air Pollution*

The following are some of the measures to be followed for controlling air pollution by automobiles.

(*a*) To check pollutants emission from vehicular exhaust,
(*b*) To control evaporation from fuel tank and carburettor,
(*c*) To use the filters, and
(*d*) To control through law—Motor Vehicles Act 1988 and other Acts of engine.

2. *Industrial Air Pollution*

Air pollution by industry and power plants waste can be checked by devising measures for removal of the particulate matter and gaseous pollutants from the wastes. The three types of equipment or devices used are—

(*a*) Cyclone collectors,
(*b*) Electrostatic precipitators, and
(*c*) Control through law—Acts of industry.

3. *Gaseous Pollutants*

The following four methods can be used to control air pollution from gaseous pollutants:

(*a*) *Wet systems:* The alkali liquid reacts with sulphur dioxide to produce a precipitate.
(*b*) *Dry systems:* Water is in contact with sulphur dioxide produces sulphuric acid.

(*c*) *Wet dry systems:* This method is very effective in dry cleaning plants, printing shops, paint factories, food processing plants, etc.

(*d*) *Control through Law:* Acts for Industries are to be enforced to prevent gaseous pollution.

HEALTH EFFECTS OF EXPOSURE TO AIR POLLUTANTS

Carbon monoxide can seriously affect the heart and brain by reducing the amount of Oxygen reaching the human tissues. This is because of the greater affinity of CO towards haemoglobin thereby forming carboxyhaemoglobin (COHb) which reduces the Oxygen carrying capacity of blood. Experiments have shown that the CO content in the blood of passenger car-drivers at a higher level.

The urburnt or partially burnt HC combined with NO_x and sunlight lead to the formation of photochemical smog. The products of photochemical smog cause irritation of the eyes, mucous membranes and respiratory system. Besides, some of the HC especially the higher molecular weight aromotic HC have been found to be carcinogenic.

Apart from its being a necessary component of photochemical smog, NO_x has a tendency to settle on the haemoglobin in the blood like CO and also join with the moisture in the lungs to cause bronchitis and complicate other respiratory system problems.

Sulphur dioxide and fog were the primary ingredients responsible for the famous 1952, London Smog. SO_2 can irritate the upper respiratory tract and cause lung damage. However SO_2 also gives rise to the formation of sulphate which settle out as particulate matter.

Certain levels of lead is highly toxic and can lead to permanent health damage or even death. The final standard for airborne lead is 1.5 micrograms per cubic metre of air in USA. Blood lead levels above 30 micrograms/decilitre of blood are associated with an impairment in cell function including the possibility of nervous system damage.

EDUCATION FOR CONTROL AND PREVENTION OF AIR POLLUTION

Education is considered as cure of all ills in the society, therefore, proper emphasis on pollution control and prevention in educational system will be very effectual because pollution is a social and human problem, hence, human attitude can change the entire situation.

Education is a powerful instrument to control social problems. Air pollution is a serious social problem of these days. Every one is concerned and effected by the problem. The air pollution and noise pollution are inter-related thus both are included under *Air and Noise Pollution Prevention Act.* The legal steps have already been taken by State and Central Government, to prevent and control the air pollutions which have been discussed in earlier paragraphs.

Education can also play a significant role in the prevention and controlling air pollution. It is very essential to provide the awareness and develop consciousness among students about air pollution and its resources and ways. Formal, non-formal and adult education programmes should provide awareness and develop feelings and attitudes or consciousness about the problem which has the serious adverse effects on human health. Charts and mottos are to be prepared on air pollutions—resources and remedial measures.

Now-a-days media and newspapers are doing the same, *e.g., 'Save the Oil'* protect the air pollution. The students should also be given this type of knowledge. The oil resources are limited and decreasing rapidly, thus the day is not for that these automobiles and aeroplanes will not be able to function.

QUESTIONS FOR ANSWER

1. *Define 'Air Pollution' and write a note on the nature and sources of pollution.*
2. *Write a note on 'Air Pollutants' and enumerate the nature of automobile air pollution.*
3. *Enumerate various adverse effects of air pollution.*
4. *Write short notes on the following:*
   (*a*) *Industrial Air Pollution.*
   (*b*) *Thermal Air Pollution.*
   (*c*) *Role of Education in Pollution Control and Prevention.*
   (*d*) *Health Effects of Air Pollution*

13

Water Pollution

A brief account of water pollution has been given in chapter one of this book, therefore, hereunder we will discuss other required aspects of this concept

INTRODUCTION

Water is the most important element in the biosphere because on one hand it is vital for the maintenance of all forms of life and on the other hand it helps in the movement, circulation and cycling of nutrients in the biosphere. It is found in various phases and in various storages such as (*i*) in liquid phase (storages such as rivers, lakes, seas and oceans, soils, living organisms etc.), (*ii*) in solid phase (storages such as glaciers and ice sheets and ice caps like ice caps of Arctic region, Greenland and Antarctica and mountain glaciers *e.g.* Alpine glaciers, Himalayan glaciers etc.). Water is also essential for power generation, navigation, irrigation of crops, disposal of sewage etc. It may be pointed out that only one per cent of the total amount of water of the hydrosphere is available to human beings and other biotic communities from various sources such as ground water, rivers, lakes, soils, atmosphere and biological system but groundwater provides the largest amount of water. Increased demand of water consequent upon increasing population and industrial expansion has degraded the quality of water considerably. Though water like other natural substances has self purifying capacity during recycling processes but when the amount of foreign undesirable substances added by the man to the water exceeds the tolerance level and self purifying capacity of water, it gets polluted.

MEANING AND DEFINITION

Water pollution refers:

- deteriorate physical, chemical and biological quality of water,
- causes the harmful effects on man, animals and vegetation and also quality of environment,
- due to natural (*land slides, volcanic eruptions, dust, soil erosion*) and human activities (*industry, agriculture, urbanization, radioctive mining, etc.*), and
- deteriorate quality of environment.

Water pollution may be defined as 'alteration in physical, chemical and biological characteristics of water which may cause harmful effects on human and aquatic life.'

Report, 1965, Restoring the Quality of Our Environment, President's Science Advisory Committee, Washington, USA.

'Foreign materials either from natural or other sources are contaminated with water supplies and may be harmful to life, because of their toxity, reduction of normal oxygen level of water, aesthetically unsuitable effects and spread of epidemic diseases'.

—World Health Organisation (WHO), 1966

Water pollution is defined as 'a natural or induced change in the quality of water which renders it unsuitable or dangerous as regards food, human and animal health, industry, agriculture, fishing or leisure pursuits.'

—P. Vivier, 1958

The term water pollution 'refers to deterioration in chemical, physical and biological properties of water brought about by human activities and/or by natural (*e.g.* hydrological processes which induce decomposed and vegetable materials and weathering products of rocks etc.

—C.S Southwick, 1967, Ecology and the Quality of Our Environment, New York.

A comprehensive definition of water pollution encompassing all aspects is given below:

'Water pollution refers to deterioration of physical (such as colour, odour, turbidity, taste, temperature etc.), chemical (such as acidity, alkalinity, salinity etc.) and biological (presence of bacteria, Coliform MPN, algae etc.) characteristics of water from various storages (such as river water, lake water, pond water, groundwater) though natural (*e.g.* fallout of volcanic dust, landslides near the water bodies, sediments supplied by soil erosion and weathering processes) and anthropogenic (*e.g.* industrial, urban, agricultural, domestic, radioactive, mining sources etc.) processes to such an extent that it becomes harmful to human beings, plants and animal communities'.

— *Savindra Singh*

SOURCES OF WATER POLLUTANTS

The substances which degrade the quality of water are called water pollutants. The water pollutants are created from two basic sources *e.g.* (*i*) *Natural Sources*—of water pollutants include soil erosion, landslides, coastal and cliff erosion, volcanic eruption and decay and decomposition of plants and animals. Excessive soil erosion in the catchment area of particular river increases the sediment load of the river and thus increases the turbity of river and lake (when silt-loaded river empties into a lake) water. Landslides near lakes pour down enormous quantity of debris into the lake and thus the lake is polluted not only through silting of its bed but also through increased turbidity. (*ii*) *Anthropogemic Sources*—It may be pointed out that natural water system is capable of taking care of natural pollutants and therefore it is the anthropogenic sources which are the real sources of water pollution. The anthropogenic sources of water pollution include industrial source, urban source, agricultural source, cultural source (congregation of large number of people during pilgrimage, religious fairs etc., for example, more than 30 million people from all over India congregate at the confluence of the Ganga and the Yamuna at Allahabad every 12 years during *Kumbha Fair* etc.

Urban source contributes water pollutants such as sewage, huge quantity of municipal and domestic garbages, industrial effluents from the industrial units located in the urban centres, fallout of particulate matter of automobile exhausts etc.

Various types of chemicals used in the chemical fertilizers, pesticides and herbicides etc. are the pollutants which are derived from agricultural sources. These chemical substances are brought to the rivers and lakes through surface runoff caused by rainfall and are also moved downward by infiltrating rainwater to reach groundwater.

Industrial sources pollute streams, rivers, lakes and coastal waters through industrial effluents, solid and dissolved chemical pollutants and numerous metals. Besides, fallout of radioactive substances is very dangerous source of air and water pollution.

In brief there are two main sources of water pollution as follows:

1. *Natural Sources*: Of water pollutants include soil erosion, volcanic eruption, land slides, coastal and cliff erosion, floods, decomposition of plants and animals.

2. *Man-induced Sources*: Of water pollutants include industrial development, urbanization, agricultural sources, cultural sources (*religious fairs and pilgrimage*) *Kumbha fair* at Allahabad is an example of cultural source of water pollution.

The main sources of water pollution are:

(*i*) Sewage and water in cities,
(*ii*) Industrial effluents and waste products,
(*iii*) Agricultural discharge, chemical fertilizers used, and
(*iv*) Thermal power plants and nuclear plants waste.

CLASSIFICATION OF WATER POLLUTANTS

Water pollutants may be divided on different bases as given below:

(*i*) On the Basis of Sources of Pollutants

Water pollutants are divided into:

(*a*) *Industrial Pollutants*: *e.g.* industrial waste water, including several chemical pollutants such as chlorides, sulphides, carbonates, ammonical nitrogen, nitrites, nitrates, heavy metals such as mercury, lead, zinc, arsenic, barron etc. organic chemical compounds synthesized for industrial purposes, radioactive wasts etc.

(*b*) *Agricultural Pollutants*: *e.g.* chemical fertilizers, pesticides, insecticides and herbicides and several other synthetic chemical compounds, weeds and plant remains.

(c) *Urban Pollutants*: *e.g.* various types of ion such as sulphate ion, nitrate ion (representing washout of air pollutants emitted from automobiles and other forms of fossil fuel combustion), chlorine ion and sodium ion (coming from deicing salts used to melt ice spread over roads and streets), calcium ions and bicarbonate ions (from lime and chemical fertilizers used in the lawns and the gardens within the city), sulphate, nitrate and potassium ions, a host of chemical ions contained in urban sewage water, household sewage stored in septic tanks, phosphate and nitrate ions from body wastes of humans and animals etc.

(d) *Natural Pollutants: e.g.* volcanic dusts, sediments due to weathering and erosion, debris caused by landslides, decayed and decomposed organic matter (both plants and animals) etc.

(*ii*) On the Basis of Physical and Chemical Properties

Water pollutants are divided into two categories *viz.*:

(*i*) *Physical Pollutants*: *e.g.* colour, taste, turbidity, sediments, volcanic dust, oil and grease, dissolved and suspended solids, total solids,

(*ii*) *Chemical Pollutants: e.g.* chlorides, sulphides, carbonates, ammonical nitrogen, nitrites, nitrates, pesticides, insecticides, herbicides, several other synthetic chemical compounds etc.

(*iii*) *Water Pollutants* are also divided into: (*a*) *Degradable* and (*b*) *Non-degradable Pollutants:* Those pollutants which are broken down and decomposed by biological means such as decomposers/microorganisms are called biodegrad-able or simply degradable pollutants. These pollutants are also called as organic pollutants. Nondegradable pollutants are those which cannot be degraded by biological means. Such pollutants are also called as inorganic pollutants. Examples of biodegradable or organic pollutants—leaf litters, sewage, garbages, plants and animals, human and animal excreta etc. Non-degradable pollutants—all of the chemical pollutants and toxic solid substances.

NATURE OF WATER POLLUTION

'The nature and intensity of water pollution is linked with many factors like waste water disposal and treatment system, hydrological conditions of diluting bodies and self-purification capacity of streams, characteristics of effluents discharging from an area, socio-economic conditions of the communities generating the wastes and, in cases, types of soil and vegetation' (J. Singh and D.N. Singh, 1988). Even rainwater is never pure because when it falls as rainfall atmospheric carbon dioxide is mixed with it and thus acidity of rainwater is slightly increased because of dissolution of atmospheric CO_2 in rainwater. When rainwater passes through several pathways such as lateral movement as surface runoff and downward movement as groundwater several contaminants mix with the water. Further, a host of pollutants are discharged from various sources *e.g.* industrial, urban and agricultural into different water storages such as river water, lake water, pond water and groundwater. All these pollutants pollute the water to various levels depending upon the nature, and amount of pollutants. It is significant to point out that unlike air water has dissolving capacity and therefore water, while moving through various pathways, further dissolves several chemical substances and thus is further polluted by numerous organic and inorganic matters.

The water pollution is assessed on the basis of certain parameters *e.g.* (*i*) physical, (*ii*) chemical, and (*iii*) biological parameters. Physical parameters used to ascertain the quality of water include temperature, colour, turbidity, conductivity, density, suspended dissolved and total solids while chemical parameters include nature and amount of soluble salts, hardness of water, acidity and alkalinity of water, dissolved oxygen (DO), biological oxygen demand (BOD), chemical oxygen demand (COD), concentration of hydrogen ion (*p*H), amount of ammonia, nitrate and nitrites, amount of heavy metals, mercury, lead chromium, chlorides, pesticides, insecticides, detergents etc. Biological parameters are bacteria, coliform MPN, algae, viruses etc. Generally, Biological Oxygen Demand (BOD), Chemical Oxygen Demand (COD), Dissolved Oxygen (DO), and *p*H value are important indicators of water quality.

SOURCES OF WATER POLLUTION

Water pollution may be divided on the basis of sources and storages of water into (*i*) *Surface Water Pollution,* (*ii*) *Lake Water Pollution,* (*iii*) *Groundwater Pollution,* and (*iv*) *Sea Water Pollution.* Water pollution may also be divided on the basis of sources of water pollution *e.g.* (*i*) sewage pollution, (*ii*) domestic waste pollution, (*iii*) industrial waste water pollution, (*iv*) solid waste pollution etc.

ECOLOGICAL EFFECTS OF WATER POLLUTION

Each type of water pollution affects the physical and biological components of various *aquatic systems* in different degrees and its ultimate effect on man remains quite drastic in medical, aesthetic and economical sense. The well known ecological effects of water pollution are as follows:

1. Sewage Pollution

The primary source of sewage pollution is the discharge of untreated sewage in water bodies, sometimes due to improper sewage. This is very common in major cities of the country.

Sewage is the waterborne waste derived from home (*domestic waste*) and animal or food processing plants. It includes human excreta, paper, cloth, soap, detergents, etc. These are a major proportion of the pollutants entering our water. There is uncontrolled dumping of wastes of rural areas, towns and cities into ponds, lakes, stream or rivers.

Due to accumulation of sewage and other wastes in these bodies, they are not able to recycle them and their self-regulatory capability is lost. The self-purifying ability of the water is lost and water becomes unfit for drinking and other domestic uses. Since decomposition of sewage and other wastes is largely an aerobic process, accumulation of these in water increases its oxygen requirements.

Phosphates are the major ingredient of most detergents. They favour the luxuriant growth of algae which form water blooms. This extensive algal growth also consumes most of the available oxygen from water. This decrease in O_2 level becomes detrimental to growth of other organisms which produces a foul smell upon decay.

The following methods are to be used to check the water pollution through sewage waste:

(*a*) The waste water must be treated before its discharge into lake or river. This would limit its nutrient input.

(*b*) To stimulate bacterial multiplication in order to reduce the amount of nutrients solubilised in water. This would help disruption of algal food web.

(*c*) To check recycle of nutrients into the water through harvest and removal of algal blooms upon their death and decomposition.

(*d*) To remove dissolved nutrients from water by physical or chemical methods. For instance, phosphorous can be removed by precipitation; nitrogen by biological nitrification and denitrification or by air stripping of NH_3 from an alkalised waste water, or by ion exchange, electrodialysis or reversesosmosis.

2. Industrial Effluents

A wide variety of both, *inorganic and organic pollutants* are present in effluents from breweries, tanneries, dying textiles, paper and pulp mills, steel industries, mining operations etc. The pollutants include oils, greases, plastics, plasticizers, metallic wastes, suspended solids, phenols, toxions, acids, salts, dyes, cyanides, DDT, etc. many of which are not readily susceptible to degradation and thus cause serious pollution problems.

Sulphuric acid waste from coal mines is a serious pollutant that increases the hardness of water, has disastrous effect on live organisms and corrodes concrete, etc. Nitrates, Copper, Chromium, Cadmium, Mercury, lead, etc., are the heavy metal effluents, discharged from industries.

3. Thermal Pollution

The two chief pollutants are heat and *radioactive substances.* These are the wastes chiefly from power plants—thermal and nuclear, which use large qualities of water. Some other industries also give our waste after use. Nuclear power plants are the source of radionuclides.

The quantity of water is highest in the *thermal power plants* in the country. This waste water is returned after use at very high temperatures to the streams—a river, lake. This affects the aquatic life in these water bodies. This is also called *thermal pollution* since heat acts as a pollutant. Similarly, nuclear power plants besides causing fall out problems, also release waste heat.

This also contributes to thermal pollution. Some plants and animals are killed outright by the very hot water. Though waste water from nuclear power plant is not as hot, but still has adverse effects on aquatic life. These are (*i*) early hatching of fish eggs, (*ii*) failure of trout eggs to hatch, (*iii*) failure of salmon to spawn, (*iv*) increase in BOD, (*v*) change in diurnal and seasonal behaviour and metabolic responses of organisms, (*vi*) significant shift in algel forms and other organisms towards more heat-tolerant forms. This leads to decrease in species diversity, (*vii*) affect changes in macrophytes, and (*viii*) migration of some aquatic forms.

4. Agricultural Discharges

It is another kind of water pollution. These include chiefly the chemicals used as fertilisers and the pesticides (*biocides*) used in disease control. Their discharges reach not the water bodies. As compared to developed nations, India has relatively a low use of these chemicals, thus discharges into water are still low. India uses about 16 kg/ha of fertilisers.

Modern agriculture rely heavily on a wide range of synthetic chemicals which include various types of fertilizers and biscides. They are dangerous, harmful and disturb the natural ecosystem. These chemicals affect the quality of the food stuffs. The chemical make water unfit for drinking and also causes diseases.

Pesticides are the chemicals used for killing the plant and animal pests. There is a wide scope of chemicals used as biocides, but these are most harmful to man by entering into *our food chain*. Pesticides create various type of diseases related to kidney, blood, urine and brain tissues. There are other sources of water pollution:

- *Ground water pollution* by septic tanks, seepage pits etc.
- *Marine water pollution:* On their way rivers receive huge quantity of sewage, garbage, agricultural discharge, biocides and heavy metals.
- *Mercury pollution:* It is through industrial effluents. It is responsible for smallpox epidemic.
- *Lead pollution:* The main source of lead to water is the industrial effluents. It causes the damage to liver and kidney.

- *Fluoride Pollution:* It is naturally present in water. The arid and semi-arid soils is due to fluoride contents. It causes the bone diseases.

ASSESSMENT OF WATER QUALITY

There are various methods and programmes have been introduced to assess the quality of water—

(*a*) Assessment of Water Quality

Under the *National Water Quality Monitoring Programme,* the water quality monitoring of rivers is being done. Till 1987 this network had 200 monitoring stations on rivers all over the country. In 1988, there were added 106 stations to the network. Thus at present there are 306 monitoring stations on river basins all over the country. This includes also 11 ground water stations and 27 stations on the Ganga under the *Ganga-Action Plan.* It is planned to increase the number of such stations to 400 by 1990. The stations monitor in respect of 19 parameters such as total dissolved solids, BOD, metals and nitrates.

(*b*) Assessment of Coastal Water Quality

The CPCB in collaboration with the *Department of Ocean Development* has identified 173 monitoring stations all along the Indian Coast to assess the water quality. Four SPCB have also been involved. Data on 25 parameters are being processed to formulate schemes to control and monitor pollution of the coastal waters.

POLLUTION PREVENTION MEASURES

Control of water pollution requires several *remedial measures* and *Central Water Control Acts.* The following measures are suggested to control water pollution:

1. Maintaining stability of the eco-system.
2. Reutilization and recycling of water.
3. Removal of pollutants.
4. Management of water pollution.

1. *Maintaining Stability of the Ecosystem:* It is most scientific

method to control and prevent water pollution. The basic principles are the reduction in waste input, thus water pollution is controlled at source. Several methods biological as well as physical can be used to restore species diversity and to maintain ecological balance in the water bodies.

2. *Reutilization and Recycling of Waste:* The various types of wastes include industrial effluents and thermal pollutants which may be reutilized. The urban waste is reused to generate cheaper fuel gas and electricity. The efforts are being made in the development of suitable technology for waste water so that it can be utilized in agriculture and prepare some useful products.

3. *Removal of Water Pollutants:* There are various types of pollutants present in water bodies which can be removed by suitable methods, *e.g.*, absorption, electrodialysis, ion exchange, reverse cosmosis, etc. This process is used for purifying water from sewage.

The *solar power* can also be used for cleaning up polluted water cheaply. Such type of experiments are being conducted in our country and also in Western countries.

LAWS FOR WATER QUALITY MANAGEMENT

There is lot of industrial liquid waste, very poor urban sewage, sewage treatment facilities which have caused heavy water pollution. There is an urgent need to maintain the quality of water at surface level as well as ground water. The Central Government has constituted *'Water Control Acts'*. Some important *'Central Water Control Acts'* have been enumerated here.

1. The Government of India has constituted *'Central Ganga Authority'* as a comprehensive plan of cleaning the polluted Ganga water under the authority of *Central Pollution Control Board.* The Ganga project includes establishment of sewage treatment plants in the major cities located at the Ganga bank before allowing sewage into the river.

2. *The Damodar Valley Corporation Act, 1948:* Prevention of pollution of water.

3. *The Water Act, 1974:* Prevention and Control of Water Pollution.

4. *The Water Cess Act, 1977:* Prevention and Control of Pollution.

The *Water Pollution Prevention and Control Act* at the

maintenance of good water quality for human use. The problem of water pollution has already assumed alarming proportion in many big cities and industrial complexes in our country such as in Delhi, Kanpur, Varanasi, Mathura, Bombay, Madras, Calcutta, etc. Even small towns and cities suffer from high level of water pollution.

5. The *Central Ground Water Board* has assisted the plan and helped in establishing more stations for controlling ground water pollution. Most State Governments have set up such stations.

The Problems of Water Quality Management

The water quality can be managed by both, short-term and long-term measures.

1. *Short-Term Devices:* Pollution control at urban settlement. Proper sewage system, sewage regulation, control at industrial source, planning of industrial estates, protection of drinking water.

2. *Long-Term Devices:* Preparation of water use map, evaluation of pollution in river basin, preparation of water quality map, water quality assessment.

3. *Rural water Supply:* The efforts are being made at global level to supply safe drinking water for all people. The hand pumps are established by the assistance of World Bank.

QUESTIONS FOR ANSWER

1. *Define 'Water Pollution' and enlist sources of water pollution.*
2. *Write a note on the sources and classification of water pollutants.*
3. *Enumerate the ecological effects of water pollution.*
4. *Write a note on legal provisions for water quality management and suggest measures for prevention of water pollution.*
5. *Write short notes on:*

   (*a*) *Assessment of water quality.*
   (*b*) *Nature of water pollution.*

14

Soil or Land Pollution

In the first chapter of this book a brief account concerning nature of soil pollution including losing forests and wildlife under threat have been given, therefore, hereunder we will discuss other aspects of soil or land pollution.

INTRODUCTION

Soils are infact the very heart of the life layer (the biosphere) because these represent a zone wherein plant nutrients are produced, held, maintained and are made available to plants through their roots and to the micro-organisms which live in the soils. Soil is also very important environmental attribute for human society because (*i*) it is the basic medium for food and timber production; (*ii*) it provides formation for building and roads; (*iii*) it is very important exhaustible natural resource because it cannot be replaced if it is destroyed or lost through excessive soil erosion caused by atmospheric activities and it is the base for the development of human civilisation.

The formation of soil is a slow process as the formation and development of one inch of soil require about one thousand years whereas the destruction of soils through erosion and pollution is quick process. The quality of soils depends upon the nutrients (both organic and inorganic), humus content, moisture, temperature etc. present in the soils.

DEFINITION OF SOIL POLLUTION

"The contamination of soil with excess of chemicals, fertilizers, insecticides, herbicides is known as soil pollution."

The decrease in the quality of soils either due to human

activities or natural sources or by both is known as soil pollution or soil degradation. The soil pollution is caused due to soil erosion, decrease in plant nutrients, decrease in soil micro organisms, excess or deficit of moisture content, high fluctuation of temperature and lack of humas content.

SOURCES OF SOIL POLLUTION

The main factors of soil pollution are accelerated rate of soil erosion consequent upon major land use changes (*e.g.*, deforestation); excessive use of chemical fertilizers, pesticides, insecticides and herbicides; polluted waste water from industrial and urban areas; a few micro-organisms; forest fires; dumping of urban and industrial solid wastes; water logging and related capillary process; leaching processes; drought etc. Following are the source of soil pollution.

1. The *Physical Source* of soil pollution is related to soil erosion and consequent soil degradation caused by natural and anthropogenic factors. The natural factors of soil erosion include amount and intensity of rainfall, temperature and wind; topographic factors; lithological factors; vegetation and soil characteristics. These factors are further accelerated by human activities such as land use changes (*e.g.* deforestation). In most of the developing countries of the tropical and subtropical regions accelerated rate of soil erosion due to rapid rate of deforestation and faulty agricultural practices has degraded the soil on a large-scale because the top fertile layer has been washed out.

2. *The Biological Sources or Agents* of soil pollution include those micro-organisms and unwanted plants which degrade the quality and therefore fertility of the soils. The soil pollutant biological agents are grouped into four major categories. (*i*) Pathogenic micro-organisms excreted by human beings; (*ii*) Pathogenic micro-organisms excreted by domestic animals; (*iii*) Pathogenic micro-organisms already present in the soils; and (*iv*) Enteric bacteria and protozoa. These micro-organisms enter the soils from various sources and degrade them. These micro-organisms also enter the food chains and thus affect human bodies.

3. *Air-born Sources* of pollutants are infact are pollutants which are released into the atmosphere by 'human volcanoes' (chimneys of factories), automobiles, thermal power plants and domestic

sources. In fact, gaseous and solid particulate pollutants emitted by factory chimneys and other sources are transported to the areas far away from the source of the emission of pollutants by prevailing wind.

The fallouts of these pollutants are deposited in the soils which are polluted due to toxic substances. Sulphur emitted from the factories causes acid rains which lower the pH of the soils. Acid rains increase the acidity of the soils. Highly acidic soils are injurious to plant growth.

Huge quantities of particulate matters emitted from cement factories, lime kilns, coal mining, loading and unloading of coal, thermal power plants etc. reach the soils and thus pollute them by altering their chemical and physical properties.

Flakes and chips of mica from the mica mines spread over the soils and pollute them. Numerous mica chips may be seen strewn all over the agricultural fields in the vicinity of Kodarma mica belt of Bihar (India).

Magnesite dusts, when mixed with soils, cause marked rise in the soil *p*H (increase in the soil alkalinity which causes salinization) and decrease in potash (K), calcium (Ca), magnesium (Mg) and phosphorous to critical lower limit. Fallouts of metallic particulate matter from metal smelters into soils damage their physical and chemical properties. For example, the soils near copper smelters are so polluted that no plant growth becomes possible.

The fallouts of mercury released from industrial processes and combustion of fossil fuels when mixed in the soils reach the food chain. Similarly, high concentration of lead pollutes the soils to large extent.

4. *Chemical Fertilizers and Biocides* have now become essential part of modern mechanized agriculture. Excessive use of chemical fertilizers to boost agricultural production causes alteration in the physical and chemical properties of soils, though chemical fertilizers act as inorganic plant nutrients.

The most dangerous pollutants are different kinds of biocides which destroy micro-organisms including useful bacteria and thus lower down the quality of soils significantly. Infact, rapid growth of population and commercialization of agriculture have been responsible for the phenomenal increase in the production and consumption of chemical fertilizers and biocides.

The use of biocides has also gained momentum in India with the Green Revolution since 1960s. According to an estimate about

100,000 tonnes of biocides are used in India annually. According to the report of World Health Organisation (WHO) about 500,000 persons become the casualties of biocides in one way or the other every year. The annual production of various biocides in India has increased from 2,350 tonnes in 1955 to 149,795 in 1983 thus registering more than 63 times increase in their production. This rate of increase continues even today. The following types of biocides (pesticides, insecticides, herbicides etc.) are generally used to get rid of unwanted plants and to kill harmful insects and destroy pests to boost agricultural production.

5. *Organic Phosphate Compounds e.g.* Malathions. These are used to kill insects by damaging their nerve systems. Frequent use of these chemicals results in the accumulation of acetylchlorine in the soils and ultimately these chemicals are transported to plant tissues. The mammals depending on these plants are thus adversely affected. *Chlorinated Hydrocarbons e.g.* D.D.T. dieldrin, aldrin etc. These insecticides are generally used to kill insects and micro-organisms. Chlorinated hydrocarbon compounds were developed as potent pesticides after World War II.

D.D.T. proved to be boon to human society in the beginning because its use helped in killing a host of disease carrier insects such as mosquitoes and millions of people could be saved from typhoid, malaria etc. D.D.T. has proved successful in eradicating malaria, incephalitis, dengu fever etc. D.D.T. was used world over to kill insects and germs upto 1971 without any suspicion but in 1972 its dangerous effects on human and animals were brought to notice in the USA and hence its use was banned by the US government. It has been found out that D.D.T. may persist in soils for 20 to 25 years and thus reach the food chains through the plants.

6. *Arsenic Containing Pesticides* reach the soils and are transported to plants and thus to foodgrains. These chemicals cause gastric digestive problems in humans. *Sodium Fluoroaccetates* are generally used to kill rodents and accumulate in the soils to reach the food chains.

The analysis of innumerable samples of food grains all over the world has shown that the human food is widely contaminated by the concentration of pesticides, insecticides and herbicides and thus these synthetic chemicals have become a part of human diet all over the world. The main culpritis are carbaryl, D.D.T., malathion, parathion, dieldrin, lindane, hepatachlor, aldrine etc.

Improper disposal of industrial and urban wastes and irrigation of agricultural fields from polluted urban sewage water near urban and industrial areas degrade the soil properties by changing their physical and chemical properties. The toxic chemical substances of industrial effluents and urban sewage enter the soils and pollute them mostly in the neighbourhood of cities and mills.

The study conducted by V.K. Kumra in and around Kanpur city reveals the following facts—(*i*) Excessive use of chemical fertilizers and improper disposal of industrial wastes in the city boundary has caused rise in the alkalinity of the soils; (*ii*) Contamination of nitrogen varies from 40 pounds per acre to 640 pounds per acre; (*iii*) Phosphorous concentration in the soil ranges between 0.03 to 0.085 per cent, (*iv*) Soluble salts range between 0.03 to 0.27 per cent, and (*v*) Soil *p*H varies between 7.32 and 10.1.

EFFECTS OF SOIL POLLUTION

Effects of soil pollution on human beings, animals and plants are far reaching. Since pollution degrades the quality of soils, soil pollution thus results in substantial decrease in agricultural production. Some forms of soil pollution even render the land unusable for crop farming. For example, soil erosion through rill and gully erosion converts the land into wasteland.

Chemical pollutants in the form of chemical fertilizers and pesticides, insecticides and herbicidcs after reaching the soils reach the human and animal bodies through food chains and cause various diseases and several deaths. According to an estimate about 500,000 persons die every year in the world because of insecticides and pesticides. Most of the foodgrains in the *USA*, mainly wheat and corn, have become toxic due to these synthetic chemicals.

It is not only desirable but is also necessary to control soil pollution because the very existence of human beings and animals depends upon soils. It is very necessary not only to maintain but also to enhance the quality of soils because the supply food for billions of world human population, fodder for animals and a host of raw materials come from soils. The following steps may be suggested to control soil pollution:

(*i*) to implement various control measures of soil erosion,
(*ii*) controlled and judicious use of chemicals fertilizers and pesticides, insecticides and herbicides,
(*iii*) development of such pesticides and insecticides which do not harm human beings,
(*iv*) proper disposal of industrial and urban wastes,
(*vi*) use of urban and industrial effluents for irrigation purposes after proper treatment,
(*vii*) proper land use and crop management,
(*viii*) education to farmers about the proper uses of fertilizers and biocides, and
(*ix*) proper researches regarding the adverse effects of soil pollutants mainly toxic chemicals on various components of natural ecosystems.

CONTROL OF SOIL POLLUTION

It is very essential to control and prevent soil pollution because the existence of man, animals and vegetation depend upon the quality of soil. It is necessary to maintain and also increase the quality of soils. The essential commodities required for man, animals and plants come from soils. The following are suggested to control soils pollution:

1. To check the soil erosion by using controlling measures.
2. To use judiciously chemical fertilizers and pesticides and insecticides.
3. To restrict the use of D.D.T.
4. To dispose properly urban and industrial wastes.
5. Crop management and proper land use.
6. To educate the farmers about the use of fertilizers and biocides.

SOLID WASTE POLLUTION

Solid waste substances are those materials which become useless and hence waste after short period of their use such as newspapers, different types of cans, bottles, broken glass wares, plastic containers, polythene bags, ashes and domestic garbages. These discarded solid substances after their uses are variously called as *Refuse, Garbage, Rubbish, Solid Waste etc*. These solid wastes require proper and ample space for their dumping and disposal. The environmental pollution caused by these solid wastes is rapidly increasing in tune with rapid rate of industrial growth and urbanization. The problem of disposal of ever-increasing quantities of solid substances has become a headache for not only industrialized and developed countries but also for most of the developing countries.

SOURCES OF SOLID WASTE

The Sources of solid waste substances may be grouped into two categories *viz.* (*i*) *Production Centres,* and (*ii*) *Consumption Centres.* Production centres may be further divided into small-scale production centres and large-scale or industrial production centres. Consumption centres contributing solid waste substances may be further divided into individual house, community centres, markets and municipal garbage centres.

Alternatively, sources of solid waste substances may be grouped into two broad categories *e.g.* (*i*) *Household/Domestic Sector,* and (*ii*) *Industrial/Commercial Sectors.* Most of the solid waste substances are not degradable such as plastics.

It may be pointed out that there is direct positive relationship between the amount of solid wastes produced and the affluence/ richness of the economically rich and industrially developed western countries as their Throwaway Culture has been responsible for the acute problem of solid waste pollution because all of the substances are thrown away after use. None of the used items is reused or recycled. On the other hand economically poor societies of the developing countries produces much smaller quantities of solid waste substances than the economically rich societies of the western developed world because they use these items several times.

TYPES OF SOLID WASTE SUBSTANCES

Solid waste pollutants are divided into several types based on their sources such as (*i*) mining wastes, (*ii*) agricultural wastes, (*iii*) industrial wastes, (*iv*) municipal wastes, (*v*) packing wastes, and (*vi*) human wastes.

1. *Mining wastes* are produced during mining operations wherein huge quantities of wastes are dumped on land surface which may be otherwise useful for other purposes. For example, for the mining of metallic ores, huge quantities of earthen materials, rocks and other wastes are created.

Similarly, for coal mining surficial crustal materials are removed to expose coal seams. The removed materials are heaped at other places. Thus mountains of waste mining materials are created which not only occupy valuable land surface but also create nuisance, because mine wastes contain, some times, toxic chemicals which pollute the nearby environment.

2. *Industrial wastes* include huge amount of abandoned items which create several environmental problems. For example, huge quantities of bagasse are produced in sugar mills during the process of sugar production. These bagasses are heaped in the vicinty of sugar mills. Thus the sugar mill overburden of bagasses after rotting stinks and spreads unbearable foul smell. Copper smelters and aluminium industry produce dangerous waste substances which are very much injurious to vegetation and soils. Many more examples may be cited.

3. *Agricultural wastes* include roots and stems of crops, straw, hay, dung, food articles etc. There is almost no problem of agricultural waste substances in developing countries because these items are used and reused in a number of ways. For example, dungs are used for compost and manures for domestic fuels etc; straws are used as animal feed; paddy plants after harvesting and separation of grains are either used as fodder or are burnt in the farm for manures. But the problem of disposal of these agricultural waste has become headache in the developed countries.

4. *Municipal wastes* include solid waste such as papers, plastics, metal cans, glass bottles, aluminium foils, metal junks, garbages mostly coming from domestic uses etc. It may be further pointed out that most of these items are reused and recycled in poor countries and therefore the problem of solid waste pollution is not so acute at least at present as it is in the developed countries.

5. *Packing wastes* include packagings of different materials such as polythene, plastics, paper board, paper, jute, flax (gunny bags) etc. These packaging are generally used several times in different forms in developings countries but these are immediately discarded after their first use and hence present the problem of their disposal.

6. *Human wastes* include sewage in the cities which is disposed off in several disposal bodies such as underground pits, lakes, tanks, rivers and seas. In the rural areas mainly in the developing countries people use open lands as lavatories and thus stools pose a serious environmental problem.

These human excreta are washed by rainwater and are carried to nearby tanks, lakes and streams. *Animal wastes* such as dungs, their skeletons and waste substances from slaughter houses pose serious disposal problems. In India dungs are picked up by farmers and are used as manures and cooking fuels. Similarly, bones of dead animals are used in fertilizer industry.

The municipal garbages of Indian cities generally comprise carbon and organic matter, compostable matter, ash, earth, moisture, stone, coal, straw, leaves, vegetables, paper, rags, cans, bottles, plastics, polythene bags etc. The municipal waste substances are also classified into (*i*) Non-combustible waste, (*ii*) Highly combustible trash, (*iii*) Combustible wastes, (*iv*) Animal and vegetable trash etc.

MANAGEMENT OF SOLID WASTE

It involves collection of waste substances and their disposal through dumping in suitable dump sites and their incineration. These are quick and efficient automatic machines for the collection and disposal of solid waste substances in the developed countries but rapidly increasing quantities of solid wastes are dangerous signs of environmental problems in near future. The dump sites in the western world are generally lakes, underground pits and sea waster. Disposal of solid wastes from various sources has created ecological problem in the littoral areas because of deaths of marine organisms including fishes and corals.

There is no proper arrangement for the collection and disposal of domestic wastes and sewage in the rural areas of India and hence these substances spread on the ground within the village and outside the village. The collection and disposal of solid wastes and domestic sewage is yet another serious problem in the small towns of the country. Dumps of domestic garbages remain at their places for several days and thus pollute the environment by foul smell and releasing harmful gases.

Collection of municipal wastes is the first step in the management of solid waste pollution. In Indian cities and towns domestic solid waste substances are generally thrown by the residents in specially enclosed masonry structures on road sides, on the roads, in the corners of the buildings, behind the boundary walls etc.

Even the residents of flats in multi-storeyed buildings throw their domestic wastes downward which come as 'missiles' on the ground while dusts and ashes spread in the air.

These heaps of municipal garbages are further spread by stray cattle, pigs, rats, rodents and poor people who collect some reusable items such as iron and aluminium junks, paper, plastics etc. These heaps of solid wastes are then collected by municipal personnel and are carried by trucks and lorries to dump sites.

The collection and clearance of municipal wastes from various collection sites in the cities are seldom performed regularly in most of the Indian cities. It is thus desired that the frequency of waste collection should be increased and properly maintained. The solid wastes should be collected by municipal personnel at least twice a day from the market and business areas mainly from fruit and vegetable markets and at least once a day from residential localities. The same norm should be applied for the clearance of domestic wastes in small towns also.

The second step of the management of solid waste pollution is the *Proper and Scientific Method of Disposal of Solid Wastes.* Garbage disposal involves (*i*) sorting of waste substances, (*ii*) dumping of non-combustible substances into suitable dump sites, and (*iii*) incineration of combustible substances.

The solid wastes are separated into the following categories of substances—(*i*) *Compostable Organic Matter,* (*ii*) *Non-Combustible Solid Wastes,* (*iii*) *Highly Combustible Waste* (*e.g.* papers, card boards, plastics, rubber etc.), (*iv*) *Combustible Wastes* (*e.g.* wood scrap, cartons, floor sweepings etc.), and (*v*) *Animal and Vegetable Wastes and Reusable Wastes.*

Compostable organic substances such as vegetables, plant leaves, animal and human wastes etc. (which are biologically degradable-biodegradable substances) should be composted either through open window composting method or through mechanical composting method and thus useful manures can be produced.

'Composting may solve twin problems of India, *i.e.* proper disposal of solid wastes and production of organic manure for increasing agricultural output. According to an estimate, a town with one lakh (100,000) population may produce 20,000 tonnes of garbage and 8,000 tonnes of night soils which can be converted into 18,000 tonnes of compost (organic manure) per year.

Non-combustible solid wastes such as metals are dumped and compacted in garbage disposal sites such as landfills, depressed ground or even in open wasteland.

Combustible substances may be burnt in specially designed incinerators such as Multiple Health Furnaces (MHF) and Fluidized Bed Furnaces (FBF). Pyrolysis is another way of treatment of solid wastes wherein wastes are broken down through the process of destructive distillation in an oxygen free atmosphere into gases like carbon dioxide (CO_2), CO (carbon monoxide), H_2, C_2H_2 ,C_2H_4 and CH_4 and into liquids like tar, light oil, water soluble distillate and solid char. Thus burning of solid wastes may solve the problem of their disposal as well as may yield energy for various uses.

QUESTIONS FOR ANSWER

1. *What do you mean by Land or Soil Pollution? Explain the sources of land or soil pollution.*
2. *Enumerate the effects of Land or Soil Pollution.*
3. *Define solid waste pollution and write a note on the sources of soil waste.*
4. *Give details of various types of solid waste substances.*
5. *Write a note on the management of solid waste for prevention and control of pollution.*

15

Noise and Radioactive Pollution

INTRODUCTION

Today, we are witnessing a fierce race for industrial supremacy, based on increasing use of energy. Noise is a factor commonly associated with production and utilisation of energy. The effects of air and water pollution are often easy to see, but noise does not leave evidence that can be seen or identified. But noise pollution in the community environments has assured dimensions of national concern world over. Pollution control laws heretofore associated with water and air pollution are now extending rapidly into the field of noise and its control. Continued exposure to high intensity on noise results in annoyance, fatigue, temporary shift of the thresh-hold of hearing and finally to permanent loss of hearing. There is increasing evidence that noise exposure causes physiological disturbances, such changes in digestion, metabolism, blood circulation etc. Studies pertaining to bio-chemical changes in man have shown that noise cause blood catecholamine, cholestrol, free fatty acids, total white cell counts, lymphocytes and neutrophills.

SOUND AND NOISE

Sound which pleases the listeners is music and that which causes pain and annoyance is noise. Sometimes, what is music for some can be noise for others. Intensity of noise can today be measured objectively in a universally accepted scale, though healthy human ears have a very wide range of sensitivity to sound, higher noise levels can be injurious to the ears and also to other body systems.

Sound may be defined as a pressure in air, water or any

medium that a human ear can detect. It is the most primitive and effective tool of communication. It becomes discordant and unpleasing to the ear when produced in irregular succession or disturbances. This is when sound becomes noise.

Sound is a special type of pressure wave which is usually transmitted through air (also through solids and liquids but with very low intensity) and is received by the receiving mechanism, the hearing apparatus (ear). In other words, 'sound, the form of energy giving the sensation of hearing, is produced by longitudinal mechanical waves in matter including solid, liquid and gas and transmitted by oscillation of atoms and molecules of matter. The intensity of sound waves, measured in watts per square meter (w/m^2), is the flow of energy per unit time ($second^{-1}$) through a unit area to the area perpendicular to the direction of propagation of waves' (K.P. Singh and S. Sinha, 1983).

The speed of sound waves depends upon the density and elasticity of the transmitting medium such as gas (air), liquid and solids. The pressure waves or sound waves after being generated in the air at sound source are transmitted through air in all directions in spherical manner. The intensity of sound waves decreases with increasing distance from the source of sound. There are certain characteristics of sound waves which must be taken into account before studying various aspects of noise pollution. (*i*) The intensity of sound waves decreases as the distance increases from the source of sound; (*ii*) After being hit by solid objects sound wave is reflected; (*iii*) Two sound waves, after being reflected by solid objects, are scattered or dispersed; and (*iv*) Sound waves are also absorbed by perferated objects.

High pressure sound or high intensity sound termed as unwanted sound is called NOISE which causes discomfort to human beings and interferes with their efficiency. In other words, noise is defined unwanted high intensity sound without agreeable musical quality. In fact, noise is that higher level of sound which becomes unpleasant, and causes discomfort and fatigue to human bodies by damaging hearing ability, brain and balancing mechanism. It may be pointed out that differentiation between sound and noise is a subjective matter is the concept and perception of sound and noise varies from person to person.

DEFINITION OF NOISE POLLUTION

Noise is an unwanted sound without agreeable musical quality. Encyclopaedia American defines noise as "Noise by definition is unwanted sound, what is pleasant to some ears may be extremely unpleasant to others, depending on a number of psychological factors". Thus noise as pollutant produces contaminated environment which becomes a nuisance and affects the health of a person, his activities and mental abilities.

Hence, "Noise pollution is unwanted sound 'dumped' into the atmosphere not-withstanding the adverse effects, it may have on living and non-living things."

Noise pollution may be defined as the state of discomfort and restlessness caused to humans by unwanted high intensity sound known as noise. Thus noise is the main pollutant of noise pollution which may be both natural and artificial. Natural noise pollution results from natural sources such as cloud thunder; high intensity rainfall, hailstorms, water falls etc. It may be widespread, sporadic, frequent or rare.

On the other hand artificial noise pollution is caused by high intensity sound created by human activities and therefore artificial or simply called as noise pollution is increasing in high dimension and intensity with increasing urbanization and industrialisation. It is apparent that the main source of noise pollution is sound which may be caused naturally or artificially. It may be pointed out that unlike other pollutants, sound/noise is not an element, compound or substance and thus it cannot accumulate and harm future generations. There is no lag-time between its generation and impact on human beings and of course on animals. In other words, noise has instantaneous effects on nearby organisms. Unlike other pollutants, it cannot be carried far away and spread from its source area.

SOURCES OF NOISE POLLUTION

On an average the sources of noise pollution are divided into three categories *viz.*—

(*i*) *Natural Sources*: such as cloud thunder high velocity wind such as hurricanes, gales, thunderstorms; high intencity rainfall; hailstorm; waterfalls, surf currents, etc.

(*ii*) *Biological Sources:* e.g. sounds of varying intentsities of wild and tame animals such as roars of lions in circus cages. Street dogs are perpetual sources of noise pollution in rural areas. Similarly, jackals cause noise pollution in the neighbourhood of villages and fringes in urban areas. Man also creates different types of sounds and noise such as during laughing, crying, singing, weeping, quarrelling etc.

(*iii*) *Artificial sources* e.g. noise created by man through his activities and creations such as musical instruments, automobiles, aircraft's, factories etc.

Sources of noise are also classified on the basis of the areas of noise such as—(*i*) Rural Sources of Noise Pollution, (*ii*) Urban Sources of Noise Pollution, and (*iii*) Industrial Sources of Noise Pollution. Rural source generates least noise pollution because of general absence of ingredients of industrial and urban areas. There are certain occasions when the level of pollution becomes higher than normal permissible level (25-35 dB) *e.g.* during festivals (Holi, Diwali, Moharram etc.), religious rituals (marriages) mourning elections, quarrels, fairs etc. Street dogs are perpetual sources of high level of noise pollution. Very often barking dogs disturb the sleep of villagers during night. Diesel engines used for pumping sets and flour mills cause high level noise pollution.

Urban Source of noise pollution includes noise produced from (*i*) automobiles (motorcycles and scooters, tempo, cars, lorries and buses, trucks, trains) and aircrafts, (*ii*) rockets, (*iii*) defense experiments, rifle shooting, motor firing, other firing explosions, (*iv*) hawkers, (*v*) vegetable and fruit markets, (*vi*) children playing, (*vii*) electioneering, (*viii*) religious propaganda, (*ix*) cultural programmes, (*x*) musical rights, (*xi*) festivals, (*xii*) worships (prayers in temples and mosques), non-stop recitation of Rama Charita Manas, Geeta, Upanishads etc. (*xiii*) advertisements, (*xiv*) mourning at the time of deaths etc. Loudspeakers are the most significant noise pollutants as these are used at large scale during all types of festivals and religious fairs of all communities, national festivals like Independence Day (15th August) and Republic Day (26th January), electioneering, advertisement, political and religious propaganda, worships, bhajan and kirtan; speeches etc.

Industrial source of noise pollution includes noise produced from factories and all other sources of noise pollution in urban areas such as noise created from automobiles, loundspeakers, defense establishment, markets, religious and cultural gatherings etc. Industrial sources of noise pollution also include noise caused by mining operations such as operations of buldozars, trucks, and machines, blasting of rocks by dynamites, operation of drillers etc.

TYPES OF NOISE POLLUTION

Noise pollution may be classified in a number of ways on different criteria. On the basis of areal source of noise, noise pollution may be divided into four types *viz.*, (*i*) rural noise pollution, (*ii*) urban noise pollution, (*iii*) industrial noise pollution, and (*iv*) mining noise pollution.

On the basis of sources of noise, noise pollution may be divided into: (*i*) natural noise pollution caused by noise created from natural sources as referred to above, (*ii*) biological noise pollution caused by noise produced by different animals including man (such as tamed elephants, lions in circus cages and in zoological gardens, dogs, jackals, donkeys, birds etc.) and (*iii*) man-made noise pollution.

Noise pollution may also be divided on the basis of periodicity and intensity of noise into (*i*) pollution caused by intermittent or non-uniform noise, (*ii*) pollution caused by continuous or uniform noise, and (*iii*) pollution caused by instantaneous or impulsive sounds such as explosions, gun shots, thunder etc. The noise pollutions caused by intermittent and continuous noise are most injurious to human beings because they are quite annoying disturbing and fatiguiing as they cause much discomfort to human health and mind. These pollutions are generally caused by the noise created from entertainment establishments (cinema halls, dance halls, etc.), public addresses by politicians, religious addresses, hospitals, schools, common vegetable fruit and fish markets, vacuum cleaner, television and radio sets, sewing machines, stereomusic players, grinder, mixer, fans etc. Sonic booms created by supersonic jet aircrafts, high intensity sound waves caused by the explosion of high power bombs, blasting of rocks by high power dynamites etc. create such powerful sound waves that even window glass panes are rattled. In fact, sonic boom is the noise which is caused by the objects travelling faster the speed of sound and is produced instantaneously. Sonic boom is expressed in *Mach Unit*. For example, the sound produced by the object travelling at the same speed of sound is termed Mach 1, while the sound created by the object travelling at the speed twice to that of sound is termed Mach 2 and so on.

MEASUREMENT OF NOISE LEVEL

The common measurement unit of sound in acoustics, the science of sound, is the decibel (dB) which is the unit of the measurement of the intensity of sound. The other unit of the measurement of sound pressure is *Weighted Sound Pressure (SPL.)* or very commonly known as dB (A) in abbreviated form. The fundamental difference between these two noise level measurements is that dB is the measure of sound intensity while dB (A) is the measure of sound pressure but dB (A) scale is more commonly used because it is quite easier to construct instruments to measure the pressure of sound waves rather the intensity of sound waves.

The decibel (dB) scale begins with 0 which represents the faintest sound being audible to a normal human ear. it is to be remembered that 'in the decibel scale each ten fold increase is represented by 10 dB'. For example, 0 is the threshold value for the faintest sound, if the sound intensity increases 10 times more than the faintiest sound, the intensity on decibel scale will be 10 dB if the sound intensity increases 100 times, it will be 20 dB; 1000 times increase = 30 dB, 10,000 times income = 40 dB, 100,000 times increase = 50 dB, 1,000,000 times increase = 60 dB, 10,000,000 = times increase = 70 dB, 100,000,000 times increase = 80 dB, 1,000,000,000 times increase = 90 dB, 1,000,000,000,000,000 times increase = 150 dB, 100,000,000,000,000,000,000 times increases = 200 dB and so on.

NOISE POLLUTION LEVEL IN INDIA

Most of the million cities of India are suffering from noise pollution because of phenomenal growth in automobiles and other noise pollutants consequent upon unchecked growth of urban population. Loudspeakers and traffic noise are the biggest nuisance in Indian cities. Every nook and corner of a city is echoed by blistering and defeaning noise created by overcrowded loudspeakers tuned at full volume during festivals of all communities, cultural programmes, public addresses, national festival, Indian victories in games and sports in international encounters etc. Most of the big cities of India have high level of noise pollution, generally above 70 dB *e.g.* Delhi (89 dB), Calcutta (87 dB), Bombay (85 dB), Madras (89 dB), Cochin (80 dB), Madurai (75 dB), Nagpur (75 dB) Trivandrum (70 dB), etc.

EFFECTS OF NOISE POLLUTION

Noise pollution or say exposure of human beings to noise of levels higher than recommended level causes a number of adverse effects ranging from mild annoyance to permanent hearing loss. The effects of noise pollution of humans are generally of four types *viz.* (*i*) General Effects, (*ii*) Auditory Effects, (*iii*) Psychological Effects, and (*iv*) Physiological Effects.

(*i*) General Effects

General effects of noise pollution on humans include speech interference, annoyance, sleep interference and related after effects and problems. Speech interference is generally caused by community noise. Speech interference simply means non-audibility of speech to a particular person due to loud community noise. In other words, in loud community noise such as in vegetable-fruit-fish markets, fairs etc. a person may hear only a few or even none of the speech sounds necessary for satisfactory intelligibility. Sleep, which is very much necessary for the good health of human beings, is not only disturbed by high noise level but its duration is also shortened. There is a negative relationship between noise intensity and sleep duration *e.g.* as the intensity of noise increases, the duration of sleep decreases. Frequent high noise disturbs the sleep and awakens the person which causes many socio-economic problems. For example, people living in the villages along the main rail routes are awakened several times during night due to high level noise produced by passing trains and hence produce more children. Sounds of all types cause annoyance and irritation in most of the people. The annoyance caused by high intensity sound some times causes mental imbalances.

(*ii*) Auditory Effects

Auditory effects include the damages done to hearing mechanism in humans due to various types of noise. Noise pollution causes hearing damages in a number of ways. The problem has been thrown with sharp focus by the discovery that some teen-agers went suffering from permanent hearing loss following long exposures to amplified rock music and by public concern about the effects of sonic booms that would be caused by supersonic transports (SST) if they were put into commercial service (P.R. Ehrlich and A.H. Ehrlich, 1970). Auditory effects may be divided into two categories *viz.* (*i*) temporary and mild damage to hearing mechanism, and (*ii*) permanent hearing loss. It has been found that even short exposures to high intensity noise may damage and rupture the ear drum and may cause temporary deafness. Experiments have revealed that noise in excess of 90 dB may produce varying degrees of impairment of hearing depending upon the length of exposure, frequency of sound waves susceptibility of the individual against noise.

It has been shown that a person subjected to exposure of 2,000 cycles frequency of noise levels of 80 dB may lose his hearing ability by 15 dB in ten years. Long and continuous exposure to high intensity sounds leads to permanent loss of hearing rendering a person deaf. An intensive study to measure the *Noise Induced Hearing Loss* (NHL) among the factory workers in the textile, automobile, fertilizers and chemical industries in the cities of Madras, Coimbatore, Madurai, Cochin and Trivandrum revealed the fact that one out of every four factory workers suffered from incurable NIHL and 10 per cent of the people such as traffic constables and pavement vendors in three cities suffered from NIHL due to their exposure to traffic noise. Community noise caused NIHL among 3 per cent of the people of these cities.

According to a survey of students between the age groups of 5-10 years in the industrial areas, railway colonies and in other areas of high noise about 60 per cent of the students could not concentrate in their classes because of high level noises produced by loudspeakers and running trains.

(*iii*) Psychological Effects

High level noise causes many behavioural changes among humans as well as animals. Unwanted noise very often causes annoyance, irritation, and fatigue which result into low performance, low efficiency and frequent errors. Further, high frequency of high level noise and exposure of human beings for long period to such high level noise may cause tension in muscles, nervous irritability and strain and neurotic mental disorder.

(*iv*) Physiological Effects

Annoyance, irritation, anxiety, strains and stresses caused by noise pollution may cause changes in harmone content of blood which in turn may introduce changes in human bodies. Noise pollution of various sorts caused by varying levels of noise may cause high blood pressure, heart diseases, dialation of pupils of the eyes, tensing of the voluntary and involuntary muscles, diminution of gastric secretion, neuromuscular tension, nervousness, stomach and intestinal diseases such as ulcer etc. Sudden very high level noise caused by sonic booms or explosion may lead to termination of pregnancy in early stages. Many cases of congenital defects in newly born babies have been reported in the areas which are generally close to high noise regions.

CONTROL OF NOISE POLLUTION

Noise is measured in the unit of decibel (db) which is a tenth of the largest unit, the *Bel.* One decibel is equal to the finest sound that can be heard by the human ear. The following are the methods to control and reduce noise pollution.

1. *At Source Control.* The gadgets are to be developed to control noise at source.
2. *Transmission Control.* The room walls can be covered with sound absorbers.
3. *To Protect Exposed Persons or Workers.* The devices as ear plugs and ear muffs can be provided to workers of industries.
4. *Plantation or Vegetation.* Trees should be planted along high ways, streets and other noise places, the big trees are good for this purpose.

5. *Through Acts or Law:* The noise pollution has now been included under Air Pollution Control Act.

6. *The Education:* By educating students and public about noise nuisance through news media.

RADIOACTIVE POLLUTION

Radioactive pollution is the product of rapid development of science and technology, which is much more harmful than any other form of pollution.

Meaning

Radioactive substances are most toxic, as compared to organic poisons which have the harmful and injurious effects. Nuclear war materials, test explosions, great rush for power plants and radio-isotope use in medicines, industry and research are the main sources of radioactive pollution that could threaten or degrade the quality of environment.

SOURCES OF POLLUTION

1. *Natural Processes in Rocks and Soil Sources*—Such as radium, uranium, thorium, potassium, carbon, etc.

2. *Human Activities.* Sources from atomic bomb, nuclear reactors and other radiation sources—radio isotopes such as iodine, strontium, plutonium, cobalt, cesium, etc. A few radio-isotopes are concerned with environmental pollution such as argon, cobalt, cesium, iodine, krypton, strontium and plutorium and plutonium.

With biotic communities and ecosystem, the radioactive elements may become accumulated or dispersed, depending upon the biological activity of the element and period of radio-activity of the isotope. These are absorbed by plants, ingested by animals which are deposited in bone tissues close to blood forming tissues and it can then be passed on to humans through milk and non-vegetarian food.

The isotopes are accumulated in human tissues as well as those of plants and animals. The isotopes in human tissues cause serious health hazards to man. Man's radiation exposure from artificial sources is already sufficient to produce serious disease problems such as bone tumors, genetic damage and infant mortality.

PREVENTION AND CONTROL OF POLLUTION

There is race the world over to develop atomic power, so experiments are being conducted by nations either in deserts or in sea or oceans. Such experiments pollute atmosphere at regional and global level. The *World Health Organisation' and United Nations Organisation* can play a significant role to check such experiments. The atomic energy may be used in industry and domestic purposes.

The education of medical science must include such environmental studies, so that proper medical aids may be provided to the sufferers. Research are to be designed for preparing effective medicine to cure such patients.

Radioactive Protection Rules have been formulated in 1962. It is known as the *Atomic Energy Act, 1962.*

QUESTIONS FOR ANSWER

1. *Define Noise Pollution. How does noise differs from sound.*
2. *Discuss various sources of Noise Pollution.*
3. *Enumerate various types of Noise Pollution.*
4. *Write a note on the effects of Noise Pollution.*
5. *Describe the 'Radioactive Pollution' Indicate the sources and methods of preventing and controlling of Radioactive Pollution.*
6. *Write short notes on the following:*
   (*a*) *Control of Noise Pollution.*
   (*b*) *Noise Pollution Level in India.*
   (*c*) *Auditory Effects of Noise Pollution.*
   (*d*) *Measurement of Noise Level.*

16

Human Ecology and Environmentalism

Human ecology is the most important aspect of environmental education. Environmental studies include—(1) Physical environment, and (2) Human Environment or human ecology. We may define human ecology as follows.

"Human ecology is an interaction between man and his living and non-living components of environment". It is based on the earlier proposition of Darwin.

'A struggle for existence and survival of fittests'.

The main theme of human ecology is that man has also to struggle in his physical environment, like other animals and plants. In the process of struggle or interaction weakers can not survive.

Human ecology is different from plants and animals because man has knowledge, scientific advancement and innovations, transformation of ecosystems according to his needs and requirement. Man is also manufacturing tools and machines, using technological advances to grow crops for his food and can import food stuff and other goods from other countries or states.

Man is not depending for his food on his physical and biological environment, therefore the principles of ecology, thus are not applicable on human ecology to the some extent like plants and animals. Man himself is a powerful instrument for changing or modifying his physical environment according to his own-needs and requirements. Thus human ecology is the study of man and his adjustment and adaptation to his physical or natural environment. Man consciously adapts himself to his environment.

MAN AND ENVIRONMENT AND HUMAN ACTIVITIES

Human ecology is the study of interaction between man and his environment because environment affects man through (*a*) Biological Factors, (*b*) Behavioural Controls, and (*c*) Natural Resources.

Note: All there aspects have been discussed in details in chapter 3 and 4 of this book. Please read chapter 3 and 4 again.

Approaches of Studying Man and Environment

The concept of environmental science and relationship between man and environment has been changing through time with the development of human society and components of environment.

Note: Approaches to the studying of man-environment relationship have been discussed in details in chapter 2 of this book. Please read chapter 2 again.

Types of Environment

1. *Physical Environment*	2. *Human Environment*
1.1 Climate	2.1 Social organisation
1.2 Natural vegetation	2.2 Religion
1.3 Soils and Minerals	2.3 Economic system
1.4 Air or Atmosphere	2.4 Political system
1.5 Water or drainage system	2.5 Literature
1.6 Topography	2.6 Language

The various ethnic groups and indigenous people have certain values, traditions to protect their environment while obtaining their fuel and other basic needs.

Human ecology serves the purposes of liberal education. It provides the awareness about man and environment at global level and to appreciate the environment affecting man and nation other than our own. It clarifies the differences in societies and cultures in different regions of the earth

SOCIAL AND CULTURAL DETERMINISM

The modification of an environment mainly depends on our ideas, values, perceptions and decision-making processes. "Our thoughts determine our acts and our acts determine the previous nature of the world." There is great variation in human interest, desires, prejudices and values among people of the world. This proposition advocates, "significance of man of the physical and biological features of his habitat is a function of the attitudes, objectives and technical skill of man himself."

Physchological or Behavioural Environment: The influence of environment on man can be assessed in terms of psychology or behaviour of the man. Human perception is condition for the active process of decision-making. The environmental perception is both factual experiences and a directive for human activities. It depends on the organisation or cognitive maps of a person. It is also termed as a field or life space of a person.

The concept of *psychological environment* is developed by *Kurt Lewin* the *Gestalt* psychologist. It holds the views that a person lives simultaneously in different environments—Physico-social and psychological environment.

It is the environment in which physico-social behaviour begins and decisions are taken, which may or may not be translated into overt action or behaviour in the phenomenal environment. The behavioural environment is a product of the interaction of reality and cultural values. Human actions are guided by psychology field not by physical environment.

Gestalt psychology takes into account two factors. (1) Experience or content, and (2) Situation or environment or context. It has its meaning only in the context. On the other hand *behaviourists* take into account situation or environment rather than experience while *Gestalt* takes into account both experience and situation.

The main contribution of Gestalt is perception psychology. It has two elements: *part* and *whole*. Whole depends on the perception or organisation which is conveyed by parts. *Whole* is always greater than parts. *Parts* are meaningful, they are not the substitution of whole.

Thus form quality depends on the whole perceived by mind. It is dynamic organisation which provides unique appearance. It depends on three types of factors: peripheral, reinforcing and central factors. The first two types of factors exist in the external situation and third type is persons experiences which develops mental set, values and attitude and familiarity.

Behaviourists take into account only situation or environment and do not consider the experience or the perception which is more meaningful for human activity. Every person reacts according to his own perception and experience gained through the situation: *Watson's* strongest claim for environment is that he could guarantee, is given free hand in controlling the environment, to take any normal child and train him or make him whatever type of specialist we want. Gestalt has attempted to establish relationship between man and his environment. Behaviourists do not help in this contest.

HUMANISTIC PHILOSOPHY OF ENVIRONMENT

It is another philosophical approach to state the relationship. It gives central role to human awareness or experience, consciousness and creativity. According to this approach man has a central position. The human experiences, expressions provide the awareness about environment and earth. This philosophical approach gives much more weightage to man rather than nature. The existence of nature is due to human experiences and expression. Man finds values and goals in his experiences which is the advancement of human knowledge. If man finds value and goals in his environmental awareness, is known as *environmental education.*

Influence of Man on Environment. Human ecology provides the understanding of the reciprocal interaction of man and environment. The history of Indian classics—philosophers and thinkers had the knowledge of human ecology. They have revealed in their writings in the *vedas, upnishads, puranas* and epic literature.

Our two great epics—*Ramanaya* and *Mahabharata* have shown their ecological awareness at several occasions. *Kalidas* has also shown his ecological understanding in his writings such as *'Meghdoot' 'Ritu samhar'* and Abiyyan Shakuntalam and Kautilya's Arthasastra. *Charak* considered the important factors of Vayu (*air and gases*), Jala (*water*) Desha (*topography*) and kala (*time*) in regulating the life of plants.

Determinism and possibilism are the two extreme approaches dealing the concept of *'Man and Environment'*. The eclectic approach appears to be tangible to deal this concept, *i.e.*, mutual interaction between man and environment. Nature influences both man and environment. The natural hazards and disasters affect both man and environment. Man can not prevent himself from these events. He can forecast for the precautionary measures and can prepare himself for the relief measures.

Man has influenced and modified the environment which has created several types of environmental problems. Man induced impact on environment can be prevalued by employing various types of measures, legal and administrative steps. The influence of man on environment has the following propositions.

The Propositions for the Interaction between Man and Environment

The concept of *'Man on Environment'* is based on the following propositions:

1. Man is no longer the product of his environment, he is also its creater and transformer. Man dominates the ecology since his origin on earth.
2. Environment change is a continuous process which is operating since the origin of man on earth. The change is occurring due to natural forces and man's activities.
3. Human beings must always have been concerned with their environment since it has been their immediate surroundings that provide the resources essential for their survival.
4. The factors and forces of environmental change are several and the process involved in this change are very complex.
5. The climate and humans are two major forces for the environmental change which directly influence the process operative in environmental system.
6. The changes are gradual and imperceptible or intrinsic. All natural systems are in a state of dynamic equilibrium. These system have both resistance and resilience to change.
7. Man becomes a powerful force or agent to change in the global environment. The degree and extent of man's impact on environment may be appreciable due to certain significant contributions or positive feedback. Man is most powerful present creater of environmental change.

HUMAN ACTIVITIES

The earth history, the forces of environmental changes have been the natural agents like earthquakes, volcanoes, floods, fire, storms. They produce dynamic ecosystem to maintain balance. Human agencies of environmental change have only become significant in the last ten thousand years or so, but as technological advances have made their impact termendously increased. Most of the environmental change has taken place as man has started to exploit the natural resources.

Thus one of the major reasons of *man-induced change* is to manipulate energy transfer and expansion of human population. In the following paragraph, the human factors and activities have been enumerated and discussed which have induced or are responsible for the environmental change.

Man-made sources or human activities are such as urbanization, industries, factories, aircraft, automobiles, nuclear experimentation, agriculture, power plants, tourism, means of recreation and social functions. These human activities influence the environmental components, *air, water, soil, noise; ratioactive and solid waste.* Human activities degrade the quality of the environment.

Human activities concerning following aspects have been discussed in chapter 3 and 4 of this book.

1. *Agricultural Development*
2. *Industrial Development*
3. *Deforestation* (also discussed in chapter 1 of this book).
4. *Development and Use of Automobiles*: There is very rapid increase in the use of automobiles in urban areas during this period of technological development. The development of automobiles has raised the traffic and transportation density in towns and big cities. These two and four wheelers generate tones of gaseous pollutants into the atmosphere. It has degraded the quality of environment of our big cities.

These vehicles create dust. Dust travels several thousand kilometres across the landscape. It is harmful to human health and it may lead to many types of diseases. The automobiles smoke, gases and dust have affected heavily the urban climate and environmental conditions. The noise pollution is created by these automobiles in our cities.

5. *Radioactive and Nuclear Development.* The nuclear war materials, test explosions, great rush for power plants and radio-isotope use in medicine industry and research are the main source

of radioactive pollutants which are degrading the quality of environment.

The *isotopes* are accumulated in human tissues, plants and animals. These isotopes in human tissues and animals cause serious health hazards in the biosphere.

There is a race among the nations of the world to develop atomic power, therefore experiments are being conducted by nations either in deserts and seas or oceans. These atomic experiments have affected the environment at regional or global level. It is most significant factor for the environmental change or degrading the quality of the environment. The *World Health Organisation* (WHO) and *United Nations Organisation* (UNO) can play a significant role to check such atomic experiments.

6. *Recreational and Tourism Industry Development:* Tourism has so developed that it becomes the world's third largest industry. The natural areas vegetation are damaged in the countryside for these tourism and recreation. It has accelerated the loss of soil and disturb animals. Sports, skeing, boating, camping, riding, trekking and picnicking adversely effect the landscape and environment. Thus, tourism is also bringing significant environmental change. The uncontrolled tourism destroy the landforms fauna and flora. Planning and management of tourism is very essential to continue as source of income.

7. *Population Explosions:* The growth and increase in human population has also disturbed the ecological balance of environment. The over population has created the demand of more food and shelter facilities. Therefore man has destroyed forests, vegetation and grassland for agricultural land and for establishing industries, factories, power plants, etc. As a result of deforestation some of the animals have become extinct and some are on the verge of extinction. It has caused several types of environmental changes and problems.

Most of the causes which have been enumerated in the earlier paragraphs, are due to the population explosion such as urbanizations, agricultural and industrial development, deforestation, use automobiles, nuclear development and development of tourism industry. These developments are made to meet requirements of over population but these have created environmental problems—soil erosion, floods, drought, air, water and soil pollution. The root cause for the environmental change is the explosion of human population.

There has been a rapid growth and increase of population in India. It has now crossed 100 crores which is more than 16 per cent of world population. Most of the world population lives in the developing countries. The growing pressure of the population on resource base, especially on urban level which has created many socio-economic, social, cultural, ecological and environmental problems. The environmental changes and problems vary from region to region.

The developed countries are highly industrialized and urbanized in which the per capita income is not only high, but most of the population is dependent either on primary or secondary sources. There is also the race in the developing countries for industrialization and urbanization which has caused several types of human problems and ecological changes.

8. *Process of Urbanization:* There are more facilities and social amenities such as educational institutions, universities, technical education, colleges, hospitals, banks, recreation places, electricity, transportation facilities, security, marketing, etc, are in the towns and cities. These are reasons for migrating people from rural areas or villages to urban areas.

The pressure of human population density is increasing very rapidly, in our towns and cities. It requires more facilities and social amenities in our cities, as a result the pressure of transportation, water supplies, electricity supplies, sewage system, dust, smoke of factories, automobiles, chemical effluents, traffic congestion and noise problems. Thus urban life is full of human tension which leads to physical and mental illness.

9. *Educational Environment:* The educational facilities are available in urban areas which is for 25 per cent of our total population. Thus, the rural youth has to move to urban areas which are full of problems as mentioned in the above paragraphs, but for learning congenial environment is very essential.

The institutional climate and organisation is highly polluted by lower level politics. The student-unrest is major problem of our education at all levels. Our education can not develop moral and ethical values among our students. The social and political environment is greatly influenced by our youth studying in colleges and universities.

The urgent need of the nation is to have check or control on the human population which is the root-cause for environmental changes and problems. Education can play a significant role in this context. Population education is very essential for the youth which is directly related with our development and standard of living of the people for economic and social development, there is an urgent need for imparting population education in our country.

IMPACT OF MAN ON ENVIRONMENT—AN ASSESSMENT

In order to assess the changes in the environment caused by human activities, effective and reliable monitoring systems are required to recognize and predict hazardous effects. Biological methods can be used successfully in assessing the impact of human activities particularly of pollutants well in advance since they present effective and reliable method of assessing the effect of anthropogenic substances on the living organisms. The ecological indicators can be successfully employed to assess and predict environmental changes.

The human activities have the impact on plants, animals, agriculture, soil, climate, water, deposits, etc. Thus, the following measures or indicators can be used effectively for assessing the impact of man on environment—climate, agriculture, soil, productivity of land, water, air pollution and petroleum deposits etc.

1. *Climate:* The environmental change of a region provides information on the climate of that area. The evergreen forests indicate high rainfall in winter as well as in summer. The grasslands indicate heavy rainfall in winter and low in summer.

2. *Agriculture:* Native vegetation of particular region is the safe criterion of agricultural possibilities. Thus plants growing under natural conditions provide information on capabilities of land for crop growth than information obtained through soil analysis.

3. *Soil Type and Soil Characteristics:* The growth of natural vegetation not only indicate the agricultural possibilities but soil type and its characteristics.

4. *Adequate Oxygen in Water:* Burrowing may fly indicates proper oxygen regime in the water.

5. *Petroleum Deposits:* Some protozoans as fusilinds indicate petroleum deposits.

6. *Pollution:* Presence of diatoms in water indicates pollution by sewage. Movement of fish in water indicates industrial pollution of water. Dust and smoke in the atmosphere indicates pollution in air.

Biological systems as indicators of the environment, therefore, have a remarkable potential for predicting or forecasting of disasters, prevention of pollution, exploration and conservation of natural resources, all aiming as a substainable development with minimum destruction of the biosphere.

The scientists have also developed. *'Biological Monitoring Programme'* to encourage scientists to develop and improve methods indicative of hazardous substances occurring in the environment, and to promote inter-disciplinary and international cooperation in standardizing methods and extending the use for monitoring the environmental change. Bioindicators provide a practical way of assessing the health or quality of environment. The bioindicators cover a wide range of organisms and of soil, water and air pollution serving as indicators of environment.

QUESTIONS FOR ANSWER

1. *Indicate the influence of Man on Environment. Enumerate the human activities which influence the environment.*
2. *Describe the assessment impact of Man and Environment. Suggest some measures for assessing this type of impact.*
3. *Write short notes on the following:*
   (*a*) *Humanistic Philosophy.*
   (*b*) *Population Explosion.*
   (*c*) *Psychological Environment.*
4. *Define the term 'Human Ecology'. Explain the concept of interaction between Man and Environment.*
5. *Describe the various approaches of studying Man and Environment.*
6. *Write a note on the socio-cultural determination of environment.*
7. *Discuss the propositions for interaction between Man and Environment.*

17

Environment: The Interdependency

The Food Chain, Food Web and Remedies

Environment and ecology are sometimes used interchangeably, though they are not as such, therefore, we will study the interdependency aspect of environment.

Ecology is a vast and encyclopaedic biological subject. It is the study of ecosystems or the interaction between living organisms and their environment. These physical and biological factors are interacting and maintain ecological balance.

The ecosystem is an organizational unit which includes living organisms and non-living substances interacting to produce an exchange of materials, the living and non-living parts. The ecosystem has two aspects—*structural* and *functional* aspects. The *interdependency* in environment deals the *functional* aspect of ecosystem. An ecosystem contains various population of different types of plants, animals and microbes, all are interacting with one another as community and with the physical environment as well. It includes not only the physical space occupied by an organism but also its functional role in its trophic position and its position in environmental factors—temperature, moisture, soil and other conditions of existence. This interdependency in environment reveals the life-forms of the plants which influences the nature and life cycle of animals.

An ecosystem includes abiotic and biotic factors. The main aboitic factors are—*climatic factors* as solar radiation, temperature, wind, water rainfall; *physical factors* as light, fire, pressure, geomagnetism; *chemical factors* as acidity, salinity and inorganic nutrients required by plants. The biotic factors of ecosystem are—all living organisms as plants, animals, bacteria and viruses.

ENVIRONMENT—THE FUNCTIONAL ASPECT

The interdependency of abiotic and biotic factors provides the functional awareness of an environment. The ecosystem is divided into three types of organisms from the energy point of view—*producers, consumes,* and *reducers.* These producers provide the food to all the organisms directly or indirectly. *Consumers* are herbivorous, carnivorous and omnivorous animals. The consumers eat the organic matter produced by other organisms. *Reducers* are heterotrophic organisms like animals; there are fungi and bacteria that decompose dead organic matter. The ecosystem is composed of organisms eaten by or eating other organisms. Species are related to their feeding behaviour in food chain or food webs or food cycle.

1. Food Chain

The process of energy transfer from producers to consumers and then to decompose is called *food chain.* In the biosphere the energy flows from producers to primary consumers; from primary consumers to secondary and from secondary consumers to decomposers, is known as *food chain.*

The consumers food chain includes the sequence energy flow—Plants producers and Animals consumers.

Producers → Herbivore → Carnivore → Reducer

(*i*) Grass → Sheep → Lion
(*ii*) Grass → Deer → Lion

The entire zone of water, air, soil which can sustain life is known as biosphere.

2. Biogeochemcial Cycle

Organisms take inorganic nutrients from soil, water and air; they eliminate their wastes and their bodies are rendered into inorganic molecules once again. The water and minerals shuttle among air, land, and water with an occasional pause in an organism. Such cycling of nutrients in circular path in between biotic and abiotic components of the ecosystem are called *biogeochemical cycles.*

3. Biological Clocks

A biological clock is hypothetical internal mechanism by which an organism can keep track of time and governs its activities. It is predictable for a given area and depends upon rainfall, temperature and soil conditions. It is an ecological succession change of organisms.

Ecology is broadly divided into two aspects:

(*i*) *Autecology*, and (*ii*) *Synecology:*

(*i*) *Autecology*

It deals with the ecological study of one species of organisms. *Autecology* is concerned with the study of the interrelations of individual organisms with the environment. Autecology is experimental and inductive.

(*ii*) *Synecology*

It deals with the ecological studies of communities or entire ecosystems. *Synecology* is philosophical and deductive. It is concerned with the study of groups of organisms—the community, hence, it is called community ecology.

Autecology is concerned with the relationship of an organism to one or more variables such as light, temperature, moisture and salinity, is easily quantified and subject to experimental design both in the laboratory and in the field. Autecology has borrowed techniques from physical sciences.

Autecology is also important for soil conservation and wild life conservation. There is an intimate interrelationship between the individual organism and its surrounding environment. The life cycle of a plant is highly influenced by a number of environmental factors and conversely, species does modify continuously the environment. Autecology is based on the study of the ecological life history which is concerned with the activities of species throughout its life cycle and in relation to its adjustments to natural conditions.

The niche is the property of the community and it represents the place of the species in the formal community structure. The position of functional roles in the community can be considered as *niches* as the community can be viewed as an aggregation of niches. The term niche is used in the area of ecology for a variety of meanings.

ECOLOGICAL PRODUCTION AND PRODUCTIVITY

The green plants use solar energy to convert carbon dioxide and water into carbohydrates and other biochemical molecules. The process of conversion of light energy into food or chemical energy is called *photosynthesis.* The organisms which produce their own food are known *Primary Producers or Autotrops.*

They are of two types—phototrops and chemotrops. The primary producers include chlorophyle in green plants, green purple bacteria, blue green algae and phytoplanktons. The production of organic matter or energy by autotrophic primary producers is termed *Primary Production.* The green plants involve the *production* activity of ecosystem.

The *productivity* of ecosystem depends on two factors:

(*i*) the amount of solar radiation available to the autotrophic primary producers, and

(*ii*) the efficiency of the plants to covert solar energy or light energy into food energy or chemical energy which is used by green plants to build up their tissues.

The *productivity* is the rate of increase of biomass of a given unit area at given time.

Biomass is the quantity or weight of living matter per unit area, per unit time and is represented in terms of dry weight. It includes plants and animals; therefore it is of two types—*Plant Biomass* and *Animal biomass.*

The productivity of ecosystem mainly depends on solar radiation and plants efficiency to use energy. There are abiotic factors—temperature, water, climate, chemical factors—nutrient supply.

Plants and grass are primary producers, because they convert solar energy into food.

Animals and insects are primary consumers, because they depend for their food energy on primary producers. The plants depend on solar radiation and physical components of the environment while animals and insects depend on plants and grass. There is interdependency among the environmental factors and also for the survival of the organisms.

THE FOOD CHAINS AND FOOD WEBS

The green plants are the primary producers because they prepare their own food which is the main source of food energy for all types of organisms in the biosphere. Carbon dioxide is taken by plants from the atmosphere through their leaves in day time and inorganic matter and water are taken by the roots from the soils. Plants convert water and carbon dioxide into starch and sugar with the help of sun light. The process is known as photosynthesis. Thus the green plants are *Primary Producers*. Some animals depend on plants for their food are called *herbivores*. The animals take their food from animals are known as *carnivores*. Some animals depend on both, plants and animals for their food are termed as *omnivores*.

In the ecosystem feeding process takes place in hierarchical order. The food energy passes from one group of organisms to another group which are called *Trophic Level*.

The chain of transformation of food energy in the ecosystem from one group of organisms to the other group through a series of steps or levels is called *food chain*. The transfer of food energy from one group of organism to the other group is called *trophic level or step*. The four trophic levels of a food chain have been identified as follows:

First Step of Food Chain. The base of the food chain in the primary producers is known first level of trophic. The green plants produce their food through the process of photosynthesis with the help of sunlight, water, carbon dioxide and inorganic salts and consume the produced food energy to form their tissues and grow. This level is the source of food for all other organisms of the food chain.

Second Step of Food Chain. The organisms do not produce their food themselves but depend on primary producers of first level for their food is known as second level of trophic or second step of food chain. The organisms or animals are called primary consumers (*Vegetarians*).

They basically depend on plants for their food, *e.g.*, sheep, cow, goats, deers and rabbits. Such animals are known as *herbivores*. The food energy passed on from primary producers to primary consumers is second level of the food chain. The animals are known as herbivores.

Third Step of Food chain. The trophic level where energy is transferred from primary consumers to secondary consumers is called third level of food chain. Some animals depend on other animals, are known secondary consumers or carnivores, because they depend on primary consumers or herbivores group of second level, *e.g.*, lions, leopard, beers, etc. Carnivores are land animals, soil animals and aquatic animals.

Fourth Step of Food Chain. The animals which take food either directly or indirectly from primary producers, primary and secondary consumers, are known *omnivores*. Man is the most important member of fourth level, because man takes food and fuel from the green plants, primary and secondary consumers. Decomposers also take energy from all these levels.

A simple food chain is formed with the help of four steps. It is the sequence of energy transfer from lower levels to higher levels. This chain may be summarized as follows:

1. Primary producers → Primary consumers → Secondary consumers → Higher secondary consumers.
2. Plants → Herbivores animals → Carbivores animals → Omnivores animals.
3. Grass is eaten by sheep, cows, goats (*Primary consumers*) → sheep, goats are eaten by → Tigers, Lion (*Secondary consumers*)
4. Vegetation → Vegetarian food → Non-vegetarian food → all the earlier food.

The food chain does not remain simple and linear in a natural ecosystem, sometime it becomes complicated by several inter-connected overlapping food chains. This happens when greater number of species feed on many kinds of prey. The complicated food chain is known as *Food Web*. The complicated food-web is in a polar or arctic ecosystem where there are several inter-connected food chains, as given below:

(*i*) Man eats canibours which feeds on grass
(*ii*) Man eats whales which eat crustacea which feeds on diatoms
(*iii*) Man eats polar beer which feeds on crustacea which on diatoms
(*iv*) Man eats wolf and fox which eat hares which feeds on grass
(*v*) Man eats hares which feed on grasses.

All plants are not the primary producer but some of the plant are also primary consumer are called *parasites* and secondary consumers are known *hyperparasites*.

The solar energy passes through the hierarchy of levels of food chain and food web ultimately becomes output from the ecosystem as energy is lost through respiration from each level.

Thus, *foods chain* and *food web* require sunlight or solar energy as a basic input which enters into the ecosystem. The plants are the primary producers which require sunlight, water and minerals for preparing their own foods. Thus, the food chain involves solar energy flow and biogeochemical cycle to maintain ecological balance. The brief description of solar energy flow and bigeochemical cycle have been given in the following paragraphs:

1. Solar Energy Flow

The plants prepare their food in sunlight with photosynthesis. It requires one per cent solar radiation which is received on earth. This solar energy passes through the hierarchy of levels of a food chain and food web. The solar energy is a basic input and becomes output through respiration from each level of food chain.

The process of formation of organic tissue which indicates the transformation of solar energy into food energy is known as biosynthesis. The process of decomposition of organic matter which refers to the release of nutrients and food energy in the form of heat, is called *biodegradation*. The transfer of organic molecules in the ecosystem is unidirectional or non-cycle which can not be recessed.

The solar energy is received by green plants and it is used in photosynthesis to prepare food at first level. The solar energy is transformed into organic tissues. It is the source of energy directly to the vegetarian animals of second level which are the primary consumers. The plant energy is transferred to plant-eating animals are known as herbivores. The organic tissues are formed among herbivores by eating plants.

The stored energy in the bodies of herbivores now becomes the source of energy for carnivores animals at the third level of foods chain. Some part of chemical energy is lost through respiration from herbivores at second level of food chain. The animals consume energy for their movement for getting food from green plants.

The carnivores eat herbivores at third level of food chain, thus some part of potential energy is transferred to carnivores at this level through intake of food herbivores. Some part of energy is released by herbivores as wastes and their dead bodies decompose in soil.

The stored energy in the bodies of carnivores not becomes the store house of energy for omnivores which eat both plants and animals, man is most important example of omnivores at the fourth level of food chain. The animals of the fourth level take energy from both primary producers (*plants*) and herbivores (*animals*), *i.e.*, first and second levels of food chain.

Some part of energy is released by respiration of omnivores, their dead bodies are decomposed in soil by the decomposers. The omnivores take their food directly from plants and herbivores and also from carnivores. Thus there are three ways of flow of energy under food chain and food web in a natural ecosystem—First way is as follow—

First Path—The chemical energy flows in a hierarchical order,
i.e. I level → II level → III level → IV level

Second Path—The chemical energy flows in a bypass manner,
i.e. I level → IV level

The second way of flow of energy is that animals of all levels release energy by respiration as heat which is lost in the atmosphere as output which can not be recessed.

The third way of transfer of chemical energy from dead bodies of animals and waste of plants are decomposed in soil by the decomposers at all levels of food chain. The chemical energy which is transferred by decomposers can be recessed by plants. Thus, there is cycle of flow of chemical energy.

2. Biogeochemical Cycles in Food Chains

The biogeochemical cycles include the intake of inorganic elements by plants through their roots in solution from the soils where these inorganic elements are stored. The nutrients are taken up by plants through the process of *osmosis* and prepare their own food. The chemical energy is transferred to the higher levels along the food chains and food webs through flow of energy.

The nutrients are used and assimilated in developing plants tissues and their bodies. When these are transferred and assimilated among different animals of different levels of food chains or food webs are known as organic matter.

There are three cycles through which organic elements flow in a food chain or food web.

(*i*) The *waste* materials released by plants and animals such as leaves, dung, etc., are decomposed by bacteria decomposers, are again changed into inorganic elements which is again used by plants through the process of osmosis. It is first cycle of inorganic matter to organic matter and organic matter into inorganic matter in a food chain.

(*ii*) The dead bodies of animals and plants are decomposed by the bacteria in to soil as inorganic matter. The organic materials are converted into inorganic materials in soil. It is the second cycle of biogeochemical energy.

(*iii*) The process of deforestation and burning of vegetation by lightning or accidental forest fire, the organic material are released to the atmosphere and again fall down on the ground surface, it become soluble inorganic form of element to soil which can be re-used by plants.

3. The Carbon Cycle in Food Chains and Food Webs

The carbon dioxide of the atmosphere is used in the biological cycles in food chain through the process of photosynthesis of green plants. The carbon, oxygen, and hydrogen are combined by green plants with the help of sunlight and thus organic compounds are formed by the processes of osmosis and photosynthesis of green plants.

Thus the carbon dioxide assimilated by green plants is stored in the form of bodies tissues. The green plants produce the carbohydrates as chemical energy which is consumed by herbivorous animals of the second level of food chain and by omnivorous animals at the fourth level.

The animals release carbon dioxide during respiration. The fallen leaf, animals waste and dead bodies are decomposed by bacteria or decomposers, thus carbon and carbon dioxide are returned to the atmosphere. The decomposers release carbon in gaseous form through respiration and dead organic tissues.

4. The Oxygen Cycle in Food Chain

Oxygen is very essential for the living organisms because they can not survive without oxygen. It plays a significant role in the biosphere. It is very active gas because it combines with majority of the elements in the biosphere. It is produced through the process of photosynthesis by the green plants of different ecosystems and enters into the atmosphere. The atmospheric oxygen is used by the plants and animals during the process of respiration. The process of respiration among green plants takes place during night-time. Thus the oxygen cycle includes the input of oxygen to the atmosphere by the photosynthesis of green plants and output of oxygen to the atmosphere through respiration of plants and animals in the food chain and food web.

5. The Water Cycle in Food Chain

The water, oxygen, hydrogen and carbon are the most essential elements for the survival of living organisms—plants and animals. These elements constitute 90 per cent of the organic matter in the biosphere. Hydrogen in the form of water and oxygen together constitute 80.5 per cent of the total weight of all the living organisms. The water is the combination of hydrogen and oxygen which enters into the biosphere and goes out of the biosphere in the form of moisture mainly in liquid form. The food involves the major part of water. The hydrogen cycle also represents the water cycle in the food chain and food webs. The water cycle is regulated by the solar energy.

6. The Phosphorous Cycle in Food Chain

The phosphorous is the most important second level substance in the biosphere which is most essential for the growth and development of organisms. It has very limited gaseous phase and has the main phase in the biogeochemical cycle.

The plants take up phosphorous in the form of inorganic phosphate from the soils through their roots by the process of root osmosis. The inorganic phosphates are converted into organic forms in the plants which are circulated in the food chain through different levels.

Thus, the phosphate is returned back to the soils when dead organisms and their wastes are decomposed by soil organisms. The organic compounds of phosphate are returned to the soils when these are again converted into mineral forms. This cycle is completed after a long time. The phosphorous cycle is slow and gradual.

FACTORS AFFECTING FOOD CHAINS AND FOOD WEBS

The biosphere usually contains several kinds of *food chains, food webs* and *ecosystems.* Many of these are interconnected by one or more species which in more than one food chain to form food web. These involve energy flow, bio-chemical cycles, hyroden, carbon and oxygen cycles. There is interdependency between biotic, abiotic and solar energy which maintains the ecological balance in nature. There are several factors which are affecting the food chains and may be broadly classified into two categories— (*i*) *Human Activity,* and (*ii*) *Natural Disasters* and *Hazards.* Another way to classify these factors may be the food chains.

(*i*) Disturbance of food chain, and
(*ii*) Quality of food.

Both types of the factors are inter-related and interdependent which ultimately affect the quality of food. The description of these factors have been given in the following paras:

1. Factors Disturbing the Food Chain

The food chains are disturbed by human activities; natural disaster and hazards.

(*a*) *Human Activities:* Man is trying to exploit the natural resources through industrial development, transportation and automobiles, deforestation, agricultural development use of chemical fertilizers and pesticides undiscriminating hunting animals, development of tourism, power plants, explosion of population, urbanization. These human activities have polluted heavily the environment, *i.e. air, water, soil* which have disturbed ecological balance and natural food chains.

The *deforestation* and undiscriminating hunting of animals is harmful. It is found that the removal of even one type of organism from the food chain will upset the whole ecological balance in nature. If peacocks are killed, population of snake will increase. If cats are killed, population of rats will increase, thus removal of any part of the chain organism would disturb the ecological balance in nature. The human activities have disturbed biosphere by hunting wild animals and indiscrimitive hunting any type of organism.

(*b*) *Natural Disaster and Hazards:* The natural accidents also disturb ecological balance of nature. The floods, forest fire, earthquake, storms, volcanic eruptions, etc. disturb the natural functioning of the environment. The affects of natural disasters and hazards have already been discussed in the separate chapter of the book. The forecasting preventive measures and relief measures are used to maintain the ecological balance of nature.

2. Factors Affecting the Quality of Food

Human activities and natural hazards not only disturb the ecological balance but also deteriorate the quality of food even for primary producers. These may be of two types (*a*) *Human activities*, and (*b*) *Natural disaster and hazards.*

(*a*) *Human Activities:* Man is trying to utilize natural resources as far as possible. There is explosion of human population which has increased the pressure on the natural resources through technological, industrial and agricultural development. The chemical fertilizers are used to produce crops of high yield. The pesticides are used to protect the food crops from harmful bacteria. It has increased the per acre yield of the food crops but deteriorate the quality of food.

The natural process of food chain and ecological balance also maintain the quality food. The primary producers plants are affected by harmful bacteria, if pesticides are used to kill the bacteria, the herbivores take their food from plants, they also eat pesticides which are harmful to them. Thus the adverse effect of pesticides continues to the carnivores and to human beings whether they are vegetarian and non-vegetarian.

Human activities have polluted air, water and soil through the industrial wastes and water sewage. The normal water is not fit for drinking purpose. The quality of human food is deteriorating day-by-day. The wheat and other cereals are stored alongwith sulpha capsules which are highly poisonous.

(*b*) *Natural Disasters and Hazards:* They destroy the total ecology and food system. There are epidemics after disasters and hazards because of quality of food can not be maintained.

EDUCATION—THE BEST REMEDY

Education can play a significant role through its formal and informal agencies to improve and maintain the natural process of food chain. Education can play a significant and effective role for providing the awareness of this process and developing right-type of attitude and values for this concepts. The growth and development of man and other living organisms mainly depend on natural process of food chains and food webs. Human activities can be restricted by forming legal laws, *e.g.*, deforestation is crime, family size can also be limited.

The fertile land can not be used for industrial purpose, hunting or killing wild animal is also crime, etc. There should be an effective media in the country to forecaste about disasters and hazards–earthquakes, floods, storm, volcanic eruption, etc., so that precautionary measures can be adopted and immediate relief measures can be used quickly and effectively.

(*i*) *Role of Formal Agencies of Education*: The formal system of education is classified into four levels, *i.e.*, primary, secondary, higher secondary and college and university levels. The awareness of this concept food chain and food webs may be provided at primary stage of students. The relevance for real-life situation can be emphasized at secondary stage. The conservation of natural resources are to be taught at higher secondary level. The solving problems and sustainable development attitude, values and appraisal should be emphasized at college and university level. It is an *interdisciplinary concept*, so it may be taught along related subject.

Now it is recognized that *Environmental Education* is an independent field of study or discipline. Some practical and field works should be organised to develop skills and understanding through the co-curricular activities, *e.g.*, Scouting and Girls guiding, N.C.C. camps and N.S.S. programmes so that an active participation in prevention and solving problems at their local level may be encouraged among the students. The educational programmes can promote the value and necessity of local and national levels.

At college and university level group discussions, seminars, workshops and conferences should be organised of *interdisciplinary nature*. The experts should be invited for delivering lectures and deliberations. The field work and workshop should be given priority at this level.

There should be a compulsory course at B.Ed. and M.Ed. level along with practical work on environmental problems. Teacher-education programme is also *interdisciplinary* in nature, therefore this concept is best fit in. The methodology of teaching almost of all the subjects are taught at B.Ed. level. Therefore specific and detailed awareness of the concepts energy flow, water cycles, hydrogen, oxygen, carbon cycle, and biochemical cycle, the process of photosynthesis and osmosis may be given in science teaching subjects.

(ii) Role of informal Agencies of Education: The formal and informal agencies of education have the significant role to solve problems of food chains and food webs. *Indian Environmental Society,* adult education programmes, media and other social organisations are making efforts to provide the awareness to people of the country. These agencies are also doing field work in this context.

QUESTIONS FOR ANSWER

1. *Indicate the relationship between ecology and ecosystem. Enumerate and types of factors of ecosystem.*
2. *Enumerate the functional aspects of environment. Explain the concept of interdependency in environment.*
3. *Explain the concepts of food chain and food webs in the light of interdependency of biotic and abiotic factors of the environment.*
4. *Explain the following terms and concepts:*
   (*a*) *Biogeochemical cycle.*
   (*b*) *Biological clock.*
   (*c*) *Synecology.*
5. *Describe the ecological production and productivity. Explain and illustrate procedure of food chain and food webs.*
6. *Explain the following terms:*
   (*a*) *Solar Energy Flow.*
   (*b*) *Carbon Cycle.*
   (*c*) *Oxygen Cycle.*
7. *Write a note on the factors affecting food chains and food webs and quality of food.*
8. *Describe the role of education in maintaining the natural process of food chain with special reference to formal and informal agencies of education.*

18

Explosion of Human Population: The Ecological Aspects

Twentieth century witnessed two explosions—(1) The knowledge Explosion, and (2) The Population Explosion. On account of the first explosion scientific, technological and industrial achievements have reach a height and it seems that nothing is beyond human reached but the second explosion is a controversial topic. There are people who have strong feelings about the right to have children and consider that any interference with natural birth rate in immoral. On the other side, some people maintain that continued birth rates are crime that will lead to starvation and endless misery for millions, therefore, there is a need and accordingly hereunder will consider ecological aspect of population explosion briefly.

The *explosion of human population* has created several types of problems. At present, serious problem of *environmental pollution* which is also generated by the explosion of human population. The happiness of human society basically depends on the quality of environment. There is an urgent need of *environmental management*.

It is essential to understand the terms used for studying *human population*. Therefore some important terms have been explained in the following paragraphs.

1. *Demography:* is the description and statistical analysis of the vital process and movements of human population.
2. *Birth Rate:* Number of live births per year per 1,000 of the population.
3. *Death Rate:* Number of deaths per year per 1,000 of the population.
4. *Infant Mortality Rate:* Number of deaths of children below one year of age per 1,000 of the population.

5. *Life Expectancy:* The average age at which people die. It is important to realize, however, that it is not the age at which most people die.
6. *Natural Increase.* Excess of births over deaths per 1,000 of population.
7. *Fertility:* is the actual reproductive performance of given human population? Fertility being dependent upon ecological and social factors, have varied greatly.

Human Birth Rate (natality) is the fertility expressed as the average number of live births per thousand population per year. Since not all age groups in a population have equal fertility, demographers often use more specialised measures of birth rate that relate to age groups.

Human Mortality Rate is the average number of individuals who die per thousand population per year. Again, demographers often use more sensitive measures, for different mortality rates. Both the very young and the very old segments of the population have higher mortality rates.

Human population shows uneven or clumping pattern of distribution on earth. The *density* of human population in a village, district, city, province, country or any area can be obtained by dividing the total number of persons living in the given region by the total land area of that region. The average number of people per square km unit of land area tells us how dense or sparse is the population in a given area.

The information secured from the study of human populations is known as *vital statistics.* These have many applications in our modern society. Some general findings resulting from an analysis of vital statistics are as follows:

1. Birth rates are higher in rural areas and among farming people than in cities. Furthermore, the larger the city, the lower the births rate.
2. Within a given region, such as city or a farming area, the lower economic classes have the higher birth rates.
3. More males than females are born.
4. Social and economic factors which produce low birth rates also produce low mortality rates. Mortality rates are lower in times of depression, in higher economic groups and in city dwellers.

5. Women have lower mortality rates than men.
6. Both married men and married women live longer than single persons.

China has the largest population in the world. Most densely populated country is South Korea. India is second largest population in the world. The highest density of South Korea is 345 persons per square kilometre and India's density is 182 persons per square kilometre.

ECOLOGY THROUGH AGES IN POPULATION GROWTH

Human population increased gradually in size from the time of primitive man until about the mid 1800's. Since then human population have increased rapidly. Population increase has been associated with major shifts in *man's relation to his environment*. The ecology of man and trend of growth of human population can be studied at the following three levels:

1. Ecology of Primitive Man

During man's evolutionary history, the size and functioning of human brain has developed considerably. When growth of brain size stabilised at an average of some 15 hundred cubic centimetres and constituted the modern species, the homo spacies.

Ecologically, man's primitive position in natural communities was that of particularly large, vicious land, animal with an unusually wide range of food.

For a hundred thousand generations, our ancestors lived in small, isolated, nomadic groups as hunters and food-gatherers, spacing themselves, according to the availability of wild food. Man was primary consumer or *herbivorous* and secondary consumer or *carnivorous* or both, *i.e.*, omnivorous. It does not mean that man could eat everything. Man took any kind of animal food and any kind of plant food especially fruits, seeds and tubers or starchy roots.

In fact, as long as man remained in this stage of cultural development, he was just another member of the *complex food web* of the community and populations soon reached some maximal population levels in balance with the rest of the community. All his energy requirements were furnished by plants or animals that are "*renewed*" each year by biological growth. Even when primitive man began to use fire, his fuel was wood from trees that were renewed.

2. Ecology of Agricultural Man

Agricultural man further shifted the balance of nature in the original biotic communities by killing any wild herbivores that fed on his cultivated plants and killing carnivores that preyed on him and his domestic animals.

During this agricultural revolution, a sedentary way of life evolved, which allowed the construction of permanent dwellings in which man could seek shelter from the weather. As life became safer and the food supply more stable, a large number of babies survived.

Around 8,000 B.C. the world population is estimated to be about 5 million. By the time Egypt became well established as an ancient civilisation the world population probably reached the 100 million level. By 1650 A.D., human population had climbed to 453 million. The average rate of increase during this period was about 50,000 per year.

3. Ecology of Industrial Man

As human population continued to increase, man continued to modify his environment in such a way as to permit even greater population size. With the invention of the wheel, transportation devices were developed and utilised for moving food from place to place, thus allowing for larger concentration of people in a given place. The so-called *industrial revolution* saw the development of tools and machines that resulted in the construction of more and better housing, the production of more and better food items and textiles, and the development of food storage, preservation and transportation techniques and techniques permitted medical science to greatly reduce mortality rates and the agricultural sciences to produce more and better food from cultivated plants and domestic animals.

During this period human population has increased at a rate than has become alarming to many people. By 1830, the population had reached one billion; by 1930, two billion; and by 1961, three billion. Between 1650 and 1830, the rate of increase was just over three million per year; between 1830 and 1930, about ten million per year; and between 1930 and 1961, about 30 million per year. Now it is about 6 billion.

If current birth rates and death rates are maintained, human population will reach more than ten billion by 2,025 A.D. It is estimated that a human population of only 1 billion people is the maximum supportable at U.S. levels of affluence by present agricultural and industrial resources. The much larger population now occurring are possible only because over 80 per cent of the world population is living well below these levels.

These under-privilege people seek a larger share of the world's resources and a rise in their standard of living. The option is either ruthless suppression which is unthinkable or accommodation which is applied by present Governments in the form of family planning measures.

ECOLOGY OF HUMAN NEEDS AND PROBLEMS

Man surpass animals in being able to control his environment in some degree, by (1) food production (*agriculture*) and food storage (*warehouses, canning refrigeration*) against seasonal shortage and deterioration; (2) shift in energy utilisation from solar energy→wood fire→fossil fuels→electrical and atomic energy to increase human efficiency; (3) improved shelter for adults and offspring's against unfavourable weather and against enemies (*housing, flood protection, police protection, national defense*); (4) destruction of animal enemies (lions, tigers, wolves, snakes, rats and mice, household insects); (5) reducing competition from other animals (*fencing crops and livestock*); and (6) control of diseases that attack human beings (*sanitation, immunisation*).

However, human beings are reduced in numbers by following agencies:

(1) *Food Shortage or Famines* due to crop failure as from unfavourable weather, especially in densely populated lands such as China and India where food reserves are scant or unequally distributed. Malnutrition may lead to physical impairment with greater susceptibility to disease and death. (2) *Inadequate shelter,* especially during cold or winter outside the tropics is an important mortality factor. (3) *Calamities in nature,* like floods, droughts, hurricanes, volcanic eruptions, earthquakes, etc., claim great toll

of human population. (4) *Enemies,* large predatory animals like lion, tiger and poisonous snakes, cause many deaths in less civilised regions. (5) *Wars.* Warfare is a form of competition between human races or nations for land, natural resources, trade routes, or other desired features of human environment. Wars have remained a major mortality factor throughout human history, not only by causing direct battle casualities, but also by stimulating disease and famine. (6) *Disease* is the largest single factor in reducing pollutions. Diseases like bubonic plague, cholera, typhus, small pox, malaria, yellow fever, sleeping sickness, etc., have been among the great killers of man throughout history. (7) *Explosions,* fire, popullion, shipwrecks and transportation accidents cause many death in modern civilisations.

There are two types of problems related to human population—*over populated* countries like China and India and *under populated* countries like Canada, Denmark, Australia and European countries. These have different types of problems related to human population.

PROBLEMS OF POPULATION EXPLOSION

The growing pressure of population on resources base, especially on arable land, has created many socio-economic, cultural, ecological and environmental problems. The population problems vary in space and time and differ from region to region. These problems may be more systematically examined as follows:

(*a*) *Problems of Developing Countries:* Most of the world population lives in the developing countries. China and India support about 20 per cent and 16 per cent of the total world population respectively. Taking together the developing countries have over three fourth of the total world population. The level of technological development in these countries is, however, low which is affecting the agricultural efficiency and coming in the way of industrial development, despite the availability of local resources.

(*b*) *Problems of Developed Countries:* The developed countries are highly industrialized and urbanized, in which the per capital income is not only high, but most of the population is dependent either on secondary or tertiary sector. These countries, despite high degree of development, efficient agriculture and large-scale industrial production, are also confronted with many of the population problems. Problems of *rapid growth of population,* unemployment, inadequacy of housing and health, under-utilisation of resources and slow growth of industries, have been briefly examined in the following paras:

1. *Rapid Growth of Population:* In most of the developing countries, the birth rate is high and the death rate has been checked because of the development and extension of medical facilities. Moreover, family planning in most of these countries is not practised sincerely on a large scale.

This situation has resulted into large proportion of young people who are dependent on relatively small work-force of the population. This large proportion of young population puts great pressure on the available medical, educational and other social amenities.

2. *Unemployment:* In most of the developing countries, the population is largely dependent on agriculture. The secondary (*industries and services*) are relatively less developed. There are very limited opportunities for the semi-skilled, unskilled and highly educated people. The rural areas are the places wherefrom large number of unskilled workers face the problem of unemployment. The educated and skilled technocrats also have very limited opportunities of employment. Consequently, both the educated and uneducated, skilled and unskilled workers try to emigrate to other countries in search of employment. Those who find it difficult, migrate to towns where it is often more difficult to find employment. Moreover, the towns become *overcrowded,* making living conditions poorer, and resulting into socio-economic and *environmental problems.*

3. *Poor Standard of Living and Malnutrition:* There is shortage of nourishment especially that of balanced diet in the developing countries. The standard of living is low and housing conditions are often poor. The standard of hygiene and quality of nutrition are also low, which lead to health problems. The ignorance of people, the inadequacies of medical facilities, and lack of financial resources come in the way of improving the housing and health conditions.

4. *Urbanization:* As town expands, the pressure of transport, water supplies, sewage and refuse disposal grows and creates problems. Smoke and chemical effluents from factories produce

air and water pollution. Traffic congestion and noise are other problems. Tension created by urban life lead to a far higher incidence of mental illness, heart troubles, breathing problems and madness in developed countries than that in under developed ones.

Urban sprawl and slums expansion are the other major problems which create many social and environmental problems. The highly productive agricultural land is encroached by urban houses, roads and industries.

5. *Mismanagement of Agricultural Resources:* By and large, most of the developing and under-developed countries have agrarian economy. The agriculture is mostly done by traditional methods, obsolete equipment and inadequate financial resources. Owing to the lack of funds and finances, the farmers are unable to apply chemical fertilizers and other inputs in required quantities. Consequently, the production per unit area is low.

Fragmentation and small size of holdings and land tenancy systems are also some of the serious barriers in the modernisation of agriculture.

In such countries, land, their ultimate asset, is thus either under-utilised or misutilized. Many of the farmers, being tradition bound, do not accept the innovations and new ideas and their agricultural techniques remain traditional and production much below than their potential.

6. *Slow Growth of Industrial Sector:* In most of the under-developed and developing countries, the industrial sector is generally not very strong. There is lack of local capital which makes the actual exploitation of resources or setting of factories difficult. The work-force, though large in number, is generally unskilled and has no background of industrial development. Similarly, although the large population should provide a good market for the finished goods, the majority of the people are poor and cannot afford to buy the products. The poor industrial base, lack of capital, and poverty of people create a vicious circle and the growth of industries is hampered. The pressure on agricultural resources continuously increases.

7. *Orthodoxy:* As said earlier, the people in the under-developed and developing countries are tradition bound, and less exposed to the outside world. Moreover, they are religious in their attitudes who do not accept new ideas and modern style of life.

Being religious, they do not observe family planning. Birth control is forbidden by the Catholic Church. In India, caste restrictions on occupation also help to slow down transformation of society and process of development. Most of the villagers do not adopt new cropping patterns easily. For the removal of such attitudes and for the eradication of blind faith and orthodoxy, large-scale literacy and education are necessary.

8. *Rural Population:* There are more social amenities like universities, colleges, hospitals, banks and places of recreation in the urban areas. For this reason, the rural youth outmigrate from their villages and start their career in towns and cities. The fewer, especially the old people, live in villages. The agricultural sector suffers adversely because of the non-availability of work-force. The rural areas get depopulated and consequently, less social amenities are provided in the countryside. The standard of living of the villages suffers a decline.

The education improves the standard, children remain for longer period at school and join the work-force later. The labour force expands slowly while industrial and other employment opportunities continue to multiply. Thus, work-force is another problem in rural as well as in urban areas.

POPULATION EXPLOSION IN INDIA

The world population has been increasing at an unprecedented rate since the *Second World War.* There is the fast pace of population growth at international level. Environmental *degradation* and *pollution* are directly related to extraordinary increase in *human population* during the present century. At the beginning of the 20th century, the world population was about 1.5 billion and by the end of the century it was about 6 billion, while India's population at present is more than 101 crores.

The *growth of population* has the great pressure on agriculture for more food and industries for further development, deforestation is going on at a very large scale resulting in soil erosion, change in the world climate and exploitation of natural resources. In developing countries like India domestic sewage and industrial waste are dumped into rivers resulting in contamination of fresh water.

FEATURES OF INDIAN POPULATION

In India *'National Population Education Organisation'* was introduced in 1979 in view of rapid growth of human population. It has analysed the main features and consequences of *population growth* as follows:

1. India is second largest populated country of the world. It has 15 per cent or 1/6th population of the world.
2. A child is born every one and half second.
3. The rate of increase of population per year is 2.28 and it will double upto 2015.
4. The birth rate in India is 37.10 per thousand and death rate is 14.00 per thousand while in England 16, in France 18 and in Germany 17.
5. The average age of male and females is 50 years.
6. The per capita income in India is Rs. 720 per year while in United States of America is 2,679 dollars per year.
7. The 48.13 per cent population of the country is below the poverty line. The rural population is 50.82 per cent and urban population is 38.19 per cent.
8. India has 2.50 per cent land of the world area while it has 15 per cent population of the world.
9. Indian total earning is 1.5 per cent of the world and population is 15 per cent *i.e.* ten times of its proportionate income.
10. Indian literacy has rises from 16.67 per cent to 36.17 per cent in 1981, but total population of illiterates has risen to 48.60 millions.
11. The boys and girls of (10-14) age group studying in schools are 52.90 per cent.

IMPACT OF POPULATION GROWTH IN ENVIRONMENT

Most of the *environmental problems* are caused by *human population growth.* The following are the environmental problems which have been created by population growth. The rate of socio-economic, agricultural and industrial development can not meet the demands of the country because rate of population growth is higher. The following are the major problems which are due to the rapid growth of human population.

1. *Degradation* of the quality of the environment.
2. *Detorirating the quality of food.*
3. Acquiring land for *agriculture and using chemical fertilizers* for high per acre yield. The use of pesticides for protection of crops and seeds.
4. *Urbanization population* and settlement is increasing rapidly. It has caused sewage waste, automobiles, water supply system: air, water, land and noise pollution.
5. *Industrialisation* and *technological development* is essential to meet the needs and requirements of the country. It has also caused air, water, land and noise pollution in the industrial estates.
6. *Poor standard of living* and economic status is lowering down due to the rapid growth of human population.
7. *Lack of educational facilities* for higher learning. The human population is increasing rapidly even in our towns and cities but educational facilities for higher education are not increasing. There is heavy pressure on colleges, technical, medical institutions. This is main cause of student unrest in our country.
8. *Quality of man* is also detoriating due to the rapid growth of human population. The corruption and evils of the society are increasing rapidly. There is devaluation in political, religious, social, cultural spheres of life. Therefore, main stress is being given on moral education in our schools. The human is being polluted physically, socially, psychologically and culturally due to the rapid growth of human population.

Some of our public services such as transport, water and electricity supply, posts and telegraph, health and sanitation are already over stressed resulting in rapid decline in *quality of the services.* If we have to survive and progress as a nation worth the name, the present trend of increase in the human population must be controlled and checked. Therefore, it is the duty of the Government to act and act firmly without any other consideration. The Government of India without further delay must come forward to enact laws to give the movement the required impetus to introduce a common civil code for small family norms or standard.

HOW TO CONTROL POPULATION GROWTH

There is an urgent need for *controlling population growth* to maintain the *quality of environment* as well as *quality of man.* The Government of India has been trying to check the population growth through population policy and giving stress by making provision in each five year plans. High priority was given to the family planning programme in *Ninth Five Year Plan,* but these plans could not yield significant results. It is the hope that education may contribute significantly in controlling human population growth. Thus the following measures can be used effectively for this purpose.

1. *Natural regulation* of population growth.
2. *Plan and Policy* of population of India.
3. *Legal laws* can be formulated for the citizen of the country.
4. *A separate ministry* of family planning.
5. *Role of media* in controlling population growth.
6. *Population of education, i.e.* Role of Education in controlling population growth.

The concept of natural regulation of population growth has already been discussed in the earlier paragraphs. Some steps of plan and policy of population of India have also been given in this chapter. The most important and essential steps that the government has to take in the larger national interest are to introduce a common civil code, enact laws to give incentives for small families and deterrents for flauting the small family norms.

INDIA—THE POPULATION POLICY

There are absolutely no soft options for checking population growth for the developing countries like India. The Government of India does not seem to have the will to take the problem effectively. Confucius had rightly said that unless you give the problem the right name, it cannot be solved. Though the population policy was designed in *First-Five Year Plan of India,* it was realised that the base of population is already very large and the trend of population growth can not be changed easily and quickly.

In the *Second Five Year Plan,* the voluntary sterlization population polity was introduced. The striking growth rate of population compelled the government to adopt a relatively more clear and less flexible policy of population. More emphasis was laid on the family planning programme in *Fourth Five Year Pan.* It was time bound target of reducing the birth rate from 39 per thousand to 23 per thousand by 1979.

In the *Fifth Five Year Plan,* the programme sought to integrate most of the basic social services, including education and public health services with family planning, nutrition of children and nursing mothers. High priority was given to the family planning programme is *Sixth Five Year Plan.* The plan was to integrate health, family welfare and nutrition services at all levels. The birth rate was reduced to 30 per thousand by the end of 1982-83. The *Seventh, Eighth and Ninth Plans* had more pragmatic policy of population. There is more stress now on persuasion, publicity and family and individual well-being.

All these plans and policies could not check the population growth. The population of India is growing at a faster pace and taking the shape of population explosion. It may be attributed to various physiological and socio-economic factors.

POPULATION EDUCATION—THE ONLY WAY

There is rapid growth of population in our country. It is now more than 84 crores. The rapid population growth has created several types of problems which have been enumerated in the above paragraphs. Most of the *environmental problems* are caused by the population growth. This grave problem of the country can be solved by providing population education to the students and common people through formal, non-formal system of education to make them aware and conscious about its serious consequences.

Meaning and Definition of Population Education

In India, it was *Solan Wayland of Columbia University,* who gave concrete shape to the concept of population education. According to him, irrespective of the nomenclature, we are concerned with the fact that the public policy on family planning, nation and family, the desirability of family planning, etc., should be comprehended under the counselling system in formal education. At the same time, studies should be conducted into the economic and social development of education, size of the family, and the dynamism of the qualities of a nuclear family. Hence, it is necessary to develop a special method of education at the school level under the linguistic provisions in a particular society.

Population education refers to the development of a healthy and positive attitude among citizens about the family norms and size. There is dire need to make them aware about its utility and outcomes. The problem is directly related with the standard of living of the people. Knowledge of population education results in the development of the personality of the members of the family in an upright and balanced way and helps establishing nuclear family. *V.K.R.V. Rao* had been of the view that—

> "For economic and social development, there is an urgent need to provide population education in the country. It acquaints people about the realities of life and relieves them from the bondage of the narrow ideology of fatalism."

According to the seminar organised by UNESCO in Bangkok in 1969, "Under population education, we study about the conditions of family, society, nation and the world. It aims at the development of responsible attitude, desirable behaviour and sound reasoning among citizens in general." Another seminar organised by NCERT in (1979) on population education aimed at developing knowledge about "controlling the size of the family, its limitations and economic consequences".

Population education is the awareness of knowledge relating to population. It has three purposes, (1) Educationists and others concerned with them should understand the importance of population, the disadvantages of its nature, (2) Teachers and students should understand the nature of their own tendencies, and (3) Education has to provide the awareness and understanding of human population growth and its consequences so as to develop the feelings and attitude for the betterment of family life. The main purpose of population education is to control the size of the family.

NEED OF POPULATION EDUCATION

It is a natural question to ask why we should have population education. The answer is very obvious. Today, population is increasing at such alarming rate that material resources have completely failed to keep pace with it. There is a complete imbalance between material resources (*food, clothing, housing*) and the size of the population. The existing situation naturally encourages exploitation and misery, thus leading to increasing social injustice.

In order to face and overcome these conditions, educationsits and demographers have come to feel that the problem must be given the form of a revolution in ideas. This implies that the problem of population must be given the form of a revolution in ideas. This implies that the problem of population must be integrated with education. In India, the task of educating people about the problems of population is being done by the governmental agency. NCERT, and the informal agencies—*Family Planning Association, All India Federation of Education Association,* etc.

These programmes are directed at—(1) schools, colleges and other educational institutions, (2) those who have left school or have not received any education, (3) those imparting training to teachers, teachers themselves and those who impart education through training, counselling and guidance and the media can be effectively used for providing awareness and understanding of population growth and its consequences along with remedial measures to have a small family size.

OBJECTIVES OF POPULATION EDUCATION

Population education is essential for the reconstruction or restructuring of our modern, rapidly changing society. The NCERT has set up a special wing entitled *Population Education.* It has set out the following objectives of population education:

1. Orientation of the school teachers towards preparing training units on which students will obtain information about the increasing population and the problems created by it and also take interest in finding solution to the problem.
2. Conducting experiments in extra-curricular courses in selected schools, and implementing similar experiments on a larger scale if successful.
3. Preparation of suitable teaching material for population education in schools.
4. Making provisions for research and study concerning

population education in schools and making the programme more effective.

5. Evaluating the productiveness of students covered by the programme and developing the necessary skills.

The above objectives have been formulated to solve the problem of population growth. The objectives may contribute in the following ways to control the rapid population growth of the country.

(*a*) The main purpose of population education should be—control on the size of the family.

(*b*) It helps in raising the standard of living of the family.

(*c*) To create awareness among citizens that increase in the welfare of the society is possible through population education.

(*d*) It increases happiness and progress of the family and thus establishes sound marital relationship.

(*e*) Upbrining of children and care of old can proceed in a better way through population education.

(*f*) It helps in developing a healthy attitude and broad outlook among citizens towards life.

(*g*) Population education would result in the longevity of life of the individual.

(*h*) It helps to foster ideal home relationship in the members of the family.

It is evident from these objectives that in the programme of population education, it is necessary to keep in mind the ecological complex. *According to Duncan, Ecological Complexes* are built up out of changes in the environment, changes in the structure of population measures for fighting the problem of population and the mutuality of factors, and an account of these complexes amounts to population education.

In the same way, *Chauls* has expressed the following opinion on population education. He says that population education should comprehend the culture of the students, the population situation of their society, their own views about the existing situation, their logical, reasoned and organised ideas on the situation of the population and its effects.

The UNESCO workshop defined population education in the following terms—"Population education is our educational programme which provides for a study of the population situation in family, community, nation and world with the purpose of developing in the students rational and responsible attitudes and behaviour towards coping with the situation.

THE COURSE CONTENTS

The above objectives can be achieved by developing the course content and programmes for *population education*. The *Family Planning Association of India* has developed the following *course-content* of population education.

1. Population, Factors and—(*Rates of birth, life and increase*).
2. Human, situation and environment—(*Population, reduction in consumption, production*) and environmental problems.
3. Social, economic and development aspects—Production, national production, health, education, housing, employment, per capita income, economic, social status.
4. Family life and the individual aspect—(*Family and social institutions, education for family life, sex education, position of women*) and concept of small size of family.
5. Fundamental values and qualities of life—Objectives of society, techniques, a consumer's society, utilisation of resources.
6. Measures for controlling population growth to have small family size.

These programmes will be implemented through studies, discourses, regional schemes and research.

At present, the *Population Education* Department has taken the following steps under the aforementioned programme—(1) preparation of context books, *hand-books and publications*, (2) preparation of *teaching material*, (3) *publication* of a monthly magazine, (4) *establishment of libraries and information centres*, (5) issue of *teaching materials* to schools at low prices, and (6) preparation of *kits for population education*.

IMPORTANCE OF POPULATION EDUCATION

Population education emphasises the importance of nutritious and balanced diet among citizens and thus helps to develop good habits with regard to the rules of health and hygiene. It results in proper economic and social development of the individual. The study of social studies is of immense help in this matter. In rural areas, through the display of audio-visual material, its advantages can be properly demonstrated to the general public. There is an urgent need to incorporate population education as a subject in the training programmes of both *primary* and *secondary* teachers, so that through teaching they would be able to create an awareness among children with regard to the harm caused by tremendous *population growth* and the advantages of small family.

This would go a long way in developing proper awareness and attitudes among them. Ministry of health with its peraphernalia can render much help in this stupendous task of reconstruction. A cell of population education had also been set up in NCERT to prepare guidelines and useful materials in this respect. Similar, cells can also be created at the state level. This would help provide proper motivation and desirable attitude and behaviour towards population problem among citizens of India.

Population education programmes and its awareness of youths and general people may be helpful to check the population growth. Ultimately the *quality of environment* can be raised and maintained and the quality of man will also be improved.

HOW TO MAKE POPULATION EDUCATION EFFECTIVE

Today, the crowds in universities are growing larger, colleges lack even an inch of spare space. Our population annually increases by 13 millions, which is equal to the entire population of an Australia. In the next twenty-five years, our population will double itself. In order to solve the problem of the future, we should adopt the following programmes—

1. Departments of education should make arrangements for *in-service taining, research* and *programme* implementation of population education programmes.
2. Various departments of universities should conduct research and prepare desirable literature on population education.
3. Departments of science should conduct factual experiments into the evil consequences of rise in population.
4. Various programmes of population education should be

implemented through seminars, conferences, workshop exhibitions, etc.

5. Population education course-content should be introduced from primary to university levels.
6. The print and non-print media can be made more effective for educating masses about population growth and its consequences.

The following programmes may also be introduced to accelerate the process of population education.

(*a*) *Introduction and Sensitivity of Groups (Village/City)*

1. The objectives outlined above will be achieved with the help of the ministries of education and health and other ministries, administrators, educationists, principals and teachers.
2. Arrangements will be made for discourses, contact with the people, publication, guidance cells, training syllabi, etc.

(*b*) *Introduction of Future Schemes*: (Syllabi, extra-curricular activities, etc., in village/city)

1. This programme will be implemented through the medium of schools, colleges, social education classes, adult education classes and classes for the employed.
2. For this purpose, arrangements for reading class units, context books, hand-books, audio-visual material, information centres and library facilities will be made.

(*c*) *Active Research and Study*

1. Studies into marriages in villages and cities, sex, family life, population problem, awareness of the population problem and the attitudes towards it.
2. A survey of guardians of school-going children for an understanding of begetting of children, sex, family life, population awareness and study of problem.
3. A study of the knowledge of teachers with a view to introducing population awareness, marriage, family life, sex relations, begetting of progeny etc., into the syllabus.
4. A study of the leaders of education in the contexts outlined above.

5. Active research into teaching methods and techniques, pertaining to sex, family planning, population education, problems, etc.

For all these programmes, close contacts will be established with educational research institutions, teachers' training institutions, social welfare institutions and voluntary agencies so as to impart speed to these programmes.

Learning Exercises

1. Give a brief account of *human population* from primitive man to industrial man.

QUESTIONS FOR ANSWER

1. *Discuss in brief the growth of human population through ages.*
2. *Write a note on the ecology of human needs and problems.*
3. *Discuss various problems created by population explosion.*
4. *Write a note on population explosion in India and India's population policy.*
5. *Discuss the impact of population growth on environment.*
6. *Define the term 'Population Education' and write a note on its need in India.*
7. *Write a note on the course contents and objectives of population edication.*
8. *Write your views on 'How to make population education more effective'.*

19

Educational Environment: The School

The aims and objectives of environmental education can best be realised through formal and informal system of education, which is the prime responsibility of the society as it establishes schools for the purpose. The quality of education depends upon the quality of educational environment as well as social ecology and family situations.

INTRODUCTION

A child's family is the primary environment from which he gets primary needs, drives, raw for growth and development. The home environment is created by parents. The mother is equivalent to hundred teachers, if she is able to provide a conducive environment for brining desirable modification and change in his/her behaviour. The social behaviour, conduct and attitudes of a child indicate the impact of his home environment.

Even before a child enters school, he benefits from parents, family, peers and society contribute a lot for creating educational environment by their appreciation, encouraging, approval and showing positive attitudes, sympathy and empathy towards children. Educational environment minimises the psychological inhibition and complexes of these children. Thus the child may learn formally and informally many things without hesitation through congenial educational environment.

By enriching the educational environment with broad base and special curriculum, methods of teaching, co-curricular activities, teaching aids, library, laboratory, effective teachers and the dynamic administrators can maximise the potential of children.

Child development requires an environment which may be confluence of physical and social environment. Such confluence of natural and human managed environment may be designed so as a child may get maximum possible freedom to learn or to develop. The social-emotional climate is the important component of the educational environment of a school or college. The most significant contribution of human being is to develop education system.

Education is powerful instrument for social change as well as social control. Man has significant impact on the environment. Human activities have created various types of problems which have been discussed in the chapter of *'Human Ecology'*. These environmental problems may be solved by designing appropriate educational programmes.

AREAS OF EDUCATIONAL ENVIRONMENT

Educational environment is broad and wide concept which is related to total educational organisation, ranges from primary to university education, formal and informal education system, conventional and distance education. There are several types and areas of educational environment. It is difficult to cover or describe all types of educational environment. The educational environment refers organizational set up which creates its own organizational climate.

Each educational institution has its own unique type organizational climate. Therefore, in this chapter the concept of organizational climate, organizational health, classroom climate have been discussed in general not in specific area which seems relevant to the title of the book.

SOCIAL ECOLOGY AND ORGANIZATIONAL CLIMATE

The movement to make effort to improve the quality of man, has created strong concern for upgrading the quality of social environment. It has introduced the new concept of *'social ecology'*. Social ecology is defined as the *'interdisciplinary approach to study the influence of man on physical and social environment.'*

The concept of *'personality'* has no meaning without the social environment. Scientific studies of environments are used for accelerating the human efficiency. These assumptions have evolved the concept of *'organizational climate'*, and have drawn the attention of behaviour scientists. It is an important aspect of social environment, environmental management and organisation.

DEFINITION OF ORGANIZATIONAL CLIMATE

The educational environment refers to the concept of *'organizational* climate'. Several terms are used such as—Social interaction, institutional climate, social-emotional climate, organisational atmosphere, interpersonal relationship, psycho-social environment, cultural environment. Thus, social scientists have used various terms in different contexts with different meanings. It is difficult to define the concept of organizational climate.

"The organizational climate is reinforcing force for shaping the behaviour of children in which they act or perform learning tasks."

—*B.S. Bloom (1968)*

"The organizational climate is a result of the interpersonal behaviour, attitudes, perception and values of the individuals who are working in the organization."

—*C.G. Miskel (1977)*

"The interpersonal climate includes openness of communication or freedom of expression and confidence among teachers and administrator".

—*C.G. Miskel (1979)*

"Organisational climate is the institutional climate" characterised by the teacher-taught, teachers-administrator and students-administrator interactions, their feelings, attitudes, behaviour, values and approaches, their actions and reactions.

The term *'organizational climate'* refers to *'organizational morale'*, *'organizational rapport'*, social-emotional climate, and psycho-social environment. It is generalized attitudes towards various practices and components of educational institution life which the students, teachers and administrators working with organisation sharing with each other in spite of their individual variations.

The attitudes and expectations of teachers and administrator influence their organizational behaviour creating social climate which is fairly stable and establishes the norms and standard of an institution. Thus climate indicates the norms and values of the form system of an organization.

MAIN CHARACTERISTICS OF ORGANIZATIONAL CLIMATE

Following are the characteristics of organizational climate for proper educational environment.

1. It is a reinforcing force for shaping the behaviours of the children.
2. It includes interaction, openness and freedom of expression among teachers and students.
3. It also refers to organizational health or quality of an institution.
4. It is a result of interpersonal relationships, attitudes, feelings, perception and value of the individuals working in the organization.
5. It is an organizational morale, rapport, and psycho-social climate of an institution.
6. It mainly concerns with social-emotional climate of an institution and classroom teaching.
7. It depends on the expectations and attitudes of teachers and administrator.
8. It is a generalized attitude towards various practices and aspects of an institution.
9. It indicates the norms and values of the system; standard of an institution.
10. It refers the personality of its own which varies from organization to organization.
11. It is formed by the behaviours, attitudes and expectations of teachers and the principal.
12. It is highly individualized, each organization develops its own culture or climate with its own locality. It possesses cultural heritage, feelings and beliefs.
13. Its quality depends on the conscious and unconscious efforts and interpersonal relationship of the workers.
14. It provides the basis or frame of reference for interpreting and assessing the efficiency of the functioning of an institution.

The social scientists have used different methods and components for characterizing organizational climate. *R. Mors* has also enumerated five features:

1. Physical or ecological components,
2. Psychological aspects,
3. Behavioural surroundings and factors,
4. Components of organizational structure, and
5. Personal and behavioural situations of the workers.

A.W. Halpin and C.W. Crofs (1963) have identified eight dimensions of the organizational climate in context of educational organisation, *e.g.*, behaviours of principal and teachers

(*a*) *Principal's Behaviour*—(A_1)—Production, (A_2)—Emphasis, (A_3)—Thrust and (A_4)—Consideration.
(*b*) *Teacher's Behaviour*—(B_1)—Disengagement, (B_2)—Hinderance, (B_3)—Esprit and (B_4)—Intimacy.

Organizational behaviour is the central reference point in the approach of *Halpin* to understand its nature. It also indicates the 'Intellectual climate', achievement standards, supportiveness, orderliness, practicalness and impulse control. These characteristics may be classified into two categories—developmental behaviours and controlled behaviours.

DETERMINANTS OR DIMENSIONS OF EDUCATIONAL CLIMATE

The most important characteristics of *organizational climate* is that it is highly individualised concept. The climate of organizations varies from institution to institution. This variation can be identified or studied with the help of factors or determinants of organizational climate. The effectiveness of an organization can be assessed in terms of realization of its objectives or social environment. There are certain factors which operate as determinants of organizational climates and that they vary in their impacts and cause of variations in their environments. A number of such external and internal factors; *developmental and controlling* factors have been identified which have been enumerated as follows:

1. Organization size and structure.
2. Organization policies and legal issues.

3. Leadership or personality of administrator.
4. Economic or financial conditions.
5. Attitudes and values of the workers.
6. Aptitude and vocational interest of the workers.
7. The norms and standard of the organization.
8. Availability—physical and social conditions.

These are the determinants of *organizational climate* which differentiate the nature and aspects of the environment. *Determinants* are the causes while dimensions are the components of organizational climate. The social climate of the organisation is the result of the relationship of factors that affect it. The classroom is the unit of organization.

A good socio-emotional climate of the classroom is an important variable for school learning. The classroom climate is assessed in terms of teacher-taught interaction, pupils attitude and achievement as studied by Ned A. Flanders.

ORGANIZATIONAL HEALTH

The organizational climate concerns with the quality of an institute in terms of norms, standing of pupils performance; attitudes and expectations of teachers and principal. These factors form health of the organization. The working efficiency and standard of an organization is based on its physical and psychological health. It is a new concept for understanding and assessing the efficiency of the organization climate.

The *organizational health* refers to the efficiency of an organization. There are three main indicators for assessing it.

1. Realize the objectives of the organization,
2. Maintain the interpersonal relationship among its pupils, teachers and principal, and
3. Adaptation of people to its environment.

The efforts are made by the principals in their organizations to ensure about these indicators through various measures. A healthy organization not only survives in its environment but continues over long period for maintaining its standard.

The *organizational health,* but eduational environment should cope with changes and to adopt the social future demands. The following are the specific indicators for assessing quality of *organizational* health of an institution:

1. Goals and objectives of the organization.
2. Level of morale of the workers.
3. Adequacy of commercial system of the organization required for the working of the people.
4. Proper use of technology and equipment.
5. Problem-solving abilities among teachers and principal.
6. Level of aspiration and expectations of teachers and principal.
7. Freedom of expression and working for the people.
8. Facilities of educational and vocational guidance services.
9. Achievement and attitudes of the students.
10. Adaptation to changing environment and future needs.

DIMENSIONS OF DEVELOPMENT OF ORGANIZATIONAL CLIMATE

The education has to face with and meet the requirements of the society. The social system is very dynamic. Development of *organizational climate* is a response to change the beliefs, attitudes, values and structure of organization so that they can better adapt new technologies, challenges and complex educational strategies.

The concept of development is associated with total system planned change efforts. The planned change is concerned with the following dimensions of the organizational climate:

1. *The goals and objectives:* There is rapid change in society and have varied demands of the nation which are to be met by our educational system.

2. *The attitudes and values system:* There is also change in our values. The economic and political values have important place in our society.

3. *Introduction of systems approach:* There is an urgent need to employ systems approach for inducing any change in our education system as well as organizational climate of any institution.

4. *Orientation programmes and refresher courses:* (For teachers and principals.) They should be aware about change and about the new approaches, methods and devices so that they may adopt to the new changes.

5. *Use of proper communication strategies:* The openness and freedom of expression and communication will bring desirable

change in their attitudes, values, feelings of people or workers. The development requires to improve the quality of teachers and principals.

6. *Scientific attitude towards the problems of organizational climate:* The real problems and their causes should be identified. The pressing problems should be given priority and efforts should be made to solve them scientifically.

7. *Involvement and expectations of teachers and principal*: The teachers and principal should have high level of aspirations and expectation about the quality of their products. It will provide an insight and practical ways and means to improve the organizational climate.

Thus, *organizational climate* development and improvement may be a process for accelerating and increasing the self-renewal capacity and resources of an organization. In order to introduce the above programmes and objectives, we have to employ various types of strategies. The organizational development is *multi-dimensional* such as—

(*a*) *Physical dimension* requires sanitation of surroundings, plantation, development lawns, playground facilities, prevention from air and noise pollution, drinking water purity, etc. The building conditions, classroom should be airy and light. The furniture and seating requirement should be well maintained.

(*b*) *Social dimension* is related to the interpersonal relationship among students, teachers with principal should be congenial. The teachers and principal should have high moral and religious values rather economic and political values. The principal should be democratic in his behaviour.

(*c*) *Psychological dimension* includes the level of aspirations, expectations and involvement of teachers and principal in organizational functioning. Such behaviours of teachers and principal will reinforce the students in their studies.

(*d*) *Educational dimension* is related to curricular and co-curricular activities of the organization. The courses should be properly completed by teachers before the final examination. There should be monthly tests in courses to make the students study regularly. The new courses, vocational and technical courses should be introduced. There should be adequate facilities of library, reading room, laboratory and field work.

The co-curricular programmes should be well organized, such as, assembly debates, discussion, seminar, cultural programmes, educational excursion, sports and games. The teachers should be encouraged to participate in the workshops, seminars and upgrade their qualification through inservice programmes—distance education, correspondence education.

FACTORS INFLUENCING ORGANIZATIONAL CLIMATE

Some important factors influencing organizational climate of the school or institution are given hereunder:

1. *Population Explosion:* There is a rapid increase in the human population but expansion of education facilities is very slow. There is heavy pressure of population on our educational facilities. The students and their parents want to get the admission anyhow for their wards which has spoiled the tone of the organization in general.
2. *Urbanization:* The rural youth is migrating into cities and towns due to facilities of medical, transportation and education. The educational institutions which were situated out of the locality, now are in the heart of cities due to urbanization. The physical and social environments are highly polluted of the surroundings which has influenced *organization climate* and health of the educational institutions.
3. *Industrialization:* The industries and factories are also increasing in cities and towns. There are industrial estates in big cities which have polluted the physical environment of cities and the organization climate of educational institutions.
4. *Development of Transportation and Automobiles:* The big cities have created the demand of transportation facilities, as a result automobiles are used. The educational institutions are generally situated on main routes which have the heavy traffic. It creates smoke, dust and noise thus, air and noise pollution influence the climate of the institutions. The climate is not conducive for teaching and learning.
5. *Social Functions and Election Campaign:* Similarly social functions and election campaign use loud speakers which disturb the teaching learning situation which creates the noise pollution in the climate of the institution.

6. *Students Unrest and Agitation:* The educational institutions are considered temple of learning but now these are used for emerging leadership. There are students unrest and agitation in these institutions which have influenced the social climate of the institutions.

7. *Teachers Alienation:* The teachers are alienated from their duties and functioning of their institutions, whatever is the reason for their alienation. The classroom teaching and social-emotional climate are generated by the teachers which is most important component of organizational climate. An alienated teacher can not create conducive teaching-learning situation in his classroom.

8. *Personality and Leadership Quality of a Principal:* The most important and crucial factor which is the determinant of organization climate and health is the personality and leadership qualities of an administrator. Physical and social structure of an organization remain the same but change of the principal, head, and vice-chancellor influence the climate of the institution. The research studies related to organizational climate revealed this fact that leadership qualities, democratic attitude, values, problem-solving abilities, the way of dealing with teachers, parents and students influence the social-emotional climate.

The organizational climate and health is the dynamic concept which mainly depends on the leadership qualities of a head of the institution. Thus studies of organizational climate are the case studies and difficult to generalize.

Secondly organizational development also depends on the planning and foresight of the principal. The functions of an administrator are organization, execution, supervision and planning. The level of these functions evolve the climate of the institution. Thus leadership qualities are highly related to organizational development and its climate.

9. *Educational Policies:* The educational policies have curtailed the autonomy of the institutions in appointing teachers, payment salaries, admission procedure. Reservation policy for admission have also influenced organizational climate adversely. There should be provision for *equalisations of educational opportunities'.* Moreover we talk about national system of education but education is concern of state.

10. *Teachers Involvement in Politics:* Teachers are involved in politics and take part activily in their party, so they exploit students

and also create political environment rather than conducive to teaching-learning. Thus the teachers attitudes and beliefs play a significant role in the organisational climate.

11. *Students Unions and Teachers Associations:* The organizational climate of educational institutions is influenced by students unions and teachers associations bécause their main job is to oppose administrator/principal who is supposed to provide leadership to an organization but students and teachers dictate the principal. Thus, social climate and functioning of an organization are governed by students and teachers. In this way principals have no freedom to administer and execute their programmes which may improve the climate.

EVALUATION OR ASSESSMENT OF ORGANIZATIONAL CLIMATE

The organizational climate may influence the attitude, achievements, values and other aspects of students personality. These are the criteria for an effective organizational climate. The leadership qualities of head of the institution are responsible for the quality of organizational climate. It also contributes for high or low morale of teachers.

The pioneer work of *Halpin and Crofs* is the field organizational climate assessment. They have defined climate of an organization with reference to teachers and principals behaviours. Organizational behaviour is the basis for assessing the effectiveness. They have developed a tool—*Organizational Climate Description Questionnaire* (OCDQ) to measure the eight dimensions and types of climate:

1. Intimacy,
2. Aloofness,
3. Production,
4. Disengagement,
5. Hindrance,
6. Esprit,
7. Thrust, and
8. Consideration.

Halpin, George Stern and *Carl Steinhoff* worked independently to measure it and they have used different approaches to measure organization climate. The schools and colleges are distinctly dissimilar in many ways, the kinds of students they attract, the values and goals of students, types of courses and faculties, etc. It is also termed as college characteristic index and high characteristic index. Faculty has *Press Scales and Department Press Scales. Chattopadhyaya* and his associates have constructed an *Organizational Environment Questionnaire.* U.P. Singh has developed *'A Human Relations Inventory'* for measuring movement from one's own position towards norms.

The classroom social and emotional climate is the important aspect of organizational climate. *Ned A. Flanders* developed an observational technique, for measuring social-emotional climate of classroom teaching later on it was discovered that it measures the *'Verbal Interaction'* of classroom teaching. A large number of studies have been designed and conducted in India by using *Flanders Interaction Analysis Technique* in classroom teaching. *Withal* developed a tool for *Non-verbal Interaction Analysis Technique;* Non-verbal interaction contributes significantly for creating social-emotional climate in classroom.

The review of literature on the measurement of organizational climate reveals that various approaches, methods and tools have been developed in this context. The following aspects have been considered to measure the organizational climate of an institution:

1. Leadership Qualities of head of institution which also include level of aspiration and his expectations.
2. Teachers morale, attitudes, values and their aspiration and expectations about their students.
3. Students attitudes and achievement in their study subjects or performances.
4. Classroom climate or social-emotional climate which includes verbal and non-verbal interaction. The quality of content or content analysis of classroom teaching.

The organizational climate is considered as a factor of the organizational health of an institution. It may be used as an index of the organizational health. Under organizational development, efforts are made to improve the health of an organization.

QUESTIONS FOR ANSWER

1. *Describe the meaning, need and area of educational environment. Differentiate it from environmental education.*
2. *Define and explain the term 'organizational climate'. Enumerate the characteristics and dimensions of organizational climate.*
3. *Explain the term 'organizational health' and procedure of development. Differentiate it from organizational climate.*

20

Educational Environment: The Teacher and Classroom

This is a basic fact that quality of the teacher and his dedication to his job and pupil as well as the class atmosphere are the basic determinate of the educational environment of the school, therefore, hereunder we will discuss this aspect and its various points, very briefly:

TEACHER

The status of the teacher in the system of education is of pivotal nature, therefore, his quality, devotion and dedication to his job and upliftment of his pupil makes him ideal for his pupil. Hereunder, we will discuss some of the basic aspects concerning teacher's role in the educational environment of the school.

TEACHER—THE CLASSROOM LEADER

Some pattern of leadership is bound to emerge, either organized around you or organized without respect to you. You will also have to exert some leadership either through one approach or through another. Finally, there is the real obligation to help the pupils develop greater skill as leaders.

Emergent Leader

As the power structure begins to develop within a group, one person will seem to acquire more than his share of influence. He may exert this influence by contributing ideas and information, by providing a friendly atmosphere, by making decisions, or by verbalizing decisions toward which the group is moving, or by sheer labour. At times the group may elect such a person to some office, or higher authority may appoint him to position of official influence. But even if neither of these things occur, the person is clearly exercising leadership. Such a person is called an *emergent leader.*

The *emergent leader* is likely to have a general feeling of security. In a minor emergency, for instance, while most of us stand around wondering what to do, the potential leader is likely to move confidently and unhesitatingly toward some proposed solution. More often the proposed solution is reasonably effective.

The teacher of course, is neither an emergent nor an elected leader but some one who is appointed. It is not necessary that appointed leader is able to demonstrate his ability to exert influence, but the teacher is assigned this responsibility to perform in his class. He is also considered the ideal for his students. Usually the students try to imitate the behaviours of his teacher.

CLASS STRUCTURE—THE TEACHER'S PLACE

The place of a teacher in the structure of the class is most important. The climate of the classroom safely depends on the behaviour of teacher in the classroom. The social and emotional climate of the classroom is generated by teacher behaviour.

1. The teacher's age, size and legal status would point to him as a key figure in the power structure. Very often he does the talking. Pupils, when they speak, typically address their remarks to the teacher. When they do speak to each other, their eyes are often on the teacher. Many people, impressed by the talk about democratic practices, are somewhat surprised by the marked concentration of influence in the person of the teacher. But some degree of concentration seems inevitable and desirable. After all the teacher should have more to contribute and should have a surer sense of the direction the class should be taking.

2. The teacher can never forget his very real legal and moral responsibilities to the adult community. He is legally entrusted by some agency to accomplish a set of fairly definite objectives. He is also given enough authority to permit him to carry out his assignment. He can delegate much of his authority if he so chooses. But he cannot actually relinquish either the authority or the responsibility.

3. The responsible role assigned to the teacher by law and by social expectation fits in with the influential role that many teachers automatically adopt. This extensive influence, however, is somewhat at odds with the more democratic role which is advocated by many theorists and to which many teachers profess allegiance.

Whenever the teacher's inclinations and the practical circumstances permit, there are some gains to be had from a moderate dispersal of authority. *Glidewell* and his colleagues hold that such diffusion of authority or influence among pupils themselves is associated with greater independence, greater flexibility in thinking processes, less anxiety, and a greater feeling of moral responsibility. Naturally, such a dispersion also involves more direct interaction between pupil and pupil. This is likely to have an effect, one way or the other, on the feelings pupils have for each other.

4. The teacher can get better results by decentralizing authority, increasing independence of students. The teacher must pay proper attention to the comments and questions of the students. He should encourage students to participate in group discussion in the class and outside the class. Group action is facilitated when teachers use indirect rather direct influence in the classroom teaching.

5. The classroom group organisation may be either *teacher-centred* or *reality-centred*. A teacher-centred classroom is one in which teacher makes the major decision about content, activities and individual's roles to be played. In such classroom-organisation, the teacher is the judge for punishment and reward and is responsible the group.

6. The *reality-centred* classroom is characterised by students' participation in decisions regarding content, actions, methods of teaching. Students set the standard of behaviour and enforce it. The teacher points out and justifies limits. He expects pupils to act within limits.

7. In recent years there has been great emphasis on *reality-centred* classroom where students' active participation in teaching-learning process is encouraged and the teacher acts as a guide to promote learning.

The scientific and objective system of observations have been developed by *Flanders* and others to analyse the interactional procedure in the classroom. The classroom teacher behaviour also includes the students participation in classroom activities.

TEACHER'S ROLE IN THE CLASSROOM

An *effective teacher* employs the knowledge and understanding of educational psychology in organizing his classroom teaching and dealing the problems of the students. But he must understand that his main task is to promote the social learning or group learning. The social learning emphasizes the immitation learning. Therefore his significant role in the class is that he should be the model or ideal for his students.

The teacher must improve and create conducive emotional climate and cohesion in the class as a group employing techniques developed by research workers in the field. Now spread of education to all sectors of society necessitate the development of researches and interest in group dynamics. It has been incorporated as an integral part of teacher-education programme. It has been further established that central principle of group formation and improvement of classroom climate depends to a great extent when the adolescent boys and girls are taken into confidence and things are decided on democratic principles and decisions are made in consultation with them. The following methods can be used to improve the classroom climate.

Teacher is a model for the students. His behaviour should be impartial, his handling of problems should be psychological. He should provide help to individual students who need it. He should not tame *'pets'* because sometimes pets become the cause of conflicts among the students of the class and the teacher. The whole climate of the classroom as a social group is charged with emotions.

To improve the classroom emotional climate, free discussion should be occasionally arranged for the group. The suggestions should be invited from students to improve upon the existing conditions. It is desirable that racial prejudices, religious beliefs which are prejudicial to a community should not be discussed in the class.

Sometimes lack of proper communication causes disruption in the class. The teacher should help students to understand each other in formal and informal meetings. They must be encouraged to meet each other and the teacher freely. If any misunderstanding is created, it should be immediately clarified. The classroom communication should be a two-way process. Students should not remain passive listeners in the class.

Teacher should encourage the feelings of cohesiveness among the members of the class through effective communication. Though in classes where students of various communities and religions study, it becomes very difficult for the teacher to create cohesiveness.

Recent findings in group dynamics emphasize the role of counselling to disturb pupils in the class. Teacher can also use group counselling to improve the emotional climate of his class.

The teacher can organize educational tours, picnics and excursions to bring the students more close to each other. These activities give an opportunity to understand each other and improve the emotional and social climate of the class as a group.

The teacher should know how adolescents form group and what is the structure of groups or forces in general and other behaviour mechanisms operating in group situation. The teacher with the knowledge of group dynamics at different levels of growth and development of students can improve the social and emotional climate of the class. He can maintain the mental health of isolates of the class.

Theory of *teacher-behaviour* of *D.G. Ryan* indicates that the teacher behaviour is modifiable. *Flanders* interaction analysis measures the social and emotional climate of the classroom. It can also be used for the modification of teacher behaviour in desired direction. *C.P. Hill* technique is used for measuring the classroom content analysis behaviour of the classroom. The techniques are used modifying the classroom behaviour of teachers.

CLASSROOM CLIMATE

Classroom climate is the most important component of organisational climate discussed in the last chapter. Hereunder, we will discuss various aspects of this concepts.

DEFINITION OF CLASS

The class is collection of individuals or students. The class may be regarded largely as an assemblage of individuals, each of whom be taught. It is also a social group, having a structure and an organisation of forces which give it a measure of unity and coherence. The class may have a character of its own. The class has its norms of behaviour or performances. The class has a planned and well organized interaction. It has its own former *leader, i.e.,* teacher. The class as such may have a marked influence on its members.

The group has been defined as follow:

"A class is social unit consisting of a number of individuals who stand in role and status of relationship to one another, stabilizing in some degree at the time and process a set of values or norms of their own behaviour, at least, in matters of consequence to the group"

—*Sherif and Sherif*

"A class is an organized system of more individuals who are related to one another so that it performs some functions, it has a standard of role relationship and has a set of norms that regulate the function of the group."

—*McDavid*

The term *'class'* has been defined by distinct social psychologists by emphasizing its different aspects. These definitions emphasize the following characteristics:

1. It is an assemblage of individuals or students.
2. It stands in role and status of relationship to one another.
3. It has its own standard and norms of behaviours or performances.
4. It performs some specific functions.
5. It has its own structure and organisation of forces.
6. It provides motivation and satisfaction of needs of the members.
7. It has its goals and objectives.
8. It provides the awareness of members by the process of interaction.
9. It has a common fate or future. The members are interdependent.
10. It has dynamic process of social and emotional development of the member.
11. It has own leader, may be formal, *i.e.*, teacher, or informal.

A teacher always deals with some actual class of students, he has several opportunities to help the students to develop skills in working with class. Experience in such group work is inevitable.

A teacher can make sure by providing little guidance that the group experience is very useful. The teacher may be able to use a few powerful group forces to accomplish other purposes, such as the desirable attitudes, values or the attainment of social maturity.

CHARACTERISTICS OF CLASSROOM

The class is also a working group. The students assemble on call for a particular purposes or series of purposes. They do not drift together out of sociability or mutual attraction. The classroom group is much more of a business group than is any other group. The activities taken by the class are largely well organised and well planned for achieving specific objectives. The classroom group has the following characteristics:

1. It has the specific objectives and goals.
2. Class is the well organised group.
3. It is formal group well planned and well maintained.
4. The teacher is the leader of the class.
5. The class has its own structure.
6. It has the motivational base or level of aspiration.
7. It has the common purpose or goal of the students in a class.
8. Its process is the interaction between teacher and students in the classroom, which creates social emotional climate.
9. Its basic nature is developmental.
10. It is formed for about one year duration in general and has its own norms or level of performance.
11. The basic activities of the class are teaching tasks and learning activities, both these activities go side by side.
12. The class has its fixed schedule and programmes.

PROBLEM OF IDENTIFICATION AND INTERACTION IN THE CLASSROOM CLIMATE

The child entering school brings him a host of anxieties, desires, fears and attitudes which he has learned and found rewarding from his parents and family. In this context, the actions of the teacher are likely to influence strongly the subsequent attitudes toward school and teacher. Social-class differences are consistently found, and tend to increase by grade, in factors such as achievement, anxiety about achievement, attitudes toward education and pressures from peers and classmates. These exert direct tough pressures on the role played by the student and subsequent role necessary to the teacher.

As the child matures, his increased contracts exert influence on his values, the amount and direction of such influence depending on the reinforcement system and interaction procedure. By the time the child enters school, he brings with him an elaborate, complex, but efficient series of needs and means of reinforcement.

CLASSROOM CLIMATE

Many people, impressed with the fact that the class is a group rather than a collection of individuals, have stressed the general group climate within the class. Does the teacher permit some diffusion of authority, for instance, or is all the authority tightly concentrated in his hands? Does the group take any part in setting the goals? To what extent can we see group forces in operation?

1. *The Group-Centred Approach:* According to the proponents of the *group-centred approach,* it is not enough that the teacher encourage the group to take as much responsibility as possible in making the major decisions. He must also provide emotional support for the students. He should accept each suggestion seriously, making liberal use of praise and encouragement. He may ask questions to be sure that the suggestion is completely understood or that it really contains what is in the students' mind. And, naturally, the spirit of the group process would be nullified if the teacher had to call attention to his own status or authority, or if he had to act defensively, or to show that a certain suggestion is just what he had been trying to advocate all along.

2. *Effect on Group Relations:* Although there are some exceptions the general trend of the early evidence has suggested improved group relations associated with the *group-centered approach.* There seems to be more group cohesion. It is shown by the fact that pupils readily accept group decision as their own and feel a personal responsibility to carry out the wishes of the group. On the whole, however, the really inscientious use of the group-centered approach may be more useful than only the presentation of subject matter.

3. *Mastery of Subject Matter:* There would be higher achievement

when pupils are working in a happy classroom and are working towards goals of their own choosing rather than conforming to goals imposed from above. It appears that achievement is just about the same in group-*centred and teacher-centred approach.*

4. *The Inconsistency of Climate:* The curriculum can make a difference to the climate. The students are exposed to the new discovery-oriented science courses, for instance report climates which are more democratic, more flexible, less threatening, and which permit more flexibility and diversity.

To use the *group-centred approach* you must be democratic and supportive and tolerant of diversity. This may be true, of course, that each of these qualities is necessary. The teacher who has a strong need for considerable distance may not relish some features of group-centred approach of teaching. He may be more effective, if he uses *teacher-centred approach* of teaching.

Discipline and the Group Process: Teachers talk about the discipline, they refer to problem of maintaining classroom order or the *code and conduct* of the class. It also refers the *'norms'* or standard of the class. The narrowest sense of the word discipline means punishment. The term *'self-discipline'* means to regulate his own behaviour to fit in with his own purposes and the needs of others. In the democratic set up, the teacher should develop the concept of self-discipline among the students. Teacher should assign some tasks which are to be performed by students themselves. The *project-method* is the best way to self-discipline.

Types of Disciplinary Problems of the Class: Teachers make most frequent rapport of some disciplinary problems—lateness, truancy, general disturbances, *i.e.* making noise, disobedience (to comply with teacher directives) and disrespect. These behaviours of the students are natural and frequent in adolescence. Naturally the reports stress behaviour likely to occur in the classroom and are less likely to include such things as smoking, serious fighting, gambling, drinking, or theft. Presumably these things, along with drug abuse, are offences for the corridor, playgrounds or washrooms.

The Dimensions of Problem Behaviour: Obviously there are many kinds of problem behaviour, and psychologists have tried to classify these to see if some can be legitimately grouped together or perhaps placed on a few separate dimensions. First of all, there has been an attempt to set separate dimensions. First of all, there has been an attempt to set separate problems into two broad classes: the personal or psychogenic problems on the one hand, and the conduct or sociogenic problems on the other. Basically, of course, the two types may be closely *intertwined.*

Among the problems in the conduct area, *Philips* (1968) has suggested a number of dimensions. One of these is diffuse hyperactivity and involves restlessness, disorderly behaviour, compulsive talking, and interrupting. It also includes embarrassing things like belching and nose-picking. A second factor is overt derogation of others. This is shown by tattling, overcritical behaviour, jealousy, and expressions of contempt. A third factor in the area of conduct is labelled aggression with independence strivings. It includes impertinence, rudeness, sullenness, defiance, resistance to authority, quarrelling, and fighting.

The *Role of Circumstances:* Disciplinary incidents are more likely to be reported in some situations than in other. Rapports are more likely to come from required courses than from elective courses. Women issue more rapports than men. More problems are reported in classes where there are many failing pupils. There are many more groups than for the middle-class student.

It is difficult to know the causal pattern underlying these relations. Some teachers may be quite free to make rapports, others more reluctant. Female teachers, who give more disciplinary rapports in general, may be especially perturbed by the misbehaviour of boys. Some teachers may expect poorer behaviour from certain minority groups and may then see what they expect to see. Academic failure may lead to misbehaviour. Misbehaviour may lead to poorer performance or to poorer grades assigned as punishment. The same unfortunate background condition may be responsible for both failure and misbehaviour.

Preventive Measures for the Classroom Problems

The following measures should be adopted for preventing classroom problems:

1. Teacher should be of *task-oriented* attitude.
2. He should manifest his *confidence* in the classroom.
3. He should avoid unnecessary ambiguities of teaching content.

4. He should minimise unfavourable conditions of the class.
5. He should reduce the confusion and make clarity.
6. Teacher should feel concern with problems of the students.
7. He should maintain the rapport with every student by having direct contact with the students. Each student should be given due weightage in classroom.

QUESTIONS FOR ANSWER

1. *Write a note on Teachers' place in the class structure and his role in the classroom.*
2. *Define class and write its characteristics.*
3. *Write a note on the problems of identification and interaction in class.*
4. *Discuss various aspects of classroom climate.*

21

Environmental Aspect of Human Growth and Development

INTRODUCTION

Environment and Education have the same functions: growth and development. Environment includes physical, social, cultural and psychological components, similarly the educational process contributes in physical, social, emotional and mental development of child. The environment components contribute jointly in the development of child. The cultural and psychological environments play the significant role in social, emotional and mental development. The physical growth and development relates to physical environment and the heredity of the child.

There are two factors: *heredity* and *environment* which have main influence in growth and development. The growth and development concern with the structure and functions of environmental components when a child is in the process. The mental and physical aspects of a child are related to more heredity and less environment.

The environment has the major role in social, cultural and emotional development. The great philosopher *Rouseau* states that the evils in the child come from society while nature of child is basically pure-free from evils.

NATURE OF DEVELOPMENT

As the number of environmental reinforcers increases, the child identifies himself with models who satisfy his needs. If adults fail to present desirable models then child identifies himself with his peers. The child acquires social, religious, political and economic values from his environment.

The theories of child development, its nature have been studied and explained. The review of these theories indicate the two main aspects—*structural* and *functional* development. Some of these theories have stressed upon the structural changes and others have emphasized the functional changes. Under these the following characteristics have been enumerated.

Piaget has used the term *schemes* or *cognition* terms of five operations—sensorimotor, symbolic, concrete, initiative thoughts and general operations under the process of development.

Havinghurst emphasized tasks in two stages. He has enumerated list of tasks of different stages from walking to develop attitudes, and values towards life.

Freud's theory is known as *psycho-sexual* development. He has explained the function or role of *libido* at different stages. In the process of development he considered, ego, super-ego and id formations.

Erikson's theory is psycho-social theory of child development. He has considered four stages relating four types of development a sense of trust, autonomy, initiative and industry.

The functional theories of child development have educative value. A teacher can plan and organise his teaching activities to develop the operation and can provide situations for performing the tasks at different stages of development by the students. They have emphasised the role of environment in the process of development of the child.

DIMENSIONS OF DEVELOPMENT

In the process of development two interrelated factors are at work: *learning* and *maturation*. Experiences that provide a basis for learning are necessary for normal development. In the training of children it is important to take account of the factor of maturation and to adjust requirements and opportunities for learning to the child's readiness.

The *training* and *learning* are planned processes which are organized by the teacher in school and classroom situations. Therefore, it is essential for him to understand the four dimensions of development and their components or characteristics of a child.

1. Physical and motor development,
2. Emotional development,
3. Social development, and
4. Mental development.

The nature of development has been studied in these four dimensions or characteristics with reference to three stages of development—*Infancy, Childhood* and *Adolescence.* A brief summary of the dimensions and their components has been given:

Structure of Growth and Development

	Dimensions	*Components or Characteristics*
1.	Physical and motor development	Growth of anatomy, body size, height, weight, muscle, teeth, sex-organs, change in voice, face bones, head, body proportion.
2.	Emotional Development	Excitement, fear; affection, pleasure, anger, happiness, jealousy, capacity to suppress the emotion, difficult to control emotion, expression of emotion.
3.	Social development	Like, mother, social responses, sympathy, friendship, competition, aggression, leadership, social behaviour.
4.	Mental development	Memory, reasoning, language development, concept for mature fluency moral concept, creativity, day dream, problem solving, abstract thinking.

PHYSICAL AND MOTOR DEVELOPMENT

Physical and motor development are important both from the point of view of physical well-being and from the point of view of behaviour and adjustment.

Measuring of Physical and Motor Development: The general pattern of growth in stature, weight, and in the dimensions of various parts of the body tends to be similar in different individuals, but there are many individual variations with respect to the age at which growth is most accelerated and the age at which the maximum growth is attained.

The process of development of motor behaviour consists both of the differentiation of individual or separate movement patterns out of previously more generalized and diffuse activities and also the combining of such movements into new systems.

Gains in speed, strength, and precision of movement appear throughout the period of childhood, but the rate of gain is not consistently uniform.

Infancy Stage: During the first year of life a larger proportion of children show predominant use of the left hand than will be the case at later ages. Since the child is moving into a predominantly right-handed world, practical steps that may be taken to encourage right-handedness at an early age may be to his advantage. However, the practical value of being right-handed is not so important as to justify an effort to change children who have a strong disposition to be left-handed.

Stage of Childhood: During childhood years girls are somewhat more *'mature'* than boys of the same chronological age and they show many of the physical changes associated with puberty at an earlier average age. But boys tend to surpass girls in a majority of the motor activities and skills involved in children's outdoor games and athletic contests. The superiority of the boys before the adolescent period seems to be influenced in part by the fact that boys receive more practice.

According to studies of children at the adolescent level, the differences between the sexes in motor performances become so prominent that beyond the junior high school age there are not many conventional athletic activities in which boys and girls can compete on equal terms.

From about the age of eight years there is a falling off in the number of physical activities in which children engage. As children move on toward the adolescent level many of them tend to become more sedentary and to become *spectators* rather than *participants.* This tendency continues through the high school and college levels. A part of the decline in motor occupations occurs by virtue of the encroachment of other interests.

General Characteristics of Physical and Motor Development: Individuals who stand high in mental ability also tend on the average to be somewhat superior in motor abilities, but the correlation between mental and motor abilities, although positive, is so low that superiority in one sphere does not imply superiority in the other. A child who is average or backward mentally may equal or surpass brighter children in many other activities.

An individual may be quite uneven in his motor abilities. It is true that if an individual stands high in one kind of motor performance he is more likely to be competent than incompetent in other skills, but the relationship is so low that an individual's ability in one performance does not provide a reliable index to ability in other performances.

The motor and physical activities in which children engage in connection with their play cover a wide range of occupations at different age levels. However, they tend also to be influenced by prevailing customs and to fall into conventional patterns. At all the age levels from a pre-school period onward the average child has potentialities for mastering a larger number of useful and enjoyable motor skills than have been provided for in the usual educational programme or in his opportunities in every day life.

The motor activities and manual skills that adults adopt as hobbies or leisure time occupations are determined to a large degree by the opportunities that were provided at the elementary or high school level for acquiring such skills. The evidence from many angles suggests that in the education of children we tend to fail to capitalise the potentialities for motor learning that would provide enjoyment and wholesome exercise at the childhood level and that also would be advantageous from the standpoint of health and recreation at the adult level.

EMOTIONAL DEVELOPMENT

Emotion is not heredity characteristic but it is almost environmental *component*. The emotions are acquired from the environment. The term emotion denotes anger, fear, joy, amusement, grief, disgust and other conditions in which an individual is excited. The emotional behaviours are called by definite name.

Meaning of Emotion: Components of emotional experience include feelings, impulses, and physical and physiological relations.

The development of emotional behaviour parallels and is interrelated with other aspects of a child's growth. During the first days of life the infant shows much behaviour that seems to have an emotional tone, but his behaviour seems to be more in the nature of *'general excitement'* than in the nature of patterns that correspond to fear, joy, affection. Moreover, the infant appears to be impervious to many stimuli that eventually will arouse him.

With the passage of time the child's emotional behaviour becomes more clearly differentiated. However, at no time of life is this differentiation so complete that there is any one emotional state that can be defined in terms of symptoms and expressions that are unique and distinct from the expressions that occur in other states. The varieties of emotional behaviour are almost infinite and emotion pervades all thought and action.

Development of Emotions: As he grows in his ability to discriminate and to understand meanings associated with happenings that occur, as he enters into a wider range of social contacts, as he acquires the ability to imagine, to lay plans for the future, and to anticipate the future, and as he gains in competence and familiarity in dealing with everyday happenings in his immediate environment, there is a falling off in some emotional reactions that appeared at an earlier age and in increase in his susceptibility to other circumstances. His emotional susceptibility will be bound to his hopes and aspirations and what he personally has at stake.

Stage of Infancy: With advancing age during late infancy and pre-school and elementary school years, there is a shift from *'Whole hearted'* to more graded or subdued forms of response. In keeping with this change there is a noticeable decline in crying. Overt signs of fear such as flight or clinging to adults tend to diminish. Explosure symptoms of anger give way to more subdued expressions.

He may entertain fears that are not recognised even by those who daily associate with him, and harbor resentments which are difficult for another person to detect and which influence the child's behaviour in ways that are devious and hard for his associates to understand.

Stage of Childhood: An important feature of the child's emotional life is the affection that he receives from others and the development of his own affection for other persons. Children who are rejected, or who feel that they are not wanted and that no one is fond of them, are likely to encounter many problems of adjustment.

On the other hand, a display of anger or the harboring of

resentments frequently merely aggravates, rather than solves a person's difficulties. Likewise, a person may be burdened with fears quite out of proportion to what seems needed to promote caution and prudence.

Development of Emotion: It would be impossible completely to prevent the occurrence of anger, fear, or other forms of emotional distress. However, in everyday life such emotional reactions frequently are aggravated by interference, threats, examples, and various forms of intimidation that could be avoided. In like manner, it has been emphasised that in promoting wholesome satisfactions and pleasures it is important, among other things, to give the child an opportunity to enter into activities that provide an appropriate challenge to his growing abilities.

It is also important to help the child to overcome remediable weakness, to help him by degrees to acquire understanding of his emotions and competence and skill in coping with problems in his environment that cause anger by reason of his inability to solve them, or that cause fear by reason of his actual or imagined inability to deal with circumstances which he regards as a threat to his safety.

AFFECTION—TWO WAY PROCESS

But the need for affection, and the values that accrue from it, do not flow in only one direction. Even during the first year of life children show affection for adults who care for them. Moreover just as the affection of an adult is important to the child so also the affection of a child is important to an adult. Affection is important not only to the child but also to any human being at any time of life.

The values of an affectionate relationship are indicated, as noted above, by the unfavourable turn a child's behaviour sometimes takes if he is not in friendly hands or if he is actually disliked. According to one study lack of an affectionate relationship with his parents may be a factor contributing to delinquency.

Children likewise desire acceptance and affection from their teachers, councillors, club leaders, and other adults who substitute for parents. There is, of course, much overlapping between the characteristics of a good teacher and those of a good parent. In a study in which children described the teachers whom they liked best, a large percentage of the replies dealt with qualities that characterize an agreeable human being in any walk of life, including items such as kindliness, sympathy, a genuine interest in children as children, and fairness combined with firmness.

Observations such as the foregoing suggest that it would be well for all who have children in their care, at home, at school, in camps, in hospitals, and other places, to allow themselves not only to feel but also to show in their whole manner a warm hearted attitude toward children. This does not mean, of course, that a feeling of affection will solve all problems. An affectionate teacher still needs to know the knack of good teaching. The fact that he is fond of children will help, but will not, in itself, automatically make him a wise teacher.

HUMOUR AND LAUGHTER

Unfortunately, there are no neat rules that can be offered concerning how a person can cultivate or utilize a "*sense of humour*" in his dealings with others. The most common (*and most futile*) admonition is that one should not take oneself too seriously. There are, however, a few rather simple generalizations that can be made. One rather obvious generalisation is that most children, even at an early age, welcome an opportunity to laugh.

At the school-age level, pupils are only too pleased to find something to laugh at, although frequently the atmosphere at school is so solemn that children hesitate to laugh when something funny occurs, unless the teacher gives a signal, such as smiling or laughing himself.

SOCIAL DEVELOPMENT

The development of a person's behaviour as a social creature proceeds apace with the development of this individuality, his status as an independent creature, distinct from others, socialization and individualization are complementary features in the development of personality.

Meaning and Definition of Social Development: The phenomena such as affection, shyness, zealously stage fright and sympathy are treated as social forms of behaviour.

According E.B. Hurlock "Social development means acquisition of the ability to behave in accordance with racial expectation." *I.L. Child* says "Social development is the process by which an individual is led to develop actual behaviour according to the standards the group."

The social development has following characteristics:

(1) Social responses, (2) Responses to other children, (3) Group activities (4) Social perception, (5) Resistant behaviour, (6) Fights and quarrels, (7) Sympathy, (8) Cooperation, (9) Competition, and (10) Leadership.

Factors Influencing Social Development: There are several factors which influence the social development. The most important factors are as follows: (1) Socio-economic status, (2) Leadership, (3) Emotions, (4) Games and Sports, (5) Peer group or gang. These factors lead to social maturity. Thus the following are the social development norms.

1. Social interaction,
2. Social adjustment,
3. Social participation,
4. Social conformity, and
5. Social maturity.

The social development concerns with personality development. The personality is more social and less psychological. In the absence of social group the concept of personality has no significance.

Stage wise Social Development: The social development can be studied into three stages of life—infancy, childhood, and adolescence.

Stage of Infancy: During the first days of life the child shows little behaviour that can be called "*social,*" but from the beginning his everyday experiences and his daily survival are rooted in associations with other persons. Within a few weeks after birth, he not only is the passive recipient of attentions from others but also is active, in his own way, as a social being. The widening of his stage of social activities parallels and is interwoven with other features of his growth.

The development of a person's behaviour as a social creature proceeds apace with the development of his status as an independent creature, distinct from others. As a child matures, he becomes increasingly able to enter into various forms of *'sociable' behaviour,* to cooperate to join with others in common endeavour.

In due time, he cooperates, from friendships, and acquires, with the passage of time, a degree of sensitivity to the wants of others and a degree of sympathy with their concerns. Eventually also he becomes able to participate in complex teamwork, to develop loyalties on an extensive scale, to identify himself with the interests of a community or of a nation and to be concerned with the welfare of the larger society of which he is a part. The *"other centered"* and *"self-centered"* forms of behaviour, involving, on the one hand, varying degrees of collective thought and action and, on the other hand, varying degrees of self-assertiveness and individualism, are normal and complementary features of the child's social development.

Stage of Adolescence: There is an advance with age from the infancy to the adolescent level, when children acquire a capacity for group behaviour and for identifying themselves with group interests. In the early elementary grades the child does not seem to be able to encompass intellectually, or to identify himself in a practical manner with the interests of a community as large as the enrolment of an average class, unless under direct adult supervision. At about the junior high school level, children's contributions in class discussion show decidedly more preoccupation with the larger affairs in the community or in the world at large, and there is also more continuity as children contribute jointly to the development of a topic or theme as distinguished from independent testimonials from individual members of the group.

MOTOR SKILLS AND SOCIAL DEVELOPMENT

During childhood much of child's social activity with other children takes place through play and a child's competence in motor activities has an important influence on his social adjustment.

His plight is especially unfortunate if his motor deficiencies are combined with a strong desire for social contacts and social approval. This does not mean, of course, that every child must be a robust athlete to achieve normal social adjustment, for some children gain acceptance and satisfying social contacts by other means, especially if they are bright or have other outstanding talents. In the case of the usual child, however, the acquisition of motor skills is of value not only from the point of view of the personal satisfactions that accrue from competence in self-help and independence of adult aid, but also from the point of view of good social and emotional relations with others.

Trends of Social Development: Developmental trends can also be noted in other aspects of social behaviour. Resistant or *negativistic"* behaviour is displayed by practically all children, beginning some time in the first year and reaching the peak by about the age of three and a half years, but prevailing thereafter in varying degrees in years to come. Resistant behaviour is a normal feature of social behaviour. Children also show varying degrees of aggressive behaviour, most overtly during the pre-school years, and in more subdued ways during later years.

Aggressive behaviour may serve varying functions in different children. In the case of a child hitherto has been shy and withdrawing a display of aggressiveness may be a temporary expedient and it may be a welcome and wholesome symptom of improving adjustment. There is evidence which indicated that rigid and autocratic practices in dealing with children are likely to arouse aggressiveness (*or apathy*) to a greater extent than do less rigid, more democratic, man-to man procedures.

Aggressive, resistant, and other forms of self-assertive behaviour frequently receive more notice and seem to be more conspicuous than co-operative, sympathetic, and friendly forms of conduct. However, research findings indicate that in the behaviour of normal children friendly responses quite out unfriendly responses. Friendly, kindly cooperative behaviour is no less natural, no more a product of training, than is aggressive, unsympathetic, and competitive behaviour.

Shyness or *"withdrawing"* behaviour is shown by many children in varying ways at different age-levels. Apart from attention to factors in a child's everyday life that would have the effect of subjecting him to continued failure or of lowering his confidence in himself, there is much that can be done in school and in other group situations to aid the child to find his way by degrees into group activities through helping him to use and to improve skills and interests that he already possesses or through helping him to acquire the skills that are useful in social intercourse but which he happens to lack.

School Age: In many occupations, especially those in which an individuals' performance is graded or marked in terms of comparison with others, the average child is likely to exert himself more when working for individual honours than when working for the group. However, the child is likely to exert himself relatively more when working on behalf of congenial group of his own choosing or on group projects that enlist his interest, than when working with an arbitrarily designated group or on group projects that have been arbitrarily assigned.

Competitiveness is encouraged by the adult practice of comparing children with one another and by emphasizing the importance of being a winner as distinguished from playing the game. School marks, rating system, the practice of giving extraneous prizes and rewards may also accentuate children's competitive activities. The competitive urge of parents and teachers are often deeply involved in the child's progress at school, especially in connection with the conventional school subjects.

In their *own social groups* children come to recognize, more or less clearly, that members of the group possess varying degrees of ability, popularity, and prestige.

Children's social behaviour is likely from an early age level to show the influence of the customs and standards of the social group to which their elders belong. Standards and customs vary more or less at different socio-economic levels and in different ethnic groups within a single community. It is important for adults to remember this fact if they would understand a child's behaviour.

Training for leadership is an important responsibility of education. Leaders among children usually are somewhat superior in ability to the average of the group especially in the sphere in which they are recognized as leaders. However, ability is not alone the determining factor. To be a good leader a child should also be able to be a good follower in the sense that he should be responsive to the needs and wishes of his follower and able to participate whole-heartedly in their interests and concerns.

Friendships or affinities between individuals are apparent from an early age in the social behaviour of children. Friends tend, in general, to resemble each other more than they tend to differ from each other in their abilities and in their personality traits, although there are many exceptions to this. This factor of propinquity, or nearness in geographical space, is obviously important in determining the range of individuals from among whom the children's friends will be chosen.

All children, in one way or another, desire some degree of *recognition, acceptance,* and prestige in their dealings with others. Even a bad child wishes to be liked, and sometimes the punishment inflicted upon such a youngster merely widens the social distance between him and his fellows and intensifies his unacceptable forms of behaviour.

EDUCATIONAL IMPLICATIONS

The school should offer, as far as possible, a variety of opportunities for leadership. An educational policy which keeps the same pupils together from year to year under the same teacher and in much the same educational programme may provide as imbalance of continuity and security. Needless to say, it is not possible to arrange matters so that every child is a leader. Many children and adults do not seem particularly to desire to assume direction of others as long as they can be left to their own interests. Apart from desire, there are differences in ability to assume leadership. However, even though an individual may not aspire to leadership, he still likes to be noticed once in a while.

Nursery School: Nursery schools promote a child's ability to enter into social contacts with others, and at the same time to promote his ability to assert his independence. The effects of such opportunities will vary with different children. However, if a child's opportunities to associate with other children are delayed, he will eventually be at a loss, especially if, in the meantime, he is not acquiring the skills and play techniques that are used by the group that he ultimately has to join.

Camp experience or other opportunities for acquiring independence away from home likewise have been found to be of value to individual children, especially if they are overprotected at home and can be helped during the transitional period or if, in their regular environment, that prevent them from developing their social potentialities.

MENTAL DEVELOPMENT

The child's mental world consists in the development of ability to respond in terms of events which are remote in time as well as removed in space. The mental changes—memory, reasoning, imagination, languages, ability and concept formation are associated with increasing maturity.

Piaget has contributed significantly in area of mental development. *Cattle's theory* of intelligence is also associated with process of mental development. *Cattle* considers two aspects of intelligence *biological* and *social* factors. The biological factors of intelligence are concerned with growth and heredity while social factors depend on *environment* or social climate of the child in which he lives. Thus, it is termed a *fluid theory* of intelligence. Mental development can not be described in terms of distinct stages, but it is true that certain features of behaviour and certain mental trends are more conspicuous at one mental age level than another.

Stage of Infancy: It has been noted many of the changes take place in the intellectual life of the child as he develops from infancy to maturer years. At birth the child is responsive to some forms of sensory stimulation but he does not have the sensory acuity that he will acquire in time. His *"mental world"* at the start seems to consist primarily of experiences arising through direct physical contacts with the environment and through the sensation. With the passage of time impressions received through the *"distance receptors"*—the eyes and the ears—gain increasing prominence. Through the accumulation of experiences he becomes able to differentiate between phenomena that earlier were not distinguished from one another. There is an increase in his capacity to respond to symbols or *"reduced cues."*

A majority of persons are unable to *recall* with any degree of accuracy events that befall them before the age of about three, and even then their recollections are scanty compared with the sum total of their experience.

In the process of growth the child's mental world expands in many dimensions. As he moves from the cradle to the larger world his mental horizons widen. With the development of the imaginative abilities and the ability to plan, the dimensions of the child's mental world are extended into anticipation of the future.

Through the use of make believe he is able to enter vicariously into a wider range of experience and to transcend, in part, his own limitations. Related to his own private day-dreams is his interest in vicarious experiences that are provided for him by way of his reading, and way of radio programmes and motion pictures.

Trend of Mental Development: With advancing age there tends to be an increase in the child's ability to concentrate over longer periods of time. The ability to give sustained attention varies with the nature of the task. The child's span of attention is likely to be longest in the case of activities that he himself has chosen or that are undertaken in connection with his own designs.

The Development of Children's Ability to reason is gradual and continuous rather than characterized by distinct stages. However, there are changes with age in the range and complexity of problems which engage the attention of children and to which they will apply themselves. The younger the child, the more his everyday thoughts tend to concern with events related to his own immediate experience and well-being; as he grows older, he becomes increasingly able to occupy himself with more remote issues and to deal with abstractions as distinguished from concrete experiences.

DEVELOPMENT OF MORAL CONCEPTS

Child's first ideas of right and wrong are determined largely by the verdict of his parents concerning acts that are forbidden or permitted. Throughout life an individual's moral code continues to be determined to a large extent by rules in the form of conventional standards and, directly or indirectly, the teachings of religion.

Even from a rather early age, however, the child is able to formulate some *moral principles* in terms of the reasons that lie behind them and to adopt them as his own rules rather than simply as edicts that have to be obeyed because others have so told him.

In childhood as in later years, a person's ideas as to what constitutes proper conduct are likely to show many irregularities and inconsistencies. He may have rigid principles concerning the wrongfulness of cheating, stealing, and mayhem under some circumstances and yet condone such acts in other circumstances in which his principles should apply with equal force. The consistency with which he exercises his moral code will depend in part upon specific learning, in part upon the likelihood of direct retaliation, in part upon the remoteness of the issue from his own daily life, and, in large part, upon his desires and prejudices.

Integrated Process of Development: The social, emotional and mental development are highly correlated to one another. The development of one aspect helps or includes the other aspect. In thinking and reasoning emotional factors play important role in the person's behaviour. *Moral concepts* include social and mental development. The process of child development in various dimensions goes side by side, hence the components of one aspect help or involve the components of other aspect. The motor skills help in social adjustment.

EDUCATIONAL IMPLICATIONS OF MENTAL DEVELOPMENT

In the *development of information and concepts* it is likely that child's knowledge or grasp will vary considerably in the case of different topics or areas of experience. Depending upon his past opportunities for learning he may be well informed and be able to reason out effectively in connection with one topic and not in connection with another. Accordingly, he may seem very naïve and illogical in dealing with one problem and quite logical in dealing with another. However, changes that normally come with added maturity cannot be brought about simply by giving the child concentrated experiences or special training over a short period of time.

Concentrated periods of practice or instruction at a given stage of growth cannot bring about the changes that take place over a period of years through the joint influence of growth and such indirect instructions as everyday experience affords.

Studies of children in the elementary and high school grades indicate that pupils frequently are called upon to deal with *abstract* and *complex problems,* especially in the field of the social sciences, before they have the background of experience adequately to grasp the subject-matter. When such is the case, much of what a child learns is primarily of a verbal nature, divorced from realities or practical applications to the decisions that are made in everyday life.

As children grow older, there are changes, not only in their information about affairs in the world at large, but also in their attitudes toward such affairs. Frequently there is little relationship, however, between a child's attitude (the stand which he takes for or against, the liking or disliking, prejudice or tolerance which he exhibits) and the amount of knowledge he possesses concerning a matter at issue. His thinking, like the thinking of adults, will be influenced to varying degrees by his desires, his fears, and other emotional tendencies. One of the most difficult problems in education is to provide teaching that does not consist in passing adult preconceptions on to children but that stimulates children to make free use of their intelligence in meeting the problems of everyday life.

A teacher should always keep in his mind that social, emotional and mental development are highly related to one another. The components of these dimensions are inclusive. The thinking process is governed by emotional factors such as prejudices of a child and depends on attitudes and values of an individual.

QUESTIONS FOR ANSWER

1. *Define the term 'Growth and development' and enumerate the principles of development.*
2. *Define the term 'maturation' and indicate the characteristics of maturation. Compare with learning.*
3. *Indicate the stages of development and forms of development. Describe the factors influencing development of an individual.*
4. *Enumerate the methods of studying development. Give a brief description.*
5. *Enumerate the dimensions and their components of development.*
6. *Describe physical and motor development at different stages of life and its educational implication.*
7. *Describe emotional and social development of child and its problems.*
8. *Enumerate the characteristics of mental development. Indicate some educational implications.*

22

Psychological and Ecological Environment for Mental Health

INTRODUCTION

Human psychology has been drastically changing the ecological balance of practically every component of the environment—atmosphere, climate, hydrosphere, lithosphere, social and cultural and biosphere. The efforts are being made on global level for *environmental management*. The education has to play the very significant role for providing the awareness, and developing skills, attitudes and values of students since primary and pre-primary stages to university level. The action aspect of the programme requires the good physical and mental health and for this following socio-cultural conditions are vital for the children.

1. The working efficiency of a person, are greatly influenced by the climate of the country. The advanced and developed countries of the world have the climatic conditions which are suitable for high working efficiency of the people.
2. The extent to which social centres, recreational facilities and social agencies exist.
3. The extent of racial prejudice. The racial differences are governed by physical conditions of the country. White race is in cold countries. Yellow race and black race are in hot countries.
4. The degree of freedom allowed to the persons to work according to their abilities and potentialities.
5. The extent of tolerance or intolerance of religious sects.

HUMAN ECOLOGY

The education has the interaction between student and teacher. The teacher provides the situations—social and emotional for the experience and activities which result in learning or modification of behaviour or development. In the teaching-learning process mental health of teacher and pupils play the significant role to realize the desirable objectives.

There has been a great deal of talk in recent years about the *"population explosion"*. It is said that the human population is increasing so rapidly that widespread famine is inevitable in the near future. There is much fierce debate about the methods that should be used to slow down or stop the growth of the human population. The ecology of human population has to play a vital role in a number of socio-economic and cultural problems both national as well as international levels.

The human ecology concerns with the *mental health.* It is said that healthy mind is in healthy body, the reverse is also true. The physical and psychological components are interdependent. Therefore, in the present chapter the *'mental health* of students and teacher has been discussed. The problem of students and teacher has been discussed. The problem of mental health has acquired importance in the national development programmes. The mental hygiene is the means for assuring the adjustment.

DEFINITION OF MENTAL HEALTH

Mental health is like physical health, consists of the absence of serious defects or mental ailments. It is the approach of physician who gives you a physical test. He has a checklist of the defects or ailments considered to be serious. If a person is free from these ailments or symptoms is considered healthy. Ill health implies a departure from the normal or undesirable or troublesome departure from the normal.

Another approach to mental health is a number of feelings, attitudes or ways of behaving which lead to distress or interfere with larger goals and which are unusual or inevitable. These conditions are abnormal in the sense that there is departure from normal behaviour.

Health is also considered as positive attainment. Mental health should not be measured by evils we avoid but by positive steps we take toward our true potential. In this view, descriptions of the healthy person are almost descriptions of the ideal person.

1. Enlarged concept of mental health is considered as attainment of positive values and attitudes. He has enjoyable experiences, happy, zestful and creative person. He has the potentialities for effective functioning in day-to-day life.
2. Minimal concept of mental health is considered as the absebce of illness. It is the freedom from ailments, absence of mental disorder. He has the good resistance to stress.

MENTAL HEALTH AND EDUCATION

During the present days mental ailments have increased tremendously and have involved serious problems at the national level in industrial development, social and economic changes. The problem of mental health has required importance in the national developmental programmes.

It is difficult to define the *term mental health* comprehensively. The definitions of mental health have great variations but the fundamental elements are more or less the same, in spite of wordings used in their definitions.

Norma E. Cutts and *Nicholas Mosely* have defined the term *mental health* comprehensively—

> "Mental health is the ability to adjust satisfactorily to the various strains of the environment, we meet in life and mental hygiene as the means we take to assure this adjustment."

In the process of education mental health plays significant role. The sound mental health is the first condition for the education. Mental health is most important condition for effective teaching and learning. It is said that *"sound mind in sound body."*

Thus, mental health and education are closely related to each other. The students learning or achievement depends on their sound mental health. It is a crucial condition for education.

The following *criteria* have been identified of mentally healthy student or person:

1. Possesses socially adaptable behaviours.

2. He is emotionally satisfied.
3. He possesses adaptability and resilient mind.
4. His desires are in harmony with socially approved norms.
5. He is enthusiastic and reasonable.
6. He possesses good habits and constructive attitude.
7. He has insight into his own conduct.
8. He has own philosophy and values of life.

It is a fact that healthy person is in conscious control of his life. There is consistency in his behaviour and conduct. A healthy person is aware about his own strength and weakness. Healthy person does not live in the past but he always plans and thinks for future and acts accordingly. His future orientation is very realistic according to his own capacities and resources.

MENTAL AILMENTS

There are many positive aspects of mental health, the avoidance of specific ailments may not be the objective of mental health but is one of important objectives. There are several types of ailments of mental health.

(*a*) Distortion of reality,
(*b*) Unusual difficulties with anxiety,
(*c*) Difficulties with self-control, and
(*d*) Inadequate relation with other persons.

(*a*) *Distortion of Reality or Denial:* An important feature of mental ailment is a distorted view of important facets of the world. The person may refuse to face his own hates, or fears or off beat desires.

(*b*) *Unusual Difficulties with Anxiety:* Anxiety is no mark of mental ill health. The lack of anxiety would, in fact, suggest an unhealthy refusal to face the reality of the situation. Under these circumstances, real anxiety as it is termed would be normal. It is only when such anxiety seems out of proportion to the menace that would consider that something is wrong. Such neurotic anxiety is unhealthful in and of it-self. It brings serious distress.

(*c*) *Difficulties with Self-Control:* The self-control is regarded as the key test of emotional adjustment. Mental ill health may be associated with both the amount of control maintained and the type of the control that is used. The self-control can not eliminate the basic urges or drives. On the contrary, the wholesome personality is endowed with strong urges or drives. The happy, admirable person is well equipped with vigorous appetites and a full quota of needs. In a proper balance between drive and control there should be evidence of a happy and spontaneous energy.

(*d*) *Inadequate Relations with other People:* Social relations are related to mental health in at least two ways. First of all, to avoid ill health, we must have made some kind of adjustment to other people. Second, our relations with other people often cast some on other aspects of adjustment. They serve as an index by which other facts of mental health may be observed.

ATTRIBUTES OF MENTAL HEALTH

In describing some of the mental conditions are to be avoided and our attention should be on positive attributes which are as follows:

1. *A Positive View of the Self:* The feeling about himself should be based on a view of himself that is reasonably free from distortion. He should have some general notion and the notion should not be too far from the objective truth or reality of life. He must also recognize the significant traits that give him concern his poor eyesight, his fear of rough and tumble games, his tendency to stammer. Self-acceptance has an intimate relation to freedom from distortion.

2. *Striving Toward a Confident Mastery:* One of the attributes of positive mental health is that of commitment and striving. The healthy person does not merely avoid evils and handicaps, nor does he deal with them by simple retreat. As he gains success in these enterprises, he gains confidence in his ability to master other problems.

3. *Specific Positive Goals:* The several psychologists who put forward the goals of positive mental health have, in total proposed a long list of desirable attributes.

4. *Mental Health, Character and Morality:* Mentally healthy child is the good child. The positive mental health called for a reasonable degree of socialization and sensitivity to the needs of others. Mentally healthy child generally possesses good character and morality.

ATTRIBUTES OF SUPERIOR MENTAL HEALTH

The following are the main indications of superior mental health:

1. *Adaptiveness and Flexibility:* This includes ability to deal with the world, to specific objectives and to carry them out, being guided by the results of the efforts.

2. *Capacity to Gratify one's needs:* It means spontaneous actions in the relaxed enjoyment of life, has sexual capacity, ability to work for one's own interests.

3. *Competence and Good will in Dealing with other:* He takes part in productive work and meets responsibility in a manner approved by others and fulfills the commitments to others ability to accept help. Trust and liking for people. He is capable of intimacy and warmness.

4. *Intellectual Ability:* He is accurate in his perception of reality and of self, ability to solve problems, rational much common sense. He has broad comprehensive view of life.

5. *Emotional Control:* He is capable to handle anxiety and frustration, moral and conscientious. He is courageous and of high morale.

6. *Autonomy, Productivity and a Sense of Worth:* He takes initiative, self-reliant in making contributions, emotionally independent, detached strong sense of identity and feeling of self-determination. He seeks self-actualization, sense of achievement and self-respect.

7. *Integration and Equilibration:* He maintains balance and consistency in dealing with opposing forces, mature unifying view of life and gives impression of maturity.

THEORY OF MENTAL HEALTH

There are various theories of psychology which deal the concept of mental health. Theory related to the needs provide the basis of mental health.

Maslow's Hierarchy of Needs: Maslow (1948) developed hierarchy of needs with the primitive needs at the base and deferrable needs superimposed. There are five levels of needs—*Physiological, safety needs, love* and *belonging needs, esteem needs, self actualisation needs.* Next to physiological-needs involved in avoiding danger or securing safety. One step beyond this is the need for esteem. Esteem need includes both the good opinion of other people and self approval. When pressure from these needs is partially relaxed tha' the individual can get on with self actualization.

Throughout the hierarchy, any second order need will be at a disadvantage in competing with first order need. A fairly strong urge toward artistic creation, for instance, might be ruled out by weaker but more primitive need to avoid the contempt of others. When the basic needs are satisfied to some degree that the student can hopefully address himself to the more ambitious goals of competences and achievement.

EDUCATION AND MENTAL HEALTH

The teacher of course, can not be the key person in helping the student meet the basic needs in such a way that he will be free to go on to higher level achievement. The teacher can, however, do much toward providing the student with some of the esteem and affectionate regard so important to his well-being. The teacher's warm emotional support can help make the classroom a less stressful place and enable him to take the risks necessary for self-actualization.

The Hygiene Theory of Motivation

Frederick Herberg (1966) formulated a new theory of motivation. He has explained the *'Need of Theory'* and classifies human needs into two categories:

1. Hygiene factors, and
2. Motivators.

1. *Hygiene Factors*: These hygiene factors are involved in the learning environment. These factors refer to the following components of learning situation—

(*a*) Working conditions,
(*b*) Administrative norms of school,
(*c*) The form of supervision of school, and
(*d*) The safety and standard of school.

These factors provide the encouragement to the students to work hard. These factors are related to the environment or working conditions. These factors are pre-requisite for higher order of learning.

2. *Motivators*: These factors are related to the activities and behaviour of the learners rather than the *environment* of learning, verbal praise, recognition, success, knowledge of result and novelty. These factors are of four types:

(*a*) Achievement and performance,
(*b*) Recognition and responsibility,
(*c*) Advancement and freedom, and
(*d*) Personal growth.

The factors have the permanent influence on the change of behaviour of the students whereas hygiene factors have temporary effect. The internal motivation is more effective than external one which is helpful in satisfying higher needs of esteem and self actualization. A teacher's responsibility is in both factors hygiene and motivators. The hygiene factors are related to the *school environment* and *organisational climate.*

The teachers and principal have to manage and organise hygiene factors in the school campus and in the classroom. The students are encouraged and praised by the teachers for their good performance and desirable behaviour in the class and school by establishing rapport with them. These factors contribute to their mental health.

FACTORS INFLUENCING MENTAL HEALTH OF CHILD

There are several factors which influence the mental health of child. The influence of parents and family life of the community and of school practices upon the personality or mental health of the child. The following are the main factors and areas of these influences:

I. Influences of the Parent and Family life.
1. *The influence of poverty on the child's personality*
   (*a*) A feeling of insecurity.
   (*b*) A feeling of inferiority.
2. *The parents who reject the child*
   (*a*) Effect of Rejection on the child.
   (*b*) Expression of Rejection by the parents.
   (*c*) Origin of Rejection in the parents.

(*i*) Unattractive children.
(*ii*) Relationship between husband and wife.
(*iii*) Immature parents.

3. *Parents who over-protect the child*
   (*a*) Expression of over protection by the mother.
   (*b*) Effects of over protection on the child.
4. *Parents who show favouritism.*
5. *Parents who have high moral standards.*

II. The influences of the community on mental health.

III. Effects of school practices organisational climate on mental health of children and their personality—

1. The effect of overcompetition in school
2. Over-restriction in the classroom.
3. Unsuitable curriculum.
4. Teacher's method of handling the class.
5. The effect of the teachers personality on the class.
6. Teachers report of behaviour problem in the classroom.
7. Treatment of behaviour problem in the classroom.

I. Influences of the Parents and Family Life

1. The Influence of Poverty on the Child's Personality

An excellent description of the effect of poverty on the personality of the child has been made by *Plant*. He points out that *"hardening"* of personality results from constant financial strain. He feels that *"this is not a mechanism of resignation but the development of patterns of response...that prevents each experience of want (it matters little how drastic) from resulting in the emotional reverberations which accompanied the first such experience."* Thus the child attempts to make himself unassailable, in effect, by erecting a wall between himself and the environment.

(*a*) *A feeling of insecurity* is a second resultant, according to Plant. Children who have suffered repeated and serious blows to their sense of adequacy from a long-continued real fear of cold and hunger are likely to show a picture of anxiety and panic. This feeling becomes so firmly bound up with the personality structure that later acquisition of a sufficient income will not remove it.

(*b*) According to *Plant* a third resultant is a feeling of *inferiority.*

This may be found in children above the lowest economic levels; it occurs whenever there is a marked discrepancy between the economic status, reflected in type of home, clothes, belongings, etc., of the child and that of other children with whom he is in contact. This feeling is likely to become heightened during adolescence when material and social problems are more in the focus of a child's interest.

2. Parents who Reject the Child

A child is said to be rejected when he is disliked or not wanted by one or both parents, a situation which inevitably results in insufficient meeting of the child's needs for affection and belongingness. Children whose parents strongly dislike them at times but love most of the time are not considered to be rejected; consequently the following discussion is not applicable to them.

We cannot distinguish as yet the supposedly different effects on the child of (*i*) rejection by both parents as opposed to rejection by one, (*ii*) the sex of rejecting parent in relation to the sex of the child, and (*iii*) the degree of affection shown by the non-rejecting parents.

(*a*) *Effect of Rejection on the Child:* The pattern of behaviour the rejected child is reported to depend primarily on one or more of these factors: (1) *a desire to win affection* or at least attention, (2) *a wish to retaliate against people* for the hostility shown to him by the parents, or (3) *feelings of worthlessness and anxiety*. It is, of course, incorrect to attribute his behaviour entirely to one or another of these categories since, for example, *one* form of behaviour (that is, activity calculated to annoy) may be based on a desire for attention plus a wish to retaliate.

(*b*) *Expression of Rejection by the Parents:* The signs of rejection exhibited by the parents vary from those which are obviously unequivocal to those which might possibly indicate dislike for the child. *Rejection* is easily diagnosed when the parents's feeling is fully conscious and when there is no attempt to conceal it; not so easily diagnosed otherwise.

Getting rid of the child is one of the most obvious signs of rejection. *Harsh treatment*, being very strict with the child, using severe physical punishment, are all too frequent practices. Some of the more subtle methods of expressing rejection are (1) expecting the child to live up to standards that, is much too high for him, (2) never saying anything favourable about the child, (3) comparing him unfavourably with siblings or children in the neighbourhood, (4) responding with surprise to favourable statements made by other about the child, (5) taking conscientious care of the child's needs but with an air of martyrdom.

(c) *Origin of Rejection in the Parents:* The soil from which rejection grows is likely to be an *unsatisfactory marital adjustment*. The mother's feeling towards a disliked husband may be extended to the child. The husband may dislike the child of his unloved wife. *Interference with the sources of satisfaction* of the parents is an important cause. In homes of low economic level, the birth of a child means cutting down on necessities of life for the family in order to meet the baby's needs; on a somewhat higher level, parenthood often means giving up the possibility of further education, or drastic reduction in accustomed comfort.

(i) *Immature fathers and mothers* who are still dependent on their own parents and who tend to take more interest in dancing, entertaining, and having a good time than in child-rearing are likely to continue to resent the presence of a son or daughter.

(ii) *Unattractive children* are likely to be rejected. A special quality or lack of it may make the child seem unattractive to his particular parents—a boy to parents who keenly hoped for a girl; a frail child, even though charming, to parents who emphasize strength and agility; a slow child to parents who think quickness is the *summum bonum;* even minor matters such as a lack of interest in music when the parents put a high premium on this art—these traits and others may constitute special kinds of unattractiveness.

(iii) *The relations between the husband and wife*—For example, when one parent becomes so occupied with the child that the previous degree of affection for the spouse seems to be lacking or to be greatly reduced—the child may be rejected by the offended parent. The situation may be even more critical when step parent enters the home. It is normal to easily begin to believe that the child is preventing a happy relationship between husband and wife.

3. *Parents Who Over-protect the Child*

A child is said to be over-protected when he is excessively cared for, shielded, and loved. As very little is known about over-protection by the father, probably because he assumes the responsibility for the child's care so rarely, this discussion will deal with the over-protective mother.

(*a*) *Expression of Overprotection by the Mother:* Over-protection may result from either domination or indulgence, or vacillation between the two. In any type of over-protection, however, the mother characteristically spends a great deal of time with the child, takes excessive care of him, and as a result succeeds in preventing the development of his independence. Specifically, she is likely to sleep with the child for years, amuse, play with, and fondle him for hours at a time.

(*b*) *Effects of Over-protection on the Child:* Children of both dominating and overindulgent mother often lack self-reliance. In both cases they have been for so long dependent on their mothers that they are unlikely to be able to assume responsibility for tasks or for minor life problems. They continue to find their security in the presence of their mothers, in whose absence they find it difficult to cope with the world.

4. *Parents Who Show Favouritism*

When a strong preference is shown by the parents for one child the effect on both the favoured and the unfavoured child (*for simplicity of discussion, only two-child families will be considered*) is likely to be unfortunate. The favoured child may reflect, though in a mild form, the characteristics of the over-indulged child. The unfavoured child is practically certain to show form of jealousy. Young children often make bodily attacks on the *sibling*, although direct aggression against the sibling is not always shown in their behaviour. Because of the feeling of injustice and lack of sufficient, affection, they may exhibit negativism, restlessness, fighting and attention-demanding activities especially in relation to their parents but also in relation to other adults and children.

5. Parents Who have High Moral Standards

Children from homes with moral standards much more rigid than those of the rest of the community may be taught that sex is evil, that one thousand and one normal activities are sinful, *e.g., smoking, card-playing,* going to the *movies* or the *theatre, dancing,* and reading modern *novels.* The most serious result is that children who accept this teaching acquire such severe conscience that they believe they are continually failing to live a proper life. Normal social relations are almost impossible for them in an average community and, all too frequently, they develop neurotic tendencies.

The effects of the home broken by divorce or separation are too familiar to relate. The poverty, rejection, over-protection, favouritism and other specific conditions cause for the ailment of mental health.

II. Influences of the Community

Community influences on child personality adjustment are so multiform and the literature dealing with them is so indefinite that it is impossible to treat the topic adequately in short space. Some community conditions obviously important to children are (1) the extent to which recreational facilities, social centres, and social agencies, exist, (2) the degree of freedom allowed children by community folkways, (3) the disparity in economic levels, (4) the extent of race prejudice, (5) the extent of tolerance of intolerance of religious sects. These are only a few of many community factors which indirectly affect the favourable or unfavourable development of children's personalities.

III. Effect of School Practices and Organizational Climate on Children's Behaviour and Personality Development

The school practices have significant influence on the children behaviour and their personality development. The important practices have been discussed in the following paragraphs:

1. *The Effect of Overcompetition and Examination in School:* Many authorities feel the whole system of grades, examinations, and marks tends to place an undue emphasis on competition. The result in many cases is to discourage the slow learners and even many average pupils. The relatively fast learners are likely to get inflated notions of their own abilities. Excessive competition tends to breed an indifference to the welfare of others and to enhance self-interest.

Examinations, especially long ones, when used as even or partial basis for marks in a highly competitive atmosphere, are likely to cause an undue strain and fatigue in many children.

The attendant strain may be increased in schools in which the results of examinations are used as the primary criterion for rating the effectiveness of the teacher without taking into account the level of ability of the class. When examinations are used primarily for diagnostic purposes—to detect areas of weakness in the children's knowledge and skill so that subsequent work may be better directed—then they are serving a worthy purpose.

2. *Unsuitable Curriculum:* If the curriculum has little relation to the life problems of the children and makes no contribution to their present needs, many unfortunate effects are produced. Antagonism to the school accompanied by misbehaviour may be expected, and a desire to *"quit school"* at the earliest legal age is likely to be born and nourished. Inquiries into the cause of *delinquency* have shown that some bright delinquents were first attracted to the questionable thrills of stealing as a result of their intense boredom with the curriculum of their school.

3. *Overrestriction in the Classroom:* Many elementary and secondary schools restrict the behaviour of their pupils. The ideal of many schools is pin-drop quietness and a *"place for every child and every child in his place."* The traditional recess periods and the occasional *"working at the board"* are far from sufficient for most elementary school children's need for movement and activity. In the primary school, the needs for both activity and rest are usually handled satisfactorily.

4. *Teacher's Methods of Handling the Class:* The teacher's methods of handling pupils can be considered primarily a function of his personality and his knowledge. His skill is dependent not only upon knowledge of child in general, but also upon knowledge of the individual child in general, but also upon knowledge of the individual children in his class and knowledge of how to meet

the personality needs of children and control their behaviour in ways beneficial to them. There is likely to be a close relationship between the teacher's personality and the methods of controls he naturally tends to use.

5. *The Effect of the Teacher's Personality on the Class:* It may be summarized that the best liked teachers provided a warm, friendly and relaxed classroom atmosphere in which the children could not only do their best work and have the most enjoyable time, but also would have opportunity for wholesome personality development. The least liked teachers probably had the opposite effect.

Some teacher really enjoy teaching and their devotion to their job of teaching which has positive effect on the class. The involvement in teaching according to *Morrison* also contribute in the involvement of the class in their teaching activities.

6. *Teacher's Rapport of Behaviour Problems in the Classroom:* Wickman study which demonstrated that teachers tended to consider violations of classroom order, dishonesties, and immoralities as more serious than recessive and withdrawing personality traits, while the opposite was true of mental hygienists, has had wide publicity. Although this study has been justly criticized as being unfair to the teachers because they were asked to rate the items on the basis of their seriousness in class.

7. *The Treatment of Behaviour Problems in the Classroom:* The kinds of treatment techniques used are even more revealing of the lack of appreciation of mental hygiene principles. A combination of categories I, II and III, all essentially punishment, totals 56 per cent of techniques used. Constructive or non-punishment techniques comprise approximately 25 per cent. Deprivation—a method of meeting the immediate situation which may or may not have beneficient effects, depending upon the circumstances and type of deprivation—was employed 19 per cent of the time. *Campbell* comes to the following conclusions:

(*a*) The teachers apply direct measures as punishment or reward for treating undesirable class room behaviour of children. *Skinner* is of this view that undesirable behaviour should be ignored and desirable behaviour should be immediately rewarded or reinforced. This treatment avoids the adverse effect of punishment.

(*b*) The teachers are rated highly successful in classroom control who use rewards or reinforcement and provide direct help more frequently than other teachers. The results the *Skinner's thesis* of ignoring undesirable behaviour, he is not in favour of the punishment to students in the classroom.

PROBLEMS OF ADJUSTMENT—THE CAUSE OF MENTAL AILMENT

There are some special problems of adjustment of children which cause the ailment of mental health. These have been listed as follows:

1. *The Physically Handicapped Child:* Physically handicapped children because of their condition suffer more frustrations than the average child. They miss the usual play and social activities and are usually slower in their school work. Besides having fewer immediate opportunities for social recognition, most of them must look forward to a vocational future that is far from satisfying.

A wise handling may do much for the physically handicapped child. To avoid in a natural manner, calling attention to his defect while at the same time arranging for special ways for him to receive merited recognition usually aid markedly in his adjustment.

2. *The Sickly Child:* The sickly child cannot play as vigorously or do his school work as efficiently as the average child. He is likely to be considered lazy because he tires easily. Either as a reaction to the specific nature of his discomfort or because of the pampering he receives at home, he may be easily irritated. When a severe illness keeps him out of school for a considerable length of time, he is likely to be unusually worried and tense about the work he has missed. The child who has been sickly but has since become healthy has special problems, too. Often it is harder to convince the parents than the child that he is really well.

3. *The Child with Sensory Defects:* Of the possible visual defects in childhood the most common are nearsightedness (*myopia*) and farsightedness (*hyperopia*). The effect on the personality is likely to be more serious for unsuspected

hyperopics than for myopics because in addition to the inferiority feeling likely to result from repeated failures in school work and in sports, farsighted children are plagued with headaches and often with nausea. These conditions can make their school experience so unpleasant that truancy may result. The child with unsuspected defective hearing is like wise handicapped in those phases of school work which depend upon the auditory sense and in games and social relations with his peers. The most frequent reaction to defective hearing is excessive shyness and a tendency to withdraw.

4. *The Intellectually Gifted Child: Louttit* has very aptly enumerated the most frequent sources of difficulty in the adjustment of the superior child:

(*a*) Lack of teacher's recognition of superiority leading to an antagonism toward the school as an institution.
(*b*) Lack of parental recognition of superiority with resulting lack of stimulation or positive discouragement.
(*c*) Superiority over available associates so marked that social adjustment is extremely difficult.
(*d*) Development of poor study or work habits because of lack of stimulation of classroom work.
(*e*) Development of inferiority feelings because the child's interests and activities are not socially recognized by his group.
(*f*) Development of a boastful, conceited personality because of unwise emphasis by adults.
(*g*) One-sided personality development because of lack of normal social activities resulting from parental intervention or from (*c*) above.

5. *The Dull Child:* Dull children, sometimes called *"low-normal"* or *"dull-normal,"* those with I.Q.'s roughly from 75 to 90, are confronted with unusually severe hazards in the ordinary public school. Few schools have a programme which meets their needs. Usually they are left to sink or swim (*usually sink*) in classes too large to be handled satisfactorily even for the average child. The difficulty of the academic work, the speed expected of him as well as frequent inability, because of lack of facilities, to demonstrate what talents he has, constitute the major sources of frustration in the school life of the dull child.

6. *The Isolated Child:* On the transfer parents family moves, the child friendship in school and neighbourhood are interrupted, and it is not easy to form new friendship in a neighbourhood or in school. The child feels isolated. The broken home make him isolated child.

Isolated children often feel their plight keenly. They lack the status conferred by valued membership in a group and are likely to give up attempts at friendships and retire into a world of unreality.

7. *The Delinquent Child:* The *"typical"* delinquent is a boy who lives in a *"blighted area"* of a city in a home of low economic level with low moral standards as well. His parents are either not living together or are antagonistic to each other. They either utilize psychologically poor methods of discipline or reject the child altogether. His I.Q. is between 80 and 90 and he is retarded in school. *Delinquency,* however, may be found in children in whom not one of these factors is present.

8. *The "Inferior" Child:* Children with a persistent feeling of inferiority are by no means rare in our school systems. The inferiority complex stems from large discrepancies between a child's level of achievement and his level of aspiration. Any factors which depress the first or raise the second enhance the suffering of the child. Some of the most important factors which tend primarily to lower the achievement level are (1) real of imagined physical defects, (2) poor health, below average mentality, (3) low social or economic status, and (4) continued failure. Factors which tend primarily to raise the level of aspiration are: an undue emphasis on the child's natural inability to do things as well as older children or his parents; excessive competition in school or sport; and insistence by parents or teachers on too high standards.

Therefore school has the responsibility of providing a hygienic, friendly environment with understanding teachers; or aiding the continuation of sound personality growth in well adjusted children; and of assisting the children whose personalities are already warps. Overcompetition, unsuitable curriculum, Overrestriction, and poor methods of handling children are some of the factors which tend to retard personality development in any child.

MENTAL HEALTH AND SCHOOL

The role of parents and family is significant in the personality development of children. The teacher and school assume great responsibility in the process of development of children. They spend day time in school and the main focus of the school is to develop the potentialities by satisfying their needs. The school provides the proper climate for their physical, social, emotional and intellectual development. The following are the situations and activities organized in a good school:

1. School environment or climate.
2. Democratic environment or freedom of expression.
3. Provision for cocurricular activities.
4. Social emotional climate of classroom.
5. Guidance and counselling services in school.
6. Supervised study or provision for assimilation.
7. Tutorial system in school and remedial teaching.
8. Educational excursion or field trips.
9. Organization of debates and group discussion.
10. Scouting and girls guiding, N.C.C. programme.
11. Teacher-taught relation or rapport with students.

The above programmes and activities are helpful for generating conducive climate in the school. The students develop the positive attitude towards school and teachers. It should provide feelings of security irrespective of cast, religion and socio-economic status. The environment should be free from fear and tensions.

Teachers must have the knowledge, understanding and skill for organizing above programmes. They should know the basic principles of human behaviour, problems and ailments of mental health. He must be emotionally stable and have positive attitude towards teaching and students. It is also essential that the teacher's mental health should be normal.

The understanding of ailment of mental health is not enough for the teacher, but he should be capable of providing guidance and counselling for the problems of the students. The *educational guidance* is essential for the students. They should be given *remedial teaching* for their difficulties of learning. They should be provided recreational facilities in the school by organizing the *co-curricular activities* and educational trips, etc.

TEACHER'S MENTAL HEALTH

Mental health of teacher is much more important than the mental health of students. If a teacher is not sound in his mental health he can not do justice to his students and can not provide guidance in their problems. His maladjustment may have the adverse effect on children. Therefore, it is also essential to understand the causes of maladjustment or ailment of mental health of teachers or well as *remedial measures.*

The Sources of Ailments of Mental Health of Teacher

The dissatisfaction in teaching arises from the following important sources:

1. The heavy pressure of work load on teacher.
2. Inadequate salaries to the teacher.
3. Occupational insecurity.
4. Restriction on outside activities.
5. The lack of acceptance by the society.
6. Autocratic administration and supervision
7. The lack of orientation courses or refresher courses.

The mental health of the teacher is necessary to improve by improving conditions of teaching and conditions of services. This can best be effected by means of strong professional organization. The teacher can improve his own mental health, if he is able to increase his understanding of himself, accept himself largely as he is and take an active part in directing his life rather than being content with responding to pressures.

The Sources of Satisfaction in Teaching Profession

The following are the sources which arise satisfaction in teaching profession:

1. The socially useful character of the work.
2. The creative expression involved.
3. The stimulation of broad interest.
4. Personal growth and development in teaching.
5. The opportunity for association with youth.
6. The opportunity to influence social and national policy.
7. The merging of one's interests with those of the group.

8. The partial satisfaction of the needs for affection, respect, independence, freedom for expression and for maintaining the self-esteem.
9. Teaching is a noble profession.
10. Teaching involves a variety of activities physical, social, emotional and mental development.

HOW TO ENSURE TEACHER'S MENTAL HEALTH

There are various factors in school and outside the school which influence mental health of teachers. The listed factors help in maintaining mental health of teachers.

1. Improving teacher-principal relationship:
   (*a*) Democratic administration,
   (*b*) Impartial behaviour of principal,
   (*c*) Planning in advance,
   (*d*) Seniority should be considered in assigning responsibilities,
   (*e*) Proper distribution of work load,
   (*f*) Principal should have helping attitude towards teachers, and
   (*g*) Teacher's problems should be given due weightage.
2. Improving teachers relationship should have co-operative spirit among teachers.
3. Organizing refresher and orientation courses for the teachers.
4. Teachers should be allowed to attend seminars, workshops and conferences for their personal growth.
5. They should be encouraged for academic excellence.
6. Improving teacher community relations and community served by teacher.
7. Improving teacher taught relations, teacher should receive due regard and respect from the students.
8. Teachers should be rewarded or reinforced for better results or effective teaching or providing remedial teaching and guidance to the students by principal and school management.

There is a tendency to criticize the teachers by principal, students and other colleagues in our school system. The principal should have the leadership qualities to encourage or praise the teachers for their good work and performance.

They should be encouraged to attend refresher courses, orientation programmes and workshops organized by different agencies for the excellence in jobs. In school library and reading facilities should be maintained having up-to-date literature. Teachers should also be encouraged for experimental projects and innovative ideas in teaching learning situation. Teachers should be well informed with new trends and technology in the field of education.

In the pre-service teacher straining more and better courses should be offered in mental health and hygiene. The teachers trainees like such courses and many gain a great deal of insight through them. If in addition, enough psychological counsellors and psycho-therapists and medical services could be provided to all teacher training institutions, great efforts could be made in increasing the mental health of the profession.

The reading habit of books, provide guidance to the teacher related to his life:

1. Develop the habit of success in life.
2. Prepare teacher to face reality or hard facts of life.
3. He learns to react normally to emotional situation.
4. He begins to avoid worries of day-to-day working.

QUESTIONS FOR ANSWER

1. *Describe the theoretical basis of mental health. How does the Maslow Hierarchy provides the basis of mental health?*
2. *Enumerate the factors influencing mental health of child and suggest some remedial measures for these factors.*
3. *Describe the effect of school practices on children's behaviour and personality development.*
4. *Enumerate the special problems of adjustment of children and their relationship with mental health.*
5. *Describe the role of teacher and school programmes in maintaining the mental health of students in school.*
6. *Indicate the importance of sound mental health of a teacher in school and classroom. Describe the sources of ailments and satisfaction in teaching profession.*

7. *Describe the ways and means of improving mental health of teachers.*
8. *Describe the role of quality of environment in improving the mental health of students as well as teacher.*
9. *Explain the term 'Mental Health.' Describe the need for a teacher to have the knowledge and understanding of mental health of his students.*
10. *Enumerate the types of mental ailments as point out the indications of positive mental health or sound mental health of an individual.*

23

Environmental Education in Teacher Education Programme

Population explosion has transformed human ecology in a big way, therefore, there is a basic need of environmental education at every stage of our educational system, but this will only be possible if teachers at every stage of our educational system are inducted with the knowledge of environmental education, hence, there is an urgent need to include environmental education in the syllabi of teacher education programme at various levels, because teacher is the main agent for executing the process of education at every stage. We all know that education is a powerful instrument for social change as well as for social control and environmental education is problem centered, interdisciplinary value as well as community oriented programme concerned with man's survival.

NEED OF ENVIRONMENTAL EDUCATION IN TEACHER EDUCATION

Teacher education has always been recognized as one of the most crucial means of social and national development. Recently, the National Policy on Education, 1986 emphasised that the professional improvement and career enhancement of teachers should be addressed on a continuous basis. The *Programme of Action* of the policy highlighted the role of distance education in teacher education programmes, especially in view of

(*i*) the large number to be catered to,

(*ii*) the need to organise courses on a continuous basis in the career of a teacher, and

(*iii*) the unique potential of the distance mode of education to intervene without taking the teachers away from work, thus emerging as a better means of transferring knowledge, understanding and skill to them in their day-to-day practice.

Distance education has emerged as new mode of teaching which is known as distance teaching. It is different from conventional mode of teaching. In distance teaching media of communication is most important factor whereas in conventional teaching method and techniques are essential for effective presentation. Thus, it is evident there should be two types of teacher education programmes for preparing teachers:

1. Teachers training for conventional teaching, and
2. Teachers training for distance teaching.

Teachers in present times are looked upon as facilitators and managers of learning experiences organizers of situations and guides for the all round development of students. The *National Policy of Education,* 1986 has rightly placed major thrust on *child-centered* approach in teaching learning process. It asserts that, a human being is a positive asset and precious national resource which needs to be developed and nurtured with tenderness and care, coupled with dynamism.

Belgrade Charter Section (1976) has emphasised the need of *Environmental Education* and redefined, environmental ecology, objectives of environment and environmental education. A meeting of *Regional Asian Nations* held in 1976 at Bangkok passed 15 resolutions. These were classified into four areas.

1. Programmes for environmental education,
2. Training for personal environment,
3. Non-formal environmental education, and
4. Preparation of material for environmental education.

Tibliti conference U.S.S.R. (1977) of UNESCO had recommended medium term plans.

First Medium Term Plan (1977-82), and

Second Medium Term Plan (1984-89).

Under these plans several conferences and seminars were organised on environment at various levels.

Third Medium Term Plan (1990-95) has given priority to

Environmental Education. It has included—development of environmental curriculum, in-service and pre-service teachers training programmes.

The universities and colleges of China are providing in-service teachers training in environmental education. The following are the main objectives of the teachers training programmes.

- Graduates and post-graduate students are trained for environmental education.
- Preparing instructional material for teaching environmental education.
- In-service teachers are trained for teaching environmental education.
- Integrating environmental sciences and development.

The environmental education programmes have been introduced in other countries of the world such as Japan, Pakistan, Sri Lanka and Germany. The literature and course content of environmental education is to be developed at different levels and printed lectures are prepared for the use of teachers. The courses content of environmental education is being designed and developed for training teachers. Thus, teacher education programme has to play significant role in this context. Environmental education has the important place for pre-service and in-service school teachers training. The teacher-education institutions have to share this responsibility in the present context. Teacher education programmes have to prepare teachers by providing the awareness, skills, attitudes and values of environmental education. It is essential to develop environmental resource efficiency among teachers.

NCERT'S EMPHASIS ON ENVIRONMENTAL EDUCATION

NCERT is providing training for pre-service and is-service teachers. Environmental education is *interdisciplinary* in nature, therefore, it is essential to have some changes in teacher-education programmes. The teacher has to provide the awareness about, the problems of environment, which the students have to encounter and bear the consequences. We have five principles for developing teacher-education programmes.

1. Priority should be given for improving the quality of the environmental.
2. The basic scientific and social aspects of environment are to be taught to the pre-service teachers.
3. The environmental awareness, assumptions and course-content should be taught.
4. The environmental content should be included in school curriculum.
5. The awareness of technical impact on society and environmental problems should be given.

For the above following points need consideration:

1. Environmental education should be considered as an independent field of study.
2. The content course should be content-cum-methodology. Theoretical knowledge should be provided for all the points of environment. There should be provision for observation, exhibition, experimentation, discussion and other methods for teaching different points of environment.
3. Activity based approach should be employed to provide the awareness to the students. The competency should be developed among teachers through training programmes.
4. The lesson plans are to be developed on the content of environment during teaching practice.
5. An interdisciplinary approach should be followed for explaining the concepts of environment related to social studies, sciences, humanities, physical sciences.

ENVIRONMENTAL EDUCATION—THE MODULAR PROGRAMME AND IDENTIFICATION OF ENVIRONMENTAL NEEDS OF TRAINING

NCERT, SCERT, Directorate of Environment and other departments have tried to develop the content courses for teachers training. Those organisations have evolved some models which can be effectively used. Following types of programmes are being organized for in-service teachers.

1. There to four weeks contact programme should be

organized to orient in-service teachers about *environmental education* and different methods.

2. The in-service teachers are to be trained for developing programmed instructional material for self-learning. The instructional material on environmental education should be distributed free of cost to in-service teachers. Such workshops have been organized by NCERT and UNESCO.
3. Distance Education mode of training can also be used for in-service teachers for developing awareness and understanding of environmental education. The *print* and *non-print media* can be effectively used for in-service teachers. The correspondence courses can also be used for environmental education for pre-service and in-service teachers.
4. Mass communication can be used for in-service teachers training. Non-formal system is being used to provide the awareness and understanding of environmental problems and its consequences. The environmental consciousness can be development through mass-communication—newspapers, radio, television, magazines, publicity media, etc.
5. The seminars, group discussion, workshops and conferences are being organized for in-service teachers on environmental education.
6. In-service teachers should be encouraged to undertake action research project for local environmental problems related to their teaching subjects. There should be involvement of both teacher and students in such projects.

IDENTIFICATION OF TRAINING NEEDS

These are as follows:

- Generalization from the available literature on environmental education in general, and on the roles of differing personnel categories in particular.
- Analysis of the tasks, the problems of environment, anticipated tasks and the problems expected therein.
- Critical incident analysis, *i.e.*, an analysis of individual's behaviour in various situations, its consequences in terms

of the productivity of the task concerned; such exercises identify problems which suggest training needs.

- Case studies of successful educators help in identifying those characteristics which contribute in their success; these characteristics may then be pointed to, the tainees encouraged to develop them through training.
- Pooling the views and opinions of experienced people as to what they think and believe the training needs help in preparing a long list of possible needs, where from after further analysis dependable training needs can be identified.
- Awareness of environmental education is to be given from primary level to the university level. Therefore content and tasks are to be analysed at primary, secondary, higher secondary and higher levels so as to identify teachers training requirement at these levels.
- The same content environmental education is to be taught to realize different types of objectives. The teachers training needs are to be identified for teacher-education programmes at different levels in view to realize the objectives.

OBJECTIVES OF ENVIRONMENTAL EDUCATION AND B.ED., M.ED COURSES

N.C.T.E. has formulated objectives of teacher education programmes at B.Ed. and M.Ed. levels and prepared course content. The course content has been classified into three parts. Theoretical, community work and practical work. The environmental education should be the part of community work along with its practical work. The following are the objectives of environmental education which are to be realized through our teacher-education programmes:

1. To develop knowledge and understanding of environment and its problems.
2. To help in acquiring skills for identifying and solving environment and its problems.
3. To develop set of values, attitudes and feelings concern for the environment and to encourage for active participation in protection of environment.

4. To develop an ability for evaluating and managing environmental components in terms of social, economic and cultural factors.

These objectives can be realized by introducing the course content of environmental education since the primary stage as an integral part of education. The teachers training course should include environmental education at all levels.

Levels of Teacher Education	*Objectives*
1. Primary Teachers	Awareness of environment.
2. Secondary and higher secondary teachers	Understanding and skills for real life situation of natural resources.
3. College and university teachers	Ability for solving environment problem.

ENVIRONMENTAL EDUCATION—COURSE CONTENTS

Environmental education has its own independent course content while is interdisciplinary in nature. National and International conferences and seminars have attempted to develop the content of environmental education which is at emerging stage. The following is an outline of the course content which is to be taught at different levels of teacher training programmes.

First Part—Concept of Environmental Education

Concept of environment and its components, concept of education, meaning and structure of environmental education and as an independent field of study.

Second Part—Ecology and Environmental Pollution

Concept of ecology and ecosystem, quality of environment, pollution and degradation. Human ecology and environmentalism. Interdependency in the environment. Food chains and food webs, flow of energy and biochemical cycles.

Third Part—Educational and Psychological Environment

Concept of educational environment—organizations, climate and health, growth and development, mental health, population explosion and environmental problems.

Fourth Part—Environmental Management

Meaning of environmental management, teachers education, adult education, role of media, problems and remedies, impact of environmental education.

ENVIRONMENTAL EDUCATION—TEACHING STRATEGIES

The objectives of environmental education are very wide and *interdisciplinary* in nature. Thus, methodology of teaching of environmental education is varied in nature and teacher educators have to employ the following teaching strategies:

1. Teaching strategies for providing awareness, knowledge and understanding of environmental education.
2. Organizing some action research projects for local environmental problems or related to school organizational climate.
3. Extension programmes for the publicity of environmental education. Seminars, workshops and cultural programmes are to be organized. The various media *print* and *non-print media* can be utilized for the extension work.
4. Research studies can be undertaken at post-graduate level on environmental problems. *Interdisciplinary projects* can be encouraged for improving the quality of the environment.

The above methodology can be used for pre-service and in-service teacher education programmes. Environmenal education should be given the status of *independent discipline.* The content-cum-methodology based approach should be emphasised. The observation exhibition and educational excursions can also be employed for developing practical ability among pupil teachers. The programmed learning strategy can be effectively used for distance teacher education programmes.

There are various methods of teaching which can be effectively used in teacher education programme for awareness and understanding environmental problems, but group discussion is most suitable for the awareness and project method for the skills and practical ability.

GROUP DISCUSSION

Group discussion is considered as a democratic teaching strategy for providing the awareness and understanding of the concepts. The pupils are more active in it. It is pupil centred teaching strategy. It may be of three types: by teachers, by pupils and by both.

Objectives: The affective objectives and higher order cognitive objectives may be achieved.

Structure: The group discussion is organized in two forms: formal and informal. In formal group discussion, proper schedule is prepared and certain rules are observed.

The *group discussion* is organized on any educational problem or curriculum problem. Teacher acts as a leader of the group, but in the absence of a teacher, pupils have to select a student to act as a leader of the group. The leader of the group prepares a plan for discussion. In the group discussion, due weightage is given to the answers and questions of the pupils.

Principles: This strategy is based upon the following principles of teaching:

1. Principle of active participation,
2. Principle of freedom for work, and
3. Principle of group work and equal opportunities to ask questions and to answer them.

Advantage: The following are the main advantages of this strategy:

1. It develops the feeling of group work and group participation.
2. It develops the problem solving attitude and the tolerance to hear one's own criticism.
3. It helps in developing the creative ability and thinking among pupils.
4. It helps in developing the feeling co-operation.
5. It has the greater scope of criticism for incorrect approaches, ideas and concepts.

6. The higher order cognitive and affective objectives of teaching are achieved.

Limitations: It has the following limitations:

1. In the discussion, only few students dominate and discuss more and large number of students do not participate in the discussion.
2. Generally groups are formed in this strategy and they are critical to another.
3. It has greater chances for deviation from the main topic.
4. It involves more criticism rather than relevant discussion.

Suggestions: It may be improved and can be effectively employed by observing the following precautions:

1. Irrelevant criticism should not be encouraged.
2. Students should be encouraged and motivated to participate in the discussion.
3. Every student should be provided an opportunity to participate in the discussion.

PROJECT WORK

It is a new teaching strategy and it has been evolved as a result of social tendency of education. The advocates of the strategy are of this opinion that education should be related to life situations. It is *experience centred* teaching strategy. The exponent of project method is *W. H. Kilpatrick.* The main focus of this strategy is to socialize a child.

Objectives: It is used to achieve cognitive and affective objectives. The main focus is to socialize a child and to develop the ability of problem solving.

Structure: The teacher places the real problems related to life situation, and the learner realizes its utility in his life. The learner prepares a plan for solving the problem. The teacher's job is to provide guidance. The students collects several informations for solving the problems. The students themselves make an effort to seek solution of the problem by studying the materials.

Principles: It involves the following principles:

1. *Principle of Utility:* The problem of study is related with life situation of the learners.

2. *Principle of Readiness:* The learner becomes active in finding out the solution of the problem.
3. *Principle of Learning by Doing:* Learner has to perform certain tasks in project strategy.
4. *Learner gets Freedom to Work:* The learning situations are realistic.
5. *Principle of Socialism:* It develops the feeling of co-operation and group work.

CLASSIFICATION OF PROJECT

Kilpatrick has classified the project strategies under four types:

1. *Constructive:* In this type learner has to complete certain task.
2. *Artistic:* This type of project develops the aesthetic taste of the learner.
3. *Problem-Centred:* A problem is presented before the learner and he has to seek the solution of the problem.
4. *Group Practice:* A task is assigned in which group work is required to complete it.

Procedure of Project Strategy: Usually six steps are followed in each type of project strategy.

Step 1: To identify a problem related to life situation of the learner.
Step 2: To select and define the problem.
Step 3: To prepare a plan for finding out the solution of the problem.
Step 4: To implement the plan.
Step 5: To evaluate the workability of the project plan.
Step 6: To prepare a record of the project.

Advantages: It has the following advantages:

1. Project strategy is based upon psychological and sociological principles.
2. The new knowledge is imparted by linking it with their life situations.
3. It develops insight toward life problems.
4. All school subjects can be taught by an integrated approach.

5. Project strategy provides an opportunity for work experience, divergent thinking and social efficiency.

Limitations: It has the following disadvantages:

1. The subject-content can not be taught systematically or in a sequence.
2. The plan projects can not be designed for all school subjects and on the whole subject-matter of schools subjects.
3. It is very costly and time consuming strategy of teaching.
4. It cannot be used in teaching for higher classes.
5. All social qualities can not be developed by this strategy.

The following precautions should be taken in using this strategy to successfully realise the object of study.

1. It should be used in agriculture and technical institutions.
2. The problem of the project should be economical and useful.
3. It should be employed as a supplementary teaching technique.
4. It should be used at primary and secondary levels.

TEACHER EDUCATION INSTITUTIONS

Pre-service teachers training is organized from nursery or pre-primary teachers to college and university level.

1. Pre-primary pre-service teachers training is organized for his years duration. The environmental education course of local level should be included for teachers-trainees, along some practical works.
2. Pre-service primary teachers training is organized for one year duration, *e.g.*, H.T.C., B.T.C. and J.T.C., etc.
3. Secondary and higher secondary teachers training is organized for one year duration, *e.g.* B.Ed. and L.T. The environmental education course should be the compulsory course along with some community work related to environmental problems of local and regional level.
4. M.Ed. and M.Phil. courses should be recoganized and environmental education should be the integral part of the courses. Some project work and research work should

be conducted on environmental problems of regional and national level.

5. According to *National Policy of Education* U.G.C. has introduced academic staff college for fresh college lecturers to orient them for teaching methodology of higher level. The environmental awareness should also be provided to them.

There is very wide field for the teachers of environmental education, *e.g.* physical environment, social environment, psychological environment, biological environment, environmental geography, cultural environment. Therefore, it should be included in two forms—environmental education as core course, and specification at their subject level or at teaching subject level should be the part of the course content.

CO-CURRICULAR ACTIVITIES

In teacher education programmes various co-curricular activities and cultural programmes are organized to develop some practical abilities among pupil-teachers. The major co-curricular activities are—Scouting and Girls guiding, sessional work, preparation of teaching aids, educational excursions, social and cultural activities and daily assembly programme, etc. These programmes can be organized to develop the environmental consciousness and role of teacher in the environmental pollution, though it is the responsibility of the society as a whole, but teacher can play a significant role by providing the awareness and consciousness among the young generation at local, regional and national levels through educational excursions and contact programmes.

The co-curricular activities should be organised for environmental problems at local level. The sanitation and cleanliness of institution and locality. The public places and parks should be cleaned. The mottos of sanitation and protection of environment can be designed and placed for the public awareness. To waste material should be kept at proper place.

It is a teacher who can develop consciousness among his students and people in general by organizing different types of co-curricular activities. These activities may be helpful for the protection of physical, social and psychological environment. Some video films can be prepared for this purpose. Some organizations are preparing such video films.

ENVIRONMENTAL EDUCATION FOR DISTANCE TEACHERS

The distance teachers are prepared for organizing effective distance teaching. The distance teaching has the three dimensions—*content, presentation* and *communication.* The distance teachers training requires content, presentation and communication awareness and the practice for teaching. Distance teachers have to acquire teaching skills for the contact programme as supportive devices. Thus distance teachers need the different modes for preparing teachers.

NEED FOR TRAINING

In the context of distance education, multi-media strategies are followed, preparation and presentation of materials is systematic, student-support services are provided to make the system more effective, the design of the educational structure as a whole is much more advanced than the earlier correspondence or broadcasting education, and that the system is a deliberate effort to democratise education. In spite of these common characteristics, distance education systems differ widely in their organisation, practices and objectives, as their target clientele, their scales of operation and their structural complexities differ in essentials. However, these systems are now a major factor in educational development in many countries all over the world.

In this context the corner stone of the edifice of caution is *'trained personnel.'* The implications of what we have said above are that distance education:

(*i*) has recognisable features,
(*ii*) has diverse structure and practices,
(*iii*) is a major factor in educational development, and
(*iv*) needs to be safeguarded as a system.

Distance teachers training programmes can effectively use the print and non-print media for the awareness of environmental education. This programme has wide coverage of natural problems related to environment. IGNOU has introduce distance teachers training programme, environment education should be the core content.

NATURE OF TRAINING

In this fast changing world *'training once-in-a life-time'* has become a life-time affair for serious professionalism. Besides, the variety of the personnel to be trained is vast (*Unit*) and they are at different stages of their careers—some in permanent positions in well established institutions, some in temporary positions, some working on projects, some on long-term assignments—and all of them at differing levels of concern.

The anticipated progressive career profile suggests that those in permanent positions need revitalisation of their skills and practices, those in temporary positions will move to permanent positions; those working on projects will go to long-term assignments; and those working on long term assignments will step into permanent positions. Corresponding to this progressive upward mobility in the career prospects of a trainee, it is likely that the systems and sub-systems within a known system of distance education undergo changes—communication technology is changing rapidly, educational concepts and learning theories are breaking new grounds, etc. An effective training programme will have to take care of all the changes.

Now we need to list a few basic principles and specific activities that may be used to differentiate the various training types and the corresponding activities according to the needs of the specific groups of the personnel.

Scaling the Scope of the Programme

First and foremost the trainers or the training institution must measure the scale and judge the scope of the programme for which training is to be arranged—the training programme should suit that scale and scope adequately for a distance education project with a single specific objective, a training programme of two days may be enough to enable the personnel involved perform their tasks satisfactorily. An international agency may conduct a workshop of eight to ten days duration at a particular national centre involving trainees from a region, with the objective of achieving multiplier effect through subsequent similar workshops conducted in participating countries through the personnel trained at the international workshop.

Short and Long-term Advantages of the Programme

The second consideration is the short-term and long-term advantages of a training programme. It may be that the scale and scope of a training programme impose limited objectives and activities on it. Care should, however, be taken that a programme of limited scope builds reasonable motivation for further work beyond what the programme provides, and conversely a programme of vast scope should lay reasonable emphasis on immediate need and applications.

Catering both Institutional and Individual Needs

Both the needs of the individual participants and those of the institute should be catered to. Though a training programme always aims at achieving an objective for an institution to reinforce an existing distance education system or modify and improve such a system, the building blocks of that reinforcement and/or change are the individuals who come forward for the training. For the programme to be successful, it should be satisfying for the individuals too, though the overall objective continues to be the needs of the institute and/or the country.

Linking Past Activities/Events with Future

As stated above, training should not be *'once-in-a-life-time affair'*, it should build links with the training events that have gone before it, and create scope for other training events that may be linked to it in the future. To make this linking a possibility, each training programme must have built evaluation mechanisms which provide for follow-up changes, modifications and extensions. The ultimate result of such an approach is that the rewards of training turn to be cumulative.

Providing Models of Acceptable and Desirable Behaviour

To cover the affective domain, training should modify the behaviour of the trainees by providing models of acceptable and desirable behaviour patterns expected of distance educators. This objective can be achieved by practising what is preached about its characteristic features—it should be systematic, well planned, efficiently managed, well proportioned with regard to its components and the trainer should conduct himself admirably to set living examples for the trainees.

THE UGC AND THE NATIONAL COUNCIL OF TEACHER EDUCATION (NCTE)

Besides the States Ministries of Education, the Ministry of Human Resource Development, Government of India, the University Grants Commission, the National Council of Educational Research and Training and the *National Council of Teacher Education* are the agencies which influence the policy and practice of teacher education in India. Leaving out from our discussion the State Ministries of Education for obvious reasons, in this section we shall reflect and comment, briefly though, on the views of the latter agencies in order to arrive at the stand we may take on this issue.

GOVERNMENT'S APPROACH

Keeping in view the facts that the Government of India has established a national university not only to run various courses/ programmes through the distance mode but also to promote and determine standards therein, that efforts are on to establish, a network of distance education institutions to make the system more responsive to social needs and more cost efficient and that substantial sums have been contributed to international bodies like the COL (Canada) for the promotion of distance education, our firm belief is that the Government of India—

(*i*) strongly believes in the effectiveness of distance education,
(*ii*) makes all the efforts to promote it both nationally and internationally, and
(*iii*) is determined to use this system to improve the existing state of educational affairs in the country.

A glimpse of this concern is evident in one of their communications to the NCTE and we quote it:

(*i*) One of the important aspects of B.Ed. Correspondence programme, which needs consideration is whether correspondence B.Ed. courses should also be made available to nursery and elementary school teachers who wish to improve their qualification and thereby career prospects and if yes, what should be the eligibility criteria for this category of candidates? The considered advice of NCTE or NCERT is request on this vital point.

(*ii*) It would be helpful, if an up-to-date state of norms and guidelines could be evolved for B.Ed. correspondence courses keeping in view (*a*) the developments since 1980 (especially, the NPE and POA), and (*b*) the fact that at least for certain categories of candidates such courses will have to be run for quite a few years to come.

(*iii*) It is not clear what specific steps NCTE or NCERT has taken so far to implement the resolutions passed by NCTE from time to time for generally putting an end to correspondence courses by way of formally taking up the matter with UGC and Universities/State Governments concerned. If the matter was pursued with these bodies what stand they took?"

From this communication we conclude that the Government of India is keen not only to improve the lot of secondary school teachers but also that of the primary school teachers. Secondly, the concern is about the efficient running of distance education courses, and thirdly there is evidence that the Government favours the process of participatory decision-making. All this is commendable. However, the Government has to function through various agencies like UGC, etc. to which we turn now.

CONCERNS OF UGC AND NCTE

The views of the UGC with regard to distance/correspondence education in general are evident from the following statement:

"The Commission has been supporting the programmes of distance/correspondence courses with a view to providing a new stream of education to enable a large number of persons with necessary aptitude to acquire further knowledge and improve their professional competence".

However UGC shifted its point of view considerably in the

eighties basing it on the working of the correspondence courses and on the advice of the NCTE.

The NCTE appointed a committee in 1980 to ascertain the quality of B. Ed. programmes offered through correspondence in several universities. After looking into the operational aspects of these programmes, especially the practice teaching component the committee recommended that the programmes be confined to the respective states in which the universities concerned operate, that the programmes through *correspondence-cum-contact mode* be offered only to clear the backlog of untrained secondary and primary teachers and that the first degree in professional preparation of secondary school teachers be obtained only through a formal course. It needs to be mentioned here that of the ten recommendations made by the committee, one, recommends the correspondence mode for a specific purpose (*to remove the backlog*), two, propose to stop it altogether and seven recommend reforms to make the system effective. Interestingly, the seven reformative recommendations do not seem to have made any impact, or if any steps were taken to implement those reform they have generally not succeeded.

Subsequently, concerned about the continuing deterioration in teacher education through correspondence mode, the August 1987 meeting of the NCTE Standing Committee on Secondary and College Teacher Education concluded that B. Ed. through correspondence should be scrapped, and at the end of the meeting of Standing Committee (August, 1987) a delegation led by *K.L. Shrimali* submitted a memorandum to the ministry of MHRD, GOI, demanding that the B. Ed. programmes offered through the correspondence mode be stopped forthwith.

At this, among other things, the Government of India sent a query to the NCTE. This was done in July 1988.

The NCTE did not act in haste. Instead, giving due consideration to the feeling among many educationists that the general deterioration of standards in secondary teacher education and the proliferation of B. Ed. programmes through correspondence are casually linked and also to the fact that recently impressive developments have taken place in the field of distance education, the NCTE appointed another Committee to look into the relevant aspects of teacher education through correspondence and make recommendations on the use of distance education therein. The

Committee met on March 31, 1988 and then on June 8, 1989. It made five recommendations, the major ones being as follows:

(*i*) The teacher education curricula demand a great deal of weightage for live classroom experiences and other forms of human interaction.

(*ii*) Teacher education through distance education modes, if suitably organised can emerge as a trend setter in quality training for those working in face-to-face mode.

And to conclude, it recommended that clear and unambiguous guidelines incorporating new possibilities in distance education be arrived at. In sequence with the recommendations it presented a set of seven well conceived guidelines that could be followed in order to organise effective training programmes through the distance mode.

It needs to be stated emphatically that this committee does not only appear to be better informed about the potential of teacher education but is also positive in its approach for environmental education.

QUESTIONS FOR ANSWER

1. *Describe the need and importance in environmental education in teacher education programmes.*
2. *Identify training needs and modular programme for teachers training in environmental education.*
3. *Enumerate the stagewise objectives of environmental education in teacher-education.*
4. *Describe the structure of course consent of environmental education which is essential for pre-service and in-service teachers.*
5. *Describe teaching strategies and techniques for imparting environmental awareness used in teacher education.*
6. *Write short notes on the following:*
   (*a*) *Project-Teaching strategy.*
   (*b*) *Curricular activities in environmental education in teacher education.*
   (*c*) *Role of National Council of Teacher Education and U.G.C.*

24

Mass Media: The Instrument of Environmental Education

Population explosion has greatly created grave environmental problems. Yet the programmes of mass education may be the powerful means of creating environmental awareness. Science and technological advances have made availability of radio and television possible almost to each house, therefore, the mass media through its environmental programmes based on the principles of effective distance education programme, is a vital means of environmental education. Mass media is of two types:

1. Print Media, and
2. Non-print Media.

Hereunder, we will discuss various aspects of this concept briefly.

INSTRUCTIONAL MEDIA

The use of instructional media is an essential component of teaching learning process to realize various socio-economic, cultural and national goals. The media contribute to the efficiency as well as effectiveness of teaching learning process both in the case of face-to-face and distance education system.

These days method and media are equally important for teaching learning process. The media facilitates to overcome the distance between teacher and students. The media knocks at the door of students. The method facilitates the effective presentation of the content in face-to-face or word of mouth communication. The media also includes the method of teaching in the system of distance education.

There are various types of media which are used in distance teaching. These may be classified into two categories:

1. Print Instructional Media, and
2. Non-print Instructional Media.

The print instructional media is used in correspondence-education or postal-education. The printed matter and lessons are sent to the students through postal services.

The non-print instructional media is used in distance-teaching with the help of radio, television, computer, teleconferencing and video disc, etc. The subject-matter is communicated to the students by employing technical devices or *'electronic'* media.

Print Media

It has been found that print materials or text, although the most commonly used medium, may not be the only or the perfect medium to impart information in a distance education system. Secondly, *'non-print'* or modern *'electronic media'* have certain unique qualities which facilitate distance learning much more than the *'print'* medium in certain cases. This overview of the potentials on non-print media will lead us find that these media lend themselves particularly well to certain generalised educational purposes and provide support to print-based instruction.

Print as a medium for transmitting information has been the most important component of learning. It has been so even in the case of distance education. It is because print medium is adaptable to many different learning environments; it is economical and it has traditionally been used for pedagogical purposes. Yet it suffers from some serious limitations. The most crucial among them is that it demands the skills of literacy. The absence of literacy and of study skills on the part of a prospective learner can make the print-medium totally useless. Apart from this serious drawback, the print-medium suffers from other limitations. These limitations may be described as:

(*i*) *'print'* does not allow for immediate teacher-learner and learner-learner interaction;

(ii) *'print'* does not normally provide for *'active'* learner participation (the participation is 'passive');

(*iii*) *'print'* entails long waiting periods for feed back from either side (from learner to teacher and from teacher to learner);

(*iv*) with *'print'* it is difficult to provide individualised instruction;

(*v*) *'print'* does not help much in providing training in psychomotor skills; and

(*vi*) *'print'* entails pedagogically cumbersome length (both spatially and temporally) while instructing on subtle complex processes.

Non-Print Media

Keeping these limitations of print medium in view it seems that in future, distance education is likely to turn increasingly to the use of non-print media offered by the contemporary technological advances.

Advantages

Some of the strengths of these non-print media:

1. *They facilitate diverse learning objective:* In distance teaching the instruction moves away from the conventional face-to-face teaching mode and a reasonable reliance on various other media becomes necessary to meet diverse learning objectives.

2. *They motivate learners psychologically:* The use of electronic media has proved psychologically exciting for students—both at the preparation and the participation stage—and consequently it promotes learning. Several of the introductory functions, such as directing attention, arousing motivation, providing a rationale, etc., may be served by non-print media more effectively than by a printed text.

These media have special power to stimulate imagination and interest and appeal to the neo-literate. For example, the experience of Korea in providing non-formal education with the use of television, shows that *"the excitement of television sometimes leads participants in a projects to undertake tasks they might otherwise hesitate to attempt"*.

3. *They contribute to specific learning activities:* Certain non-print media formats and delivers systems contribute particularly well to distance students' learning activities. For example, audio tapes or computers can be used effectively to drill and practice learners

in arithmetic and language learning. Electronic media can help promote the *'discovery'* approach to learning. For example a film can be exploited for discovery teaching in the physical sciences.

Students keep watching the various sections of the film unit they perceive the relationships between self and the visuals. Then they are curious to find out the principles that explain those relationships. Likewise, in the social sciences various media types can be used to present learners with visual and auditory experiences that provide related inquiry. Films and simulations are often used to present *'real-life'* or *'laboratory learning'*.

4. *They help learners get involved:* Many studies have emphasized how the non-print media achieve learner involvement and participation and thereby facilitate learning. Some electronic media lend themselves more to student participation than the print material. The psychomotor skills are learned better if practised while watching a film in which those skills are being performed. Similarly, overt written or oral small responses during a film have been found to facilitate learning. Even convert responses like silent repetition of key vocabulary and specified points in a lesson are found to be effective. A group discussion after the use of video casette or films can also be used to enhance learning.

5. *They increase students' concentration:* Moreover, electronic media directed instruction increases students' concentration on a task because teachers employing television for instruction have found that televised instruction receives more concentration and has fewer diversions than classroom instruction. Because instruction through media is structured, the objectives are clearly defined, and the instructional environment is created to achieve those objectives. Media help provide a learning atmosphere in which students actively participate in the learning process.

6. *They accommodate individual needs:* Moreover, non-print media have the flexibility of accommodating individual needs and interests, especially through computers. The emergence of technological advances has very well coincided with the increasing awareness of individualised instruction. The variety and flexibility of new media offer the opportunity to adapt and media-combination for use in individualised instruction. For example, programmed instructions or the system of audio tutorial instructions are specifically designed for individualised learning.

By individualised instruction, it is possible to treat groups of students to suit the common characteristics they exhibit. For example, handicapped students who are in particular need, get special instructional treatment. In this way we can best adjust instructions according to the characteristics of any given group of students.

7. *They extend the role of teacher:* With the use of non-print media, the role of a teacher extends further than merely being a dispenser of information. Media utilisation permits teachers to become creative managers of the learning experience. They can find more time to spend on diagnosing students' problems, holding consultations individually, and offering counsel and guidance.

8. *They help learners monitor the information input:* Some of the technological devices like the audio cassettes and the video cassettes allow the learners the freedom of the choice and the length of information they would like to get exposed to. They also allow them the freedom to listen to and/or view the whole/part of an information pack as many times as they would like to. Besides, these technologies also enable them to choose their own convenient time to receive any given information.

APPROACHES OF INSTRUCTION AND USE

Educational planners decide that media-print should be built into the curriculum in an inseparable fashion because different media serve different educational functions. The distance learner, to a great extent, is deprived of face-to-face interaction. Combined with the print medium the non-print media can play an integrative role to compensate the absence of the normal teacher-learner relationship which is lacking in distance education and provide for the varying needs of the learner.

In practice, environmental education depends mostly on a *'master-medium'*, occasionally combined with other media. Although found desirable there is no set pattern to guide, the combination of media in distance education. Different distance teaching institutions combine various media according to their needs, target group, philosophies, resources and course contents. Various applications of approaches to combine media can be described as follows:

1. Integrated,

2. Complementary,
3. Supplementary, and
4. Independent.

1. Integrated Media Use

An integrated approach is decided at curricular level. It means that *'non-print'* media are totally integrated with the *'master medium'*—in most of the cases the master medium is the print. If we present this integration of media in mathematical terms, we can say that the hundred per cent of information is divided between the two media types. It could be 80 per cent print and 20 per cent non-print or 70 per cent print and 30 per cent non-print and so on. Both media types should be integral parts of course development and delivery.

The integration of media is such that in this approach the students recognise that *'non-print'* media also have something *'special'* to teach them and they are taken seriously. As watching TV is a part of syllabus, indirectly students are formed to watch it. There are assignments and examinations based on these *'non-print'* media parts. This media-mix is well adjusted to the time assigned to students for that course and it does not require extra timings.

2. Complementary Media Use

In the complementary approach, the decision is taken at the syllabus-farming level. It is decided that the whole information to be transmitted through print and non-print media and the division is sharply defined. For example, if 70 per cent is for print then 30 per cent is for non-print media. This division is clearly indicated in the very beginning, *i.e.,* out of ten units/ topics seven will be covered through delivered texts and three through additional media. This approach is particularly suitable for science subjects or subjects having both theoretical and practical components like engineering.

3. Supplementary Media Use

The prime aim of this approach is to enrich the experience of learners. The *'master-medium'* (*mostly, the print*) contains the hundred per cent information and some part(s) of the information is again provided through the other medium. For example, as case study might be presented on the TV for a better understanding of a theoretical principle discussed in an environment course; or, a film on sanitation or nutrition can be shown after a discussion about it in a rural development.

No planning at syllabus level is required for this type of media-mix because non-print media can be developed and delivered at a later stage.

4. Independent Media Use

By the independent approach we mean that form of distance teaching which does not use print medium to a large extent. Here again, the hundred per cent information is through non-print media (*except few media notes*). This approach is very appropriate if the target group is not well educated, or has not developed reading habits or the course itself consists of total practical training.

EDUCATIONAL RADIO

The radio is cheapest and the most easily accessible of all these means. No doubt, its potential audience is very large in comparison to the audience of other mass media. It caters to the people of different ages and levels of maturity ranging from a primary school child to its grandfather. Besides the cost-factor and the wide-ranging appeal, another reason for its popular use is the fact that it is easy to handle. While all these attributes make it a wide-reaching means of mass communication, it has a pedagogically strong reason for its use in education and that is its versatility, lending itself to serve different purposes. For instance, while it provides learners with new joys of learning, it can develop their command over vocabulary, promote concentration and critical listening, and improve fluency and confidence in speech and discussion. It can be used for formal and non-formal education. Its broadcasts can be designed to supplement/enrich the formal school subjects. These broadcasts may clarify a concept, or give additional views on a theme, or provide further illustrations and case studies related to an issue. Broadcasts under non-formal education may comprise programmes such as children's programme, women's programme, adult education programme, rural development programe and social action programmes which help equalise or enlarge educational opportunities.

The broadcast programmes of non-formal education of the AIR have recorded tremendous success in achieving worthy objectives in the areas of agriculture and rural development.

The introduction of educational radio can be viewed as follows:

1. School broadcasts,
2. Adult education and community development project,
3. Farm and home broadcasts,
4. University broadcasts,
5. Language learning projects, and
6. Environmental awareness

1. *School Broadcasts*

Even before the AIR came into existence there were occasional broadcasts for schools from Bombay and Calcutta. It was only in 1937 that organised school broadcasting started in Calcutta. Funds were allotted to schools to buy radio sets. Out of enthusiasm, the AIR authorities embarked on school programmes from Delhi, Kolkata, Chennai and Mumbai without waiting for schools to acquire radio sets. In the beginning, the school programmes were not strictly governed by the curriculum. With the passage of time and acquisition of more experience, the AIR tried to make its radio broadcasts more curriculum oriented but in the absence of common syllabi and time table in schools, even within the same state, it could not succeed in making its broadcasts fully curriculum oriented.

The AIR is assisted by various agencies in planning their educational programmes, particularly the programmes for the young—the primary and the secondary level students. For example, the Central Institute of Educational Technology (CIET); a wing of NCERT, regularly produces programmes for primary classes and these programmes are broadcast by Jaipur and Ajmer stations of the AIR.

2. *Adult Education and Community Development Project*

In 1956 attempt was made to communicate with the rural people and promote innovation through broadcasts. The programme was called 'Radio Forum'. This kind of programme was originally designed and tried in Canada. With the help of UNESCO, India decided to try it in the Indian context. *'Radio forums' (defined as a 'listening-cum-discussion-cum-action group'*) of villagers of about 20 members each were organised in everyone of the 144 villages. The members listened to a thirty-minute radio programme on some environmental or community-development practice, then discussed it and decided whether to take any action on it in their own village.

The project was a great success. Many action programmes were planned and put into practice. Members of the forum learned a great from the radio programmes. A careful research scheme revealed that persons who sat in the forum showed a substantial gain in processing information and contributing to constructive discussions.

3. *Farm and Home Broadcasts*

To improve the effectiveness of radio progrmmes in rural/social change the AIR initiated the farm and home broadcasts in 1966. These broadcasts were designed to provide information and advice on agricultural and allied topics. The aim was to educate the farmers and provide them assistance in adopting innovative practices in their fields. The broadcasts, under this programme are of immediate local relevance. They are directly linked with the day-to-day agricultural practices of the farmers. The officials also conduct occasional farm radio schools and these schools have proved to be very effective.

4. *University Broadcasts*

Radio programme on subjects of academic interest have been broadcast from the AIR stations from the very beginning of organised broadcasting. In 1965, an attempt was made to assess the impact of these broadcasts on students and it was found that there was little interest among students.

However, it was believed that the desire to expand higher education as widely as possible among the different strata of the society, could be fulfilled through the use of educational radio broadcasts. Consequently two types of programmes—*'general' and 'enrichment'* came into existence. While general programmes include topics of public interest, *e.g.*, environmental and population awareness, the enrichment programmes support correspondence education offered by universities in the respective jurisdiction. Responsibility for planning the courses rests with the academics, while broadcasting is arranged by the ratio stations in consultation with the universities. In Delhi, the correspondence school of the University of Delhi works out the details (*such as curriculum, scripting, broadcast schedule, etc.*) in consultation with the AIR to provide possibilities of using radio for its courses.

5. *Environmental Awareness and Understanding Broadcast*

Radio programmes on environmental education have been broadcast from the AIR stations, organized by government and non-government social organizations.

Programme Production

The process of preparing a good radio programme begins with the conceptualization of a given idea and ends with its presentation in the form of a programme. The presentation is preceded by the three stages of planning, production and post-production.

Planning Stage

The planning stage includes the following developmental steps:

(*i*) *Select the topic/idea:* The programme planners should know what course or subject-matter the radio programme belongs to. The scope of the programme should be defined in clear terms.

(*ii*) *State the objectives*: The objectives are set in terms of the expected behavioural changes.

(*iii*) *Analyse the target audience:* The needs and interests of potential listeners should be analysed. Age, sex, professional experience, education, availability of spare time, etc., need to be analysed to guide the making up of the programme.

(*iv*) *Analyse the content:* The content should be analysed into topics and sub-topics. The relevant information should be collected through specific research projects on the topic(s).

(*v*) *Write the script:* The content matter should be put in sequence following a systematic way. The format should also be decided at this stage.

(*vi*) *Select the music sound effects:* The music should be attractive and should suit the nature of the given content. The sound effect should provide a background reflecting the period, the locate or the mood of the content matter.

(*vii*) *Select the voice:* In radio, the *'talent'* who gives the talk or lecture, or participates in a programme is important. The *'talent'* should be an effective *'communicator'*.

Production Stage

After the planning stage is gone through, the actual production, *i.e.*, recording of the programme is undertaken. It involves:

(*i*) *Preparation of the studio and the equipment:* The studio is kept ready before the recording to adjust music, sound effects, etc.

(*ii*) *Rehearsal:* Before the final recording, *'production conference' (where everyone involved in the production is briefed on what he/she is to do)* and *'rehearsal'* are held to ensure the best possible quality in terms of content and prevention. A rehearsal help boost self-confidence of the participants and to ensure the quality of the final product.

Post-Production Stage

This is the final stage of programming. After production, the programme is reviewed and unwanted segments are edited to adjust the programme to an exact time length.

All the above steps facilitate a good production. But the creativity, imagination and sincerity on the part of programme planners, subject experts and producers play a more important role in producing a good piece. One, therefore, should not force the programmes to strictly follow all these steps one by one. He should, when he is capable of handling the situation independently, be given enough freedom to break away from the formal production process.

EDUCATIONAL RADIO—THE CHARACTERISTICS

The potentials of radio broadcastings stem from two sources:

- Its low capital requirements, low operating costs and wide coverage.

- Its pedagogical values.

We identify here some characteristics that contribute to its potential:

1. *Wide coverage:* Today we cover a major portion of our territory by radio broadcasts as the broadcast facility is available throughout the sub-continent. As such, the radio can extend learning at a distance as it can easily and quickly reach the isolated rural audiences. The AIR has many years of experience of combining the radio with correspondence and non-formal education.
2. *Easy accessibility:* In comparison to other media radio is accessible to the majority of our countrymen. Low cost transistors within the easy reach of even the economically weak people are available in the market. It can, therefore, be used as a home-based means of imparting education.
3. *Easy leaner-reception:* Radio broadcasts can be listened to even while one is doing some manual work. Distance learners can listen to programmes from wherever they desire to.
4. *Motivative supportive facilities:* Broadcasting can make education interesting and enjoyable, when it is used imaginatively. The feeling and motivation of listeners can be stimulated and directed by music and other sound effects. (*By supportive facilities we refer to music, special sound effects and such other means that make a broadcast programme effective.*)
5. *Effective thought promotion*: Radio tapes the thinking process of the learner as listening is invariably accompanied by simultaneous information processing. It can also stimulate a listener's imagination with a tactful use of music or the technique of pause.
6. *Low capital investment and operating cost:* Radio technology is comparatively cheap. In terms of installation and production of radio broadcasts it is quite economical and needs less production facilities compared to other electronic media.
7. *Easy production:* Production of creative radio programmes is simpler compared to a TV or video programme production. No complicated mechanism, nor any

sophisticated instruments are needed for such productions. It requires less man-power too, compared to the production of a television/video programme.

8. *Feasible mode of learner-enrichment:* The most common function of media in education is *'enrichment'*. This function is easy to materialise with the help of radio and with relatively little expense.
9. *Effective re-creation/transmission of reality:* A powerful *'audio'* version brings a scene into sharp focus and also establishes *'movement'* effectively. A live broadcast can make listeners share the experience of a scene of reality taking place, say, some 100 miles away. It can also make listeners partake of an experience of a scene of the past that took place, say, some 100 years ago.
10. *Direct instruction:* The use of radio for direct instruction has been tried. This however, demands intensive and systematic use of the radio. Under such schemes syllabus based programmes are broadcast for definite target groups.

Limitations of Educational Radio

The radio has its drawbacks too. We can summarise the limitations of radio as a medium of instruction as follows:

1. The doubts/queries arising in the mind of a learner cannot be attended to immediately. Thus, there is no provision for immediate feedback to the learner; nor is there any feedback on the quality of the content.
2. The radio is not a flexible medium. There is no face-to-face interaction, dialogue or discussion between the listener and the speaker/producer. In the absence of motivation, guidance and supervision, the atmosphere for learning is not very conducive and the teaching/learning process becomes a one-way transit of information.
3. It may not be an effective medium for all types of course materials; for example, the subjects which need demonstration/visual illustrations cannot be taught effectively through radio.
4. Educational radio programmes have not given adequate and appropriate broadcast time-chunk. This phenomenon

causes inconvenience to learner as they have to make themselves available during the scheduled broadcast time whatever be their engagements then.

5. There is dearth of adequately qualified personnel for producing worthwhile educational programmes. Radio programming demands experienced and creative personnel with both production and academic background. It is difficult to find the persons with experience along both the lines.
6. The span of attention of a learner is short and thus, the retention of factual information given after first few minutes of the start of the programme is generally low unless some special efforts are made to reassure attention from time-to-time. Furthermore, educational broadcast is not a priority area of programming in the radio set-up.
7. In a country like India educators have to plan programmes for heterogeneous masses (such as the illiterate, school drop-outs, the unemployed, etc.). The more heterogeneous the audience, the more difficult it is to produce a radio programme of common utility.
8. The technical staff concerned with the planning and production of radio programmes don't have adequate knowledge of the relevant pedagogical needs of the learners and their characteristics. The subject experts do not have any deep acquaintance with the complexities of programme production. So unless there is a perfect co-ordination and understanding between the two groups, no good production could never be achieved.

EDUCATIONAL TELEVISION
(As Non-print Instructional Media)

Television is one of the major means of mass communication. It has rapidly elevated itself to the level of *'big business'* and has become a very powerful medium. It has revolutionized the lives of people in the world. Technologically, as a combination of sound and pictures, it provides for the most effective temporal and spatial transmission of reality to its viewers. Due to its widespread network, it has become a major source of information and entertainment for a large number of our people.

The *Educational Television (ETV)* is a system that presents learning content in various subject areas through programmes prepared by a central agency. It is an effective means for this purpose as it has the capability to overcome many of the barriers in mass education.

It can provide direct instruction (*formal education*) as well as developmental continuing education (*non-formal education*). It can bring the world into a classroom and a classroom into a home!

The following educational television projects have been introduced in India:

1. Secondary School Television Project,
2. Delhi Agriculture Television *(DATV)* Project (*Krishi Darshan*),
3. Satellite Instructional Television Experiment (*SITE*),
4. Post-SITE project,
5. Indian National Satellite (*INSAT*), and
6. Higher Education Television Projects (*HETV*) of UGC.

The brief description of these projects have been given in the following paragraphs:

1. Secondary School Television Projects (STV)

School television programmes were started in Delhi on experimental basis from October 24, 1961 with there lessons per week in Physics and Chemistry and one lesson each in English and Hindi for Class XI. These programmes were syllabus-based and were telecast in school hours as a part and parcel of school activities. The aim of introducing television service in school system was to improve the standard of teaching in view of shortage of laboratories, space, equipments and dearth of qualified science teachers. The service was an experiment to find out what could possibly be accomplished to minimise the specific difficulties of higher secondary schools in Delhi specially in teaching science.

Commencing on the school television project, Paul Neurath (1968) stated that "by and large, the television schools did somewhat better in the test than did the non-television schools."

The main objectives of STV are two fold:

- to teach science subjects and thus improve the quality of instruction in science, and

- to overcome the dearth of adequately qualified secondary school teachers.

2. *Delhi Agriculture Television (DATV) Project (Krishi Darshan)*

Encouraged by the success of school telecast, an experimental TV programme, Krishi Darshan, was initiated on January 26, 1966 for communicating agricultural information to the farmers. Community viewing facilities were provided in 80 villages in the Union Territory of Delhi. The research on 'Krishi Darshan' reported that the experiment was successful and that there was substantial gain in the information regarding agricultural practices.

3. *Satellite Instructional Television Experiment (SITE)*

SITE, one of the largest techno-social experiments ever conducted in human communication, was started on August 1, 1975 for a period of one year. It is a landmark in the use of sophisticated advanced technology for instructional purposes. The main objectives of this experiment, conducted in 2,330 villages of six states, were to study the process of existing rural communication, the role of televisions as a new medium of education, and the process of change brought about by the community television in the rural structure. SITE has shown that it was possible with the new technology to reach a number of people in the remotest areas. Two types of programmes were telecast:

(*i*) Developmental educational programmes in the area of agriculture and allied subjects, health, family planning and social education were telecast in the evening for community viewing; and

(*ii*) The school programmes of $22\frac{1}{2}$ minutes duration each in Hindi, Kannada, Oriya and Telugu were telecast on each school day for rural primary school children of (5-12) years age group.

The credo for school telecast was "*to make children realise that science is everywhere, that their environment can be questioned, understood, explained and manipulated by them using scientific method*" *(Yashpal, 1977)*. The role of television was appreciated and it was accepted in rural primary schools as an educational force.

4. *Post-SITE Project*

A new SITE continuity project was initiated in March, 1977 when a terrestrial transmitter was commissioned at Jaipur. Developmental programmes were telecast by this project. The main objectives of SITE continuity project were to:

(*i*) familiarise the rural masses with the improved and scientific know-how about farming, the use of fertilisers and the maintenance of health and hygiene;
(*ii*) bring about national and emotional integration; and
(*iii*) make rural children aware of the importance of education and healthy environment.

5. *Indian National Satellite (INSAT)*

Instructional television has further been strengthened through the use of *satellite technology*. INSAT-1A an indigenous multipurpose satellite, launched on April 10, 1982 was declared unusable on September 6, 1982. Later on INSAT-1B, launched on August 30, 1983 became fully operational on October 15, 1983. Six states namely Andhra Pradesh, Bihar, Gujarat, Maharashtra, Orissa and U.P. are covered under INSAT service. In each state, a cluster of 3-4 districts has been selected on the basis of backwardness of the area, availability of suitable developmental infrastructure and utilisation of existing production facilities.

The prime objective of the INSAT service is to bring the rural and backward areas into the national main stream, by quickening the development activities in these areas with mass media support. Therefore, the service is aimed at making rural masses aware of the latest developments in the areas of agricultural productivity, health and hygiene.

Besides developmental programmes for community viewing educational programme *(ETV)* for two different age groups of school children *(5-8 years, 9-11 years)* are telecast daily. A capsule of 45 minutes duration consisting of two separate programmes—one for the lower age group and the other for the upper age group—is telecast regularly. Each programme runs for a duration of 20 minutes with five minutes change over time from one lesson to another

6. *Higher Education Television Project (HETV) of UGC*

The UGC-INSAT educational television project also known as

'country wide classroom' was inaugurated on August 15, 1984. The planning and production of the programme are actively managed by the University Grants Commission (*UGC*). Under this programme, the one hour programme in English is a miscellany of subjects presented with the objective of general enrichment for undergraduates, educated public and the teacher as well. These programmes are aimed at improving the quality of higher education to create a dynamic classroom situation.

In order to give impetus to this scheme, a Mass Communication Cell has been set up in the UGC and six Audio-visual Media/Mass Communication Research centres have been set up at different institutions in the country. Besides producing programmes at these centres, some programmes are imported from other countries, and are edited to suit the requirements of the Indian students. Presently a one hour programme is telecast daily between 1.00 p.m. and 2.00 p.m. barring holiday and Sundays.

These programmes are produced in English by Mass Communication Research Centres set up by the UGC at various universities such as Jamia Millia Islamia, New Delhi; Gujarat Vidyapeeth, Ahmedabd; Roorkee University, Roorkee, etc. The programmes produced by various production institutions are pooled by the UGC for reviewing their quality and handing them over to *Doordarshan* for telecast.

Indira Gandhi National Open University (*IGNOU*); besides the printed text and occasional face-to-face contact sessions, IGNOU course materials include audio and video cassettes, which are available for use at study centres and also on sale for home study. For opitmum utilisation of these audio-video components, IGNOU telecasts its video programmes for half an hour, thrice a week, from 6.30 a.m. to 7.00 a.m. on Mondays, Wednesdays and Fridays for those IGNOU students who would otherwise not have an opportunity to take advantage of these programmes.

Most of the IGNOU programmes supplement the printed texts—the master medium of learning—and cater to a specific group of learners. Of course, the general public can also view these IGNOU programmes, and they do so with great interest.

Teacher's programmes: In order to make the primary school teachers aware of the innovations in teaching-learning processes, management of televised instruction, child psychology, etc., the

Central Institute of Educational Technology *(CIET)* produces programmes for teachers, known as *'Hints for Teacher'*. Each programme of 45 minutes is telecast on every Saturday during school hours in their respective languages of instruction. Doordarshan Kendra, Bombay also telecasts a 20 minutes programme for teachers every week.

Impact of Recent Developments

There are certain advanced electronic devices which are being utilised by developed countries in their systems of teaching and learning. Though, many of these are not in frequent use in the India, you as a student of distance education, should have some basic information about those gadgets. We present in the following sub-sections information about the few of these gadgets.

Satellite Based Communication

The recent development in education broadcasting in India is the emergence of the statellite based communication. It opened the doors for a new era in audio-visual communication. The first educational experiment to exploit the potential of satellites in dissemination of information was undertaken in 1975. The experiment, popularly known as SITE, established that the remotest rural masses can also be approached through satellite based television programme. Thereafter, INSAT-1A and INSAT-1B have provided us with the means to strenghten distance education system in India. What the satellite technology available to us, India is able to beam television signals throughout the country making the benefits of the technology available at every doorstep. (*But not every home in our country has a TV set to receive the signals and thereby the benefits. The day when every home will have a set is still far off*). The INSAT telecast could help break the feeling of isolation among widely scattered communities. India is quite advanced in having her own satellite technology, and it has helped educators make comprehensive plans for education and development.

Some of the main advantages of satellite based communication systems can be summarised as follows:

(*i*) *Geographical Coverage:* In India where geographical and other factors add to the difficulties in establishing a nationwide network, satellite communication has proved more relevant and effective. It has the capacity to beam TV signals over a large distance and even in mountain areas where terrestrial system cannot serve.

(*ii*) *Impetus for Modernization:* The technology of satellite communication is very helpful in promoting faster social change/development in a country like India. By bringing the world to the villages through television, the communication system has opened the window for innovation and change and thereby quickened the process of modernization.

(*iii*) *Immediacy in Implementation:* The satellite communication system being a centralized system the planning and implementation of educational innovations require a minimum amount of time. It can reduce the implementation time of any educational scheme.

(*iv*) *Cost Effectiveness:* Satellite technology provides a cost effective alternative educational system: the characteristic of the satellite to cover large masses spread over a vast distance makes it more cost effective than the terrestrial system. Since the cost of providing signals is not related to distance, remote communities can be served as cheaply as communities in more central locations without incurring extra costs for cables, station building, etc. Besides television broadcasts, INSAT-1B is being utilized for various other purposes such as radio, telephone, disaster warning and meteorology. It has provided the facility of two transponders (*transponders are components of a satellite that retransmit signals to the earth*) simultaneously available for the television network.

Programme Production

Television programme production is a collective art. It includes personnel from software *(academicians, producers, communication researchers, artists, etc.)* and hareware (*cameramen, technicians, engineers, etc.*) All these people work in a team for the common cause of producing effective television programmes.

The process of production of instructional television programmes can broadly discussed under four stages:

1. *Planning*

It includes the following three activities:

(*i*) *Defining Goals:* This is the first step where the tangible objectives are fixed in behavioural terms. The objectives are decided on the basis of what we want the learner to accomplish after viewing the programme. The target audience is identified, for without identifying the target audience you cannot fix goals for your programme.

(*ii*) *Preparation of Programme Brief:* The programme briefs are prepared on the basis of need assessment, *i.e.*, the priority areas where television support is needed. The programme brief includes statements about objective, the take off point [the skill(s) assumed to have already been mastered by the learners], the scope of content to be included in the programme and the communication strategy, *i.e.*, the kind of treatment to be given to the content.

(*iii*) *Script-writing:* On the basis of the predetermined objectives and the content, the script is written by the professionals. The format, the length, the content load, etc. defined in the programme brief are followed while writing the script.

2. *Preproduction Preparations*

This stage includes the following steps:

(*i*) *Preparation of Necessary Support:* Preparation of personnel, collection of production facilities, arrangement of sets, sound and light and related activities are undertaken at this stage.

(*ii*) *Rehearsal:* The step is very important. It is here that the graphics, slides, etc., to be used are adjusted. The presentation, the content, the length of the programme, the suitability of artists, etc., are also judged during rehearsals.

3. *Actual Production*

Production of television programme is a complex activity involving sophisticated machines. The producer needs to be very careful during the actual production.

4. *Evaluation*

The evaluation of educational television programmes must be done continuously from the planning stage till the programme is broadcast. Such evaluation is undertaken at two stages:

(*i*) *Formative Evaluation:* This is purposive evaluation to ensure the quality of the media product. The necessary improvement/changes are incorporated based on research findings. It is undertaken during the development of the programme, before something is *'formed'*. It starts from the preparation of an audience profile, and includes assessment of informational needs, preparation of writer's briefs, script and prototype programme testing. Formative research is generally done by in-house researchers who work in close collaboration with the programme producers and the subject experts. This type of evaluation has flexibility in methodology to suit the objectives/ requirements of the problem.

(*ii*) *Summative Evaluation:* Summative evaluation is taken up after a programme is produced. The purpose of summative evaluation is to measure the overall impact of the programme which can help in framing long-range plans. It includes feedback collection, surveys and specially mounted field studies. Summative evaluation strictly follows the methodology of the fundamental research.

Advantages of Educational T.V.

From this theoretical perspective, we can state that, in favourable conditions, students learn efficiently from educational television. While television can be a powerful educational tool, its value is totally dependent on the quality of materials we transmit and the skill with which it is used.

The conclusions of research projects on educational television have shown that television is an effective tool in the hand of educators, if it is utilized imaginatively. It has proved its effectiveness/supremacy in teaching certain subjects such as agriculture, science, geography, oceanography, etc. Here we discuss the major prospects of educational television:

1. *Higher quality of instruction:* Television progammes are well planned/organised and better presented than the usual classroom instruction.
2. *Social equality of education:* Television promotes the goal of social equality in education catering to the masses of rural background and those living in slums of urban areas. Television increases the effectiveness of instruction and cuts down drop-out rates.
3. *Reduce dependency on teacher:* The students learn from television with their own efforts. They need minimum help from the teacher in case television is pressed into service.
4. *Use of the best available teacher*: Educational television makes educational opportunities equal throughout the country. The students in rural and deprived areas of the country, where educational resources are not available, get the same quality of education as their counterparts in the urban centres. The best teacher is equally available for every student. Thus television bridges the gap between the poor and the rich, the privileged and the under-privileged, the rural and the urban.
5. *Flexibility:* Rapid and continuing change in curricula and instructional methods are made possible through educational television. Courses can be constantly modified not only to update them but to incorporate the constantly changing needs of the society and the expansion of knowledge.
6. *Cost effectiveness:* If television is utilised on a large scale, it proves cost effective. It can provide education throughout the country at a minimum cost without lowering the quality of instruction. The initial expenditure, of course, will be high.
7. *In-service training:* Educational television can be used for in-service training of educators in non-school hours. NCERT is telecasting as programme per week for teachers to improve their teaching methods and skills.
8. *Stimulation:* Through educational television, we can control the stimulation (the audio and the visual) to get desired response (learning).
9. *Combination of audio and video components:* Television has

the advantage of the audio as well as the video. That is why it has a greater appeal than the radio and the print-media.

10. *Mass education:* Educational television can cater to the explosive increase in student numbers.
11. *Logistically simple:* In operating an effective distance education system, educational television is logistically very simple. The problems of planning, implementing and operating distance learning can be overcome to some extent by teaching through television.

The Limitations

As we have already mentioned, the potential of television depends on how effectively it is being utilised for educational purposes.

In spite of the numerous advantages listed above, television has its limitations as a medium of education. Some of the disadvantages are as follows:

1. *Problem of pacing learning:* The student may learn at his own speed through television broadcasts. He has to be attentive to grasp the content. The tell-teacher teaches at a speed which he assumes to be firmly suitable to an average learner of his target audience. He cannot cater to the individual differences in study-pace.
2. *Limitations of One-way-communication:* Television is essentially a one-way-communication medium and as such it does not provide for interaction/discussion and hence does not provide for immediate feedback on learners' reactions, queries and doubts. It is a *'passive medium'* as some educators would call it, as it turns learners into mere *(passive)* receivers of information. The absence of active participation and lack of provision for feedback are likely to fail to sustain the interest and enthusiasm of learners.
3. *Costly affair:* Teaching through television is a costly affair. The high sophisticated electronic gadgets demand huge amounts to be spent on the production/telecasting.
4. *Poor accessibility:* Television is still beyond the purchasing capacity of a common man. It, therefore, cannot become a medium of the masses.

5. *Insufficient viewing conditions:* There are no adequate arrangement for viewing the programmes in colleges/ schools.
6. *Visuals becoming a distraction:* Sometimes the visuals themselves create distraction and interference in learning.
7. *Difficulty to integrate:* There are difficulties in building television as a part and parcel of on-going activities of a classroom/school. The difficulties are due to absence of uniform syllabus, absence of teachers with similar training and caliber, etc.

QUESTIONS FOR ANSWER

1. *What do you mean by the term 'Media'. Differentiate between Print Instructional and non-Print Instructional Media.*
2. *Enumerate the advantages of educational television.*
3. *Write a note on some recent developments in television and their impact on education.*
4. *Write a note on various environmental educational programmes which can be given on the educational radio of A.I.R.*
5. *Write a note on the procedures of producing radio and television programmes.*
6. *Justify that radio and television are the best instruments for erecting environmental awareness.*

25

Child and His Environment

We have discussed many aspects of child development in Chapter 21 and 22 of this book, therefore, we will discuss the concept of this chapter very briefly, as follows.

IMPACT OF ENVIRONMENT IN CHILD DEVELOPMENT

Development refers to interaction of a child and his environment whose after products after exciting behaviour and response tendencies in such a way as to increase: (1) their strength, (2) the degree of differentiation, and (3) the organisation of personality. The teaching learning situations in school generate the environment for the new experiences to alter response tendencies of the children. Thus it refers to acquisition of new behaviour or desirable changes in physical, mental, social and emotional aspects for daily living. It also expands the capacities of the children.

The objectives of environmental education are directly related to the child development. The child development includes physical, intellectual, social, emotional and psychomotor development. This fact has been illustrated here.

	The Objectives of Environmental Education	*Aspects of Child's Development and Sources*
1.	The awareness of the environment *i.e.* (knowledge objective).	Mental development (Home, family and school environment).
2.	The development of skills related to environment (working efficiency).	Psychomotor development (Home, family, society and school environment).
3.	The development of desirable attitude and values toward the environment.	Affective development (Home, community society and school environment).

The child development takes place in terms of behaviour—changes or modification of behaviour. The teaching process in schools creates conducive environment for providing learning experiences to the child. The teacher activities and actions generate the learning environment for the desirable behavioural changes among students. A child lives in three environments—*physical, social* and *psychological* simultaneously. Family home, society and school environments provides learning experiences to the child. The psychological environment of a child play a significant role for his working style as well as life style. Under chapters 21 and 22, we have already discussed the role of home, family, society, community and school environments for mental, social and emotional development of a child, therefore please read chapters 21 and 22 again.

Moral Concepts

The child's first ideas of right and wrong are determined largely by the verdict of his parents concerning acts that are forbidden or permitted. Throughout his life an individual's moral code continues to be determined to a large extent by rules in the form of conventional standards, and directly or indirectly, the teachings of religion. The fact that there are ready made conventions and moral demands does not necessarily mean that aperson is being "done about" for there would be chaos if each individual, in every act of his life, were to depend solely upon precepts that he has reasoned out for himself.

Even from a rather early age, however, the child is able to formulate some moral principles in terms of the reasons that lie behind them and to adopt them as his own rules rather that simply as edicts that have to be obeyed because others have so told him. At still earlier levels children have many opportunities to learn the meaning of rules of conduct through the natural consequences of their acts, as when they learn to curb their impulse to hit another child or to snatch his possessions, in order to avoid retaliation or the discomfort of seeing another cry.

Integrated Process of Development

The social, emotional, and mental development are highly correlated to one another. The developments are aspect helps or includes the other aspect. In thinking and reasoning, emotional factors plays important role in the person's behaviour. Moral concepts include social and mental development. The process of child development in various dimensions goes side by side, hence the components of one aspect help or evolve the components of other aspect. The motor skills helps in social adjustment, as discussed in earlier chapters.

Educational Implication of Mental Development

In the *development of information and concepts* it is likely that a child's knowledge or grasp will vary considerably in the case of different topics or areas of experience. Depending upon his past opportunities for learning he may be well informed and be able to reason effectively in connection with one topic and not in connection with another. Accordingly, he may seem very naïve and illogical in dealing with one problem and quite logical in dealing with another. It is also true that when adults face a problem that is new or quite unfamiliar they will make errors and give inconsistent or illogical answers similar to those that may be offered by a child.

However, changes that normally come with added maturity cannot be brought about simply by giving the child concentrated experiences or special training over a short period of time. Many of the gains that are shown such as speed of *perceptual response,* the ability to grasp concepts relating to matters remote from the child's own immediate experience (like the concept of historical time), and the ability to learn and to master subject matter (such as long division in arithmetic) do not result from coaching alone. Concentrated periods of practice or instruction at a given stage of growth cannot bring about the changes that take place over a period of years through the joint influence of growth and such indirect instruction as everyday experience affords.

As children grow older, there are changes, not only in their information about affairs in the world at large, but also in their attitudes toward such affairs. Frequently there is little relationship, however, between a child's attitude (the stand which he takes for or against, the liking or disliking, prejudice or tolerance which he exhibits) and the amount of knowledge he possesses concerning a matter at issue. The child's attitudes may have their roots in emotional experiences which he is not able clearly to recall. His thinking, like the thinking of adults, will be influenced to varying degrees by his desires, his fears and other emotions as discussed in earlier chapters.

A teacher should always keep in his mind that social, emotional and mental development are highly related to one another. The components of these dimensions are inclusive. The thinking process is governed by emotional factors such as prejudices of a child. Moral concepts dependents on attitudes and values of an individual.

SOCIAL DEVELOPMENT

The development of a person's behaviour as a social creature proceeds pace with the development of his individuality, his status as an independent creature, distinct from other, socialization and individualization are complementary features in the development of personality.

Meaning and Definition of 'Social Development'

The phenomena such as affection, shyness, jealously stage fright and sympathy are treated as social forms of behaviour.

According to *E.B. Hurlock's* definition,

"Social development means acquisition of the ability to behave in accordance with social expectations."

I.L. Child has defined the term social development.

"Social development is the process by which an individual is led to develop actual behaviour according to the standards of the group."

The social expectations and standards of the group refer to the following characteristics:

(1) Social responses, (2) Responses to other children (3) Group activities (4) Social perception, (5) Resistant behaviour, (6) Fights and quarrels, (7) Sympathy, (8) Cooperation, (9) Competition, and (10) Leadership.

Factors Influencing Social Development

There are several factors which influence the social development. The most important factor are as follows. (1) Socio-economic status

(2) Leadership, (3) Emotions, (4) Games and sports, (5) Pear group or gang.

These factors lead to social maturity. Thus the following are the social development names:

1. Social interaction,
2. Social adjustment,
3. Social participation,
4. Social conformity, and
5. Social maturity.

The social development concerns with personality development. The personality is more social and less psychological. In the absence of social group the concept of personality has no significance. The norms are the characteristics of personality of an individual.

We have discussed all the aspects of social development including stagewise social development and problem of social adjustment in chapters 21 and 22 therefore, please read these two chapters again.

Children's Social Behaviour is likely from an early age level to show the influence of the customs and standards of the social group to which their elders belong. Standards and customs vary more or less at different socio-economic levels and in different ethnic groups within a single community. It is important for adults to remember this fact if they would understand child's behaviour.

Training for Leadership is an important responsibility of education. Leaders among children usually are somewhat superior in ability to the average of the group especially in the sphere in which they are recognized as leaders. However, ability is not alone the determining factor. To be a good leader a child should be responsive to the needs and wishes of his fellows and able to participate wholeheartedly in their interests and concerns. If children of superior intellectual ability are to capitalize fully upon their potentialities for leadership, it is important that they should have experiences that will help them to be socially acceptable to others.

Friendships or Affinities between individuals are apparent from an early age in the social behaviour of children. Friends tend, in general, to resemble each other more than they tend to differ from each other in their abilities and in their personality traits, although there are many exceptions to this. This factor of propinquity, or nearness in geographical space, is obviously important in determining the range of individuals from among whom the children's friends will be chosen.

All children, in one way or another, desire some degree of *recognition, acceptance,* and *prestige* in their dealings with others. Frequently behaviour that seems aimed to arouse hostility and to cause an individual to be rejected springs indirectly from difficulties that he encounters in his efforts to receive attention and approval. Even a bad child wishes to be liked, and sometimes the punishment inflicted upon such a youngster merely widens the social distance between him and his fellows and intensifies his unacceptable forms of behaviour.

Educational Implications. The fact that shift such as these sometime occur has a practical implication. The school should offer, as far as possible, a variety of opportunities for leadership. An educational policy which keeps the same pupils together from year to year under the same teacher and in much the same educational programme may provide a semblance of continuity and security. But such continuity may prevent many individual children from benefiting from varied contacts in new class groupings under teachers who differ both in personality and in educational practice. Needless to say, it is not possible to arrange matters so that every child is a leader. Many children and adults do not seem particularly to desire to assume direction of others as long as they can be left to their own interest. Apart from desire, there are differences in ability to assume leadership.

Role of family school and community environment in child's development have already been discussed in earlier chapters.

WHAT MAKES FAMILY, SCHOOL, COMMUNITY AND SOCIAL ENVIRONMENT EFFECTIVE FOR CHILD'S DEVELOPMENT

Some points for this purpose are given hereunder, very briefly:

1. Means to Male Family or Home Environment Influential

A child is the product of the family. The quality of family contribute significantly in development of a child. The following measures should be followed to make family environment effective.

1. The head of the family should be conscious enough to

make the family environment, healthy and conducive for learning. The family problems should be resolved peacefully. Its should try to keep the good books and other literature which have the educative value.

Mahatma Gandhi had admitted in his autobiography that his father had brought a book on 'Shravan Kumar's parents devotion'. He had learnt and develop the quality of parents devotion, respect his elders and duties towards his parents. The second book on Harish Chandra Drama which had provided the lesson of responsibility and his duty. The family environment was responsible to keep him at the place of Father of Nation.

2. The intellectual environment of family should be healthy and high.
3. The head of family should also make efforts to maintain neighbour environment healthy and conducive.
4. The community should have high cultural values.
5. A child should be kept among good things, high ideals, good persons.

The mother has relatively more responsibility for generating healthy family environment than the father.

2. Means to make School Environment Effective

The school is the second place for developing good qualities in a child. The school organization and school health are main aspects of school aspects which have been discussed else where in detail. Now there is great change in family and home environment. We do not live in joint family, mother and father are in job, there is shift towards the single family *i.e.* parents and children. Now the family or home is not sharing its responsibilities. Therefore, the school has to share this responsibility. The school has created most appropriate physical, social, cultural and psychological environment in school.

1. The school should be out side locality in open and clean physical surroundings.
2. The school plant and buildings should be open and airy.
3. There should be adequate furniture, equipment, reading room, library, laboratory, play ground etc.
4. All these facilities constitute the school environment.

5. There should be green plants and garden etc.
6. There should be sweet relations among principal, teachers and students. There should be cooperate life. It creates social environment.
7. The main emphasis should be given on academic activities. The cultural activities, assembly programmes seminar, group discussion should be organized.
8. The teachers should provide proper guidance and counselling for their problems and difficulties.

The social environment contributes in developing good qualities and values among students.

3. Role of Community

The group of persons of a place has the same objectives which are realized through co-operative life. It is difficult to plane without co-operative life. It is the second place after home for his socialization. It develops the feeling of we. It has no place for I or me. The members of the community should have the we feeling sympathy and co-operation to each other. It is a well organized aspect of society but it is not a society. The feeling of locality is developed by the community.

The community refers to a general living group which has the common objectives. It maintains all type of relations. It is the result of general life. The members of community do not have the specific goal and selfish motive. It concerns with intensive social life in which human beings are there. They are conscious enough about social objectives and motives. Thus community life generate an environment for the socialization of a child:

1. The community life creates an appropriate social environment which contributes in social and cultural development. It develops emotions, sentiments, characters as per norms of the society. The community process evolves social environment.
2. It also develops cultural environment for the values of life, and ways of expressing his emotions. It develops conduct and values of life.
3. The educative process and activities are controlled and organized by the community to meet the local requirements. The educational programmes and

curriculum are designed in view of the future requirements of the community. The educational process is made more meaningful and purposive.

4. The community organises informal activities and programmes for facilitating the child for his study by establishing library, reading rooms, museums and play grounds etc.
5. The community education includes the following affective elements:
   (*a*) The community is a small unit of a society, therefore it contributes in socialization.
   (*b*) The culture means which we follow in our daily life. The community also provides informal educational situations for developing culture and our values. The culture factor influences the community.
   (*c*) The community of today is mainly influenced by politics. It also affects our school functioning. Today's education is purely educational politics. The political consciousness is provided by the community.
   (*d*) The community development is mainly based on the financial conditions and economic factors. The community should provide some training to the children for their vocations so that they are able to earn their livings.

4. Means to Make Social Environment Influential

The social environment has significant role in the development of personality and values of a child. The personality is a social phenomenon, beyond the society individual values are important factors of personality. The process of socialization takes place in an appropriate social environment. The socializaion process takes place in an appropriate social environment. The socialization process begins from infancy to adult-age. A child has to live in society and has to acquire a place in it. *John Dewey* has emphasised on *"Social efficiency"* as main aim of Education. It is the responsibility of society and social workers to make social environment effective and conducive for learning good conduct and values. The following measures should be employed for making social environment more influential—

1. The physical environment should be made clean and free from pollution.
2. There should be good relations among the members of the society.
3. The cultural programmes should be organized on festivals and on other occasions. These should have educative value.
4. The students who perform in their examinations and good activities should be rewarded.
5. Some competitive activities should be organized, such as dramas, group discussions to develop social consciousness among young children.
6. The national festival should be organized, such as 'probably fairy' etc.

The social environment develops the higher qualities of life and certain skills which are essential for jobs and occupations. Apart from these personality development, they are provided the awareness of major social and national problems *e.g.* human population explosion and environmental pollution. It is a fact that a child has acquired the awareness and developed the consciousness of small family and its adverse effects on his life from the very beginning of his development.

Similarity it is an urgent need to provide the awareness of environmental pollution and to develop consciousness about it. They should know the adverse effects or bad consequence of environmental pollution on his life as well as on society and nation from his infancy to adult age. The objectives of environmental education have been discussed stage wise. It is the responsibility of home, family, school, community and society to provide the learning situation at their own field, to provide the awareness of pollution to develop consciousness about its adverse effects. Thus, social environment may contribute significantly in the development of a child.

QUESTIONS FOR ANSWER

1. *Write short notes on the following*
   (*a*) *Role of home and family environment in the development of a child.*
   (*b*) *Role of school environment in the development of a child.*
   (*c*) *Role of community and social environment in the child development.*

2. *Write a note on the impact of environment in the development of the child.*
3. *Define social development and enumerate factors which effect social development.*
4. *Write short notes on the following.*

   (*a*) *Educational implications of mental development.*
   (*b*) *Means to make family environment influential.*
   (*c*) *Means to make school environment influential.*
   (*d*) *Means to make social environment influential.*

26

Adult Education for Environmental Awareness and Social Forestry

INTRODUCTION

The situation of our country is worse from environmental point of view. More than 70 per cent population lives in rural areas and 40 per cent population is below the poverty line. A large population has migrated to big cities but they are deprived of necessities such as water, electricity, residence, etc. They live in *jhuggi and jhopri* or on roads. They are mostly illiterates and have no idea of environmental awareness. They are polluting environment through their day-to-day activities. Therefore, it is the responsibility of society and nation to provide the environmental awareness to such adults.

Education is also sharing this responsibility by introducing *'Environmental Informal Education Programme'*. This is a very challenging task for education because they had never been in school and remained busy for earning their living since very childhood. Since independence *'Adult Education'* or *Social Education* programme has been introduced but could not yield good result. Thus, Environmental Awareness and consciousness can also be included in the following informal education programmes.

1. Environmental Awareness and Adult Education.
2. Environmental Awareness and Non-formal Education.
3. Environmental Awareness and Women Education.

The concept, procedure and programmes for the above informal education systems have been provided in the following paragraphs:

ENVIRONMENTAL AWARENESS AND ADULT EDUCATION

In India, adult education is of prime importance in eradicating illiteracy. The Constitution of India is based on democracy and in that framework through equality, liberty, fraternity and social justice, progress is the sole aim. It is a sovereign democratic republic and a secular and welfare state striving for establishing a socialistic pattern of society. This is possible when the life of an individual develops to its full stature and he is able to perform his duties and functions in accordance with his interests, ability and efficiency. To bring light to the majority of illiterates, there is need to develop a systematic plan of education. In fact, the existence of democracy is based on healthy development of adult literacy and education.

Concept and Objectives of Adult Education

In the words of *S.N. Mukerjee*, "Social education consists of three main types—(*i*) to provide literacy to illiterate adults, (*ii*) to develop an educated mind in the absence to literary education, (*iii*) to acquaint people with the rights and duties pertaining to citizenship." Thus by social education we mean 'the education of the complete man'. This includes his physical, mental, intellectual, moral, social, economic and cultural development. For establishing democracy on sound footing in the country expansion of social education is of paramount importance.

> "The function of adult education in a democracy is to provide every adult citizen an opportunity for education of the type he wishes and which he should have for his personal enrichment, professional advancement and effective participation and social and political life."
>
> —*Recommendation of Kothari Commission (1966)*

Objectives of Adult Education: The following are the objectives of adult education:

1. To acquaint the adults with the rules of health and sanitation, education of culture and recreation and make them literate through fictional education.

2. To make them conversant with the rights and duties of citizens.
3. To develop a healthy and scientific attitude so as to understand the realities of life and thus enable them to solve the problems of life with courage, conviction and devotion.
4. To arouse a feeling of dignity and respect among individuals for one another and to impart education without discrimination.
5. To create awareness among the masses and develop individual's personality.
6. To inculcate the 'live and let live' ideal of democracy among citizens.
7. To motivate people to rise above and work for general welfare. There is urgent need to have the main objective of adult education.
8. To provide the awareness about environmental pollution and their role by developing the environmental consciousness among the adults.

Five-Point Programme of Adult Education Needs Modification

The new concept of adult education, *i.e.*, social education should thus consist of a five-point programme. This is very necessary for all round development of an adult. In a democratic set-up for developing a healthy citizenship and to acquaint individuals with the different facets of life is of paramount importance. The new concept includes the following:

1. *Spread of Literacy:* The literacy programme should not be confined to the education of three R's, *i.e.*, reading, writing and arithmetic. As per needs of the adults proper place should be assigned to maths, history, geography, civics, religious and moral education, general knowledge, literature, agriculture, science and cottage industries etc. in the curriculum. Activities like debates, talks, lectures, discussions, seminars, etc. should also be organised so that adults may be properly educated. The use of magazines, newspapers and other journals would also prove beneficial in this respect.

2. *Health and Hygiene:* Adults should be acquainted with the rules of health and hygiene and habituated to attend to the health

of the members of the family. It is their duty to keep their house, neighbour and village neat and clean and thus save it from disease. For leading a happy civic life, good health is of utmost importance.

3. *Cottage Industries:* For economic progress of adults, a working knowledge of cottage industries is essential. It is generally said that Indian farmer remains idle for about six months. If we provide him necessary knowledge for starting cottage industries he can make proper use of his leisure time and earn something. This will improve his economic condition and thus raise the standard of living. According to the local needs and circumstances any cottage industry can be started. This may include activities like sewing, making of ropes, mats, fans, baskets, clay modelling, carpentry, leather and cardboard works, making of candles, chalk, polish, ink, soap and pickles, etc., according to their convenience. These efforts will help to strengthen the economic condition of adults.

4. *Recreational Activities:* To get education through recreation is a modern method of teaching. Like children adults also need recreation, but it should be according to their tastes and interests. The use of radio, cinema, T.V. and arranging of drama, festivals, national days and organisation of cultural activities, is very necessary at this age. Furthermore, fair, exhibition, folk songs and games like wrestling and kabaddi, etc., provide enough recreation and education to adults. They get sufficient knowledge through the organisation of such activities. Some T.V. programmes and drama should also be organized related to environmental problem and their effects on human life. Media can be effectively used for this purpose.

5. *Education of Citizenship:* Education for citizenship includes the knowledge of the rights and duties of citizens, ways of acquiring healthy citizenship, rule of the road, good behaviour, social service, *shramdan* and sanitary drive, etc. Everything pertaining to the democratic principles of equality, liberty, fraternity, justice and development of healthy citizenship, etc., come under its purview. Education for citizenship renders immense help in making adults healthy and efficient citizens. It develops in them the power of leadership which enables them to shoulder varied responsibilities in future life.

It is also the prime duty of a good citizen to maintain the quality of the environment. He should have environmental awareness at local, regional and national level. General awareness of air, water and land pollution should be provided to them. Some idea of food chain and food webs should also be given. There should be some minimum outline of environmental content which directly relates to them.

Thus, the five points programme of adult education should be restated and re-organized by incorporating the essential content of the environment.

National Board of Adult Education and many more agencies are working with devotion to educate the adults but without much success, as discussed in earlier chapters, therefore need of the hour is that the environmental awareness and education is to be organized at three levels.

1. *Local level*—Environmental problems should be taken up by the local agencies such as schools and colleges and other private agencies.
2. *Regional level*—Environmental problems should be taken up by the regional agencies—distance education, mobile libraries.
3. *National level*—Environmental problems should be taken up by the National Agencies and National Board of Adult Education.

There should also be co-ordination among these agencies of various levels. Some evaluation programme should be organized to assess the impact of environmental education on the adults in their day-to-day working.

ENVIRONMENTAL AWARENESS AND NON-FORMAL EDUCATION

All those people who either could not study at all or were compelled to give up education without completing it, irrespective of their age, sex or class, it is necessary to provide opportunities for education as a part of their working conditions. These opportunities are known as Non-formal Education in the light of universal education.

Meaning of Non-formal Education

In the modern world, non-formal education is making rapid

progress all over the globe. It has come to be believed that the aim of education is to make the individual for the fulfillment of personal, national and global needs. Useful individuals make their country useful and their nation strong.

The following suggestions were preferred for acceptance at the 28th all India Indian Adult Education Conference, (1975) held at Jabalpur—"Within the framework of adult education, non-formal education puts forward a new organisation. It is neither an alternative for formal education, nor an attempt to displace it. It offers an alternative to those who could not take advantage of formal education or abandoned their education without completing it."

In keeping with its nature, non-formal education attaches the maximum importance to the various forms of a flexible mode of operation and the environment of the individual. It is wrong to conceive of it as the second class of education. Instead, it would be far better to see it as a new form of education. It possesses the capacity to help an individual derive the maximum benefit from formal education.

Thus, non-formal education finds its expression in the following programmes:

1. Education for the 6-14 age group.
2. Education for the 15-25 age group in which functional literacy is inherent. It is suitable for both rural and urban areas.
3. Increase in the skill and productivity of urban workers.
4. Education of women through useful education.
5. Continuous education organised by universities and all classes and institutions.
6. Programme of civic education.

It is the need of the day that non-formal education should give the prime importance to environmental education in its programmes. It is the universal and international problem to maintain the quality of the environment.

Characteristics of Non-formal Education

Non-formal education is a universal education and internationally used system of education. The UNESCO has given the following recommendations.

Philip H. Comb and C. Roy have conducted a survey of non-formal education, reported in their work entitled, "*New Path of Learning*". In the preface to this report, the following concepts have been accepted:

1. Education is a life long process, which cannot be tied to place, time and circumstances.
2. It is necessary for every individual to be aware of the minimum kerning skills, who include—(*a*) creative attitude, (*b*) creative litercy and organisation, (*c*) scientific attitude, and shackling of the process of nature, (*d*) earning wealth, civic co-operation and raising the standard of mutual exchange.

In order to make the programme of non-formal learning a success, it is necessary to provide pre-school education to prepare children for school, to make arrangements for a desirable and parallel system of non-formal education and to make these arrangements operative with full dedication and devotion.

There is need to launch a country-wide movement for providing awareness of environmental pollution and degradation along with eradication of illiteracy. The environmental pollution is the national as well as international problem. Therefore efforts should be made to seek an active co-operation of all sections of the society. The teacher voluntary organizations, state, centre and local self-governments should work jointly.

Objectives of Non-formal Education

Non-formal education has the following objectives:

1. Understanding of the environment and conditions, and arousing awareness of the need to make changes in it.
2. Generating faith in science and technological knowledge and encouraging the individual to adopt their skills.
3. Creating the capacity to learn by working and to increase one's skill.
4. Utilising acquried experiences in new situations.
5. Performing the role of an agency for bringing the desired changes in society.
6. Generating a desire to participate in and contribute to the general development of the country through the democratic method of working.

7. Developing the tendency to continue for ever one's own learning and teaching others, and generating a suitable atmosphere therefore.

The non-formal education has the first objective for providing the understanding of the environment. Thus, programmes of non-formal education should be planned and organized to realize the first objective.

Kothari Commission—Non-Formal Education

The Kothari Commission has defined non-formal education in the context of education. As is the case with innumerable other thinkers, the Kothari Commission also sees education as a life-long process. It has laid stress upon the following programmes for non-formal education—

1. *Education of Illiterate:* The full time or part time general as well as vocational education for the (15-35) age group should be organized by making the use of television, radio, films and other teaching aids.
2. *Continuous Education:* It is necessary to evolve education as a continuous process for the latest developments and environmental problems along with the vocational education.
3. *Distance Education:* The print and non-print media are best used in distance education for the formal and non-formal education system. It is also cheaper than the formal school/college education.
4. *Libraries:* It is recommended to set-up libraries all over the country and these should be well equipped with useful literature of environmental awareness and general literature necessary for the adults.

In view of bad effects of pollution it is very necessary to introduce some programmes in non-formal education to check it. They should be made conversant about the evils of pollution. They should be advised to make the environment healthy and clean. There should be more parks and garden. The idea of social foresty should be provided to adults. Drinking water is to be drawn from greater depth. Rivers and ponds are to be protected from dirty water. Vehicles are to be checked from emitting smoke.

There should be certain programmes for local environmental pollution.

AFFORESTATION AND SOCIAL FORESTRY

In the first chapter of this book we have discussed the problem of losing forests and its environmental implications which include the problems of environmental pollution and ozone depletion therefore, for upgrading the environment there is an urgent need to implement the programmes of afforestation and social forestry with proper care to achieve a balance between socio-economic development and ecological environment. Hereunder we will discuss the role of afforestation and social forestry very briefly which is possible through environmental awareness, as part of adult education.

Compensatory Afforestation and Community Efforts

After 25.10.1980, any mining activity on forest lands has to be compensated by new afforestation of particularly those species which were cut on 'Land for Land' basis. This has been questioned and even legally challenged by a number of mining companies and leasees. In some cases, genuine difficulties have also been experienced in identifying equivalent lands but mostly the reluctance and reservations are because of the additional costs involved and introduction of a new culture from viewpoint of environmental and ecological upgradation.

The Government Agencies and village Panchayats engaged in the implementation of the poverty alleviation schemes under the 20-point programme, voluntary Agencies, parent Coal and other mining companies and a panel of responsible citizens of the locality (including a good number of enlightened ladies and wives of executives) have to draw out comprehensive plans for integrated area development and compensatory afforestation in particular. The financial, material and human resources pooled for such community based projects have to be visualised and defined clearly, good schools, medical and family welfare activities. Promotion of sports, Child Development, Women and Adult Education Programmes, IRDP, TRYSEM, JAWAHAR ROJGAR YOJANA spreading branches of commercial and co-operative banks. Improvised ovens and alternate energy system including community bio-gas plants, waste water and waste/by product utilisation schemes etc.

SOCIAL FORESTRY

The *'social forstry'* is not a new concept, it is a very old Indian method. All the plans are covered under social forestry. The public has the emotional attachment with social forestry, it provides fodder for animals, wood for fuel and oxygen for life.

Our government had spent about four hundred crores rupees during (1950-80) on social forestry. During (1980-85) about several hundred crores were spent on this plan. This plan has been introduced in 13 states of our country by taking loan of Rs. 780 crores from the World Bank. This plan is being implemented with the help of foreign agencies to make it more useful and effective. The efforts are being made to cover 20 lac 30 thousand hectare land by social forestry.

Objectives of Social Forestry

The following are the main objectives of social forestry:

1. To fulfil the needs and requirements of forest products of rural and urban population.
2. To develop the forest area by plantation on the rural and urban boundaries.
3. To fulfil the fuel requirements so that dung of animals can be used for making the soil fertile.
4. To check the process of deforestation which will check the soil erosion.
5. To provide the employment for poor and landless villagers.
6. To raise the standard of living by economic advantages of social forestry.
7. To maintain ecology of the environment and improve the rural economy.
8. To improve the quality of the environment and have balanced development.

Need and Importance of Social Forestry

There are various types of environmental problems due to

explosion of human population. The deforestation has created the problem of soil erosion and expansion of desert area. The forest and forest products are very useful for the needs of human population and also maintain the ecological balance. Therefore, every member of the society must take an active part in social forestry and take advantage of its products, fodder for animals, wood for fuel for the villagers, wood for agricultural tools, straw for huts and fruits and food for human population. It also provides the opportunities for the employment for poors and landless villagers. It checks the environmental pollution. It will encourage the tendency of reforestation by plantation which is the need of the day.

Role of Social Forestry

The social forestry aimed at has fixed the following:

(*a*) To meet the most urgent requirement of fuel wood in shortest possible time and to provide poles, timber, bamboo, fodder, fruits and other minor forest products for basic requirement of rural population.

(*b*) To provide employment to the unemployed and under employed local people, particularly the landless agricultural labours including tribals, scheduled caste and other traditionally weaker section of the rural communities.

(*c*) To induce community participation in creating, maintaining and protecting plantation programme under a joint management system with share of benefits of the produce raised.

(*d*) To improve the environmental condition by creating green belts in urban and industrial areas thereby ensuring aesthetic and recreational facilities.

(*e*) To supply improved variety of seeds, grafts, seedlings for increased production and upliftment of the economic standard of local people.

Various objectives have met with commendable success in this state. Some tangible benefits have occurred due planting on non-forest land where soil and water conservation status are improving the quality of life.

Social Forestry in Tribal Areas

(*i*) Social forestry has so far not been a promising tool for socio-economic and ecological development, continuous employment, for better nutrition, higher quality of clothing, home better health and recreational facilities in tribal areas. Bulk tribal population has not been covered under direct and immediate micro-level benefits to resource—poor and economically disadvantaged rural dwellers, as well as bring forth long-term, macro-level resource—conservation type advantages that Government agencies try to achieve. Neither, it has proved useful, as a small-scale landuse operation ranging from pure forests to integrated agro forestry in tribal areas; nor it has initiated inter-action between the forest ecosystem and human social systems in tribal inhabited area. It has yet to deal with broad aspect of human ecology in tribal areas.

(*ii*) Social forestry and tribal areas will need to consider social factors such as cultural knowledge and values regarding forestry, availability of resources land, capital, materials and labour, social constraints on resource management, social competition and conflict over resources.

(*iii*) Social forestry, is considered a major element in India's over all record development but it has to cover bulk rural areas of central India.

Role of Panchayat in Social Forestry

The village panchayats have got the powers, authority and finances. Therefore panchayat should play significant role in social forestry and environmental ecology and its balance. The forest and grazing land are under the control of village panchayats. The following steps may be taken by village panchayat for social forestry.

1. The village panchayat should take help of the forest department. Panchayat should hand over temporarily to the forest department for reforestation. There should be some contact between panchayat and forest department.
2. The forest department should advice and suggest a guideline for the plantation according to soil and climate of the area to the village panchayat.

3. The village panchayat can take help of the forest department for protection of the plants so that plants can develop and grow safely. The animals and villagers may not harm the plants.
4. During the period of development of plantation by forest department, some products, grass and other products can be used by the villagers.
5. The forest department should employ the villagers of the same area for plantation and their lookafter.

Social Forestry on Personal Land

The social forestry can also be encouraged and developed on personal land. The land can be allotted at personal level for such programme of social forestry. Two types of social forestry can be organized at personal level (*a*) Agricultural forestry, and (*b*) Agriculture of plants.

(*a*) *Agricultural Forestry:* Under the scheme personal land is used for plantation purpose. The forest department encourages villagers for developing nursery and can supply plants free of cost. The plantation can be done on the boundaries of their fields and also along the drainage system. These are useful for the villagers for fuel, tools, building material etc.

(*b*) *Agriculture of Plants:* The less furtile land can be best utilized for this scheme of plantation. The agricultural plantation will add to the economy of the villages and also improve the quality of environment. It will check the soil erosion. This scheme should be implemented on hill areas, along the roads boundaries and canal side. This scheme should not be used for fertile land, but popular plants are grown along the crops on the boundaries of the fields.

Advantages of Social Forestry

The following are the main advantages of social forestry scheme:

1. It will improve the economic status of rural population.
2. It will improve the quality of the environment by maintaining environmental balance.

3. It will check the urbanization and industrialization of urban population.
4. It will maintain the ecological balance of the environment of the country at local and regional level.
5. It will check the problem of soil erosion of the country.
6. The expansion of desert areas can also be checked by the scheme of social forestry.
7. It will meet the demands of rural population, *e.g.*, fuel, tools, building material and fodder for animals.
8. It will provide the opportunities for employment of poor and landless villagers.

Limitations of Social Forestry

This scheme is indeed very useful for rural population and maintaining the quality of the environment, but following are the limitations at the implementation stage.

1. The World Bank is assisting this scheme of our country. The forest department is not making its proper use except by growing Eucalyptus plants which are very useful.
2. The economically well to do persons of the villages are taking the advantages of the scheme. It is not reaching to the poors and landless villagers.
3. The plantation is being done on fertile land.
4. The villagers have no trust or faith in workers of the forest department.

NEW STRATEGY NEEDED

Various environmental, social and economic problems and hazards suffered by the tribals have been enumerated in broad outlines in the foregoing paragraphs. It is obvious, the most serious of the hazards are faced by those tribals residing in the central and western India.

The author considers that in the present economic situation of the country only the forestry sector can bring about a miraculous and most effective changes in the habitat and ameliorate the hazards of day-to-day life of the tribal communities working in more than 5,000 mines in the country.

But the job will be extremely challenging as the tribals are sensitive to any drastic change in the habitat, the soil is sterile and the task of revegetation is frought with various problems. In selecting species various factors enumerated about soil plant interactions have to be considered.

Social forestry will have to devise planting techniques and choose proper species to check erosion in quarry site, over burden dump, soil dump, abandoned quarry, tailing dams and revegetate all such areas. For improving quality of life there will be need for planting flowering trees, fruit tees, create horticultural garden, mini zoo, demarcate nature reserve and plant various species to supply M.F.P.

Suitable species have to be selected to build-up sound and dust barriers. Proper use of scientific methodology in creating shelter belts in all vulnerable areas has to be made. Various low cost soil conservation engineering designs in controlling gully, sheet erosion, controlling nullah river banks have to be made.

AN ESTIMATE FOR PROPER CONSIDERATION

There is 15 per cent land of our country, under the forest, while there is need of 30 to 33 per cent land for the forest, so that environmental balance can be maintained in our country. There is 320 lac hectare lands of the country under the desert which is in Rajasthan, Gujarat, Haryana, Karnataka and Andhra Pradesh. There is urgent need of plantation in these states. The following suggestions have been given for developing social forestry in the country:

1. The awareness and utility of social forestry is essential for rural and urban adults through adult and non-formal education system.
2. The adults of rural and urban area should be encouraged to develop the nursery for regional plants with the help of forest department.
3. The plantation and development of nursery and not sufficient programmes, but the basic need to develop the irrigation facility during the dry season. Some steps have been taken for the desert areas. Rajasthan canal is one of the facilities.
4. The adults should be given training for plantation and

developing their own nursery. It will add to their economy and employ the adults for the purpose.

5. The interested persons should be given awareness of seeds and their growing seasons. They should be well acquaint about the variety of plants and utility for the human population.
6. The schemes are implemented in the different areas of the country. There is great variation of soils. Therefore the adults should know the nature of their soil and its suitability for plants.

QUESTIONS FOR ANSWER

1. *Describe the role of adult education for providing environmental awareness. Suggest some programmes for this purpose.*
2. *Point out the role of non-formal education in the environment awareness and consciousness among adults.*
3. *Explain the term Social Forestry. Mention its objectives, need and importance.*
4. *Describe the* role of Panchayat *and non-formal education in developing the scheme of Social Forestry. Indicate its advantages and limitations.*
5. *Write short notes on the following:*
   (*a*) *Adult Education and Environmental Awareness.*
   (*b*) *Non-formal Education and Environmental Awareness.*
   (*c*) *Social Forestry and Quality of Environment*
   (*d*) *Role of Social Forestry in the Ecology of the Environment.*

27

Environmental Management: A Social Concern

As the "Frontier" theory suggests, America, under Regan's administration started to contemplate on the issues of environment as early as in April 1970. Known as environmental decade, the year's after 1980 saw many events at different levels. By the middle of 1980's the issues concerning environment slowly acquired a multi-disciplinary dimension developing its own philosophy, ethos, economics etc. The study of Management of Environment thus enlarged itself covering various chemical, physical, socio-economic and political colours thereby becoming central agenda of the twentieth century to be carried on for the future of the humanity. The policy took note of these social changes and brought environmental issues under its broad umbrella and projected its own agenda at the national and international levels taking into consideration the geo-political and environmental *status quo* concerns.

Consequently peoples and industry also took note of the change in the stand of the governments. Bureaucracy by then had taken serious note of it and was prepared with a heavy hand to deal with those who had scant respect for the environment. All these internal changes in the attitude of the people and the governing bodies across borders thus lead to a new awakening in the people thereby pushing the agenda of environment even to the bottom level administrative machinery.

The establishment of council on environmental quality, safety and health administration, regulatory commissions, so on and so forth, establishment of environmental offices at district level and at the state level.

Much publicised United Nations Conference on environment and developments held in Rio de Janerio in fact rejuvenated the larger consciousness of nations and people's around the globe. Particularly so, the youth. Agenda 21, gave comprehensive blue print for global development. It also established the rights and responsibilities of the state. It also set before them a series of principles to support the sustainable management of the environment. In doing so they in fact demolished the theories of boundaries and sovereignty.

The present global climate and the threat for the biological-diversity even in the traditional societies, made countries like India to play a vital role in these global pronouncements. In fact at Rio there were about 150 countries as signatories. India was one of them. Subsequent to Rio-India has brought about quite a lot of changes in the basic laws concerning environment apart from its constitutional stud. However, the reports of 1997, special session of the General Assembly of UN on environment did not in reality, enthuse the larger sections of global population as it did in 1992. This convention of 1997 on the other hand only helped to establish some safeguards to the world threatened by the loss of bio-diversity. Further, 1992 Rio summit's central theme, popularly known as "Agenda 21", had its drawbacks and could show little progress by 1997 as assessed.

Plants and animals which evolved in a specific abiotic environment forms an ecosystem such as forest ecosystem. Until the beginning of this century man had not experienced the unclean air, water and non-productive land. However, during the last two or three decades, there has been a gradual degradation of environment to a level of threatening the very survival of human race itself. As analysis of the reasons for this environmental degradation with a view to seeking solutions to this problem, would reveal to us, some of the major causes for environmental degradation. They are:

1. Increased population; this has put severe strain on the land for agricultural production and its sustenance as fertile soil.
2. Demand for fodder, timber and other industrial products in equal proportion to population is contributing to deforestation.

3. Growth of industry has necessitated power and power generation has lead to pollution of sorts.
4. Industry itself is polluting air, water and degrading the environment.

When we talk about industrialisation, we must remember that it is associated with the national development. There is always some amount of environmental degradation if a nation plans to industrialise.

Now let us see how abiotic and biotic environment is polluted and how we can overcome them.

In our country, mostly it is domestic waste, thermal power, industry, irrigation, exhaust from automobiles emissions and abuse of agricultural chemicals that contribute to the pollution of environment. Today there is an increase of 0.01 per cent of Carbon-dioxide in the atmosphere causing variation in the rain-fall and atmosphere temperature. There is an increase of about 3 to 4 lakh tons of Chloroforo Carbon in the atmosphere which has created holes in ozone layer causing skin disease in countries like Australia. Thus, the cautious environmental management is a very essential item on the agenda for the future.

If we keep the annual population growth at 1.8 per cent per year, then every 40 years the country's population will be double of the present population. To fend them, Scientific and Industrial revolution comes in handy. Jobs in urban centres where industries are centralised therefore attracts a steady flow of people from rural to urban centres.

The net result of it is the growth in slums in urban areas with no basic amenities of any kind. This degradation of human settlement thus further contributes to the environmental degradation. This concentration of people in their working places therefore leads to boom in automobile industry with little or no efficient public transportation traffic regulatory systems.

Concentration of major air pollutants and suspended particles like oxides of Sulphur, Nitrogen, Carbon and Hydrocarbons is causing different kinds of respiratory diseases.

Noise pollution is of recent origin, jet planes, motors, railways, factories, generators, construction machinery, television, radio sets and public address systems all cause noise pollution. Noise is quantified in terms of decibal scale. Zero dB is threshold of hearing and 130 dB is pain to the ear. Ticking of watch is around 30 dB. Normal conversation is 60 dB and Jet engine/rail engine noise is 100-130 dB. Exposure of noise level exceeding 75 dB for more than 8 hours can cause deafness.

Continued noise pollution can cause hypertension, sleep disorders and these are the major health problems in the modern world. Though one will not be in a position to point his figure at these pollutants of noise in ones daily life as they indirectly harm the health of the individuals in the society thereby weakening the progeny. Adding to these, are the problems of water pollution.

India is basically a country with more than 70 per cent of the people living in villages and nearly 40 per cent of the people are living below the poverty line. India has about 6,00,000 villages and these villages largely depend on the supply of water from ground water resources. Contamination of this water is because of seepages of sewage water and other acidic pollutants due to unplanned industrialisation leads to serious health hazards. Pollution of Tungbhadra River Water by Harihar Polyfibres is a well known case in the State of Karnataka. The industrial effluents like Mercury, Chromium, Cadmium and hosts of other organic chemicals compounds which are hazardous to life have caused the death of a large number of fishes in Tungbhadra river. Water pollution through pathogenic micro-organisms cause dysentery, cholera, giardiasis, amoebosis, typhoid etc. Latest in the series are hepatitis A, B and food poisoning.

Global warming in this direction is the most recent phenomenon. Debate on this issue is still on. Earth is protected by a thin layer of ozone in the atmosphere. If we compress this 0 at normal pressure and temperature it will form a 3 mm layer around the atmosphere. Yet, this ozone layer filters all the UV-B rays from sun reaching the earth. The UV-B rays are harmful to all living organisms. They cause irritation in plants and animals and also cause skin cancer in humans. The ozone depletion can cause rise in the temperature of earth leading to global warning. This warming can cause serious damages to what has been identified as the large network of bio diversity spread over through the process of evolution of 200 million years.

There are 2,50,00 species of flowering plants and 4,170 species of mammals on this earth. India alone has 6 per cent of total forests of the world. Increased demand of civilisation for timber, industrial products, mega dams, mining have already denuded vast tracts of forests. Satellite imagery has shown that every year in India alone 1.5 k.m. of forest is being lost. Adding to this is the natural forest fires as the one that occurred in Indonesia recently.

Well, this being the present problem currently faced the world over, retaining the nature and natural environment and the struggle for better life continues. As Gandhiji has rightly put it "Earth has enough for every one's need and not for every ones greed" it is our duty to save it for our future generations before we consume it. The natural environment on earth is not the artificial creation of man but is a product of evolution of many million year.

When we are aware that we have little strength or capacity to create the environment as the one we have today do we have the moral courage to destroy it? If everyone of us think on these lines and make a judicious use of what is bestowed upon us, then alone we can sustain our beautiful "life". If we are moved by the craze for material well being, our dooms day will not be far off. Hence we need to control the environmental destruction, degradation and pollution and manage it as a part of bio-diversity.

For this management one need not be qualified specialised professional, but one definitely has to be genius. Recycling of waste water, attempting to stop mobility of pollutants, prevention of pollution, strict implementation of laws of the state, joint action of people and governments, regulatory measures be observed.

For proper environment management, environmental education/awareness through voluntary organisation, educating the children through curriculum, updating laws are the needs of the day. Sundarlal Bahuguna, Meda Patekar only to name a few shall be the role models, for those who have genuine commitment to nature.

Government of India enacted environmental laws from time to time—namely in 1974 Preventive and Control of pollution Act, 1977 Water Cess Act, 1981, Air Pollution Act and in 1986 Comprehensive Environmental Protection Act. In fact most of the progressive states have separate ministry of environment to control, monitor and regulate the environmental issues. But all said and done it is ultimately the people who will have to do the real job in all the environmental matters, we must be aware that it controls the destiny not of a man but of the "man kind"—as poet

Shelly said. In spite of all our misdeeds against nature and natural environment, it is the nature that will have the last laugh over man. Therefore, it is better we act soon and save our environment. The man and the environment are inseparable and each depends on the other for ones survival.

Environmental management is not your job, not my job, or his/her job nor is in the job of the Government and Voluntary Organisations but it is our responsibility collectively. We must act collectively to save ourselves or else our selfish and short sighted acts will see the end of the man kind sooner or later. Let us all act together and save our environment.

QUESTIONS FOR ANSWER

1. *Justify that environmental management is basically a social concern.*
2. *"Human misdeeds against nature would make the nature to have last laugh over man". Justify this statement and enumerate the effects of pollution on mankind.*

28

Global Perspectives on Environmental Management

GLOBAL ISSUES AND CONCERNS

The discovery of the steam engine in the early eighteenth century ushered in an era of industrialisation and mass exploitation of natural resources. As a consequence there has been considerable degradation of eco systems and an exponential increase in pollution of the environment. Though environmentalism emerged in the West, in the nineteenth century, and demands for clean air and unpolluted water were made in the early twentieth century, the priority given to economic growth overshadowed thoughts relating to preservation of the environment.

Global concern regarding the steadily deteriorating state of the environment was first seriously manifested in the form of the United Nations Conference on Human Environment, held in Stockholm, in June 1972. It focused attention of the dangers posed to the quality of human life, and to survival itself, by continuous degradation of ecological assets, and by pollution due to industrial effluents. It tried to find ways by which the precious environment could be preserved. The conference highlighted the divergence in the viewpoints of the developed and developing nations.

Sandbrook (1992) pointed out it was *"a dialogue of the deaf between the rich and the poor"*. For the rich developed nations, the main concern was the cleaning up of the *'effluence of affluence'*. They advocated that the cleaning up be taken up by all nations simultaneously so that the additional cost of cleaning operations should not place any country at a disadvantage in a competitive international market.

For the developing world, seeking the fruits of industrialisation, pollution was relatively unimportant, the first priority being the alleviation of poverty. As Indira Gandhi tensely pointed out *"of all the pollution we face the worst is poverty"*. The Stockholm Conference opened the eyes of the North to the problems of the South. It also saw the adaptation of rules and regulations to cover environmental ills—at least in the developed countries. More importantly it led to the establishment of the United Nations Environment Programme (UNEP).

The World Commission on Environment and Development (Brundtland Commission) was established in December 1983, and it presented, in 1987, a remarkable report *'Our Common Future'* which *"tried to balance the arguments concerning North/South responsibility and suggest ways forward"*. It concluded that *"if we continue to use up natural resources as we do at present, if we ignore the plight of the poor then we can (only) expect a decline in the quality of life."*

The Brundtland Report (1987) suggested that the concept of sustainable development should become an acceptable principle of both national and international development and policies; and that national governments should begin a systematic integration of economic and environmental considerations. It described sustainable development as *"development that seeks to meet the needs and aspirations of the present generation without compromising the ability to meet these of future generations"*.

The very significant conclusions of the Brundtland Report were extensively discussed, and a debate in the United Nation (1989) led to the UN Conference on Environment and Development, better known as *Earth Summit 92* at Rio de Janeiro, Brazil, in June 1992. At this conference a comprehensive, and far reaching, programme for sustainable development was agreed upon in the form of Agenda 21 comprising of 38 chapters. All countries are now apparently committed to the protection of the environment and to the principle of sustainable development.

The road beyond Rio has however, been far from smooth. The bio-diversity convention remains unsigned by the United States, and binding targets for lowering greenhouse gas emissions of the developed north are yet not set. There is dichotomy in North-South thinking on important matters related to the environment. Who is responsible for the degradation of the environment—the rich or the poor? Which is more polluting—affluence or population? Who should pay for ecoprotection/ecopreservation? What should be the form of aid to the developing country for programmes related to the environment? Will international free trade, as embedied in General Agreement on Trade and Tariffs (GATT) harm or help the environment? Discussions and consensus on these issues are vital for evolution of an effective global policy on environment and its management.

The major problems on global scale faced by us today are those relating to:

(*i*) global warming, greenhouse effect and climate change.
(*ii*) depletion of the ozone layer.
(*iii*) the phenomenon of 'acid rain'.
(*iv*) preservation of bio-diversity.
(*v*) depletion of plant genetic resources.
(*vi*) destruction of tropical forests.
(*vii*) pollution of oceans.
(*viii*) loss of top-soil and desertification.
(*ix*) development of zero-polluting energy sources.

Because of constraint of space it is not possible to discuss, in detail, any of these problems. All decisions and actions relating to them will necessarily be based on international agreements and treaties.

TOOLS OF ENVIRONMENTAL MANAGEMENT

Effective management of the environment at local and regional levels requires the use of various management tools including environmental monitoring, environmental audit, environment impact assessment, and environment management system.

Environmental Monitoring (EM)

Environmental Monitoring involves the systematic collection of data on noxious and toxic elements present in the environment. In India the responsibility for recording and analysing data on toxic substances in air, water, soil and living beings is vested in the Pollution Control Board at central and state levels. Standards have been established for some selected atmospheric and hydrospheric parameters including SO_2, SPM, NO_x, HC, *p*H, BOD and COD.

Presently data is being recorded for these few parameters, at a 'limited number of stations, mostly in the cities, and sometimes away from the most-polluted areas. Moreover, no data is collected on DDT, the more vicious DDE, dangerous metallic and non-metallic trace elements or smog ozone (Oestereich, 1994a).

Professional monitoring by government agencies needs to be supplemented by surveillance by non-governmental agencies including educational and research institutions, and voluntary citizen's organizations. If properly co-ordinated this will add to the data base. Moreover a correspondence of data obtained by government and non-government agencies will help allay fears of possible connivance between representative of industry and individuals working in the PCBs.

Environmental Audit (EA)

The series of activities undertaken to evaluate the environmental performance of an industrial unit or organisation is called an environmental audit. It systematically examines, evaluates and documents all policies, equipment, methodologies and procedures of production that have an impact on material production. There are no standardised procedures for environmental audit but ideally a manufacturing or producing organisation should account for the environmental impact associated with the entire life-cycle of the product—from procurement of raw materials, to manufacturing of products, to their use and disposal (Agarwal, 1995).

The environmental audit, that a company is required to submit every year, must include information regarding the consumption of raw material, the amount of toxic wastes produced, and the methods adopted for pollution control and environmental protection. Rajaraman (1997) points out that an environment audit should include a formal policy statement of the management regarding its commitment to the environment, and should clearly identify the objectives of the audit programme. The audit should be performed by personnel with technical training and proficiency in auditing.

They should possess an understanding of relevant regulating requirements, relevant environmental technologies, and of operations and procedures. The auditing system requires the auditors to base their findings on facts, and to document these facts. Environmental audits, to be successful, must be structured and utilise checklists and questionnaires that provide details. Environmental audit is a well respect management tool that helps management's to formulate effective environmental practices, and assess the degree of compliance with regulatory requirements, and with the organisation's stated environmental objectives.

Environmental Impact Assessment (EIA)

Environmental Impact Assessment is today a mandatory process in the formulation of major development projects. Rao (1997) points out that "*EIA is an important tool for integrating the objectives of environmental management with the requirements of economic growth and social development*". He believes that it is "*the most invaluable, interdisciplinary and objective decision-making tool with respect to alternate roles for development, process technologies and project sites.*"

In EIA quantitative values are established for critical parameters that indicate the quality of material systems before, during and after the proposal developmental activity. EIA takes into consideration the impact a project is likely to have on:

(*i*) soil, water (ground and surface) and air quality,
(*ii*) forests, landuse, agriculture, fisheries, tourism etc.,
(*iii*) population in terms of social and economic levels and health,
(*iv*) flora and fauna especially endemic and endangered species, and
(*v*) displaced persons.

The procedure for EIA includes screening of sites, determination of impacts, collection of baseline data, prediction of imports, evaluation of impacts, formulation of Environmental Management Plan (EMP), and post-project environmental monitoring. Further, as Rao states, EIA is cyclical or reiterative in nature. As more information becomes available the assessment can become more derailed and the likely effects predicted with greater accuracy and confidence.

Environmental Management System (EMS)

An Environmental Management System is a structured system voluntarily developed by a producing concern to ensure compliance with the company's own stated environmental policies and objectives. It is 'watchdog' system integrated with all other operations of the company. The main elements of an EMS are the organisational structure, responsibilities, practices, procedures and resources relating to environment to environmental matters viewed in relation to existing environmental legislatures. It is internationally recognised that developing an EMS is the most effective way of reducing a producing unit's impact on the environment.

However, industrial houses are reluctant to develop one because of the high development and maintenance costs. The situation is, however, changing with the establishment of the ISO 14000 series of standards relating to EMS and the indications that some countries plan to adopt them as laws, or use them as a basis for doing business. At a seminar on ISO 14000 in Malaysia some expects were of the view that Asian companies could out on future trading opportunities (for example in textiles) because ISO 14000 certification is increasingly being applied in Europe and the United States (Diayo, 1997).

QUESTIONS FOR ANSWER

1. *Write a note on Global perspective on environmental management.*
2. *Write short notes on the following:*
   (*a*) *Brundtland Commission 1983.*
   (*b*) *Earth Summit 1992.*
   (*c*) *General Agreement on Trade and Tariffs.*
3. *Write a note on 'Tools of Environmental Management'.*
4. *Write short notes on the following:*
   (*a*) *Environmental Monitoring.*
   (*b*) *Environmental Audit.*
   (*c*) *Environmental Management System.*

29

Environmental Management: Meaning and Definition

It may be pointed out that ecological balance and ecosystem stability are duly maintained by the nature itself but the emergence of modern industrial society has disturbed the ecological balance and ecosystem stability through heavy industrialization, technological revolution, faster growth of means of transportation and communication, rapacious exploitation of natural resources, large-scale land use changes, unplanned and unchecked expansion of urban and industrial complexes etc. In other words, human activities of modern 'economic and technological man' have disturbed the harmonious relationships between the environment and man.

Environmental management is, thus, the process to improve the relationship between man and environment so that the quality of both, the environment and human society, may be improved. This improvement of relationships between man and environment may be achieved through check on destructive activities of man, conservation, protection, regulation and regeneration of nature.

Environmental management, thus, is related to the rational adjustment of man with nature involving judicious exploitation and utilization of natural resources without disturbing the ecological balance and ecosystem equilibrium. It may be pointed out that since the development of society in terms of socio-economic framework has to be maintained and hence it is imperative to utilize natural resources.

Environmental planning and management is, therefore, compromise between ecosystem and ecological balance and human material progress and the environmental management must take into consideration the ecological principles and socio-economic needs of the society.

Environmental management, thus, involves socio-economic development of the society on the one hand and maintenance of environmental quality, on the other hand. It may be further pointed out that the term 'environmental quality' is also difficult to be defined because it is a subjective term and is interpreted differently by different groups of people ranging from 'zero population growth' to simplicity of life for decent human existence, from the survival of human species to an environment that not only sustains life but enriches life, harmonising the work of man and nature for the greater good of all.

Environmental management, therefore, involves (*i*) protection of environment through putting curb on rapacious utilization of natural resources and unscrupulous activities of man, control and lowering down of pollution level, control of the rapid growth of human population and environmentally harmful technologies; (*ii*) enhancement of economic value of the environment and its resources; and (*iii*) preservation of the environment for our future generations.

"Conservation of resources and control of pollution are the essential pre-requisites for environmental planning. Conservation does not mean stoppage of development activities; rather it adds value to the available resources through appropriate technology and, thus, accelerates growth processes. In fact, conservation and development are the two facets of the same coin and thus are complementary to each other. No growth in true sense would be attained unless appropriate technology is evolved to get maximum return out of a tiny bit of resource and avoid wastage and depletion (of natural resources) and devise scientific methods of recycling so as to cause least burden over the environmental system".

—*L.R. Singh*

Environmental management involves two major aspects viz. (*i*) socio-economic development, and (*ii*) stability of the biosphere in general and survival and stability of individual ecosystems in particular. "There are healthy signs that decision-makers responsible for environmental planning and management are becoming increasingly aware that the stability of the biosphere in general and the survival and stability of individual ecosystems in particular, are criteria which need careful consideration when environmental management policies and priorities are being evaluated and implemented".—*C.C. Park*

Thus "environmental planning implies the optimal utilization of the earth's resources, both renewable and non-renewable, for development activities, conservation of what is rare and precious in nature and preservation of the quality of environment for the healthy growth of life—*R. Singh*

"Management implies a conscious choice from a variety of alternative proposals and further more that such a choice involves purposeful commitment to recognized and desired objectives. Wherever possible, management implies to the deliberate adoption of a strategy or number of strategies designed to meet realistically short-term objectives, yet specifically providing sufficient flexibility for the preservation of longer term options."—*T.O. Riordan*

According to Dennis Meadows "the concept of environmental management is generally related with the environmental model which assures that food supply will grow with increased capital, annual agricultural inputs, and land development; but on the other hand it also includes important limits to all these factors, challenges to be faced and the policies to overcome the problem."

ASPECTS AND APPROACHES TO ENVIRONMENTAL MANAGEMENT

On an average environmental management involves (*i*) judicious and gainful utilization of natural resources for socio-economic development, and (*ii*) maintenance of environmental quality by pursuing ecological principles. Broader objectives of environmental management include

(*i*) to restrict and regulate the exploitation and utilization of natural resources, mainly non-renewable natural resources;

(*ii*) to regenerate degraded environment and to renew natural resources (renewable);

(*iii*) to control environmental degradation and pollution;

(*iv*) to reduce the impacts of extreme events and natural disasters;

(*v*) to make optimum utilization of natural resources by

recycling and reusing waste materials produced from one activity to another economically and environmentally viable activity;

(*vi*) to assess the impacts of proposed projects and activities on the environment;

(*vii*) to review and revise the existing technologies of production in terms of their adverse effects on the environment; and

(*viii*) to formulate laws and regulations for the implementation of environmental protection and conservation programmes to maintain the environmental quality.

Further, environmental planning and management should include the whole biological world because environment belongs to man and all living organism which except man do not know any artificial boundary whether regional, national or international. But the same strategy for environmental planning and management may not be applicable to all the regions and all of the ecosystems because human interests differ in different regions and ecosystems.

For example, overpopulation and related problems (*e.g.* economic poverty, retarded economic development, social and educational backwardness etc.) are the main areas of concern in the developing countries whereas high level of pollution and environmental degradation caused by advanced technology, increased production, materialistic outlook and resource depletion and the immediate issues to be tackled in the developed industrialised western countries.

COMPONENTS

The components of environmental management may include five basic aspects *viz.* (*i*) Environmental Perception and Public Awareness; (*ii*) Environmental Education and Training; (*iii*) Management of Resources; (*iv*) Environmental Impact Assessment and (*v*) Control of Environmental Degradation and Pollution. These broader aspects of environmental management may be further elaborated as given below:

Environmental Perception and Public Awareness

(*i*) Sources of environmental perception and public awareness;
(*ii*) Level of environmental perception, and
(*iii*) Role of environmental perception in environmental planning and management.

Environmental Education and Training

(*i*) Environmental education at School, College and University levels, and
(*ii*) Environmental training by professional institutions.

Resource Management

(*i*) Classification of natural resources,
(*ii*) Survey and evaluation of ecological resources (inventory and evaluation of ecological resources),
(*iii*) Preservation of ecological resources, and
(*iv*) Conservation of energy resources, mineral resources, soil resources, water resources etc.

Environmental Impact Assessment

(*i*) Appraisal of existing environmental conditions,
(*ii*) Appraisal of existing and proposed production methods and technologies,
(*iii*) Methodologies and procedures,
(*iv*) Probable impacts of existing and proposed projects on environment, and
(*v*) Review of technology and required improvement—modification and improvement in production technology, development of conservation techniques, development of defensive techniques and development of ecological techniques.

Control of Environmental Degradation and Pollution

(*i*) Regeneration of degraded environment,
(*ii*) Control of environmental pollution, and
(*iii*) Reduction of natural hazards and disasters

The aforesaid aspects of environmental management may be

put under three major components of environmental planning and management *viz.* (1) *Resource Management, (2) Environmental Impact Assessment, and (3) Control of Environmental Degradation and Pollution and Major Environmental Programmes.*

APPROACHES TO ENVIRONMENTAL MANAGEMENT

The strategies of environmental management may be formulated on two considerations, namely (*i*) spatial consideration, and (*ii*) methodological consideration. Environmental planning may be approached at local, regional, national or international levels as regards the spatial dimension and the management strategies may be chalked out on the basis of needs, aspirations, perceptions, priorities and inhibitions of the individuals, society and the government. For example, the problem of ozone depletion and its probable consequences have, no doubt, become an environmental issue of global concern but there is difference in the outlook between the western developed world and developing world regarding the control of ozone depletion.

The western developed countries are giving top priorities to tackle the problem of ozone depletion caused by the release of chlorofluorocarbons and halogen gases because they are going to be immediate victims of increased ultra-violet solar radiation and increased incidence of skin cancer whereas the developing countries are reluctant to stop the production and consumption of ozone depleting substances (chlorofluorocarbons—CFCs) because they believe that by doing so they will remain undeveloped and will be deprived of modern amenities which the western developed countries are enjoying since long.

As regards the methodological consideration, there are two approaches to environmental planning and management *viz.* (*i*) *Preservative Approach, and (ii) Conservationist Approach.* Preservative approach to environmental management advocates non-interference of man with nature or say physico-biotic environment and complete adaptation by man to natural environment.

This preservative approach is, in fact, not practicable because non-interference with natural environment would lead the humanity to complete starvation and even extinction. If man has to survive he must derive some thing from the nature and even the exploitation of minimum resources from the natural environment to fulfil the basic needs of human society would cause disequilibrium of some sort in the ecological balance and ecosystem stability resulting into environmental degradation and pollution.

The second approach of environmental management, *viz* conservationist approach advocates for adjustment with physico-biotic environment in terms of technological and behavioural institutional adjustments. In other words, the environmental resources may be utilized for the socio-economic development of human society but efforts should also be made to maintain ecological balance, ecosystem stability and environmental quality as far as possible by adopting suitable and pollution-safe technologies and by making the society answerable to any maladjustment in the natural ecosystem.

Thus the conservationist approach to environmental management is based on two broader perspectives *viz.* (*i*) to restrict and minimise adverse effects of human activities during utilization of natural resources on environment, and (*ii*) to optimize the productivity of natural environmental, ecosystems by adopting environmentally safe technologies. This approach also formulates several alternative strategies for environmental management.

ECOLOGICAL BASIS OF ENVIRONMENTAL MANAGEMENT

Any environmental planning and management whether at local, regional, national or international level (involving the whole atmosphere and the hydrosphere) must be based on fundamental ecological principles if we are interested in the survival of human beings and if we do not want to be cursed by our future generations and thus the stability of the biosphere in general and survival and stability of individual ecosystems in particular should be maintained.

The fundamental ecological issues to be considered for environmental management include (*i*) components and dynamics (energy flow and circulation of elements in the ecosystems of biospheric ecosystem; (*ii*) form, function and equilibrium of ecosystems; (*iii*) ecological changes through time (evolution of plants and animals in historical perspective and space (disposal and distribution of plants and animals; (*iv*) exploitation and utilization of ecological resources; and (*v*) impacts of human activities on environmental leading to environmental degradation and pollution.

The fundamental ecological principles govern various aspects of natural ecosystems and organisms therein such as (*i*) evolution, dispersal and distribution of plants and animals; (*ii*) extinction of species; (*iii*) biological succession; (*iv*) transfer, circulation and consumption of matter and energy in the different components of natural ecosystems; (*v*) cycling and re-cycling of organic and inorganic substances in the natural ecosystems through biogeochemical cycles; (*vi*) stability and instability of ecosystems; (*vii*) life cycles of organisms; and (*viii*) interrelationships among organisms and between organisms; and physical components of the environment.

The following basic ecological principles must be taken into consideration before formulating any environmental management strategy—(1) Biotic and abiotic components of the biospheric ecosystem and subsequent smaller ecosystems are interconnected and intimately related to large-scale biogeochemical cycles. (2) Sustained life on the earth is a characteristic of ecosystem. (3) Nothing actually disappears when we throw it away. (4) All systems and problems are ultimately interrelated and so we should not solve problems one by one. (5) Resources of planet earth are finite. (6) Nature has spent millions of years to create resources and in refining a stable ecosystem. (7) When biological processes are associated with physical events more severe hazards are created (floods-diseases). (8) All living organisms and physical environment are mutually reactive. (9) Energy pattern and flow in the ecosystem are governed by the first and second laws of thermodynamics. (10) Ecosystem productivity depends upon availability of solar energy and the efficiency of plants to convert solar energy into chemical energy.

APPROACHES TO RESOURCE MANAGEMENT

Resource management on the basis of ecological principles to achieve sustainable socio-economic development of human society through purposive and judicious utilization of environmental/ natural resources and to maintain, simultaneously, the environmental quality is infact and inter-disciplinary field. The emergence of Resource Science involving the study of classification, evaluation, utilization and management of environmental/natural resources has opened a new vista in environmental studies in general and environmental management in particular.

In spite of the development of resource science there are still certain problems in the field of resource management because of difference of opinions and concepts of various aspects of resources and their management between different academic disciplines, between resource scientists and decision and policy makers, and between social groups and environmentalists/conservationists' groups and decision and policy makers.

Similarly, there is difference of opinions among resource scientists about the approaches to resource management because of the fact that many of the ecological problems are of global nature or of long-term dimension and many of the problems are multi-dimensional. Thus there are two approaches to the resource management based on the dimension and multiplicity of ecological problems arising out of resource utilization:

(*i*) *Holistic Approach*—advocates to consider all the ecological problems coming out of resource utilization together and thus all problems should be solved together and not one by one. This approach is no doubt ambiguous one and aims at long-term solution of problems and ecological balance and technological infrastructure.

(*ii*) *Monistic Approach*—advocates for narrow solution/short solution for specific problems. In other words, efforts should be made to tackle one problem at a time rather than tackling all the problems together at the same time.

Another approach to resource management is the system modelling on the basis of characteristics and functioning of biosphere ecosystem and ecological principles and of course general principles of system analysis. Consequently, J.N.R. Jeffers has formulated a *Five-Stage Iterative Planning Process* for land use planning and resource managements. It is apparent that the resource management model of Jeffers is iterative, dynamic and continuous process. There is ample scope in the model for further improvement and modifications in the light of changing socio-economic conditions and changing demands and value of resources.

ENVIRONMENTAL MANAGEMENT FUNCTIONS AND CHARACTERISTICS

Briefly these are as follows:

1. The main function is to maintain ecological balance and ecosystem stability for the welfare of man.
2. It is related to the rational adjustment of man with nature.
3. It involves socio-economic development of society and maintenance of *'environmental quality'*.
4. It compromises between ecological balance, ecosystem stability and socio-economic development of man.
5. It has two major aspects:
   (*a*) Socio-economic development, and
   (*b*) Stability of ecological balances and stability of individual ecosystem in particular.
6. The essential prerequisites of environmental management are the *conservation of resources* and *control of pollution.*
7. Environmental management has *three* main functions—
   (*a*) Protection of environment and lowering down the level of pollution,
   (*b*) Enhancement of socio-economic values of the environment and its resources, and
   (*c*) Preservation of the environment for future generation.
8. It evaluates the policies, plans, priorities implemented for the maintenance of the ecological balance and stability of ecosystem in view of the human development.

Dimensions of Environmental Management

There are various approaches which are employed for five *basic aspects* of environmental management.

1. *Environmental Awareness:* sources, levels and role of the environmental awareness.
2. *Environmental Education:* at different levels and environmental training.
3. *Resource Management:* survey, and classification natural resources preservation of ecological resources and conservation of energy resources.

4. *Environmental Impact Assessment or Evaluation:* methods, procedures, production, development, realization of objectives, and
5. *Control of Environmental Pollution:* regeneration, control and reduction of natural disasters.

INTERNATIONAL AGENCIES AND PROGRAMMES OF ENVIRONMENTAL MANAGEMENT

There are number of international agencies and programmes involved in different areas of environmental management, but hereunder we will discuss only the most important such bodies in which the U.N. and India are directly involved.

1. *Human Exposure Assessment Location (HEAL):* The project is a part of the Health Related Monitoring Programme by WHO in co-operation with UNEP. This project has three components, viz. (*i*) air monitoring, (*ii*) water quality monitoring, and (*iii*) food contamination monitoring on a global basis.

2. *International Union for Conservation of Nature and Natural Resources (IUCN):* An autonomous body, founded in 1948, with its Headquarters at Morges, Switzerland, that initiates and promotes scientifically based conservation measures. It also co-operates with United Nations and other intergovernmental agencies and with sister bodies of World Wildlife Fund (WWF).

3. *International Marine Consultative Organisation (IMCO):* It regulates the operation of ships in high seas, from marine water pollution viewpoint.

4. *South Asia Co-operative Environment Programme (SACEP):* This has been recently set up for exchange of professional knowledge and expertise on environmental issues among member countries—Afghanistan, Bangladesh, Bhutan, India, Iran, Pakistan and Sri Lanka.

5. *United Nations Educational, Scientific and Cultural Organisation (UNESCO):* A United Nations agency, found in 1945 to support and implement the efforts of member states to promote education, scientific research and information, and the arts to develop the cultural aspects of world relations. It also holds conferences and seminars, promotes research and exchange of information and provides technical support. Its Headquarters are in Paris.

Independently as well as in collaboration with other agencies like, UNEP, it supports activities related to environmental quality, human settlements, training to environmental engineers and other socio-cultural programmes related to environment.

6. *United Nations Environment Programme (UNEP):* A UN agency, Co-ordination of inter-governmental measures for environmental monitoring and protection. It was set up in 1972. There is a voluntary United Nations Environmental Fund to finance environmental projects. There is an Environmental Coordination Board, to co-ordination the UNEP programmes. Its Headquarters are in Nairobi, Kenya. UNEP was founded to study and formulate international guidelines for management of the environment. UNEP is assisting many such programmes in India.

7. *World Commission on Environment and Development (WCED):* This is a 23-member commission, set up in 1984 in pursuance to a UN General Assembly resolution in 1983 to re-examine the critical environmental and development issues and to formulate proposals for them. This is a call for political action to manage better environmental resources to ensure human progress and survival. The commission makes an assessment of the level of understanding and commitment of individuals, voluntary organisations and governmental bodies on environmental issues.

8. *Earthwatch Programme:* A worldwide programme, established in 1972 under the terms of the Declaration on the Human Environment. It monitors trends in the environment, based on a series of monitoring stations. Its activities are co-ordinated by UNEP.

9. *Man and the Biosphere Programme (MAB):* The programme is the outcome of International Biological Programme (IBP) that has already concluded its activities. MAB was formally launched by UNESCO in 1971. There are 14 project areas under this programme. We shall provide here the details of MAB with special reference to major activities in our own country so far done under the same, and the priority areas for future.

10. *Tehri High Dam Project (India):* It is one of the most controversial river projects in world as regards the conflicts between environmentalists, local people, project authorities and government. It is being constructed on the Ganga river below the confluence of its two main tributaries—Bhagirathi and Bhilaganga at Tehri of Uttar Pradesh. *Tehri Hydro Dam Corporation* (THDC)

was formed in 1989 and construction work was taken over by Union Government of India with Soviet technical and economic aid. It is 260.5 metre highest rock fill dam in the country.

Before planning this dam, proper assessment was not done to visualize the probable adverse effects. This area is seismically active zone, any strong earthquake will cause dam failure and disaster for mankind apart from other issues of the dam, it has the major issues to complete this project.

11. *Man and the Biosphere Programme (MAB):* MAB was conceived at the International Biosphere Conference of UNESCO in 1968 and was officially given shape by the General Conference of UNESCO at its 16th Session in 1970. The programme was formally launched by UNESCO in November 1971, when the MAB International Co-ordinating Council held its first session and identified 13 project area of cooperative research.

At *international* level MAB is guided by International Coordinating (ICC) which is inter-governmental and representative in character. ICS is made up of 30 countries elected by the General Conference of UNESCO. It meets after every two years to review and evaluate the programmes being made in implementing the programme. A MAB secretariat, provided by UNESCO ensrues overall coordination at international level. The National MAB Committees are the agencies through which the entire programme is operated globally. MAB National Committees, so far have been set up in 101 countries, including India. A national committee has scientists from universities and research institutions and public or private bodies' representatives concerned with environmental management. This committee directs and supervises the programme.

MAB cooperates closely with several other organisations as United Nations Environment Programme (UNEP), Food and Agricultural Organisation (FAO), World Health Organisation (WHO), International Council of Scientific Unions (ICSU) and International Union for Conservation of Nature and Natural Resources (IUCN).

In India, the MAB programme is serviced and funded by the Department of Environment, Forests and Wildlife. The national committee, Indian National Man and the Biosphere Committee, was first constituted in 1972, which supervises and directs the programme. The usual term of the members is two years. The members are taken from universities and other scientific organisations. The committee functions as an advisory/ recommendatory body to the Department of Environment, Forests and Wildlife for the MAB programme and catalyses actions on the issues related to this programme.

MAB is a problem-oriented programme. It is interdisciplinary in approach and emphasises the collective efforts by natural and social scientists. The programme aims to provide scientific basis to solve real practical problems of resource management through understanding the environmental problems in the ecosystem context. Finally, it intends to follow a system approach to find the best possible solution under a given set of conditions. Thus MAB helps bringing together the planners, policy makers, managers and scientists for arriving at a national decision on the issues of resource management.

Project Areas of MAB

Research under MAB has been divided into *fourteen broad areas* which are listed in the following paragraph:

1. Ecological Effects of increasing Human activities on Tropical and sub-tropical Forest ecosystem.
2. Ecological Effects of different Land Uses and Management practices on Temperate and Mediterranean Landscapes.
3. Impact of Human Activities and Land Use Practices or Grazing lands. Savana and other Grasslands.
4. Ecological Effects of Human Activities and Value and Resources of Lakes, Rivers, Estuaries and Coastal zones.
5. Impact of Human Activities on the Dynamics of Arid and Semi-arid zones to effects of Irrigation.
6. Impact of Human Activities or Mountain Ecosystems.
7. Ecology and Rational use of Island Ecosystems.
8. Conservation of Natural areas and the Genetic material they contain.
9. Ecological assessment of pest Management and Fertiliser use on Terrestrial Aquatic Ecosystems.
10. Effects of major-engineering works on man and his environment.
11. Ecological aspects of Urban systems with particular emphasis on Energy Utilisaiton.

12. Interaction between Environmental Transformation and the adaptive, Demographic and Genetic structure of human population.
13. Perception of *'Environmental quality'*.
14. Research on Environmental Pollution and its Effects on the Biosphere.

A number of research projects on these aspects have been sponsored. A Unit of Genetic Toxicology is established at Calcutta University to study (*i*) the chronic effects of sub-toxic doses of pollutants on human systems in relation with different modifying factors as genetic polymorphism, nutrition, etc., and (*ii*) identify the species of vegetation genetically tolerant to various pollutants.

A project is initiated to study the effects of SO_2 and particulate matter on vegetation in the urban and industrial areas. The project is designed to focus on specific (*industrial emissions*) and unspecific air pollution. The organisations involved are, B.H.U., Varanasi; J.N.U., New Delhi; N.B.R.I., Lucknow; N.E.E.R.I., Nagpur; University of Calcutta; Vikaram University., Ujjain and B.S.I. Calcutta.

There is wide diversity in our country. It has been divided into the following regions:

1. High altitude mountainous region—Forestry, road, dams, mining.
2. Mountains of Peninsular region—Forestry, mining projects.
3. Indo-Gangetic Plains—Population density, irrigation, cultivation.
4. Vindhyan and Daccan Highland Plateau—Forestry, mining and grazing.
5. Semi-arid Deserts of Western India—Irrigation, grazing.
6. Coastal regions—Industrialisation, urbanization, mining.
7. Oceanic Islands—Tourism, evergreen forest.

The MAB has focused much attention on these regions in view of its predominant natural ecosystems and human stresses or exploitations of resources.

INDIA'S ENVIRONMENTAL POLICIES

A concern for the environment is ingrained in India thought and is reflected in *"the pro-nature pantheism in Indian culture and Gandhian thought"* (Inamdar, 1989). India has incoporated in its Constitution a commitment to environmental protection and improvement. The country has enacted laws like the Water (Prevention and Control of Pollution) Act, 1974 as amended in 1988; the Air (Prevention and Control Pollution) Act, 1974 as amended in 1981 and 1987; the Forest (Conservation) Act, 1980; the Motor Vehicle Act, 1980; the Environment (Protection) Act, 1986; the Factories Act, 1988 the Liability Insurance Act, 1991 and the National Environment Appellate Act, 1997. It has formulated a National Wildlife Action Plan (1980) a Biosphere Reserves Programme, and a National Forest Policy (1988). A Central Water Commission, a Board for Waste land Development, Pollution Control Boards, and Institutes for research on environment, and for planning and development of different aspects related to it, have been established. National programmes for integrated (ecological and economic) development of areas constituting unique ecological systems, and for control of pollution in rivers, are being implemented. Respective examples are the programmes formulated during the Sixth Five Year Plan for the development of hill areas (Himalayas and Western Ghats) and for cleansing of the Ganges. A National Biodiversity Authority is sought to be created under a draft legislation, that has been prepared by the Ministry of Environment and Forests, for regulating the country's Biodiversity.

The Tata Energy Research Institute, New Delhi has undertaken a project called Growth with Resource Enhancement of Environment and Nature (GREEN India, 2047) with the object of evaluating the damage to our natural resources that has taken place during the fifty years since independence; and determining the likely trend, upto 2047, if the present pattern of exploitation and growth continues (Pachauri, 1997). The results are disturbing. For example, the availability of renewable fresh water resources, per capital, fell from 6000 cubic metres per annum in 1947 to 2,300 cubic metres per annum in 1997 and is likely to further fall to 1,600 cubic metres per annum in 2017. Other changes anticipated between 1997 and 2047 are increase in urban municipal waste from 48 million tonnes per annum to 300 million tonnes per annum; increase in water-logged soils from 12.7 million hectares to 396 million hectares; and increase in soil erosion from 166 million hectares per annum to 200 million hectares per annum.

The inability to check deterioration of the environment is attributed to a number of factors, including a burgeoning population, rapid and unplanned urbanisation, substantial increase in the quality of fossil fuels utilised for energy requirements, great increase in the number of polluting industries, ever-increasing use of wood and other national resources, and continued loss of top soil. The inputs into environment protection programmes, from government and industry, are nowhere near requirements. Add to this a general apathy on the part of both government and society, and rampant corruption, and the picture is complete. As Valiathan (1993) pointed out in another context, *"knowing what to do and not doing it has cost a shadow on (our) national endeavours"*.

ENVIRONMENTAL MANAGEMENT IN INDIA

Most of the governmental bodies involved in environment studies are either put under the administrative control of, or assisted by the Department of Environment, Forests and Wildlife (D.O.En.) in the Ministry of Environment and Forests, Government of India.

The national environmental management is done at three levels:

1. Environmental Protection Law,
2. Governmental Organizations and agencies,
3. Non-governmental organizations and voluntary organisations or agencies.

Environmental Protection Laws

Several laws pertaining to the protection and conservation of wildlife have been formulated. India was probably the first country to enact a Wild Life Protection Act.

The Wild Birds and Animals Protection Act was passed in 1887 and repealed in 1912. For game protection in the states, in 1927, the Forest Act XVI was enacted. India Board for Wild Life was established in 1952 and this was followed by setting up of Wild Life Boards in different states. In 1972 new wild life Protection Act was passed. Under this Act possession, trapping shooting of wild animals alive or dead; serving their meat in eating houses; their transport and export are all controlled and watched by special staff (Chief Wild Warden and authorized officers). This Act prohibits hunting of females and young ones. Under this Act threatened species are absolutely protected and the rest afforded graded protection according to their state of populations size.

Protected Species of Indian Wild Life

These wild animals have been enlisted as threatened and protected species: White eyed buck, Indian antelope or black buck, Four horned antelope, Bharal, Swamy deer, Eastern pangolin, Elephant, Indian gazelle or Chinkara, Mask deer, Serow, Tahr, Godden cat, Snow leopard, Great Indian Bustard, Pink headed duck, Peafowl, Moval pheasant, Koklas pheasant, Chir pheasant, Horned pheasant, Monitor lizard, Water lizard Gharial, Marsh crocodile, Python, and Leathery turtle; Albino and melanic individuals of all species of wild animals are also protected.

Establishment of Sanctuaries and National Parks

In India, nearly 200 sanctuaries and national parks have been established for wild life management. Sanctuaries are places where the killing or capturing of any animal is prohibited except under orders of the authorities concerned. They provide protection and optimum living conditions to wild animals. National Parks are set up for preserving flora, fauna, landscapes and historic objects of an area. Some well known wild like sanctuaries and national parks of India are as follows:

1. *Bhagwan Mahadev wild life santuary:* It is located in North Goa and has an area of 240 sq. km. and supports fauna almost similar to Cotigao wild life sanctuary.

2. *Sesan Gir:* This famous wild life sanctuary for the Asiatic lion is situated in Gujarat state, 468 km. from Ahmedabad and 43 km. from Veraval. It has an area of 1,295 sq. km. of semi-arid country with patches of thorn shrub and deciduous trees. Its fauna includes Asiatic lion, spotted deer, blue bull (Nilgai), four-horned antelope, chinkara, striped hyena, wild bear, procupine, langur, python, crocodiles and birds like green pigeon, partridge, rock-grouse, etc.

3. *Kanha national park:* This national park was established in 1955 in former Banjar Valley Reserve (Madhya Pradesh). This park has an area of 939.94 sq. km. and includes hilly terrains and streams.

It is 175 km away from Jabalpur and has forests of sal trees. Its typical fauna includes animals like tiger, chital, panther, sambhar, black buck and bara singha.

4. *Guindy deer park:* It is situated near Madras city and has mainly chitals and black bucks. A new albinos of black buck are also found here.

5. *Point calimera wild life sanctuary:* This is situated at the southern tip of the Thanjavur district of Tamil Nadu abutting the Palk strait. Its back water and lagon is visited by flamingos and black bucks, chitals and wild boars.

6. *Mundanthurai sanctuary:* It is established in 1962 in Tirunelveli district of Tamil Nadu and has an area of 520 sq. km. It has evergreen forests and Tamaraparani river flows through this sanctuary. Its typical fauna includes panther, tiger, sambhar and chital.

7. *Periyar wild life sanctuary:* This is situated in Kerala State and has an area of 777 sq. km. It was established in 1940 around the artificial lake which arose behind the dam built across the Periyar river in 1990. This sanctuary of great scientific beauty supports a fauna of wild elephants, gaurs, leopards, sloth bear, sambhars, barking deer, wild dogs, wild boars, black Nilgiri langur and water birds like grey hornbills, egrets.

8. *Kaziranga wild life santuary:* It is established in 1926 in district Sibsagar, sub-division Jorhat (Assam) on the south bank of the Brahmputra river. It consists of 430 sq. km. of forest grasslands and swamps and supports a fauna of 700 rhinoceros, besides elephant, wild buffalso, bison, wild boar, gibbon and birds like pelican, stork and ring-tailed fishing eagles.

9. *Manas wild life sancutary and Tiger reserve:* It is located in district Kamrup in Assam, has an area of 540 sq. km. and is situated at an altitude of 80 metres. River Manas passes through it. It contains the following wild animals: tiger, panther, wild dog, wild boar, rhinoceros, gaur, wild buffalo, sambhar, swamp deer and golden langur.

10. *Jaldapara wild life sanctuary:* It is situated in Jalpaiguri district of West Bengal and is a 65 sq. km. stretch of grassland. Its wild life fauna includes animals like rhinoceros, gaur, elephant, tiger, leopard, deer, and a variety of birds and reptiles.

11. *Palamau national park:* It is situated in Daltongunj district in Bihar and has an area of 345 sq. km. Its flora is thick tropical forests.

The fauna of this park includes tiger, panther, sloth bear, elephant, chital, gaur, nilgai, chinkara, chowsingha and mouse-deer.

12. *Hazaribagh national park:* This national park was established in 1954 in Bihar. It has an area of 184 sq. m. of thick tropical forests. The typical fauna of this park includes wild boar, sambhar, tiger, leopard, sloth bear, hyena and gaur.

13. *Simlipal national park:* It is situated in district Mayuri Bhanj in Orissa and has an area of 2,750 sq. km. It is covered over by dense sal forests and is chosen for project tiger. Its typical fauna includes tiger, elephant, pea fowl, taking maynas, chital, sambhar, panther, gaur, hyena and sloth bear.

14. *Chilka lake:* This largest inland lake has an area of 1000 sq. km. and is about 100 km. from Bhubaneshwar (Orissa). Its typical fauna includes water fowls, duck, cranes, ospreys, golden plovers, sandpiper, stone crulews, flamingoes, etc.

15. *Kolameru bird sanctuary:* This is a small bird sanctuary n ır Tadepallegudam in Andhra State. It is a breeding place for pelicans and many marine birds visit this place.

16. *Vedanthangal bird sanctuary:* This small-sized but very old sanctuary extend over a lake of about 0.30 sq. km, 85 km south of Madras. Many migratory birds regularly visit this temporary lake. The regular visitors of this lake are birds like spoon bill, open billed stork, egrets, ibis, cormorant, darter, grey herom, pelican, snipes and dab chick.

17. *Tandoba national park:* Its is located in Chandrapur district (Maharashtra) and has an area of 116 sq. km. Its typical fauna includes tiger, sambhar, sloth bear, bison, chital, chinkara, barking deer, blue bull, four horned deer, langur, peafowl and few crocodiles.

18. *Sariska:* This is one of the most beautiful wild life sanctuaries of Rajasthan near Alwar. It has an area of 800 sq. km. and dense Dohokra and Solar forests. Its typical fauna includes tiger, leopard, spotted deer, jungle cat, four horned antelope, langur, porcupine, hedghog, pea fowl, etc.

19. *Bharatpur bird sanctuary (Koeldeo Ghana):* It is located at Bharatpur (Rajasthan), has an area of 29 sq. km. and harbour all kinds of indigenous nesting water birds, water side birds and migratory birds. More than 328 varieties of birds including cormorants, spoonbits, white ibis, Indian darters, egrets, painted storks, open billed storks, great black necked storks, etc. Many

migratory birds like ducks, geese, siberian cranes, etc., regularly visit this sanctuary. Drier parts of this marshy sanctuary have animal like spotted deer, black buck, sambhar, blue bull, wild boar and python.

20. *Sultanpur lake bird sanctuary:* This small sized (2 sq. km. area) bird sanctuary is located in Gurgaon district (Haryana) about 30 km. from Delhi. Its typical avian fauna includes crane, sarus, spot-bill, rudyshel and drake.

21. *Ranganthittoo bird sanctuary*: It covers an area of 166 sq. km. and includes a series of islands in the Cauvery river 15 km. off the Bangalore, Mysore Road, near Shrirangapattam. Its avial fauna includes open bill strock, while ibis, egret, spoon bill, wild duck, pea fowl, night heron, etc.

22. *Randipur wild life sanctuary:* This sanctuary was established in 1941 by the then ruler of Mysore (Karnataka State). It is situated 80 km. south of Mysore city enroute to Ootacamund. It has an area of 874 sq. km. and is at an altitude of 1,454.4 metres. Its forest is very thick and has plenty of rain fall. Its wild life fauna includes plenty of gaurs and animals like elephant, leopard, sloth bear, wild dog, chital, panther, barking deer, porcupine and langur.

23. *Cotigao wild life sanctuary:* It is located in South Goa and has an area of 105 sq. km. It has wet evergreen forest of Elve and Berla trees and supports rich fauna of the following animals: gaur, sambhar, chital, hog-deer, barking deer, wild boar, hyena, panther, leopard, jackal, otter, porcupine and birds like parakeet, lorikeet, woodpecker, kingfisher, bulbul, jungle fowl, egret etc.

24. *Shikari Devi wild life sanctuary:* It is located in Mandi district in Himachal Pradesh. It has an area of 213 sq. km. and has the following animals: snow leopard, flying fox, black bear, barking deer, musk deer, chakor, partridge. etc.

25. *Bir Motibagh sanctuary:* It is located near Patiala in Punjab. The typical fauna of this wild life sanctuary includes black buck, blue bull, hog deer, hare, jackal and birds like peafowl, partridge, sparrow, babbler, myna, parakeet, pigeon, dove, etc.

26. *Dachigam wild life sanctuary:* It is established in 1951 in Kashmir, 26 km. away from Srinagar. It has an area of 89 sq. km. and has two levels: upper Dachigam at 3,692.3 metres altitudes and Lower Dachigam at 1,846.2 metres altitudes. It mainly preserves hangul of Kashmir stag, but also have animals like musk deer, leopard, black bear, brown bear and baboon.

27. *Corbett national park:* It is one of India's most famous wild life sanctuary and was constituted in 1935 as the first national park of India. It is situated between Nainital and Garhwal districts in Uttar Pradesh. It has an area of 525 sq. km. and is located within west-to-south bend of river Ramganga. It supports a rich and diverse fauna of the following animals: tiger, panther, sloth bear, hyena, elephant, blue bull, swamp deer, barking deer, Indian antelope, porcupine, birds like bulbul, woodpecker, barbet, babbler and bee eater, and reptiles like crocodile, python, etc.

28. *Shivpuri sanctuary:* It is located in Madhya Pradesh and is an asylum for tigers.

29. *Anamalai sanctuary:* This sanctuary was established in 1972 in the southern part of Coimbatore district in Tamil Nadu. It has a vast area of 958 sq. km. and supports rich fauna of animals like elephant, gaur, sambhar, spotted deer, barking deer, Nilgiritahr, lion-tailed macaque, tiger, panther sloth bear, langur, porcupin and pangolin.

In addition to the above about 200 sanctuaries, national parks and other miscellaneous national areas have been established in our country to provide protection to wildlife of different categories. Sanctuaries having natural habitats provide maximum protection and optimum living conditions to animals and birds.

WORKING STRUCTURE OF THE MINISTRY OF ENVIRONMENT AND FORESTS

The Department of Environment was set up in 1980 to serve as the focal point in the administrative structure of the government for planning, promotion and coordination of environmental programmes.

The present integrated Department of Environment, Forests and Wildlife (D.O. En) in the Ministry of Environment and Forests was created in September 1985. The ministry serves as the focal point in the administrative structure of the Central Government for the planning, promotion and coordination of environmental and forestry programmes. The Ministry's main activities are, the survey and conservation of flora, fauna, forests and wildlife, prevention and control of pollution, afforestation and regeneration of the degraded areas of the environment. These are to be achieved through impact assessment, support to organisations implementing the programmes, environmental and forestry research, extension, education and training to augment the requisite manpower, collection, collation and dissemination of environmental information and creation of environmental information and creation of environmental awareness.

The following items of work are allocated to the ministry:

1. Invironmental and Ecology.
2. Botanical Survey of India and Botanical Gardens.
3. Zoological Survey of India.
4. National Museum of Natural History.
5. The Water Pollution Act, 1974, 1977.
6. The Air Pollution Act, 1981.
7. The Environment (Protection) Act, 1986.
8. Biosphere Reserve Programme.
9. National Forest Policy and Forestry Development.
10. Forest Policy.
11. Indian Forest Service.
12. Wildlife Preservation.
13. Fundamental Research in Coordination with Higher Education in Forestry.
14. Padmaja Naidu-Himalayan Zoological Park.
15. National Land Use and Wasteland Development Council.
16. National Wastelands Development Board.
17. Central Ganga Authority.

Ministry's is different Divisions and Agencies are shown. It may be seen that there are (*i*) Ganga Project Directorate, (*ii*) National Wastelands Development Board, and (*iii*) Eighteen Divisions under the Department of Environment, Forests and Wildlife.

Ganga Action Plan: The Central Ganga Authority was constituted in 1985 to guide and oversee the implementation of a programme for restoring the quality of the river, Ganga. The Ganga Project Directorate (GPD) of the Ministry coordiantes the implementation. The State Governments of U.P., Bihar and West Bengal are to coordiante the Action Plan Work.

National Wastelands Development Board (NWDB)

NWDB was set up in 1985 with the following main objectives:

- to increase tree and other green cover on wastelands;
- to prevent good land from becoming wasteland; and
- to formulate within the overall Nodal Policy, perspective plans and programmes for the environment and development of the wastelands in the country.

There are 18 Divisions. There are three wings for Impact Assessment Divisions. These are, Impact Assessment I (A-1), II (A-II) and III (A-III).

There are 7 associated units under the administrative control of the Minitry. Of these, two (Botanical Survey of India; Zoological Survey of India) are under Conservation and Survey Division; two (Indira Council of Forestry Research and Education; Indira Gandhi National Forest Academy under Forest Research, Education and Training Division; one (Forest Survey of India) under Forest Survey and Utilisation Division; one (National Zoological Park) under Wildlife Conservation Division; and one (National Museum of National History) is under the Education and Information Division of the Ministry. There are five Institutes under the Indian Council of Forestry, Research and Education.

There are 11 Autonomous Agencies assisted by the Ministry. These are attached with different Divisions.

1. Salim Ali Centre for Ornithology and Natural History (*Conservation and Survey*).
2. Andaman and Nicobar Islands Forests and Plantation Dev. Corp. Ltd. (*Forest Survey and Utilisation*).
3. Wildlife Institute of India (*Wildlife Conservation*).
4. Padmaja Naidu Himalayan Zoological Park (*Wildlife Conservation*).
5. Central Pollution Control Board (*Control of Pollution*).
6. Centre for Ecological Research and Training (*Research and Eco-Regeneration*).
7. Centre of Mining Environment (*Research and Eco-Regeneration*).
8. Gobind Ballabh Pant Himalayan Paryavaran Evam Vikas Sansthan (*Research and Eco-Regeneration*).
9. Indian Institute of Forest Management (*Forest Research, Education and Training*).

10. Centre for Environment Education (*Education and Information*).
11. C.P. Rama Swami Environment Education Centre (*Education and Information*).

Other National Organisation

There are many other governmental and non-governmental organisations/agencies involved in environmental issues. Some of the important ones are as follows:

1. Advisory Board on Energy (ABE).
2. Bombay Natural History Society (BNHS).
3. Central Forestry Commission (CFC).
4. Department of Non-Conventional Energy Sources (DNES).
5. Industrial Toxicology Research Centre (ITRC).
6. National Environmental Engineering Research Institute (NEERI).
7. National Dairy Development Board.
8. National Natural Resources Management System.
9. National Wetland Management Committee.
10. State Pollution Control Boards (SPCB).
11. Tata Energy Research Institute (TERI).
12. Several Research Institutes under I.C.A.R. including I.G.F.R.I., Jhansi, Central Soil Salinity Research Institute, Karnal.

ASSESSMENT OF ENVIRONMENTAL IMPACT

It is an important aspect of environmental management, because under this aspect plans, projects and programmes are assessed to evaluate or visualize the adverse effects on the quality of the environment. The effects of human activities regarding the use of natural resources on the quality of the environment is known *'environmental impact'*. The evaluation of environmental affects of human activities are called *'environmental impact assessment'*. It attempts to produce estimates of future environmental changes accountable to a plan or proposed project action, *i.e.*, environmental consequences. It also estimates the possible adverse effects of these environmental changes. It is the most important aspect of *'environmental managements'*.

Procedure of Environmental Impact Assessment

The major objective of the assessment is to promote efforts and to prevent damages or adverse effects to the environment and stimulate the health and welfare of man. It also examines the ecological balance and stability of ecosystem as a result of implementation of plans and projects. The following steps are employed in the procedure of assessment—

1. To describe the present nature of environment.
2. To indicate the project and its needs and objectives.
3. To explain the effects of the project/programme.
4. To estimate the impacts, both short-term and long-term.
5. To propose and compare alternatives of the project.
6. To present a projection of the future of the site with and without the project.
7. To provide the remedial measures and feedback mitigating activities.

The different methodologies and procedures for '*Environmental Impact Assessment*' have been devised by scientific research organizations because the nature of projects and programmes are different in the areas of environment.

CONTROL OF ENVIRONMENTAL POLLUTION AND DEGRADATION

The assessment aspect of environmental management indicates the causes, processes and adverse effects on the quality of environment. It suggests the remedial measures for improving the quality of environment.

It has been emphasised by the scientists that increasing impacts of human activities on natural environment have caused environmental degradation and pollution at global, regional and local levels. Thus the lowering of environmental quality has aroused international awareness about man-environment interactions and it has caused environmental crisis of global concern. Consequently, a number of plans, programmes and projects have been designed by the international organizations to control the environmental problems caused by man also by natural process. The following are the important national and international programmes which aim at the study of man-environment interaction, the environment problems emerging therefrom and possible solutions and remedial measures thereof:

1. International Biological Programme (IBP).
2. Special Committee for International Biological Programme (SCIBP).
3. Man and Biosphere Programme (MAB).
4. International Hydrological Programme (IHP).
5. Integrated Project on Arid Lands (IPAL).
6. Scientific Committee on Problems of Environmen (SCOPE).
7. United Nations Environmental Programme (UNEP)
8. Scientific Committee on Oceanic Research (SCOR)
9. Scientific Committee on Water Research (SCWAR).
10. International Centre for Integrated Mounta Development (ICIMOD).
11. International Decade Disaster Reduction (IDDR).

There are many more organizations, programmes and projects which are actively engaged in the study of man environment relationships, the effect producing from such interactions and their possible remedial measures at national and international level. These have been enumerated as follows:

- Atomic Energy Commission (AEC).
- Botanical Survey of India (BSI).
- Central Arid Zone Research Institute (CAZRI).
- Chlorofluorocarbons (CFC).
- Council on Environment Quality (CEQ).
- Canadian International Development Agency (CIDA).
- Convention of International Trade in Endangered Species (CITES).
- Central Pollution Control Board (CPCB).
- Department of Non-Conventional Energy Sources (DNES).
- Department of Science and Technology (DST).
- Environmental Impact Assessment (EIA).
- Environmental Information System (ENVIS).
- Environmental Protection Agency (EPA).
- Environmental Protection Council (EPC).
- Food and Agriculture Organisation (FAO).

- Global Environmental Monitoring System (GEMS).
- Human Exposure Assessment System (HEAL).
- International Atomic Energy Agency (IAEA).
- International Biological Programme (IBP).
- International Centre for Integrated Mountain Development (ICIMOD).
- International Council for Research in Agro-Forestry (ICRAF).
- International Council of Scientific Unions (ICSU).
- International Union of Biological Sciences (IUBS).
- International Union for Conservation of Nature and Natural Resources (IUCN).
- Man and the Biosphere Programme (MAB).
- Minimal National Standards (MINAS).
- National Committee of Environmental Planning (NCEP).
- National Environmental Engineering Research Institute (NEERI).
- National Environmental Policy Act (NEPA).
- National Land Use and Wasteland Development Council (NLUWDC).
- National Wastelands Development Board (NWDB).
- South Asia Co-operative Environmental Programme (SACEP).
- Scientific Committee on Problems of the Environment (SCOPE).
- State Pollution Control Board (SPCB).
- Swedish International Development Agency (SIDA).
- National Committee on Environmental Planning and Coordination (NCEPC).
- United Nations Environment Programme (UNEP).
- United Nations Educational, Scientific and Cultural Organisation (UNESCO).
- World Commission on Environment and Development (WCED).
- World Conservation Strategy (WCS).
- World Health Organisation (WHO).
- World Wildlife Fund (WWF).

ENVIRONMENTAL EDUCATION AND TRAINING

It is the most important aspect of *'Environmental Management'*. The main objectives of environmental education is to improve the quality of environment, to provide an awareness among the people on environmental problems and conservation and to generate an atmosphere so that people participate in decision-making and evaluating the programmes. All resources are finite and there is also limit to the growth of living system. Thus, the environmental education helps in—

1. Acquiring awareness of total environment.
2. To gain variety of experiences and understanding of environmental problems.
3. To acquire a set of values and feelings for the environment production.
4. To acquire skills for solving environmental problems.
5. To evaluate environmental measures and education programmes.
6. To provide an opportunity for active participation for solving environmental problems.

The above objectives can be achieved by developing programme of environmental education from primary level to the college level. NCERT has been playing vital role in designing syllabi and text books and other material of teaching. UGC is looking after environmental education at university and college level.

The environmental management also involves the environmental training programmes by professional institutions. As we have discussed that environmental awareness is of interdisciplinary nature. Therefore, the awareness of environment can be provided through the various subjects—botany, zoology, chemistry and geography, etc. The skills, attitudes and values are to be developed for the protection of environment in the teacher-education programmes and other professional institutions.

Environmental Education and Training Centres

There are two types of education centres of environment—formal and non-formal education centres. These may be classified into two categories—Government organisation and non-governmental organizations.

1. *Centre for Environmental Education, Ahmedabad:* Educational teaching material and teaching aids are developed at this centre. Audio-visual materials for media, mobile exhibitions are organized by experts.

2. *Centre for Training senior Executives/Administratiors:* The regular courses are organised and arranged for various institutions imparting such training. The foundation courses should be developed for the I.A.S., I.P.S, I.F.S. and I.E.S. candidates to their area of work. There should be training programmes for the trainers, professionals, technical personnel and legal experts.

3. *Centres for Excellence:* Department of Education has established two centres of excellence in the country. They generate knowledge and methodology of training in areas of Tropical Ecology, Bangalore and Environmental Education at Ahmedabad.

4. *Eco-development Camp:* The Department of Edcuation has prepared guideline in (1984) to help in sound rural youth development. The main purpose is to identify root cause of ecological problems as related to human activities and solve the local environmental problems.

5. *Environmental Information System (ENVIS):* It was set up in 1982 under Department of Education plan programme. There are ten such centres on diverse areas of environment established in specialized institutions in the country.

There are more than 200 non-governmental organizations which are engaged in environmental education awareness and training youths on different areas—pollution control, rural development, wildlife conservation, afforestation, floristic and faunal studies, waste utilization and eco-development.

ENVIRONMENTAL MANAGEMENT—VITAL PRIORITY AREAS

This is high time to work for environmenal management, proper resource use and resource management. India in several ways is indeed a unique country among developing countries. In this context the following are the environmental problems and issues where priority action is needed in our country—

1. Environmental education and awareness,
2. Population stabilisation,
3. Integrated land use planning,
4. Healthy cropland and grassland,
5. Conservation of biological diversity,
6. Control of water and air pollution,
7. Human settlement,
8. Development of non-polluting renewable energy system
9. Updating environmental law, and
10. New dimensions of national security.

These are the issues that are posing threat to our environment as a whole, and to sustainability in particular. The concept of sustainability in fact is much more applicable to non-renewable resources, *i.e.*, coal, oil, gases and minerals than the renewable ones.

THE ROLE OF THE JUDICIARY

Industrial units, both large and small, are primarily responsible for environmental pollution in India. A majority of them seem not to bother about their primary responsibility of ensuring that effluents and emission are within permissible limits. There are over 300 central and state legislations, including about 30 major enactments, for the protection of the environment. One would think that these were sufficient to enable administrators and monitoring agencies to keep a check on pollution. However apathy, helplessness or (possibly purchased?) sympathy for industrialists has brought about a situation wherein little action is forthcoming from the government or its agencies. The judiciary has had to step in with increasing frequency and today we are witnessing judicial activism in matters related to the environment (Bharucha, 1994; Banerji and Martin, 1997).

Bharucha (*op. cit.*) points out that time and again the Supreme Court has legislated on environmental matters. It has closed down quarries and polluting industrial units, or ordered their shifting. It has issued orders restricting developmental activities. Banerji and Martin (*op. cit.*) list 14 significant environmental decisions taken by the Supreme Court in 1996 alone. The Apex Court has gone to the extent of ordering the constitution of 'green benches' at the High Courts at Calcutta and Chennai to hear environment related petitions.

Judicial actions install in the public a sense of awareness of their rights and encourage individuals to give up apathy, and to fight from their rights. But there is a limit to activism of the courts. The number of offences are large, and the judicial process both costly and slow. The overall impact is next to negligible.

Banerji and Martin (*op. cit.*) have highlighted the fact that the Apex Court, while acting against the offenders, has let off the monitoring agencies very lightly. They believe that '*the present situation of grossly threatened environment has come about as the agencies charged with ensuring that industry operated within the prescribed rules, had abdicated their duties*".

In defence of the monitoring agencies it may be stated that they are ill-equipped in terms of staff and technical expertise, and are short of funds. Moreover, there are numerous loopholes in the legislations that can be exploited, and the Boards lack the authority to take action. For example 'non-point source emissions', (including agricultural emissions, domestic emissions and emissions from small-scale industry) are excluded in legislations. By implication it is only the pollution from the bigger industries that can be controlled by legislation (Oestereich, 1994b). However, a recent positive step is a decision of the cabinet to authorise the Central Pollution Control Board to take steps for the abatement of environmental pollution in accordance with the Environment Protection Act, 1986.

CITIZENS' PROTESTS

There is a sharp increase in people's awareness about their rights relating to matters of the environment. More important is the fact that they are willing to fight for them. Two examples from two decades are illustrative. In 1989 the people of Bichhri village, near Udaipur in Rajasthan, forced the administration to order the closure of a chemical factory whose effluents had polluted the ground water of the area—an action subsequently upheld by the Supreme Court (Banerji and Martin, 1997). Likewise, in 1996, a people's protest, at Vidisha in Madhya Pradesh, against the pollution of the river Betwa led to the closure of a distillery owned by a powerful industrial house (Banerji, 1997). These examples show that people's protest is a powerful tool which can make recalcitrant industries see reason. Many industrial houses have now realised that it is in their interest to integrate environment policies with their business strategy.

QUESTIONS FOR ANSWER

1. *Define the term environmental management and write a note on the functions and characteristics of environmental management.*
2. *Write a note on various approaches employed in environmental management.*
3. *Explain various approaches to resource management.*
4. *Write a note on ecological basis of environmental management.*
5. *Write short notes on:*

   (a) Assessment of Environmental Impact.
   (b) Environmental Protection Laws.
   (c) Man and Biosphare Programme (MAB).
   (d) India's Environmental Policies.
   (e) Judiciary and Environmental Management.

30

Status of Environmental Education in India

INTRODUCTION

Global consciousness on the importance of environment was so aroused by the Club of Rome (CR) activities, United Nations Conference on Human Environment (UNCHE) at Stockholm and United National Environment Programme (UNEP) during 1965-72 that many countries have launched ministries of Environment well before the next UNCHE Conference at Nairobi in 1982. India was one among these, where environmental concerns have graduate into an all encompassing activity after the Rio conference. Added to these the recent globalisation of Indian economy and the GATT impacts on our policy have deep environmental and ecological implications.

If the challenges are not well responded, the consequent inequalities may unleash enormous violence that ever before. Even if it succeeds bringing social uplift and international respectability, environment here will deteriorate depleting natural resources and disruption balances. To preempt and manage these portents new thrusts of activity are warnated. These are best done through education at higher level that supplies all the levers and agents of change for the country. Therefore a stocktaking of the present and past is an urgent responsibility, so as to do better in future, *vis-a-vis* higher education pertaining to environment and ecology. If we do not improve on this front the ecological and environmental challenges from the anticipated acceleration of economic activity cannot be met, letting down the country.

The Department of Environment of the Government of India initially discouraged the establishment of separate sectors of environmental studies in the Indian Universities during mid 1970s.

Yet three Universities initiated Schools or Departments of Environmental Science (1975-80) while there is no such science. Everyone found or made to find a "relevance" there and now there are nearly 60 educational establishments in India with outfits prefaced "Environmental". While environment and ecology is everything, they became different to different people, some assumed "omnoscience" and became 'omnipotent' and 'omnopresent'. The ecological wisdom that has taken deep roots in the developed North, is yet to seed fruitfully on our campuses. Our objective is therefore to take stock of the whole gamut of higher education in our campuses and suggest approaches to reforms and inputs in the light of hindsight wisdom, ground realities and future needs.

HERITAGE AND TRADITION

Though the educational efforts started in mid 1970's, research activities on various aspects of Environment and Ecology have been existing for long. It is appropriate to briefly summarise these as a backdrop and to assess if the traditions bequeathed to us have been followed, for these will have telling effect on the quality of education.

Right from the time of British East India Company information on resources, environment and ecology were getting documented. Surveys of flora, fauna, native people, other natural resources like water and minerals have gradually intensified. By the time of political freedom from the British, enormous informations accumulated on our plants, animals, lakes, river, etc. All these and the departments of agriculture, forestry and fisheries, had bequeathed very valuable knowledge for their conversion into wisdom to guide the destinies of our country. People like Misra, Santapau, Agharkar, Salim Ali, Bharucha and Mani began their every valuable careers followed by Ganpathy, Panikkar etc. on several aspects of ecology and environment.

ENVIRONMENTAL STUDIES: IDEAL AND THE REAL

The environmental study is the Science of Nature as well as of Society culminating in an understanding of human ecological predicaments. Environment will not become a concern unless ecology of its resources is affected nor pollution would bother us unless toxic either to us or our resources. Therefore controversies or debates on these are irrelevant yet a Vice Chancellor thought it fit to debunk a department of his own university recently along with the faulty member-despite both being parties! Queer sense of ethics indeed.

Thrusts of Environmental activity in University systems, as the possible best, should cover the natural resources, regional institutional facilities and the ethos of the local leadership based on global knowledge to meet regional challenges. Therefore the subject of environment deals with most branched in a University. Ideally, there should be only a holistic education on environmental issues through a coordination of efforts. In delineating the details however the ideals may be supplanted by the local forces of expediency and opportunism.

Yet when the subject, as an ultimate outcome of academic exercises, is offered to students it embodies the twin content of Student Needs and Faculty Resourcefulness. Thus a programme on Environment—be it called Studies or Science, must be imparted by working out a golden mean between students needs and faculty resources. Both these influence development of the curriculum. The final outcome should be far away from the initial ideal. As we have seen, University systems are not all that good as one hopes for and therefore must be put to public gaze by adding surveys of and services to local environments in the curriculum by involving and interacting with regional facilities. Keeping all these the following proposals are made.

IMPERATIVES

1. Philosophy

The criteria for identification of courses and formulation of curriculum and programme may be idealistic or opportunistic. Current wisdom may opt for the expediency in the name of realistic solutions are the idealistic ones. Even if everything is lost in society, university still shall keep the asphidistra flying with an objective and hope of retrieving the society. It should ventilate and articulate the eternal social values. A kind of perennial philosophy has to be upheld against the myraid ephemeral ones coexisting even within a single campus. All this is a challenge to the leadership. Despite my experience I am for the idealistic one because I do not wish the intellectuals continuously fail the society. This should be reflected in the most important discipline of educational endeavours—environment.

Social Sciences and Geography have been lately begun taking interest on environmental issues. This development is expected to have a salutory effect on the environment education. For an overall well being in this very vital area of education medical disciplines have also to come off age just as engineering and agriculture. Then alone a holistic subject will develop for a proper comprehension of the problems of nature and their management. Of course this is a very challenging task.

2. General Suggestions

(*a*) Out of 200 + institutions of higher learning about 150 + offer courses in Botany and Zoololgy. And all these have an ecology environmental biology as a paper. This needs to be revised, updated and perhaps a common paper can be formulated as in the case of Genetics and cell biology.

(*b*) Out of 10,000 colleges in India, most of them offer B.Sc. courses with Biological components in which ecology is included as a part of syllabus of a paper. This needs an upward revision with greater coverage and emphasis.

(*c*) In every department one can have some environmentally oriented components Botany, Zoology, Chemistry, Physics and so on. Ecology and environment being most holistic in nature than any other subject, education must necessarily reflect this, specialisations depending on the trainees choices.

(*d*) Separate syllabi need to be prepared for social sciences and humanities at college and university levels to increase the levels of their awareness and make the students and teachers realise who valuable their own disciplines are *vis-a-vis* the environment.

Checklists of courses and syllabi are therefore to be prepared based on the following criteria:

1. Global Perspectives.
2. Natural Resources of the Region.
3. Institutional Facilities in the Region.
4. Existing Opportunities in the State.
5. Regional and National Manpower Needs.
6. Existing Man Power.

7. Existing grants.
8. "Hares and Hounds" out look.
   - Plan for the students and the teachers and the authorities do in other Universities in the State

Schedules or Streams of Courses

(*a*) *Primary*: This consists of the usual M.Sc., with 4 semesters—the last semester devoted entirely to dissertation project. Each semester shall have devoted entirely to dissertation project. Each semester shall have 5-7 paper chosen from the suggestions given here subsequently. The stream will be manned by the entire faculty within or across the school.

(*b*) *Secondary*: This consists of an M.Phil., of 2 semesters in a major branch of Ecology/Environment. A few faculty can offer such a programme covering their disciplines such as Environmental Toxicology, pollution, etc., This may further be in collaboration with the extra-university facilities available in the region. Thus M.Phil., in several subjects can be offered.

(*c*) *Tertiary*: When the faculty gradually become experts they should be able to offer a Certificate (1 Semester) or a Diploma (2 Semesters) Programme of teaching and training in their specialities.

A school thus can be very active offering M.Sc, M.Phil, Diploma and other programmes serving the regional needs with a global ethos.

As Environmental studies are diverse, some courses cannot be structured by any of the exiting methods. Such ones may have to be organised into 4+ or 8+ week courses instead of the customary 16 + week schedules. Fresh looks on all aspects of these including syllabi formats for practicals and surveys are warranted.

Models

Approaches to Programming: Over all three approaches of higher education on environment are discernible. In the holistic approach everything is included in the menu of Curriculum. In the Stream approach the holistic programme is delineated into physical, biological and social sciences. The sectorial approach, by far the most common, concentrates only on that part of environment in which the department running it is interested.

The foundations—basic course, applied subjects, in-depth specialities, in theory, practical in lab, library and field, surveys in the habitats and society can be structured and offered as curriculum for Post-graduate Programme in four ways. In each model any set of courses can be chosen to form the module. From these very same, M.Phil. modules, Diploma modules, Certificate courses can be chosen. Foundation courses had to be covered first Semester and Basic Ecology, Applied Ecology and Specialities in the 2nd, 3rd and 4th Semesters respectively. Practicals and surveys will be spread out all semesters and Dissertation in the Fourth Semester.

(*a*) *One/Three Stream Programmes*: The components of the four semesters will be so organised that it should mostly suit for students of any back fround with the aid of some foundations. Conversely the components of I, II, III and IV Semesters will be different depending on the background of the students. Thus we can envisage three streams each for students with the backgrounds of Biological Sciences, Physical and Chemical Sciences and Social Sciences, Practicals and Surveys will be different.

(*b*) *Model* (*i*): Maximum Choice System: In this system students can choose their papers in all the four semesters.

(*c*) *Model* (*ii*): Minimum Choice System: In this Foundation, Basic and Applied courses of the three semesters are compulsory. The choice is limited to the elective in the fourth semester and the dissertation with it.

(*d*) *Model* (*iii*): Tutorial Approach—During the First semester all foundations will be taken as tutorials and exempted from evaluation. Two Basic Courses will be compulsory. Semesters 2 and 3 have only compulsory papers. In the 4th Semester Electives can be more than one and Dissertation is compulsory.

Mechanisms of Organisation

(*a*) *Holistic*

All branches of relevance to environment are brought together in a single programme. This may be done by a large school or by a small co-ordinating unit.

(*i*) *Unitary*: A full fledged school of environmental studies. All programmes—Research, Training, Extension and Education leading to M.Sc., M. Phil., Diplomas, etc., can be carried out following tow mechanisms which are in vague at present. Both are holistic in approach to education can be organised so as to be self sufficient in faculty numbers and competence to carry out all responsibilities including programmes, curriculum, programmes, syllabi, etc. But this is difficult because it entails a large number of faculty-competent enough to claim autonomy for each one.

(*ii*) *Federal System*: A nucleus or centre for Environmental Studies may be formed with a minimum faculty. All other faculty can be co-opted from other departments. Wherever there is relevance and interest they can run common programmes while each can carry out researches in their own departments. The difficulty here is that common often inspite tragedies. Accountability may become casuality.

(*b*) *Sectorial*

This consists of dealing environmental education in different branches separately. For decades ecological and environmental subjects were parts of syllabi in botany, zoology, chemistry, physics, geography, penology, geology etc. If these are strengthened in the light of current global concerns, the purposes of environmental education will be served.

Faculty

In any University the local leaderships are more important than a check list of recommendations from a workshop of Shakespeares. The leaders are expected to be master of one and jack of few trades and among the best either as a teacher or a Scientist, if not both. It is my experience that most good scientists become so mechanical in their selfish pursuits that they cannot teach. They gradually develop fear to be in a classroom! If the leadership is sensitive and idealistic, in addition, it will just be wonderful. I do not entirely believe in the selection of the "best men" and leaving the rest to them. Quite often these 'best men' developed empires, impregnable forts and even fascist tendencies due to which Science in India did not flourish while scientists did, and do still. This is mainly due to a singular lack of the 4 Es (Ethics, Ethos, Equity and Empathy) and domination by the 4 Ps (Power, Profit, Pleasure and Popularity) in our academic society to climb up social ladder in any name under any guise. One can trace all the evils of our country to this singularly Himalayan source. Therefore besides the teacher's experience and expertise, dynamism, careerism and philosophical outlook determine the fats of all programmes. They are *in-situ* agents of change.

Syllabi

Syllabi are generally brief in most Indian Universities. But this can be misleading to the student as well as the observers and evaluators but convenient to their framers and teachers. They should be elaborate and unit wise. There shall be no scope for ambiguity. Syllabi should be invariably followed by the recommended texts and incorporate besides the global status of the subjects the regional conclusions. Ecology should always maintain a golden mean between latest knowledge and regional needs.

Evaluation

The conventional examination system does not hold in toto. The evaluation need to be continuous and involve such wide varieties like library, fielnd and laboratory exercises, surveys of fields, people media and governmental record, question banks. Open book system of answering and even framing and posing questions, approaches to understand and solving problems have to be tried. Genuine social service of restorative nature in the field also reveal the ethics of the student and therefore reckoned for evaluation.

University

The University must empathise with regional problems of environment and people and apply global knowledge by taking up relevant projects for research, development, education, extension, etc. This is the only way to develop an ethos for people oriented educational ethic. The chief thrust of Environmental Studies should be conservation of natural resources and ecology followed by their staggered utilization-i.e. ecological development.

MODEL CURRICULUM OF MASTERS DEGREE IN ENVIRONMENT AND ECOLOGY

1. Theory

(*a*) *Foundation Courses (based on the Needs of the student):* Basic knowledge of several subjects is necessary to understand the ramifications and implications of studies on any component of environment and ecology. These will however vary depending on the background of the student and objectives of institution.

(*b*) *Basic Courses (Pristine Ecology)*: What are the scenarios, constituents, interactions, interrelationships, productivities and ultimately the balances if the habitats and ecosystems are not affected. Assessing these are a prerequisite to understand the historical implications of exploiting Nature. Therefore the products of evolution and the underlying principles and mechanisms must be thoroughly understood. Therefore Basic Ecology is a must for any study on the environment.

(*c*) *Applied Courses (Habitat Perturbances)*: What are the consequences of direct human actions on the ecosystems and their indirect consequences in time and space. The statuses of these pervasions need to be studied for standing on a firm ground so as to manage them. And there are a myriad of these generally considered to constitute environmental studies.

(*d*) *Specialities (based on the speciality of the faculty)*: Having been exposed to a basic knowledge of a whole gamut of environmental and ecological issues, there is necessity to specialise. This may be on the local systems—Marine, Riverine, Moutain, Desert, Grassland, Wetland, Forest, etc. or on the ecology of specific taxonomic groups—Insects, Birds, Grasses, etc. These may also involve social problems—Pollutions, Toxicology, Agro-ecosystems, etc. ultimately all these will depend upon the specialisation of the faculty and therefore will vary from place to place.

2. Parcticals

(*a*) *Laboratory Objectives*

1. Observations and deduction
2. Experiment and analysis

(*b*) *Field Outlook*

1. Surveys of flora, fauna, populations, resources, degradation, etc.
2. Studies on Pollution, Toxicity, Perceptions, etc.
3. Interactions among plants, soil, water and animals.
4. Data collection from records and analysis.

(*c*) *Extension Work/Social Service*

1. Restorative Practices.
2. Educational Practices.
3. Awareness Campaigns.

(*d*) *Research Projects*

1. Association with an on-going scheme anywhere in India.
2. Association with a local problem.

CONCLUSIONS

1. Pioneering Efforts

Some of the suggestions made here are neither new nor novel as they are advanced or carried out by UGC, AIU, and IGNOU in other fields, a few of which have relevance to Ecology and Environmental studies. But this is the first time that an exhaustive analyses of the problem of higher education on a vital field like Environment is made—assessment of the current scenari and consequent imperatives for action. The difference between the presently advocated approaches and the beaten tracks, lies in the stress on developing a national ethos and interests. Only a patriotic effort on the part of the responsible institutions and senior teachers and scientists can salvage the country's current efforts from the mess on environmental education. My efforts constitute a beginning in this direction.

2. Holistic Practice

Environment appears many things to many people. There will be as many opinions as there are Environmentalists. As in the "elephant and the blind men" and 'experts' may pursue only their personal interests. It is therefore imperative on the leadership to be honest with themselves and the very restive but impressionable youngsters. These present and future leaders have to cultivate a holistic philosophy towards the Nature and its components in a historical perspective, lest they fail our country forever, and never to be resurrected!

3. Leaderships

All said it should be realised that reviewing the status of higher education in India is a very tall task for an article. It just consumes a space that befits a book or booklet. The work done in India is a major aspect that needs to be surveyed. So is the work done by Indians. There are many Institutions especially under CSIR and ICAR that is partly or greatly ecological in nature. A new dimension is added by the gradual and increasing entry of NGOs into the areas of ecology and environment. They influence the education and also influenced by it in turn. As a corollary comes in the role of foreign agencies and foreigners, more so in this age of globalisation and remote sensing. Unless a great feeling of self preservation and patriotism pervades the veins of Indian enthusiasts of environment, India may turn out once again a land of open veins! Adding to this are the ever increasing corruption in the grating and conduction of research projects, publication of papers and books and awarding of degrees. In this background can we expect correct choosing of courses, or making syllabi, or teaching what to talk of improving them. The culture of practice schools in business management is needed in ecological and environmental practices, in addition to introspection on our duties to wards the country, the people and future generations—nothing short of a spirit that pervaded India under the leadership of Mahatma Gandhi some decades ago can redeem Indian environment for which the need of appropriate higher education in this field is pivotal.

Note: Please have a look at Table 8.1 and 8.2, in chapter 8 of this book, which enlists institutions, in India, providing higher education in various aspects of environmental education, studies and sciences

QUESTIONS FOR ANSWER

1. *Write a note on the status of environmental education in India.*
2. *"The study of environmental education/science in vital for national good". Justify.*

Bibliography

(BOOKS AND JOURNALS)

Ashby, W.R. (1958), *An Introduction to Cybermetics*, John Wiley and Sons, Inc., New York.

Ager, D.V. (1963), *Principles of Palaeccolony*, McGraw-Hill, London.

Ager, D.V., (1976), *The Nature of Fossil record*, Proceedings of the Geologists Association.

Allen, J.R. (1975), *Physical Geology*, George Allen and Unwin, London.

Arvill, R. (1967), *Man and Environment*, Crisis and the Strategy of Choice, Penguin, Hamondsworth.

Ash, M. (1972), *Planners and Ecologists*, Town and Country Planning, Vol. 40.

Atkinson, B.W. (1981), *Precipitation in Man and Environmental Processes* edited by K.J. Gregony and D.E. Wailling, Butterworths.

Bahuguna, S. (1990), Tehri—The Dam of Discontent, *Yojana*, Vol. 34(10), pp. 9-12.

Begon, W.D. and Mortimer, M. (1981), *Population Ecology*, Blackwell Oxford.

Bharucha, M.P. (1994), Environment Compliance Litigation, *Chartered Secretary*.

Bhatnagar, R.P. and V. Agrawal (1995), *Educational Adminsitration*, R. Lall Book Depot.

Billings, W.D. (1964), *'Plants and Ecosystem'*, MacMillan and Co., London.

Bird, E.C.F. (1981), *Coastal Processes in Man and Environmental Processes* edited by K.J. Gegory and D.E. Wareling, Butterworths, pp. 82-101.

Botkin, D.B. and Keller, E.A. (1982), *Environmental Studies*, C.E. Merrill Company.

Botkin, D.B. and Keller, E.A. (1982), *Environmental Studies*, C.E. Merrill Publishing Company, A Bell and Howell Company, Columbus, p. 505.

Bridge, E. (1978), *World Soils*, 2nd edition, Cambridge University Press.

Brock, T.D. (1967), *The Ecosystem and Study of State,* Bioscience, Vol. 17, pp. 166-9.

Browen, H.J.M. (1966), *Trace Elements in Biochemistry,* New York, Academic Press.

Brundtland Report (1987), *Our Common Future,* Report of the World Commission on Environment and Development, Oxford University Press, p. 383.

Bryan, R.B. (1981), *Soil Erosion and Conservation in Man and Environmental Processes* edited by K.J. Georgoy and D.E. Walling, Butterworths.

Cain, S.A. (1971), *Foundations of Plant Geography,* Hafner Publishing Co., New York.

Cariquist, S. (1974), *Island Biology,* Columbia University Press, New York.

Clapham, W.B. (1973), *'Natural Ecosystem',* MacMillan, London.

Clark, G.L. (1954), *'Elements of Ecology',* John Wiley and Sons Inc., New York.

Cloud, P.E. (1969), *'Resources and Man',* W.H. Freeman and Company, San Francisco.

Cole, M. (1971): *Plants, Animals and Environments,* Geographical Magazine, Vol. 44, pp. 230-31.

Dassaman, R.D. (1976), *Environmental Conservation,* Wiley, New York.

Daubernmire, R.F. (1974), *Plants and Environment,* 3rd ed., John Wiley, New York.

Deshbandhu and G. Berþeret (1987), *'Environmental Education for Conservation and Development'* Indian Env. Society, New Delhi, p. 537

Det Wyer, T.R. and Marcus, M.G. (1972), *'Urbanization and Environment',* Duxbey Press, Belmont, California.

Det Wyler, T.R. (1971), *Man's Impact on Environment,* McGraw-Hill, New York.

Dikshit, R.D. (1984), *'Geography and Teaching of the Environment'.* Poona University, pp. 68-83.

Elton, C.S. (1967), *Animal Ecology,* University of Washington Press, Washington.

Elton, C.S. (1989), *The Ecology of Invastion by Plants and Animals,* Methuen, London.

Embleton, C. (1989), *Natural Hazards and Global Change,* ITC Journal (1989), pp. 169-78.

Etherington, J.R. (1975), *Environment and Plant Ecology,* Wiley, New York.

Furley, P.A. and Newey, W.W. (1983), *Man and the Biosphere,* Butterworths, London.

Garg, R.K. and Prakash Tatair (1988), *Paryavan Shiksha'* Community Centre, p. 36.

Goel, M.K. (1995), *Apna Paryavaran,* Vinod Pustak Mandir, Agra, p. 314.

Goudle, A. (1984), *The Nature of the Environment,* Basil Blackwell Publisher Ltd., p. 331.

Govt. of India, (1986), *The Environment (Protection) Act 1986,* Ministry of Environment & Forests, GOI, New Delhi, p. 14.

Gregory, K.J. and Wailing, D.E. (1981), *Man and Environment Process,* Butterworths, London.

Hewitt, K. and Hare, F.K. (1973), *Man and Environment: Conceptual Frameworks,* Commission on College Geography Resource Paper 20.

Holliman, J. (1974), *Consumer's Guide to the Protection of the Environment,* Ballanine, London.

Hutchinson, G.E. (1978), *An Introduction to Population Ecology,* Yale University Press, New Haven.

Jeffers, J.N.R. (1973), *System Modelling and Analysis in Resource Management,* Journal of Environmental Management, Vol. 1, pp. 13-28.

Kendeigh, S.C. (1974), *Ecology with Special Reference to Animal and Man,* Prentice-Hall, New Jersey.

Kerbs, C.J. (1985), *Ecology,* 3rd ed., Harper & Row, New York.

Khoshoo, T.N. (1984), *Environmental Concerns and Strategies,* Indian Environmental Society.

Komondy, E.J. (1969), *Concept of Ecology,* Prentice-Hall, New Jersey.

Kumar, V.K. (1982), *A Study in Environmental Pollution,* Tara Book Agency, Varanasi, p. 205.

Lee N. and Wood, C. (1972), *Planning and Pollution,* The Planner, Vol. 58, pp. 153-58.

Lohani, B.N. (1984), *Environmental Quality Control,* South Asian Publishers, New Delhi, p. 448.

Marsh, G.P. (1984), *Man and Nature* (Physical Geography as modified by Human Action), Charles Scribner, New York.

Mishra, R. (1968), *Ecology Work Book,* Oxford & IBH, New Delhi.

Nelson, I.G. and Byrne, A.B. (1986), *Man as an Instrument of Landscape Change,* Alberta Geog. Rev., Vol. 58, pp. 226-38.

Nicholson, M. (1972), *The Environmental Revolution,* Penguin, Harmondsworth.

Odum, E.P. (1979), *Fundamental of Ecology,* Saunders, Philadelphia.

Odum, E.P. (1983), *Basic Ecology,* Holt Saunders Intle ed., Japan.

Odum, H.T. (1971), *Environment, Power and Society,* Wiley Interscience, New York.

Oestereich, J. (1994a), The Concept of Environmental Monitoring in the Indian Context, *Productivity,* 35(2) : 185-191.

Pal, B.P. (1981), *National Policy on Environment,* Deptt. of Environment, Government of India, New Delhi, p. 15.

Pal, S.K. and Malhotra, Sudha (1994), *Environment Trend and Thoughts in Education*, Vol. XI, 1994, Published by Innovative Research Association, Allahabad.

Paric, C.C. (1980), *Ecology and Environment*, Longmans, Londons, p. 272.

Pattern, B.C. (Ed.) 1971, *Systems Analysis and Simulation in Ecology*, Academic Press, London.

Phillipson, I. (1986), *Ecological Energetics*, Arnold, London.

Pimm, S.L. (1982), *Food Webs*, Chapman & Hall, London.

Rao, K.L. (1975), *India's Water Wealth*, Orient Longman Limited, New Delhi, p. 235.

Rao, M. Sitaram (1987), *Introduction to Social Forestry*, Oxford & IBH, p. 87.

Ricklefs, R.E. (1979), *Ecology*, 2nd ed. Chiron Press, New York.

Rouse, W.R. (1981), *Man-Induced Climates in Man and Environmental Process* (ed.) Walling Butterworth, pp. 38-54.

Sandbrook, R. (1992), *From Stockholm to Rio*, in *Earth Summit 92*, Regency Press Corp. London.

Sapru, R.K. (1987), *Environmental Management in India*, Ashish Publishing House, p. 288.

Saxena, A.B. (1986), *Environmental Education*, National Psychological Corporation, Agra, p. 191.

Sharma, C.B.S.R. Panneerselvam, N. and Arumikkili, K. (1985), *Environmental Genetic Toxicology in India*.

Sharma, P.D. (1990), *Ecology and Environment*, Rastogi Publishers, Meerut (U.P.).

Sharma, R.A. (1995), *Distance Education—Theory, Practice and Research*, Meerut, p. 392.

Sharma, R.A. (1996), *Fundamental of Educational Psychology*, Surya Publication, Meerut.

Sharma, S.P. (2003), *Teacher Education—Principles Theory and Practice* Delhi, p. 574.

Sharma, Y.K. (2002), *Fundamental Aspects of Educational Technology*, Delhi, p. 454.

Simmons, I.G. (1974), *The Ecology and Natural Resources*, Edward Arnold, London.

Singh, S. (1995), *Environmental Geography*, Prayag Pustak Bhawan, Allahabad, p. 517.

Singh, S. and Dubey, A. (1989), *Environmental Management*, Geography Department, Allahabad University.

Strahler, A.N. and Strahler, A.H. (1986), *Geography and Man's Environment*, John Wiley, New York.

University of Poona (1981) *Integrated Studies in Western Ghats*, University of Poona Press.

Valiathan, M.S. (1993), *Presidential Address, 68 Annual Meeting, Association of Indian Universities,* AIU, New Delhi.

Verma, P.S., and Agarwal, V.K. (1993), *Environmental Biology (Principles of Ecology),* S. Chand & Company, New Delhi, p. 592.

Vernadsky, W.I. (1884), *Studies in Geochemistry,* Leningrad.

Vyas, A.B. and Golley, F.B. (1975), *Ecological Principles,* International Publication, Jaipur.

Vyas, H. (1995), *Paryadvaran Shiksha,* Vidya Vihar, New Delhi, p. 288.

Webster's Seventh New Collegiate Dictionary, (1970), *Environment,* p. 278, G. & C. Merriam Co. Massachusets, p. 1221.

Whittaker, R.H. (1975), *Communities and Ecosystem,* 2nd ed. MacMillan, New York.

Wilson, E.C. (1975), *Sociobiology: The New Synthesis,* Harvard University Press, Cambridge, Mass.

Woodbury, A.M. (1974): *Principles of General Ecology,* McGraw Hill Book Co., New York.

Zelinsky, W. (1986), *A Prologue Population Geography,* Prentice-Hall, Englewood Cliff, New Jersey.

Index

Acid Rain 7–8
Africa 12, 13
Air Pollution Act 425
Atomic Energy Commission 429
Autecology 131

Barrows, Harlan 20
Bates, M. 36
Belgrade Charter at Belgrade 94, 100, 320
Biogeochemcial Cycle 222, 228
Biological Clocks 222
Biosphere 3
Botanical Survey of India 429
Botkin, D.B. 26
Bowmanm, Isiah 20
Bruhnes, Jeans 20
Brundtland Report 398
Bulgaria 30

California 13, 30
Canada 348
Canadian International Development Agency 429
Carbon Cycle 4, 229
Central Ground Water Board 188
Central Institute of Educational Technology 346, 357
Centre for Environment Education 113
Charles Drawin 18
Child Development 364
Child, I.L. 287, 367
Clarke, G.L. 127
Classification/Types of Degradation 157
Cloud Seeding 29
Cole, M. 36
Conservation and Management 111, 113
Control and Prevention of Air Pollution 174
Council on Environment Quality 429
Cutts , Norma E. 298

Damodar Valley Corporation Act 187
Darwin 126, 211
Davies , B.E. 36
Davis, W.M. 18
Deforestation 29
Delhi Agriculture Television Project 353–54
Delinquent Child 313
Derrick, E.H. 36
Development
  and Human Growth 279
  Dimensions 280
  Emotional 283
  Nature 279
Dewey, John 64, 372
Difference Between Ecology and Ecosystem 143
Dixon, D.M. 148
Domestication of Animals 26
Dull Child 312

Earth Summit 1992 398
Earthwatch Programme 414
Eco-development Camps 115
Ecological
  Balance 2
  Climate 36
Ecology 91, 125, 211
  Definition 125
  of Agricultural Man 238

of Human Needs and Problems 239
of Industrial Man 238
of Primitive Man 237
Economic Determinism 21
Ecosystem 2, 136, 221
and Education 144
Artificial'Ecosystem 139
Classification 138
Functioning Process 140
Kinds of Aquatic Ecosystem 143
Natural Ecosystems 138
Education
Adult Education 115, 375
Aims 70
and Ecology 134
and Ecosystem 144
and Mental Health 298, 302
Basic Concepts 61
Commission 120
Data 65
Inter-Disciplinary Approach 78
Meaning 61
Parts 69
Some Conclusive Aims 72
Task 88
Educational Excursion Method 118
Environment
Aspect of Natural Resources 39, 57
Basic Characteristics 43
Biological and Physical Component 48
Classification 43
Components 2, 45
Definition 41
Degradation 146–147
Education 91
Educational Aspect 59
Geographical Aspect 56
Ingredients 1
Meaning 40
Physical 44
Political Aspect 55
Psychological 44
Social and Cultural 44
Social Aspect 54
Environment (Protection) Act 425
Environmental
Awareness, 93–94
Degradation 155
Causes 156
Engineering 111, 113–14
Health 111, 113
Information System 121, 432
Pollution 146
Protection Laws 419
Science 114
Studies 114
Environmental Education 106, 319
Aims and Objectives of 101
and Environmental Awarenes 96
and Training 431
and Training Centres 432
Centre for 101
Characteristics 98
Definition 92
Methods and Techniques of Teaching 117
Present Status 121
Status 436
Teacher's Role 103
Utility and need 99
Environmental Management 397
Approaches 405, 408
Dimensions 412
Ecological Basis 409
Functions and Characteris 412
Meaning and Definition 403
Plan 401
System 401
Tools 399
Evolution of Species 126
Eysenck, H.S. 86

Fishery 133
Fixed Energy 137
Food and Agricultural Organisation 415
Food Chain 6, 221–22, 224
Factors Affecting 231
Factors Disturbing 231
Food Gathering Period 24
Forest Act 419

Forestry 133
Frederick Herberg 302
Frontier theory 391

Gandhi, Indira 100
Gandhi, Mahatma 370
Ganga Action Plan 425
General Agreement on Trade and Tariffs 399
Geographical Climate 36
Gestalt 213
Gifted Child 312
Green House Effect 9
Green Revolution 191
Grossman 19
Gulf War 8, 11

H. Comb, Philip 381
Hexicology 125
Higher Education Television Project (HETV) of UGC 355
Horticulture 133
Human Ecology 92, 297
Human Exposure Assessment Location 413
Hungary 30
Huntington, E. 18, 19
Hurlock, E.B. 286
Hydrogen Cycle 5
Hydrosphere 3
Hygiene Theory of Motivation 302

Indian Institute of Forest Management 113
Indian National Satellite (INSAT) 353, 355
Indira Gandhi National Forest Academy 113
Indira Gandhi National Open University (IGNOU) 333, 356
Industrialization 28, 269
Inferior Child 313
Inter Governmental Conference on EE 100
International Council of Scientific Unions 415
International Marine Consultative Organisation 413
International Union for Conservation of Nature 16, 413, 415

Japan 32
Jawahar Rojgar Yojana 383
Jersild, T. 86

Keller, E.A. 26
Kothari Commission 101, 376, 382
Krebs, C.J. 127

Lewin, Kurt 43, 44
Limnology 133
Linguistic Jingoism 77
Lithosphere 3

Macfadyen 127
Man and the Biosphere Programme 414, 415
Man-Environment Relationship 35
Mass Media 339
Massachusetts Institute of Technology 150
Maturation 86, 87
Mental Health/Ailment, 299
  Attributes 300
  and School 314
  Cause of 311
  Factors Influencing 303
  Mental Development 292
  Theory 301
Micro-climate affects 36
Modern Education 67
Motor Skills and Social Development 288
Mukerjee, S.N. 376
Municipal Corporation of Delhi 33

National Council of Teacher Education 335
National Dairy Development Board 427
National Environment Awareness Campaign 116

National Museum of Natural History 115, 425
National Policy of Education 320, 331
National Social Scheme 120
National Thermal Power Corporation 171
National Wastelands Development Board 426
Nationalistic Chauvinism 77
Natural Environmental Research Council 148
NCERT 112, 252–53, 257, 321–23, 336, 348, 361, 431
NCTE 336, 337
New Zealand 15
Newman 114
NGOs 115
Nitrogen Cycle 4
Nunn, T.P. 52

Oceanography 133
Odum, E.P. 126
Oecology 125
Oxygen Cycle 5, 229
Ozone Deplition 10

Phosphorous Cycle 230
Physical and Motor Development 281
Pincent, R.J.F.H. 36
Plant Domestication 27
Pollutants 149
  Air 150, 169
  Biological 150
  Water 150
    Classification 180
  Cultural 150
  Environmental 151
  Gaseous 150
  Invisible 149
  Land 150
  Man-Made 149
  Natural 149
  Physical 150
  Solid Particulate 150
  Types 150
  Visible 149
Pollution
  Air Pollution 9, 166
    Automobiles Air Pollution 170
    Industrial Air Pollution 170
    Meaning and Definition 166
    Nature 167
    Sources 168
    Thermal Air Pollution 171
  Classification 153–155
  Definitions 148
  Location 154
  Medium 153
  Nature 153
  Noise Pollution 12
    and Radioactive Pollution 200
    Control 208
    Definition 202
    Effects 206
    Sources 202
    Types 204
  Radioactive Pollution 209
  Role of Education 163
  Soil or Land Pollution 189
    Control 194
    Definition 189
    Effects 193
    Sources 190
  Water Pollution 11, 177
    Ecological Effects 183
    Nature 181
    Sources 179, 182
Population Education 251
  Importance 256
  Need 252
  Objectives 253
Population Explosion 217, 240, 246, 269, 297
Post-SITE Project 353, 355
Protected Species of Indian Wild Life 420
Provincialism 77

Radiant Energy 137
Radio Forum 348
Rain Forests 13
Raymont, T. 65
Religious Fanaticism 77

Roy, C. 382

Satellite Instructional Television Experiment 353–54
Sauer, Carl 20
Saxena, M.C. 32
SCERT 322
Secondary School Television Project 353
Semple, E.C. 18
Shrimali, K.L. 337
Social Development 286, 367
Social Ecology 111, 113, 260
Social efficiency 372
Social Forestry 384
  Advantages 387
  in Tribal Areas 386
  Limitations 388
  Need and Importance 384
  Objectives 384
  on Personal Land 387
  Role of Panchayat 386
  Role of Social Forestry 385
Socially Useful Productive Work 120
Solar Energy 227
South Asia Co-operative Environment Programme 414
Soviet Union 30
Space-ecosystem 139
Sri Lanka 14
Stone National Park 16
Strahler, A.H. 30
Strahler, A.N. 30
Switzerland 30
Synecology 131

Tantham, G. 20
Tata Energy Research Institute 418, 427
Taylor, L.R. 127
Teacher Education Programmes 114
Tehri High Dam Project 414
Tibliti conference 320
Tiwari Committee 100

UK 47
Ultraviolet Radiation 34
UNESCO 92, 101, 252, 255, 320, 323, 348, 380
United Nations Conference of Human Environment 94, 397
United Nations Conference on Environment 398
United Nations Educational, Scientific and Cultural 414
United Nations Environment Programme 94, 398, 414, 415
United Nations Organisation 223
University Grants Commission 112, 335, 336, 431
Urbanisation 33, 269
USA 31, 32, 47, 192, 207
USSR 33

Vidal de la Blache 20

Water Act, 1974 187
Water Cess Act, 1977 187
Water Control Acts 187
Water Cycle 230
Water Pollution Act 425
Water Pollution Prevention and Control Act 187
Wild Birds and Animals Protection Act 419
Wild Life Protection Act 419
World Commission on Environment and Development 398, 414
World Environment Day 116
World Health Organisation 47, 210, 217, 415
World Wildlife Fund 16, 413

Yogoslavia 30

Zelinsky, W. 21
Zoological Survey of India 425